Anglo-Saxon Studies 24

THE DATING OF *BEOWULF*

Anglo-Saxon Studies

ISSN 1475–2468

GENERAL EDITORS
John Hines
Catherine Cubitt

'Anglo-Saxon Studies' aims to provide a forum for the best scholarship on the Anglo-Saxon peoples in the period from the end of Roman Britain to the Norman Conquest, including comparative studies involving adjacent populations and periods; both new research and major re-assessments of central topics are welcomed.

Books in the series may be based in any one of the principal disciplines of archaeology, art history, history, language and literature, and inter- or multi-disciplinary studies are encouraged.

Proposals or enquiries may be sent directly to the editors or the publisher at the addresses given below; all submissions will receive prompt and informed consideration.

Professor John Hines, School of History, Archaeology and Religion, Cardiff University, John Percival Building, Colum Drive, Cardiff, Wales, CF10 3EU, UK

Professor Catherine Cubitt, Centre for Medieval Studies, University of York, The King's Manor, York, England, YO1 7EP, UK

Boydell & Brewer, PO Box 9, Woodbridge, Suffolk, England, IP12 3DF, UK

*Previously published volumes in the series
are listed at the back of this book*

THE DATING OF *BEOWULF*

A REASSESSMENT

Edited by Leonard Neidorf

D.S. BREWER

© Contributors 2014

All Rights Reserved. Except as permitted under current legislation
no part of this work may be photocopied, stored in a retrieval system,
published, performed in public, adapted, broadcast,
transmitted, recorded or reproduced in any form or by any means,
without the prior permission of the copyright owner

First published 2014
D. S. Brewer, Cambridge
Paperback edition 2016

ISBN 978 1 84384 387 0 hardback
ISBN 978 1 84384 449 5 paperback

D. S. Brewer is an imprint of Boydell & Brewer Ltd
PO Box 9, Woodbridge, Suffolk IP12 3DF, UK
and of Boydell & Brewer Inc.
668 Mount Hope Avenue, Rochester, NY 14620–2731, USA
website: www.boydellandbrewer.com

A CIP catalogue record for this book is available
from the British Library

The publisher has no responsibility for the continued existence or
accuracy of URLs for external or third-party internet websites
referred to in this book, and does not guarantee that any content on
such websites is, or will remain, accurate or appropriate

Typeset by Frances Hackeson Freelance Publishing Services,
Brinscall, Lancs

Contents

List of Tables		vii
List of Illustrations		viii
List of Contributors		ix
Acknowledgements		x
	Introduction Leonard Neidorf	1
1.	*Beowulf* and Language History R.D. Fulk	19
2.	Germanic Legend, Scribal Errors, and Cultural Change Leonard Neidorf	37
3.	Names in *Beowulf* and Anglo-Saxon England Tom Shippey	58
4.	The Limits of Conservative Composition in Old English Poetry Megan E. Hartman	79
5.	The Date of Composition of *Beowulf* and the Evidence of Metrical Evolution Thomas A. Bredehoft	97
6.	*Beowulf* and the Containment of Scyld in the West Saxon Royal Genealogy Dennis Cronan	112
7.	History and Fiction in the Frisian Raid Frederick M. Biggs	138
8.	'Give the People What They Want': Historiography and Rhetorical History of the Dating of *Beowulf* Controversy Michael D.C. Drout with Phoebe Boyd and Emily Bowman	157
9.	A Note on the Other Heorot Joseph Harris	178
10.	*Beowulf* and Conversion History Thomas D. Hill	191
11.	Material Monsters and Semantic Shifts Rafael J. Pascual	202

12.	Scandals in Toronto: Kaluza's Law and Transliteration Errors *George Clark*	219
13.	Afterword: *Beowulf* and Everything Else *Allen J. Frantzen*	235
Index		249

Tables

4.1	Incidence of Type C, D, and E verses in *The Battle of Brunanburh* and *Beowulf*	85
4.2	Incidence of Type C, D, and E verses in *Judith*, *The Battle of Maldon* and *Beowulf*	86
4.3	Use of traditional diction in *Judith*, *the Battle of Brunanburh*, *the Battle of Maldon*, and *Beowulf*	89
5.1	Proposed Sequence for Metrical Innovations: Innovations Plotted Against Chronology	107

Illustrations

8.1	Date Ranges for *Beowulf* in Articles not Directly Concerned with the Date of the Poem, 1970–80	162
8.2	Date Ranges for *Beowulf* in Essays in *The Dating of Beowulf* Proceedings Volume	165
8.3	Date Ranges for *Beowulf* in Articles not Directly Concerned with the Date of the Poem, 1980–90	168

Contributors

Frederick M. Biggs is Professor of English at the University of Connecticut.

Thomas A. Bredehoft is an Independent Scholar.

George Clark is Professor of English, Emeritus, at Queen's University, Kingston.

Dennis Cronan is Associate Professor of English at the University of Nevada, Reno.

Michael D.C. Drout is Professor of English and Director of the Center for the Study of the Medieval at Wheaton College, Massachusetts.

Allen J. Frantzen is Professor of English at Loyola University, Chicago.

R.D. Fulk is Class of 1964 Chancellor's Professor of English and Adjunct Professor of Germanic Studies at Indiana University.

Joseph Harris is Francis Lee Higginson Professor of English and Professor of Folklore, Emeritus, at Harvard University.

Megan E. Hartman is Assistant Professor of English at University of Nebraska, Kearney.

Thomas D. Hill is Professor of English and Medieval Studies at Cornell University.

Leonard Neidorf is a Junior Fellow at the Harvard Society of Fellows.

Rafael J. Pascual is a Ph.D. Candidate at the University of Granada.

Tom Shippey is Professor Emeritus of Saint Louis University, formerly Walter J. Ong SJ Chair of Humanities.

Acknowledgements

The idea behind this book has been with me since 2010. When I began to share this idea, many scholars embraced it and helped me to make this book a reality. I thank all of the contributors in this volume for their enthusiasm and their superb scholarship.

Before it was the title of a collection of essays, *The Dating of Beowulf: A Reassessment* was the title of a conference held at Harvard University on September 23rd and 24th, 2011. Funding for this conference was provided by the Morton Bloomfield Trust, the Harvard English Department, the Harvard Standing Committee on Medieval Studies, and the Dumbarton Oaks Medieval Library. For their help in obtaining funds and running the conference, thanks are due to Daniel Donoghue, Jeffrey Hamburger, Joseph Harris, Eli Barlow Martin, A. Joseph McMullen, and Jan Ziolkowski.

For feedback and advice given to me while preparing this book, I thank George Clark, Daniel Donoghue, Allen J. Frantzen, R.D. Fulk, Joseph Harris, John Hines, Michael Lapidge, Francis Leneghan, Michael McCormick, Rafael J. Pascual, Geoffrey Russom, and Tom Shippey. Working with Boydell & Brewer has been a pleasure. I thank everyone at the press who had a hand in this book, especially Caroline Palmer, who has been a supportive and diligent editor.

Leonard Neidorf
Harvard Society of Fellows

Introduction

Leonard Neidorf

From the publication of the poem's *editio princeps* in 1815 to the emergence of the present collection two centuries later, few topics in Anglo-Saxon studies have generated as much speculation and scholarship as the dating of *Beowulf*.[1] Marshaling disparate forms of evidence and argumentation, scholars have assigned dates to *Beowulf* that range from the seventh to the eleventh century. Various individuals have been unpersuasively identified as the author of *Beowulf* and dozens of kings, clerics, and contexts have been associated with the poem's genesis.[2] Scholarship on the dating of *Beowulf* is markedly uneven in quality: alongside sober and thoughtful argumentation, there has been a great deal of improbable hypothesizing about the author of the poem or the milieu in which it was composed. Awareness of the qualitative differences in the scholarly

---

[1] For a conspectus of opinions, see Robert E. Bjork and Anita Obermeier, "Date, Provenance, Author, Audiences," in *A* Beowulf *Handbook*, ed. Robert E. Bjork and John D. Niles (Lincoln: University of Nebraska Press, 1997), 13–34. The poem's first edition is *De Danorum rebus gestis secul. III & IV. Poëma danicum dialecto anglo-saxonica*, ed. Grímur Jónsson Thorkelín (Havniae: T.E. Rangel, 1815). For other overviews of scholarship on the dating of *Beowulf*, see Claus Dieter Wetzel, "Die Datierung des *Beowulf*: Bemerkungen zur jüngsten Forschungsentwicklung," *Anglia* 103 (1985): 371–400; and Stephen S. Evans, "The Dating of *Beowulf*," *The Heroic Poetry of Dark-Age Britain: an Introduction to its Dating, Composition, and Use as a Historical Source* (Lanham: University Press of America, 1997), 41–63. For insights into the significance of the poem's date in nineteenth-century scholarship, see T.A. Shippey, "Introduction," in Beowulf: *The Critical Heritage*, ed. T.A. Shippey and Andreas Haarder (New York: Routledge, 1998), 1–57.

[2] Attempts to identify the author of *Beowulf* include: Gregor Sarrazin, "Die Abfassungszeit des Beowulfliedes," *Anglia* 14 (1892): 399–415; Felix Liebermann, "Ort und Zeit der Beowulfdichtung," *Nachrichten von der königl. Gesellschaft der Wissenschaften zu Göttingen, phil.-hist. Klasse* 68 (1920): 255–76; A.S. Cook, "The Possible Begetter of the Old English *Beowulf* and *Widsith*," *Transactions of the Connecticut Academy of Arts and Sciences* 25 (1921–22): 281–46; Zacharias P. Thundy, "*Beowulf*: Date and Authorship," *Neuphilologische Mitteilungen* 87 (1986): 102–16; Richard North, *The Origins of* Beowulf: *From Vergil to Wiglaf* (Oxford: Oxford University Press, 2006).

literature is tacitly registered in the relative frequency with which publications are cited, but these differences have rarely received explicit discussion. This introduction to the dating of *Beowulf* controversy examines the changing standards of evidence, methodology, and argumentation that have attended this topic, particularly in the past thirty years. The dating of *Beowulf* has not been a static or monolithic subject, but has undergone considerable change in the disputes it connotes and the practices it encompasses. In the following account, emphasis will be given to the reasons for prevailing opinions rather than to the multiplicity of opinions as such.

The dating of *Beowulf* was once a fairly settled matter. Prior to the 1980s, most scholars held that the poem was composed during the seventh or eighth century. No editor or translator of *Beowulf* supported a date outside the range 650–800, with the exception of Thorkelin, the poem's first editor, who imagined the author to have been present at Beowulf's funeral.[3] The following statement from J.R.R. Tolkien provides an indication of how uncontroversial and firmly established the early date had been:

> I accept without argument throughout the attribution of *Beowulf* to the 'age of Bede' – one of the firmer conclusions of a department of research most clearly serviceable to criticism: inquiry into the probable date of the effective composition of the poem as we have it.[4]

Why did Tolkien consider the idea that *Beowulf* belonged to the age of Bede (672–735) such a firm conclusion? Linguistic arguments for dating poetry had gradually emerged at the end of the nineteenth and beginning of the twentieth century,[5] but the consensus that *Beowulf* was an early composition neither originated in nor depended much upon such arguments. Well before the emergence of linguistic tests, scholars such as N.F.S. Grundtvig, Ludwig Ettmüller, and Bernhard ten Brink had already dated *Beowulf* to the seventh or eighth century, in large part due to literary-historical assumptions: they believed that a poem praising

---

[3] For this observation, see Colin Chase, "Opinions on the Date of *Beowulf*, 1815–1980," in *The Dating of* Beowulf, ed. Colin Chase (Toronto: University of Toronto Press, 1981; rev. with a new afterword, 1997), 3–8, at 8 [Chase's collection is henceforth cited as *Dating*]; for Thorkelin's view, see *De Danorum rebus gestis*, ix.

[4] J.R.R. Tolkien, "*Beowulf*: The Monsters and the Critics," *Proceedings of the British Academy* 22 (1936): 245–95, at 262.

[5] See, for example, Lorenz Morsbach, "Zur Datierung des Beowulfepos," *Nachrichten von der königl. Gesellschaft der Wissenschaften zu Göttingen, phil.-hist. Klasse* (1906): 251–77; Gregor Sarrazin, "Zur Chronologie und Verfasserfrage angelsächsicher Dichtungen," *Englische Studien* 38 (1907): 145–95; Carl Richter, *Chronologische Studien zur angelsächsichen Literatur auf Grund sprachlich-metrischer Kriterien*, Studien zur englischen Philologie 33 (Halle: Niemeyer, 1910); and Ritchie Girvan, Beowulf *and the Seventh Century: Language and Content* (London: Methuen, 1935), 1–25.

Danes should antedate the Viking invasions and that poems dealing with pagan, Germanic subject matter should be relatively early.[6] After linguistic arguments for an early date were posited, they were rarely accorded as much weight as these broader considerations.[7] Tolkien was not unusual in declining to mention any of the evidence upon which the firm conclusion of a Bedan *Beowulf* was based. The earliness of *Beowulf* was considered too secure to require technical substantiation. Scholars felt little need to assemble and analyze the various forms of evidence that might shed light on the poem's date of composition.

When pressed to offer reasons for dating *Beowulf* to the seventh or eighth century, scholars tended to emphasize the cultural suitability of the early Anglo-Saxon period. According to some, cultural suitability was not simply the best dating criterion; it was the only dating criterion. Francis Gummere, for instance, writes:

> There is no positive evidence for any date of origins. All critics place it before the ninth century. The eighth brought monastic corruption to Northumbria; while the seventh, described by Beda, with its austerity of morals, its gentleness, its tolerance, its close touch with milder forms of heathenism, matches admirably the controlling mood of the epic.[8]

The dating of *Beowulf* was framed primarily as a question to be approached through the identification of affinities between the poem and a given period of Anglo-Saxon history. The logic governing this affinity method tended to be rather simple: *Beowulf* contains an allusion to Offa of Angeln, therefore it belongs to the reign of Offa of Mercia (c. 757–96); it features a character named Wiglaf, therefore it was composed to praise Wiglaf of Mercia (c. 826–8); the poem is in some sense transitional, and so was the age of Bede, thus they belong together.[9] In

---

[6] *Bjowulfs drape. Et gothisk helte-digt fra forrige aar-tusinde, af angel-saxisk paa danske riim*, trans. N.F.S. Grundtvig (Copenhagen: Andreas Seidelin, 1820), xxvii–viii; Beowulf: *Heldengedicht des achten Jahrhunderts*, trans. Ludwig Ettmüller (Zürich: Meyer und Zeller, 1840); Bernhard ten Brink, *Geschichte der englischen Literatur, vol 1., bis zu Wiclifs Auftreten* (Berlin: Oppenheim, 1877).

[7] For a review of the objections raised in early scholarship against linguistic dating criteria, see Ashley Crandell Amos, *Linguistic Means of Determining the Dates of Old English Literary Texts* (Cambridge, MA: Medieval Academy of America, 1980), 6–8; these objections are also reviewed in R.D. Fulk, *A History of Old English Meter* (Philadelphia: University of Pennsylvania Press, 1992), 1–65 [henceforth *HOEM*].

[8] *The Oldest English Epic:* Beowulf, Finnsburg, Waldere, Deor, Widsith, *and the German* Hildebrandslied, ed. and trans. Francis B. Gummere (New York: The Macmillan Company, 1910) 1, n. 2.

[9] For the Offa argument, see *The Deeds of* Beowulf: *An English Epic Done into Modern Prose*, ed. and trans. John Earle (Oxford: Clarendon Press), lxxxv; for the Wiglaf argument, see George Bond, "Links between *Beowulf* and Mercian History," *Studies in Philology* 40 (1943): 481–93; for the transitional argument, see W.W. Lawrence, Beowulf *and Epic Tradition* (Cambridge, MA: Harvard University Press, 1928), 280–2.

his monumental synthesis of the first century of *Beowulf* scholarship, R.W. Chambers frames the question of dating in terms of "atmosphere" and prioritizes literary-historical over linguistic considerations.[10] He attributes the greatest weight to the argument that since *Beowulf* is the most sophisticated work of Old English literature, it must have been composed during the most sophisticated period of Anglo-Saxon history, the age of Bede.[11] Chambers' summary of reasons for early dating presents cultural suitability as the primary dating criterion:

> [F]rom the point of view of its close touch with heathendom, its tolerance for heathen customs, its Christian magnanimity and gentleness, its conscious art, and its learned tone, all historic and artistic analogy would lead us to place *Beowulf* in the great age – the age of Bede.[12]

Arguments of a different sort, in which linguistic, metrical, paleographical, and archaeological evidence were brought to bear on the dating of *Beowulf*, surfaced sporadically throughout the first half of the twentieth century, but these forms of evidence were rarely foregrounded in discussions of the poem's date.[13] The hard evidence was often denigrated, in fact, to such an extent that Dorothy Whitelock could assert in 1951 that the most compelling reason why *Beowulf* must antedate 835 is that no English poem praising Danes would have been composed after the arrival of the Vikings.[14]

The consensus for an early date of *Beowulf* met its unsurprising end in 1981. In that year appeared *The Dating of Beowulf*, the proceedings volume for a conference held at the University of Toronto. It included essays from five scholars – Kevin Kiernan, Roberta Frank, Walter Goffart, Alexander C. Murray, and Colin Chase (its editor) – arguing that *Beowulf*

---

[10] See R.W. Chambers, Beowulf: *An Introduction to the Study of the Poem with a Discussion of the Stories of Offa and Finn*, 3rd ed. with a supplement from C.L. Wrenn (Cambridge: Cambridge University Press, 1959; first published 1921), 322–32. Chambers concludes: "Everything seems to show that about 700 an atmosphere existed in England which might easily have led a scholarly Englishman, acquainted with the old lays, to have set to work to compose an epic," 332.

[11] "Now, whatever we may think of *Beowulf* as poetry, it is remarkable for its conscious and deliberate art, and for the tone of civilization which pervades it. And this half century [the age of Bede] was distinguished, above any other period of Old English history, precisely for its art and civilization." Chambers, *An Introduction*, 326.

[12] Chambers, *An Introduction*, 329.

[13] For linguistic and metrical scholarship, see the works cited in fn. 5; for paleographical observations, see C.L. Wrenn, "The Value of Spelling as Evidence," *Transactions of the Philological Society* 42 (1943): 14–39, at 18; for archaeological arguments, see Knut Stjerna, *Essays on Questions Connected with the Old English Poem of* Beowulf, trans. John R. Clark Hall (Coventry: Curtis & Bleamish, Ltd., 1912), 17–18, 169–71; and Sune Lindqvist (trans. Rupert Bruce-Mitford), "Sutton Hoo and *Beowulf*," *Antiquity* 22 (1948): 131–40.

[14] Dorothy Whitelock, *The Audience of* Beowulf (Oxford: Clarendon Press, 1951), 24–6.

was composed in the ninth, tenth, or eleventh centuries.[15] In the book's afterword, E.G. Stanley affirmed that he was now convinced that *Beowulf* was composed between 890 and 940.[16] Some of the contributors to the volume, such as John C. Pope and Peter Clemoes, maintained that *Beowulf* was an eighth-century poem, while others adopted a more or less agnostic position.[17] Further blows to the former consensus were dealt by the coinciding publication of two monographs: Ashley Crandell Amos's *Linguistic Means of Determining the Dates of Old English Literary Texts* (1980), which claimed that most linguistic tests for dating Old English poetry were unreliable; and Kevin S. Kiernan's Beowulf *and the* Beowulf *Manuscript* (1981), which sensationally announced that the author's examination of the manuscript revealed the poem to be an eleventh-century composition.[18] The books from Amos, Kiernan, and Chase have been regarded as revolutionary and iconoclastic works, but they were understandable and perhaps inevitable developments. The linguistic tests had never received much credence; the manuscript had been neglected as a source of evidence for the poem's date; and many scholars who dated *Beowulf* to the seventh or eighth century either felt there was little firm evidence for this position or neglected to present the evidence.

When E.G. Stanley proclaimed the formerly prevailing consensus for an early date of *Beowulf* to be "a conspiracy of romantic hopes,"[19] he was only registering an impression that several voices of the consensus had encouraged. In 1989, when Edward B. Irving, Jr. reiterated his longstanding view about the date of *Beowulf*, he presented it as if it were the product of romantic rather than scholarly considerations: "I boldly state here my own best guess, aware that the evidence for it is the merest gossamer. I think *Beowulf* is (or originally was) an eighth-century

---

[15] Kevin Kiernan, "The Eleventh-Century Origin of *Beowulf* and the *Beowulf* Manuscript," in *Dating*, 9–22; Roberta Frank, "Skaldic Verse and the Date of *Beowulf*," in *Dating*, 123–40; Walter Goffart, "*Hetware* and *Hugas*: Datable Anachronisms in *Beowulf*," in *Dating*, 83–100; Alexander Callander Murray, "*Beowulf*, the Danish Invasions, and Royal Genealogy," in *Dating*, 101–12; Colin Chase, "Saints' Lives, Royal Lives, and the Date of *Beowulf*," in *Dating*, 161–72.
[16] E.G. Stanley, "The Date of *Beowulf*: Some Doubts and No Conclusions," in *Dating*, 197–212, at 201 and 209.
[17] John C. Pope, "On the Date of Composition of *Beowulf*," in *Dating*, 187–96; Peter Clemoes, "Style as the Criterion for Dating the Composition of *Beowulf*," in *Dating*, 173–85.
[18] Amos, *Linguistic Means*; Kevin S. Kiernan, Beowulf and the Beowulf *Manuscript* (New Brunswick: Rutgers University Press, 1981; reprinted with supplements, Ann Arbor: The University of Michigan Press, 1996).
[19] These well-known words derive from the paper Stanley delivered at the Toronto conference and are cited in Murray, "*Beowulf*, the Danish Invasions," 101, n. 2.

Mercian court poem."[20] Sound reasons for dating *Beowulf* to the early Anglo-Saxon period were known prior to 1980, but they were rarely emphasized and apparently not very well understood.[21] Most scholars had framed the dating of *Beowulf* not in terms of assessing and making sense of chronologically significant evidence, but in terms of pinning the poem to a historical context they imagined to be conducive to its composition. The Toronto volume perpetuated this tendency; understandably, the late-daters played the game according to its established rules. Instead of the age of Bede providing the sophisticated atmosphere necessary to produce *Beowulf*, this was now provided by the age of Alfred. Instead of *Beowulf* reflecting the hegemonic Mercian politics of King Offa, it now reflected the politics of Anglo-Danish unification under King Æthelstan.[22] The argument that *Beowulf* is late because it fits well in a Viking-age Anglo-Danish context – an idea frequently iterated during the 1980s[23] – is methodologically identical to the argument that *Beowulf* is early because it fits well in the age of Bede. Although it might have seemed avant-garde in its moment, the theory of an Anglo-Danish *Beowulf* is as romantic as any earlier argument that dated *Beowulf* by situating it at the heart of a political drama or in the midst of a cultural renaissance.

Two distinct responses to the dating controversy have taken shape over the past three decades. One response has been to observe that there is intense disagreement over the poem's date and to deem the question incapable of resolution. Borrowing a phrase from Patrick Wormald, we

---

[20] Edward B. Irving, Jr., *Rereading* Beowulf (Philadelphia: University of Pennsylvania Press, 1989), 7.

[21] See R.D. Fulk, "Review Article: Dating *Beowulf* to the Viking Age," *Philological Quarterly* 61 (1982): 341–59, and Theodore M. Andersson, "Review Article: The Dating of *Beowulf*," *University of Toronto Quarterly* 52 (1983): 288–301.

[22] See, for example, Murray, "*Beowulf*, the Danish Invasions"; Frank, "Skaldic Verse"; and Chase, "Saints' Lives, Royal Lives." For an Alfredian context and Anglo-Danish politics, see also Roberta Frank, "The *Beowulf* Poet's Sense of History," in *The Wisdom of Poetry: Essays in Early English Literature in Honor of Morton W. Bloomfield*, ed. Larry D. Benson and Siegfried Wenzel (Kalamazoo: Medieval Institute Publications, 1982), 53–65.

[23] See, for example, Patricia Poussa, "The Date of *Beowulf* Reconsidered: The Tenth Century?" *Neuphilologische Mitteilungen* 82 (1981): 276–88; and John D. Niles, Beowulf: *The Poem and its Tradition* (Cambridge, MA: Harvard University Press, 1983), 96–117. Arguments for a Viking-age *Beowulf* propounded prior to the 1980s include: Levin L. Schücking, "Wann entstand der *Beowulf*? Glossen, Zweifel, und Fragen," *Beiträge zur Geschichte der deutschen Sprache und Literatur* 42 (1917): 347–410; and Nicholas Jacobs, "Anglo-Danish Relations, Poetic Archaism, and the Date of *Beowulf*: A Reconsideration of the Evidence," *Poetica* (Tokyo) 8 (1977): 23–43.

might characterize this response as one of "dogmatic agnosticism."[24] A clear illustration of such agnosticism is provided by the following remark from James Earl: "After reading Kiernan's book and Colin Chase's book, and articles by David Dumville and Michael Lapidge, I now consider it axiomatic that *the problem of the poem's date is insoluble.*"[25] Earl then concludes that because *Beowulf* cannot be dated, scholars are obligated to disconnect the poem from history: "*we should not build theories and interpretations of the poem that depend too heavily on an eighth-century or any other date ... we cannot assume the poem is representative of any period, or even, finally, of anything at all.*"[26] A variant form of the agnostic position is voiced by Nicholas Howe, who writes in his afterword to the 1997 reissue of *The Dating of* Beowulf: "The reader can choose a date for the poem among the possibilities argued in these essays as well as in other sources."[27] Evidently, because the poem has not been (or cannot be) dated, every date advanced can be considered to possess equal merit. The use of the word "possibilities" in Howe's statement illustrates the tendency of agnostics to focus on the wide range of possible dates of composition without attempting to narrow that range down to probable ones. For agnostics, there is no winner (or winners) among the dates proposed. According to Earl, competing hypotheses force us to interpret the poem independent of a historical context; to Howe, they permit us to read the poem in any year we desire between 625 and 1025. The majority of agnostic scholars appear to have gravitated toward Earl's position.[28]

Fortunately, the tumult of the 1980s did not turn everyone into an agnostic. The agnostic position has found favor primarily with scholars who are more eager to carry out the business of literary interpretation than to examine the increasing amount of evidence bearing on the date of *Beowulf*. I write of increasing evidence because of the other response to the dating controversy, which continues to this day. While some scholars have deemed the question insoluble, others have energetically assembled and analyzed varieties of evidence that might shed light on when *Beowulf* was composed. For convenience, we can label this the "reassessing" response. The agnostic response essentially ends with the acknowledgement of competing claims; the reassessing response begins

---

[24] Patrick Wormald, "*Beowulf*: The Redating Reassessed," in *The Times of Bede: Studies in Early English Christian Society and its Historian*, ed. Stephen Baxter (Malden: Blackwell, 2006), 71–81, 98–105, at 80.

[25] James W. Earl, *Thinking About* Beowulf (Stanford: Stanford University Press, 1994), 16–17. The italics here and in the subsequent quote are Earl's.

[26] Earl, *Thinking About* Beowulf, 17.

[27] Nicholas Howe, "Afterword: The Uses of Uncertainty: On the Dating of *Beowulf*," in *Dating*, 213–20, at 217.

[28] For substantiation of this claim, see Michael D.C. Drout's Chapter 8 in this volume.

with those competing claims and ends by weighing the merits of their evidential bases. The agnostic response maintains continuity with the discourse surrounding the dating of *Beowulf* that had prevailed prior to 1980, since the evidence here remains largely ignored and the issue of dating is again conceptualized as a historical guessing game incapable of principled resolution. The reassessing response was not new, but since the 1980s, it has become a more mainstream feature of *Beowulf* studies. Consequently, it has ushered in an era of scholarship wherein discussions of the dating of *Beowulf* have started to focus more on chronologically significant evidence than on supposedly conducive historical contexts. Through the independent efforts of various scholars, the rules of the game have been effectively changed.

One exemplary manifestation of the reassessing response is Dennis Cronan's study of poetic words restricted primarily to *Beowulf* and *Genesis A*.[29] Scholars had long been aware that *Beowulf* contained rare words that might reflect an early date of composition.[30] Cronan put the matter on much better footing by assembling the pertinent evidence, presenting it meticulously, and analyzing its implications. For example, the word *missere* ("half-year") appears only in *Beowulf*, *Genesis A*, and *Exodus*, in expressions such as *hund missera* ("fifty years") and *misserum frod* ("wise in years"). In the rest of the prose and verse of the Anglo-Saxon period, words such as *gear* and *winter* are used instead in parallel expressions.[31] The probable reason for the restriction of *missere* to three archaic poems is that the word became obsolete. Clearer chronological implications surround the word *suhtriga* ("nephew"). As a simplex, *suhtriga* appears in only two sources: in glossaries reproducing *glossae collectae* from the seventh century; and in *Genesis A*, where it is used four times as a term for Lot, the nephew of Abraham. The only other recording of the word is in the compound *suhtor(ge)fædren* ("uncle-and-nephew"), which is found only in *Beowulf* and *Widsið*.[32] The implications of the restricted use of *suhtriga* are clear: the word was a current expression for "nephew" in the seventh and eighth century, but it became obsolete sometime thereafter, having been supplanted by synonyms such as *nefa* and *broðorsunu*, which are used in texts throughout the Anglo-Saxon period. It is probable that the poets of *Genesis A*, *Beowulf*, and *Widsið* composed prior to the obsolescence of *suhtriga*. Related analyses can be extended to the words *dyhtig*

---

[29] Dennis Cronan, "Poetic Words, Conservatism, and the Dating of Old English Poetry," *Anglo-Saxon England* 33 (2004): 23–50.
[30] Lexical dating arguments are reviewed in Amos, *Linguistic Means*, 141–56; see especially Robert J. Menner, "The Date and Dialect of *Genesis A* 852–2936 (Part III)," *Anglia* 70 (1951): 285–94.
[31] See Cronan, "Poetic Words," 40.
[32] See Cronan, "Poetic Words," 35–6, and the references therein.

("strong"), *fær* ("ship"), *freme* ("valiant"), and *gombe* ("tribute"), which are restricted to *Beowulf* and *Genesis A*; as well as to the words *eodor* ("protector"), *heoru* ("sword"), *wlenco* ("bravado"), and *umbor* ("child"), restricted to *Beowulf* and *Maxims I*.[33] Studies from Andy Orchard and the present author have adduced new lexical evidence in support of Cronan's conclusions.[34]

A reassessing response similar to Cronan's, marshaling a different form of evidence, is Patrick Wormald's study of the use of heroic-legendary names in Anglo-Saxon England.[35] Again, the evidence was not utterly new. In 1912, H.M. Chadwick observed that many names from Germanic heroic legend were used by Anglo-Saxons during the seventh and eighth centuries, but largely fell out of use during the ninth and tenth centuries.[36] Chadwick presented this evidence in support of the claim that *Beowulf* was an early composition, but his argument garnered little attention, and it received no discussion in Chase's *The Dating of Beowulf*. Wormald, using new technology (the Prosopography of Anglo-Saxon England) and a greater range of sources, organized the pertinent evidence and found that Chadwick's hypothesis remains valid. Names such as Beowulf, Widsið, Ingeld, Offa, Hrothulf, Hygelac, Theodric, Sigemund, Ætla, and Wyrmhere occur predominantly or exclusively in sources reflecting the name-giving of the seventh and eighth centuries rather than the ninth or tenth.[37] The implication of this evidence is that the heroic-legendary traditions informing *Beowulf* were current and productive in the earlier Anglo-Saxon period, but became less prominent during the ninth and tenth centuries. Naturally, it is likelier that *Beowulf* was composed at a time when these traditions were flourishing rather than at a time when they were losing cultural significance. Wormald's conclusions have been supported and extended in onomastic studies from Tom Shippey and the present author.[38]

The most influential study to emerge in the atmosphere of post-Toronto reassessment is R.D. Fulk's *A History of Old English Meter*, which

---

[33] See Cronan, "Poetic Words," 45–9.
[34] Andy Orchard, "Intoxication, Fornication, and Multiplication: the Burgeoning Text of *Genesis A*," in *Text, Image, Interpretation: Studies in Anglo-Saxon Literature and its Insular Context in Honour of Éamonn Ó Carragáin*, ed. Alistair Minnis and Jane Roberts (Turnhout: Brepols, 2007), 333–54; Leonard Neidorf, "Lexical Evidence for the Relative Chronology of Old English Poetry," *SELIM* 20 (2013): 7–48.
[35] Wormald, "The Redating Reassessed."
[36] H.M. Chadwick, *The Heroic Age* (Cambridge: Cambridge University Press, 1912), 42–4, 64–6.
[37] Wormald, "The Redating Reassessed," 73–80.
[38] See Tom Shippey's Chapter 3 in the present volume; and Leonard Neidorf, "*Beowulf* before *Beowulf*: Anglo-Saxon Anthroponymy and Heroic Legend," *Review of English Studies* 64 (2013): 553–73.

has been labeled "the most complete argument of the past century for the relative and absolute dating of Old English poetry."[39] To determine whether proposed metrical and linguistic archaisms are reliable indicators of relative antiquity, Fulk examined the distribution of these archaisms throughout poems in the relative chronology of Old English poetry devised by Thomas Cable.[40] Reflecting a mixture of known dates and longstanding hypotheses, this chronology, cited below, is only the starting point for Fulk's study:

657–80	*Cædmon's Hymn*
735	*Bede's Death Song*
8th c.	*Leiden Riddle*
8th c.	*Genesis A (I and II)*
8th c.	*Daniel*
–	*Beowulf*
8th–9th c.	*Exodus*
9th c.	*Elene*
9th c.	*Fates of the Apostles*
9th c.	*Juliana*
9th c.	*Andreas*
890–99	*Preface* and *Epilogue, Pastoral Care*
897	*Meters of Boethius*
937	*The Battle of Brunanburh*
942	*The Capture of the Five Boroughs*
10th c.	*Judith*
973	*Coronation of Edgar*
991	*The Battle of Maldon*
1066	*Death of Edward*
1110	*Durham*

Fulk found that the results of different metrical and linguistic tests were remarkably consistent. *Beowulf, Genesis A, Daniel,* and *Exodus* exhibited the highest frequency and greatest variety of archaisms; *Andreas* and the poems of Cynewulf exhibited measurably fewer; and the poems composed during and after the reign of Alfred exhibited by far the fewest.[41] For example, one of the several tests deemed reliable by Fulk is the incidence of verses requiring non-parasited forms for scansion, such as *Ðær wæs hæleþa hleahtor* (*Beo* 611a). The meter reveals that the poet treated *hleahtor* as the monosyllabic **hleahtr*, the form of this word before it underwent parasiting during the seventh century. Another reliable test is

---

[39] See Joseph B. Trahern, Jr.'s review of *HOEM* in *Journal of English and Germanic Philology* 95 (1996): 103–4, at 104. Trahern is here citing and affirming the opinion of Thomas Cable, printed on the book's dust jacket.

[40] Thomas Cable, "Metrical Style as Evidence for the Date of *Beowulf*," in *Dating*, 77–82, at 80.

[41] See Fulk, *HOEM*, 348–51.

the incidence of verses requiring non-contracted forms for scansion, such as *on flett gæð* (*Beo* 2034b). For this verse to contain the four syllables necessary to constitute a metrical half line, *gæð* must be treated as disyllabic **gæ-iþ*, the form of the verb before contraction set in during the seventh century.[42] In these tests and in others such as compensatory lengthening upon loss of *h* and analogical lengthening in diphthongal stems, the results are consistent: verses requiring archaic phonology for scansion occur with the highest frequency in *Beowulf* and the biblical epics, with diminished frequency in *Andreas* and the Cynewulfian poems, and with the lowest frequency in Alfredian and later poems. The broad consistency of the results of so many independent chronological tests cannot be accidental, nor can it rationally be disregarded as a consequence of stylistic or dialectal variation. Studies from Geoffrey Russom, Michael Lapidge, and Thomas A. Bredehoft have supported Fulk's conclusions about the relative chronology on the basis of independent metrical criteria.[43]

A History of Old English Meter demonstrated that a number of linguistic and metrical criteria can reliably adumbrate a relative chronology of Old English poetry. In this chronology, it is clear that *Beowulf* and *Genesis A* are appreciably older than *Elene* and *Andreas*, which are appreciably older than *Judith* and *Maldon*. The strongest metrical evidence for the absolute dating of *Beowulf*, on the other hand, is provided by the poem's regular adherence to Kaluza's law. In brief, Kaluza's law refers to a linguistic regularity observed in two types of verses, in which syllabic sequences under secondary stress are treated as resolvable or unresolvable according to whether the desinence involved was historically long or short.[44] The *Beowulf* poet

---

[42] Fulk has offered several illuminating discussions of these phenomena. For parasiting, see *HOEM*, 66–91; see also "West Germanic Parasiting, Sievers' Law, and the Dating of Old English Verse," *Studies in Philology* 86 (1989): 117–38. For contraction, see *HOEM*, 92–121; see also "Contraction as a Criterion for Dating Old English Verse," *Journal of English and Germanic Philology* 89 (1990): 1–16. On the importance of lexical variety in the verses pertaining to these and other dating criteria, see "Old English Meter and Oral Tradition: Three Issues Bearing on Poetic Chronology," *Journal of English and Germanic Philology* 106 (2007): 304–24.

[43] See Geoffrey Russom, "Dating Criteria for Old English Poems," in *Studies in the History of the English Language*, ed. Donka Minkova and Robert Stockwell (Berlin: Mouton de Gruyter, 2002), 245–66; Michael Lapidge, "An Aspect of Old English Poetic Diction: The Postpositioning of Prepositions," in *Inside Old English: Essays in Honour of Bruce Mitchell*, ed. John Walmsley (Oxford: Blackwell, 2006), 153–80; and Thomas A. Bredehoft's Chapter 5 in the present volume.

[44] The law originates in the observations of Max Kaluza, "Zur Betonungs- und Verslehre des Altenglischen," in *Festschrift zum siebzigsten Geburtstage Oskar Schade* (Königsberg: Hartungsche verlagsdruckerei, 1896), 101–34; Kaluza, *Englische Metrik in historischer Entwicklung dargestellt* (Berlin: E. Felber, 1909), 57–9. Fulk, building on Kaluza, restricted the law's application to syllabic sequences subject to secondary stress. A historically short vowel is a vowel that either was short in Proto-Germanic or was shortened before the Old English period; a historically long vowel is a vowel that had

consistently observed distinctions of etymological length that became phonologically indistinct ca. 725 in Mercia and ca. 825 in Northumbria. He recognized, for example, that the feminine ō-stem nominative singular (*nȳdwracu nīþgrim*, l. 193a) is resolvable, whereas the feminine ō-stem genitive singular (*gearo gyrnwræce*, l. 2118a) is unresolvable. He recognized, moreover, that the masculine *i*-stem nominative singular (*frēowine folca*, ll. 430a, 2357a, 2429a) is resolvable, whereas the masculine adjective nominative plural (*frome fyrdhwate*, ll. 1641a, 2476a) is unresolvable. Even though the two endings would both come to be realized as -*e*, they were etymologically distinct, and the *Beowulf* poet recognized the distinction. Because of the unparalleled complexity and variety of etymological length distinctions observed by the poet, Fulk argued that this linguistic regularity must be phonologically conditioned, i.e., the poet must have composed before etymological length distinctions became phonologically indistinct. Because the language of *Beowulf* is less conservative than that of the Épinal-Erfurt glossary (ca. 685) and because dialectal indications point to Mercian composition, Fulk concluded that *Beowulf* was most likely composed between ca. 685 and ca. 725.[45]

Far from constituting a swing of the pendulum back to the linguistic tests of early philologists, Fulk's *A History of Old English Meter* represents a genuinely new development in the scholarship on the dating of *Beowulf*. Fulk made the case for the validity of linguistic and metrical dating criteria with a comprehensiveness that had not previously been achieved or even attempted. The comprehensive quality of the book's argumentation is perhaps the primary reason why it has persuaded many scholars. A single dating criterion, examined in isolation, can make only limited demands on credence from observers, since the phenomenon under scrutiny could conceivably be an accident of style or dialect. But when six independent dating criteria, each connected to independent chronological developments in the history of the English language, confirm each other's results, the only reasonable conclusion to draw is that these criteria are reliable indicators of relative chronology. Furthermore, building on the work of Max Kaluza and A.J. Bliss, Fulk was the first scholar to make a complete case for the chronological significance of the poem's adherence to Kaluza's law.[46] Because of Fulk's meticulous argumentation, scholars who now credit the hypothesis that *Beowulf* is a

---

circumflex intonation in Proto-Germanic and was shortened later than regular long vowels. For paradigms of the Proto-Germanic declensions, see Fulk, *HOEM*, 419–25. For a list of verses in *Beowulf* adhering to Kaluza's law, see A.J. Bliss, *The Metre of Beowulf* (Oxford: Blackwell, 1958), 27–30, and Fulk, *HOEM*, 160–2.

[45] See Fulk, *HOEM*, 330, 368–81, 390.
[46] See the references in fn. 44.

product of the seventh or eighth century do so for very different reasons than scholars who credited that hypothesis a century ago.

Just as Amos's skeptical treatment of the linguistic evidence provided an impetus for *A History of Old English Meter*, Kiernan's claim that paleographical evidence supported an eleventh-century date of composition elicited new interest in the *Beowulf* manuscript. Studies from David N. Dumville and Johan Gerritsen emerged with the explicit purpose of refuting Kiernan, and in doing so, these studies shed considerable new light on the date of the extant manuscript and the probability that it derives from an antique archetype.[47] Peter Clemoes, following Gerritsen, observed that certain transliteration errors in the *Beowulf* manuscript suggest that *Beowulf* existed in writing long before the year 1000.[48] The numerous scribal errors involving confusions of *a* and *u*, for example, were most probably induced by the use in the archetype of *Beowulf* of a letterform known as the open-headed *a*. This letterform was common in the eighth century, rarer in the ninth, and virtually unknown in the tenth; late scribes copying an old manuscript containing this unfamiliar form would naturally mistake it for *u*.[49] Building on Gerritsen and Clemoes, Michael Lapidge assembled all of the evidence pertaining to five transliteration errors – those involving *a* and *u*, *r* and *n*, *p* and *p*, *c* and *t*, *d* and *ð* – and observed that the collective presence of these errors can be economically explained with a single hypothesis: that *Beowulf* was first committed to parchment in Anglo-Saxon set minuscule script prior to 750.[50] A.N. Doane and George Clark have recently supported Lapidge's hypothesis by demonstrating that similar patterns of transliteration errors can be discerned in *Genesis A* and in the Arundel Psalter gloss, both of which appear to be preserved in late copies derived from eighth-century archetypes.[51]

---

[47] See David N. Dumville, "*Beowulf* Come Lately: Some Notes on the Paleography of the Nowell Codex," *Archiv für das Studium der neueren Sprachen und Literaturen* 225 (1988): 49–63; Dumville, "The *Beowulf* Manuscript and How Not to Date it," *Medieval English Student's Newsletter* 39 (1998): 21–7; Johan Gerritsen, "Have with you to Lexington!: The *Beowulf* Manuscript and *Beowulf*," in *In Other Words: Transcultural Studies in Philology, Translation, and Lexicology presented to Hans Heinrich Meyer on the Occasion of his Sixty-Fifth Birthday*, ed. J. Lachlan Mackenzie and Richard Todd (Dordrecht: Foris, 1989), 15–34; Gerritsen, "*Beowulf* Revisited," *English Studies* 79 (1998): 82–6.

[48] Peter Clemoes, *Interactions of Thought and Language in Old English Poetry* (Cambridge: Cambridge University Press, 1995), 32–4.

[49] Clemoes, *Interactions of Thought and Language*, 32, n. 77.

[50] Michael Lapidge, "The Archetype of *Beowulf*," *Anglo-Saxon England* 29 (2000): 5–41.

[51] *Genesis A: A New Edition, Revised*, ed. A.N. Doane (Tempe: ACMRS, 2013), 37–41; George Clark, "The Date of *Beowulf* and the Arundel Psalter Gloss," *Modern Philology* 106.4 (2009): 677–85. The Arundel Psalter Gloss had previously been adduced erroneously as evidence undermining Lapidge's hypothesis; see E.G. Stanley, "Paleographical and

Lapidge's study, like those mentioned above, represents a new development in *Beowulf* scholarship. C.L. Wrenn had briefly suggested that confusion of *d* and *ð* pointed to an antique exemplar, but he felt no need to make an extended case for this, nor did he consider related transliteration errors.[52] Lapidge took a form of evidence of which scholars were vaguely aware, assembled the pertinent evidence, and made a clear case for its chronological implications. A similar relationship to previous scholarship obtains in my study of the scribal errors of proper names in the *Beowulf* manuscript.[53] Kenneth Sisam, J.R.R. Tolkien, and Tom Shippey each observed in passing that many names are corrupted in the manuscript and that these corruptions may indicate late unfamiliarity with the ancient content of *Beowulf*.[54] In my study, I assembled and analyzed all of the errors, anomalies, and corrections pertaining to proper names, observing that there are approximately fifty such cases. These problems with proper names cannot tell us when *Beowulf* was composed, but their frequent presence supports the probability that the extant manuscript is a copy of a centuries-old poem, not of a recent composition. Like the decline in the use of *Beowulf* names observed by Wormald, the scribal errors of proper names suggest that the heroic-legendary traditions informing *Beowulf* were no longer widely known in the later Anglo-Saxon period.

Since the 1980s, there have also been several important studies dating *Beowulf* to the early Anglo-Saxon period using cultural and historical evidence. Their arguments have differed substantially from earlier ones favoring the age of Bede, in that they have focused more on specific and datable phenomena, and less on vague ideas of the early period's sophistication, gentleness, or semi-paganism. Sam Newton amassed a wide range of literary, archaeological, genealogical, and folkloric evidence in his effort to situate the composition of *Beowulf* in an eighth-century East Anglian context.[55] Tom Shippey observed that the *Beowulf* poet's *merewioing* for 'Merovingian' is the only extant etymologically correct rendering of this name, which could not derive from written sources

---

Textual Deep Waters: <a> for <u> and <u> for <a>, <d> for <ð> and <ð> for <d> in Old English," *ANQ: American Notes and Queries* 15 (2002): 64–72.

[52] Wrenn, "The Value of Spelling," 18.

[53] Leonard Neidorf, "Scribal Errors of Proper Names in the *Beowulf* Manuscript," *Anglo-Saxon England* 42 (2013): 249–69.

[54] Kenneth Sisam, "The Authority of Old English Poetical Manuscripts," *Studies in the History of Old English Literature* (Oxford: Clarendon Press, 1953), 29–44, at 37; J.R.R. Tolkien, *Finn and Hengest: the Fragment and the Episode*, ed. Alan Bliss (London: HarperCollins, 2006), 32; Tom Shippey, "Afterword," in Beowulf *and Lejre*, ed. John D. Niles (Tempe: ACMRS, 2007), 469–480, at 474–6.

[55] Sam Newton, *The Origins of* Beowulf *and the Pre-Viking Kingdom of East Anglia* (Cambridge: D.S. Brewer, 1993).

(where the name is routinely mangled), but must reflect current oral circulation in the vernacular – an improbability long after the downfall of the Merovingian dynasty in 751.[56] Rolf H. Bremmer, Jr. argued that the *Beowulf* poet's representation of Frisia as a land of immense wealth accords with seventh- and eighth-century conditions, but would have made little sense after 800, when the Frisian economy severely declined.[57] M.J. Swanton and Fred M. Biggs, moreover, have both written extensive studies of kingship and succession in *Beowulf*, arguing that the poet represented and meditated upon regnal practices that prevailed during the seventh and eighth centuries, but were less relevant during the ninth and tenth.[58] As we have seen with regard to other forms of evidence, these studies took ideas that were vaguely iterated before the 1980s – Newton building on Klaeber, Shippey on Bachlechner, etc.[59] – and made cases with greater precision and more evidence than was felt to be necessary before the eruption of the dating debate.

The studies from the past thirty years discussed above have achieved more than the advancement of our understanding of the varieties of evidence bearing on the dating of *Beowulf*. They have also effectively reframed what is meant by the phrase "the dating of *Beowulf*." Recent scholarship has demonstrated that the question of dating need not be conceptualized as a matter of finding the particular context most congenial to the poem's composition. Instead of trafficking in nebulous notions of early or late cultural sophistication, scholars have increasingly preferred to foreground and analyze forms of chronologically significant evidence that permit rational dispute. If the dating of *Beowulf* is understood to

---

[56] Tom Shippey, "The Merov(ich)ingian Again: *damnatio memoriae* and the *usus scholarum*," in *Latin Learning and English Lore: Studies in Anglo-Saxon Literature for Michael Lapidge*, vol. 1, ed. Katherine O'Brien O'Keeffe and Andy Orchard (Toronto: University of Toronto Press, 2005), 389–406, at 402. Walter Goffart, "The Name 'Merovingian' and the Dating of *Beowulf*," *Anglo-Saxon England* 36 (2007): 93–101, takes issue with Shippey's arguments, but does not address his claim concerning the etymologically correct form of the name.

[57] Rolf H. Bremmer, Jr., "The Frisians in *Beowulf*; *Beowulf* in Frisia: The Vicissitudes of Time," in *Medieval English Literary and Cultural Studies. SELIM XV*, ed. Juan Camilo Conde Silvestre and Ma Nila Vázquez González (Murcia: Universidad de Murcia, 2004), 3–31.

[58] M.J. Swanton, *Crisis and Development in Germanic Society 700–800*: Beowulf *and the Burden of Kingship*, Göppinger Arbeiten zur Germanistik 333 (Göppingen: Kümmerle, 1982); Fred M. Biggs, "The Politics of Succession in *Beowulf* and Anglo-Saxon England," *Speculum* 80 (2005): 709–41.

[59] Beowulf *and the Fight at Finnsburg*, ed. Frederick Klaeber. 3rd. ed. (Boston: Heath, 1950), xxxiii-vi; Joseph Bachlechner, "Die Merowinge im *Beowulf*," *Zeitschrift für deutsches Altertum und deutsche Literatur* 6 (1849): 524–6. Girvan, Beowulf *and the Seventh Century*, anticipates arguments connecting *Beowulf* to the politics of the early Anglo-Saxon period.

connote disputation about the chronological implications of linguistic, metrical, paleographical, and onomastic evidence (*inter alia*), then the position of "dogmatic agnosticism" begins to appear unwarranted. It is noteworthy that James Earl, in articulating his agnostic position, framed the dating controversy with the following question:

> Does *Beowulf* reflect the conversion, express the Golden Age of Bede, pay tribute to Offa or Wiglaf of Mercia, legitimize the West Saxon royal line, conciliate the Danish settlement, respond heroically to the Vikings, or praise the Anglo-Danish dynasty of Cnut?[60]

Conceptualizing the question of dating in such terms, a scholar would be bound to adopt a position of agnosticism, since there could be no principled basis for gauging the relative probability of competing hypotheses. How is one to determine rationally whether *Beowulf* feels more Bedan than Alfredian, or whether it is more probably advancing the politics of Æthelstan than of Offa? These terms are not particularly conducive to analysis, so it is natural that their prioritization should elicit agnosticism. We are on an entirely different footing when confronting the chronological implications of evidence such as transliteration errors or verses requiring non-contraction for scansion. Here scholars can gauge the relative probability of competing hypotheses rather straightforwardly by determining which hypothesis is most capable of explaining the form of evidence under scrutiny. Conceptualized in these terms, the dating of *Beowulf* should be regarded not as an insoluble mystery demanding agnosticism, but as a productive framework for examining evidence and drawing informed conclusions.

The history of the dating of *Beowulf* controversy adumbrated in this introduction has focused on publications from the past thirty years that have collectively changed the terms of the debate. The nature of the evidence, methodology, and argumentation to be found in current scholarship can now be quite unlike what they were one hundred years ago or even thirty-five years ago. Of course, some scholarship may continue to be written that ignores the probabilistic force of the evidence accumulated and prefers to date the poem by identifying particularized contexts congenial to its composition.[61] Studies of that sort, however, have become

---

[60] Earl, *Thinking About* Beowulf, 17
[61] For one recent attempt to date *Beowulf* by identifying a context congenial to the poem's composition, see Helen Damico, "*Beowulf*'s Foreign Queen and the Politics of Eleventh-Century England," in *Intertexts: Studies in Anglo-Saxon Culture Presented to Paul E. Szarmach*, ed. Virginia Blanton and Helene Scheck (Tempe, AZ: ACMRS, 2008), 209–40. Damico dates the composition of *Beowulf* to ca. 1040, against the paleographical dating of the manuscript, on the grounds that "the parallels in scene and character [between Wealtheow and Queen Emma] seem too compelling to dismiss solely on paleographic grounds," 210–11. I doubt that many scholars would share the view

increasingly rare. As Roberta Frank has observed, the two dating arguments that appear to be the most influential in recent scholarship are Fulk on Kaluza's law and Lapidge on the poem's archetype, both of which date the composition of *Beowulf* to the first half of the eighth century.[62] Frank considers the emerging consensus for an early dating of *Beowulf* to be a simple return to the fashion of an earlier era of scholarship; she compares the swing of opinion to the commercial revival of Hush Puppies.[63] This comparison misrepresents recent developments, however, because current scholars who hold that *Beowulf* is an eighth-century composition do so for very different reasons than scholars from earlier generations. Chambers, Tolkien, and their contemporaries felt that the cultural suitability of the age of Bede was the most compelling dating criterion. Their scholarship was not concerned with restricted vocabulary or with verses observing etymological length distinctions, because the chronological significance of such evidence had not yet been fully explored. The dating of *Beowulf* today is not what it was one hundred years ago.

The essays assembled in the present collection consolidate and augment the efforts of recent scholarship to advance our understanding of the dating of *Beowulf*. The contributors reassess the chronological implications of a wide variety of evidence, including, but not limited to, the linguistic, metrical, semantic, onomastic, paleographical, cultural, historical, and theological. Because it can involve so many disparate considerations, dating *Beowulf* may seem to be a daunting or impossible task. Understandably, scholars might prefer to take an agnostic position and assert that the question is undecidable rather than wade through the voluminous quantity of scholarship pertaining to the dating of *Beowulf*. By offering accounts of the various forms of evidence that are both authoritative and discriminating, this volume aims to facilitate the process by which scholars might arrive at an informed opinion about the poem's date. Whatever conclusion one reaches, the following essays will enable that conclusion to be based in reasoning rather than divination. No longer need one adopt a position intuitively and believe that "the evidence for it is the merest gossamer."[64] Due to the efforts of generations of *Beowulf* scholars, many forms of evidence bearing on the poem's date

---

that the probabilities involved in the paleographical dating of the extant manuscript are less compelling than the probabilities involved in the identification of historical parallels. On the dating of the manuscript (to ca. 1001–10), see Dumville, "*Beowulf* Come Lately."

[62] See Roberta Frank, "A Scandal in Toronto: *The Dating of* 'Beowulf' a Quarter Century On," *Speculum* 82 (2007): 843–64, at 849–54.
[63] Frank, "A Scandal in Toronto," 849–50.
[64] See fn. 20.

can be foregrounded and analyzed, and it is to be hoped that the present volume helps such evidence retain a central position in future discussions of the dating of *Beowulf*.

1

Beowulf and Language History

R.D. Fulk

It would appear that of the varied types of evidence that have been adduced to try to establish when *Beowulf* was composed, the linguistic evidence is accorded special status by most Anglo-Saxonists. There are countless signs that this is the case. For example, when Kevin Kiernan sets out to counter the prevailing attitude that the poem could not be a product of the eleventh century, nearly all the evidence he confronts, which he does at some length, is linguistic in nature, the only very notable exception being Dorothy Whitelock's contention that a poem sympathetic to Danes is unlikely to have been composed after the onset of the Viking Age.[1] It is notable how often, in the years following its publication, Ashley Crandell Amos's study rejecting nearly all linguistic bases for dating Old English texts was cited as having produced a revolution.[2] Likewise, Roberta Frank's especial focus upon, and attempt to discredit, those who would date the poem early on linguistic and paleographical grounds is surely a gauge of the seriousness of the challenge that such

---

[1] Kevin S. Kiernan, Beowulf *and the* Beowulf *Manuscript* (New Brunswick: Rutgers University Press, 1981; reissued 1996, with a new preface, an appendix, and a foreword by Katherine O'Brien O'Keeffe, Ann Arbor: University of Michigan Press), 23–63. For Whitelock's position, see her book *The Audience of* Beowulf (Oxford: Clarendon, 1951), 24–5. According to Colin Chase, "Opinions on the Date of *Beowulf*, 1815–1980," in *The Dating of* Beowulf, ed. Colin Chase (Toronto: University of Toronto Press, 1982; reissued 1997 with an afterword), 3–8, at 6, Whitelock was repeating a comment of N.F.S. Grundtvig.

[2] Ashley Crandell Amos, *Linguistic Means of Determining the Dates of Old English Literary Texts* (Cambridge, Mass.: Medieval Academy of America, 1980). Aside from the frequent citation of the book in studies concerned with dating, there is the evidence of the glowing reviews that the book received, e.g., by Matti Rissanen in *Speculum* 57 (1982): 112–14; Thomas Cable in the *Journal of English and Germanic Philology* 85 (1986): 93–5; Celia Sisam in *Medium Ævum* 52 (1983): 138–9; and M.R. Godden in *The Review of English Studies*, n.s. 35 (1984): 346–7, the last two less enthusiastic than the others, but still finding the treatment of the phonological evidence quite valuable.

evidence must be felt to pose to Frank's own ideas about the poem's date.³

The reasons for the particular importance accorded the linguistic evidence are not hard to divine. Linguistic evidence is more objective than other kinds, since language changes in predictable ways. For example, if the name *Ongenðeowes* at 2475 must be scanned with a short diphthong *eo* (about which more will be said below), it can be seen that this must be the older value, since comparative evidence points to an originally short vowel in OE *þēow* 'servant' (cf. Gothic plural *þiwōs*), and the analogical process by which the diphthong was later lengthened is readily perceivable. Such considerations raise the significant probability that the poem was composed before the onset of the lengthening process. By contrast, non-linguistic evidence usually entails no significant probabilities of this sort. For instance, it has been argued that the poem was composed as part of an effort to forge a common culture for Englishmen and Scandinavians living side by side in Britain, and thus it is not likely to have been composed before the reign of Æthelstan.⁴ This could indeed be the case, but it is of course just one among a very large number of possible contexts for the composition of the poem, and it does not even seem the likeliest of those possibilities. One difficulty is that if the poem represents a melding of English and Scandinavian influences, the recognizably Scandinavian contribution seems oddly thin. Scandinavian legends represented in the poem often differ markedly from versions recorded in later Scandinavian sources, and the names of Scandinavians in the poem are purely English in form.⁵ Especially since the linguistic evidence strongly suggests a date of composition at least a century before the Cotton manuscript was made, as detailed below, one feels that a hypothesis such as this needs to be particularly compelling to induce us to ignore the linguistic evidence.

Likewise, it could be that the erasure of folio 179 of the *Beowulf* Manuscript results from an attempt to compose a less abrupt transition between two separate compositions and thus possibly indicates that the poem is contemporary with the making of the manuscript.⁶ But that is

---

3   Roberta Frank, "A Scandal in Toronto: *The Dating of* 'Beowulf' a Quarter Century On," *Speculum* 82 (2007): 843–64.
4   This is the position advocated in several publications by John D. Niles, for example in *Homo Narrans: The Poetics and Anthropology of Oral Literature* (Philadelphia: University of Pennsylvania Press, 1999), 134–40.
5   For references to Scandinavian parallels and scholarship on them, see *Klaeber's* Beowulf *and the Fight at Finnsburg*, ed. R.D. Fulk, Robert E. Bjork, and John D. Niles, 4th ed. (Toronto: University of Toronto Press, 2008; corrected reprint 2012), li–lxvii. For references to scholarship concerning the English form of Scandinavian names in the poem, see R.D. Fulk, "Review Article: Dating *Beowulf* to the Viking Age," *Philological Quarterly* 61 (1982): 341–59, at 344.
6   Such is the argument of Kiernan, Beowulf *and the* Beowulf *Manuscript*, 219–70.

not the only plausible explanation; neither is it really the *most* plausible explanation, since in those few instances in which the letters of the original writing on the leaf can be made out, the words do not appear to be substantially different from those of the rewritten text.[7] Moreover, a fair amount of evidence has been amassed to show that linguistic and stylistic features of the parts of the poem before and after the erased leaf are markedly similar, and they are different from features found in other poems: for example, *Beowulf* is the only poem that faithfully observes Kaluza's law in regard to etymologically light endings, as discussed below, and the two portions of the poem observe it with equal fidelity. It is thus hard to believe that *Beowulf* represents two independent compositions spliced clumsily together.[8] And the rewritten text on the erased leaf is in places such bad Old English that it is thoroughly implausible that an Anglo-Saxon could have written it.

Similarly, in regard to the theory that the poem betrays evidence of the influence of skaldic poetry upon its diction and thus must be a fairly late composition: this could indeed explain the small number of similarities that have been identified.[9] But there is nothing in this theory to make us think that this explanation is more probable than certain others. The similarities all have to do with cognates and may thus be due to commonalities in verse traditions that antedate considerably the advent of the Viking Age. Moreover, skaldic diction was still relatively young at the time when the *Beowulf* Manuscript was made (and the poetry of the earliest skalds is quite unlike the poetry that Frank supposes influenced the *Beowulf* poet), and since we have good evidence of English influence on

---

[7] See R.D. Fulk, "Some Contested Readings in the *Beowulf* Manuscript," *The Review of English Studies*, n.s. 56 (2005): 192–223, at 208–23. The response of Kevin Kiernan, "The *nathwylc* Scribe and the *nathwylc* Text of *Beowulf*," in *Poetry, Place and Gender: Studies in Medieval Culture in Honor of Helen Damico*, ed. Catherine E. Karkov (Kalamazoo: Medieval Institute Publications, Western Michigan University, 2009), 98–131, even if it were thought persuasive in regard to analyzing the writing on the relevant leaf, would not obviate this difficulty.

[8] For references to linguistic scholarship on the poem's integrity, see *Klaeber's* Beowulf, ed. Fulk, Bjork, and Niles, lxxxviii–xci.

[9] The influence of skaldic diction on the poet has been urged in several articles by Roberta Frank: "Skaldic Verse and the Date of *Beowulf*," in *The Dating of* Beowulf, ed. Chase, 123–39; "Old Norse Memorial Eulogies and the Ending of *Beowulf*," in *The Early Middle Ages*, Acta 6 (Binghamton: CEMERS, 1982), 1–19; "Did Anglo-Saxon Audiences Have a Skaldic Tooth?" *Scandinavian Studies* 59 (1987): 338–55. For a particularly effective response to Frank's claims about skaldic influence on Old English poets' employment of the "beasts of battle" topos, see Joseph Harris, "Beasts of Battle, South and North," in *Source of Wisdom: Old English and Early Medieval Latin Studies in Honour of Thomas D. Hill*, ed. Charles D. Wright, Frederick M. Biggs, and Thomas N. Hall (Toronto: University of Toronto Press, 2007), 3–25.

some skaldic compositions already by the middle of the tenth century,[10] and most skaldic poetry was composed much later than the beginning of the eleventh century, one would rather expect that similarities between the two poetic traditions would be due to the influence of English upon Norse compositions, rather than the reverse. At all events, there does not seem to be any good reason to think that Norse influence upon English poetry is the *most* plausible explanation. Dating evidence such as this is plainly unlike linguistic evidence in respect to probabilism.

The kinds of probabilities associated with the linguistic evidence are not of such a statistical nature as to require any mathematical measure of significance, but they may be freely intuited on the principle that some hypotheses are by their very nature more probable than others. This point about probability may sound so obvious that it does not need to be made, but in fact to many scholars it is not at all obvious. In literary studies a high value is placed on undecidability: texts are assumed to have multiple meanings, often contradictory ones, and literary scholars for the most part frown on the notion that any one interpretation should be privileged over all others. As a consequence, many hermeneuts assume as a matter of course that the mere existence of competing interpretations entails undecidability.[11] This is not to say that in literary studies probability plays no role; E.D. Hirsch, for example, under the strong influence of John Maynard Keynes's *Treatise on Probability*, identifies "an interpretive hypothesis" as "ultimately a probability judgment that is supported by evidence," with all the detailed relevance of inductive methods that that identification implies; and even Hans-Georg Gadamer's fundamentally opposed theory of hermeneutics proceeds from the observation that inductive methods are the foundation of *Geisteswissenschaft*.[12] But in literary pursuits the distinction between probability and proof is nonetheless

---

[10] See Dietrich Hofmann, *Nordisch-englische Lehnbeziehungen der Wikingerzeit*, Bibliotheca Arnamagnæana 14 (Copenhagen: Ejnar Munksgaard, 1955).

[11] This issue is treated at some length in R.D. Fulk, "On Argumentation in Old English Philology, with Particular Reference to the Editing and Dating of *Beowulf*," *Anglo-Saxon England* 32 (2003): 1–26. Several of the points raised in the ensuing paragraphs are treated in greater detail in that article. That the date of *Beowulf* is undecidable is just one instantiation of this common misunderstanding about how to regard competing claims in philological argumentation. Examples are myriad; for a relatively recent instance in regard to a different issue, see Oren Falk, "Beowulf's Longest Day: The Amphibious Hero in His Element (*Beowulf*, ll. 1495b–96)," *Journal of English and Germanic Philology* 106 (2007): 1–21, at 2.

[12] Hirsch draws out the considerable methodological implications of his analysis in detail in *Validity in Interpretation* (New Haven: Yale University Press, 1967), especially 164–207, here at 180; for Gadamer's views, see *Truth and Method*, 2nd ed., trans. Joel Weinsheimer and Donald G. Marshall (New York: Continuum, 1989), 3–9 et passim. Hirsch offers an enlightening critique of Gadamer's views in *Validity in Interpretation*, 245–64.

widely misunderstood. For example, in a recent article, Walter Goffart says that "R.D. Fulk and Michael Lapidge ... both believe that they offer strict proof, philological and paleographic, that *Beowulf* is a product of, at latest, the eighth century."[13] Strict proof is impossible, for reasons to be explained in a moment, and obviously it is untrue that either Lapidge or the present writer ever made such a claim. Goffart apparently does not comprehend the distinction between deductive and inductive reasoning, though the logical result of confusing probabilistic reasoning with "strict proof" is to ignore the force of probabilities in the absence of proof. Likewise, Goffart cites Eric Stanley in regard to the apparent reference to "the Merovingian" in *Beowulf* 2921, who says, "Some single, odd, ancient-looking spelling provides no firm basis for early dating."[14] Stanley is right that it does not provide a firm basis for dating, but to reject it as he does is as much as to say what Goffart implies: that probabilistic evidence, because it is not proof, may be dismissed out of hand, no matter how cumulative the probability may be. To the contrary, although the reference in line 2921 does not prove early composition, neither is it void of significance.

Attitudes are rather different in regard to the status of probabilistic evidence in the field of philology, which is to a great extent a branch of historical linguistics, a field that professes to be governed by scientific principles. Hypotheses do not merely coexist but are always in competition with other hypotheses, jockeying for position, always aiming to come out on top. And although a hypothesis can never be proved correct, by various means it can be rendered so very probable that it demands credence. This is why, for example, proponents of intelligent design are right when they say that natural selection is only a hypothesis; but to suppose that because it is only a hypothesis it demands no greater credence than a literal reading of the Book of Genesis is to misunderstand fundamentally the nature of science. Philology is thus by nature very much at odds with what many literary scholars believe, because the purpose of philology is to narrow the range of possible interpretations rather than to treat all reasonable ones as equal.[15]

---

[13] Goffart, "The Name 'Merovingian' and the Dating of *Beowulf*," *Anglo-Saxon England* 36 (2007): 93–101, at 94. The study by Lapidge to which Goffart is referring is "The Archetype of *Beowulf*," *Anglo-Saxon England* 29 (2000): 5–41. Goffart's failure to comprehend the distinction between probability and proof is particularly disappointing because more than a little care was taken at the outset of the very book he here criticizes, *A History of Old English Meter* (Philadelphia: University of Pennsylvania Press, 1992; here at 6–24), to explain the distinction.

[14] Stanley, "The Date of *Beowulf*: Some Doubts and No Conclusions," in *The Dating of Beowulf*, ed. Chase, 197–211, at 201.

[15] For an excellent, concise summary of the principles of empirical methodology in linguistics, along with a fine demonstration of their application to a particular case, see

One means of rendering a hypothesis probable is to show that it explains a wider variety of facts than any competing hypothesis. What this means in regard to philology and the dating of *Beowulf* is that if there are linguistic features of an archaic nature in the poem, the greater the number of such features that can be identified, the likelier the explanation that they result from the poem's first having been committed to parchment at a relatively early date. The hypothesis that the poem is an early composition can never be proved, first of all, because no hypothesis can be proved conclusively, but secondly and more particularly because it is possible that the *Beowulf* poet simply knew more about the ancient traditions of verse composition, and about the Old English language, than other Old English poets. Some scholars seem to believe this latter possibility is correct, but it should be recognized that it faces certain obstacles. One is that it involves a certain kind of special pleading in the form of an unusual circumstance, and so it is the more complex hypothesis, and Occam's razor tells us that, *ceteris paribus*, the simpler hypothesis is to be preferred. A more estimable problem is that if the *Beowulf* poet were a late *scop* who happened to use rather archaic language, it is surprising that he never makes the mistake of mixing undeniable neologisms into his verse. And the greater the variety of archaic linguistic features there are to be found in the poem, the more difficult it is to believe that the poet's knowledge of archaic language was wholly artificial.

There are some more particular reasons to doubt this hypothesis, one of which will soon become plain. But at this point it may be useful to summarize some of the more significant kinds of linguistic evidence. Some of it is detectable only on the basis of poetic meter, but by no means all of it. Of the evidence that depends on meter, two sorts may be mentioned that seem particularly significant. Here they can be described only briefly; they involve technical problems of some interest and complexity, but the present purpose is to portray the range of evidence available on a linguistic basis, and so details must be sought elsewhere.[16]

First there is non-parasiting. In prehistoric times, words like *frōfr* and *wolcn* were monosyllabic, and only later did they develop into disyllables when the final resonant became syllabic. In the meter of poetry, such words must frequently be treated as monosyllables, although no poem of an estimable length treats them consistently as such. This must therefore be regarded as an archaism artificially preserved in verse, rather like the treatment of *heaven* and *never* as monosyllables in some Victorian poetry.

Sherrylyn Branchaw, "Principles of Methodology: A Case Study from the History of English," forthcoming in *English Language and Linguistics*.

[16] Unless an alternative reference is given, the linguistic issues treated in the following paragraphs are all discussed, with references, in Fulk, *A History of Old English Meter*.

Beowulf is the most conservative of any Old English poem in regard to this feature, which is quite rare in texts usually assumed to have been composed later in the Old English period, such as *Andreas* and the works of Cynewulf. It is particularly notable that in these later poems the rare non-parasited forms are used only in formulaic expressions, whereas in *Beowulf* the contexts are much more varied. This tells against the supposition that the *Beowulf* poet was a late poet who just happened to know more about archaic language than other poets, since it suggests development in the poetic tradition rather than a mere disparity in knowledge about the grammar of poetry.[17]

Second there is metrical non-contraction, whereby two vowels that have undergone contraction, usually after the loss of intervocalic /h/, must be treated metrically as if they had never undergone the process. For example, the word *sēon*, which is a monosyllable with a long diphthong, must be treated as if it were a disyllable *seohan, as it was in prehistoric times. *Beowulf* is not quite as conservative as *Genesis A* or *Daniel* in regard to this feature, but it is much more conservative than poems usually assumed to be later compositions, once again such as *Andreas* and the works of Cynewulf.

Some other linguistic archaisms of particular interest may derive support from the meter but do not depend entirely on scansion. One of these is the spelling of the names *Ecgþēo*, *Ongenþēo*, and *Wealhþēo*, which are diphthongal stems.[18] Roughly half the time in *Beowulf*, these names are spelt without *w*, in both inflected and uninflected forms. Etymologically, the second element of these names originally contained a short *e* before *w*. In the uninflected forms, *e* + *w* changed to a long diphthong *ēo*, whereas *w* remained before an inflection, so that the paradigm included forms like nominative singular -*þēo* and genitive singular -*þewes*. Then analogy set in, such that the long diphthong of the uninflected forms was extended to the inflected ones, and, conversely, the *w* of the inflected forms was extended to the uninflected ones. As a consequence, the word *þēow*, meaning 'servant', is usually spelt with a diphthong, and almost always a *w*, throughout the paradigm in Old English. There are just three instances of spellings of the simplex without *w* in the *Dictionary of Old English Corpus*, two of them in quite old texts, the gloss on the Vespasian

---

[17] The relation between linguistic evidence of this sort and the evolution of oral tradition, and why it tells against the supposition of a late, extraordinarily conservative poet, is discussed in R.D. Fulk, "Old English Meter and Oral Tradition: Three Issues Bearing on Poetic Chronology," *Journal of English and Germanic Philology* 106 (2007): 304–24.

[18] In addition to what is said about such diphthongal stems in Fulk, *A History of Old English Meter*, 146–52, see now *Klaeber's* Beowulf, ed. Fulk, Bjork, and Niles, 327–8.

Psalter and the laws of Æthelberht.[19] The likeliest explanation for the frequency of the archaic spelling without *w* in personal names in *Beowulf*, when it is so rare elsewhere in the OE corpus, is that the scribes were copying an archaic exemplar. This explanation is reinforced by the meter of the poem, in which the word root in inflected forms must sometimes be scanned as light and is never required to be scanned as heavy, showing that the poet used the older forms, which were in use before the analogical lengthening took place. It should be added that the names *Ecgþēo* and *Ecglāf* suggest a further archaism, inasmuch as three times the first scribe spells the first constituent of these names *ec-* rather than *ecg-* (correcting to *ecg-* in one instance). Three instances suggest that this is not a random scribal error but that the scribe's exemplar spelt it *ec-*. In that event, the likeliest explanation is once again an archaic exemplar, since *ec-* is a frequent spelling of this name-element in the eighth-century Cotton and St. Petersburg manuscripts of Bede's *Historia ecclesiastica*, a spelling still found occasionally in the Namur manuscript (probably of the ninth century, though some date it to the eighth), which is also encountered in some early entries in the Anglo-Saxon Chronicle.[20]

Beowulf is almost our only source for another linguistic archaism, the preservation of the original genitive plural of light-stemmed *i*-stem nouns. The original form ended in *-ia*, but like most *i*-stem inflections, this was replaced by the *a*-stem inflection, in this case simple *-a*. Examples of the original inflection are frequent in *Beowulf* because *Dene*, meaning 'Danes', is a light-stemmed *i*-stem, and it occurs often in the genitive plural in *Beowulf*. But the genitive plural *wini(g)a* meaning 'of friends' also occurs twice. There is just one other probable instance of such an old genitive plural in Old English, in *Guthlac B*, and in *Beowulf* itself the newer, analogical form *Dena* appears about as often as the older form. The use of such archaic forms almost exclusively in *Beowulf* certainly reinforces the impression that the poem's language is archaic.

---

[19] See Antonette diPaolo Healey, ed., *Dictionary of Old English Web Corpus*, 1 CD (Toronto: Dictionary of Old English Project, 2009). Also available on line by subscription at http://www.doe.utoronto.ca/pages/pub/web-corpus.html.

[20] The manuscripts are, respectively, London, British Library, Cotton MS. Tiberius C. ii; St. Petersburg, National Library of Russia, MS. lat. Q. v. I 18; and Namur, Public Library, Fonds de la ville 11. The spellings in *ec-* are preserved in the later Namur manuscript probably because the Continental scribe, not knowing English, could not update the spellings, as the English scribes of other post-eighth-century manuscripts could. On the readings of the Cotton and Namur manuscripts, and in the Chronicle, see Hilmer Ström, *Old English Personal Names in Bede's History: An Etymological-Phonological Investigation* (Lund: Gleerup, 1939), 134–5. On the readings of the St. Petersburg manuscript, see O.S. Anderson (Arngart), *Old English Material in the Leningrad Manuscript of Bede's Ecclesiastical History* (Lund: Gleerup, 1941), 84.

Kuhn's first law has generated a fair amount of discussion in recent years. It states that a particle – that is, a word of variable stress, such as a pronoun or a finite verb or an adverb without a suffix – may remain unstressed only if it appears in the first drop of the clause.[21] Otherwise it must be stressed. Recent discussion has pertained chiefly to how rigid the law is and whether the law is an independent principle of verse construction or a natural consequence of factors inherent in the language. What has not been contested, however, is Hans Kuhn's assessment that *Beowulf* is the most conservative poem in respect to the law in any West Germanic language. It is demonstrably more faithful than, for instance, any of the known works of Cynewulf. The principle appears to be a very ancient inheritance in the Germanic languages, to judge by patterns of clausal accentuation in other Indo-European languages, and so *Beowulf* would seem in this respect to reflect a linguistic state of affairs reminiscent of ancient times.

The significance of syntactic patterns involving the use of the weak adjective is widely misunderstood. Kevin Kiernan charges that syntactic patterns involving the weak adjective are credible evidence only in the eyes of those who are already convinced that the poem is an early composition.[22] But this is not a just assessment, since it is undeniable that the use of the weak adjective before a noun without a preceding demonstrative is exceptionally common in *Beowulf*, which is by far the poem with the greatest incidence of such constructions, even in proportion to the length of the poem. It is true that the incidence of this feature in various poems does not support a chronology of the sort usually assumed for OE poetry. For example, if this were a reliable indicator of chronology, *Genesis A* would appear to be younger than *Andreas*. But it has frequently been pointed out, for example by Ashley Crandell Amos, and by Frederick Klaeber long before her, that because such constructions are unusual in prose, it is not unlikely that scribes should have altered them, either adding a demonstrative or making the adjective strong.[23] The low incidence of the construction in a poem thus need not indicate late composition. Amos herself refuses to grant any preference to either of the two most plausible explanations for the exceedingly high incidence of the older construction in *Beowulf*, either that it is a stylistic matter or that it is a sign of the antiquity of the poem. But this is not an

---

[21] For discussion and references to scholarship on Kuhn's first law, see Haruko Momma, *The Composition of Old English Poetry* (Cambridge: Cambridge University Press, 1997) and, for references to subsequent work, *Klaeber's* Beowulf, ed. Fulk, Bjork, and Niles, 324.
[22] Kiernan, Beowulf *and the* Beowulf *Manuscript*, 24.
[23] See Amos, *Linguistic Means*, 121, and Klaeber, Beowulf *and The Fight at Finnsburg*, 3rd ed. with 1st and 2nd supplements (Lexington, Mass.: D.C. Heath, 1950), cviii–cix.

impartial view of the matter: although it is possible that it is a stylistic trait, we can be certain that it is an archaic syntactic pattern. To consider the stylistic explanation as likely as the other is (to turn the tables on the objection raised by Kiernan and mentioned above) to look at the evidence from a rather willful perspective, since it should be apparent by now that *Beowulf* shows many very conservative linguistic features – so many that it is hardly plausible that they should be merely the stylistic traits of a late poet. The poem contains linguistic archaisms: to explain them all away as stylistic quirks reveals a definite bias.

There are many other linguistic features of *Beowulf* that appear to be archaisms. Dennis Cronan, for instance, has done some excellent work on the semantics of Beowulfian vocabulary, and Geoffrey R. Russom on metrical change.[24] But these few examples already mentioned ought to suffice to illustrate the point made above about probability. Even just two or three such archaic linguistic features might be difficult to ignore, but when so many aspects of the language of *Beowulf* are of this conservative nature, producing what in the sciences is referred to as the cumulative effect of evidence, any explanation other than the most natural assumption – that *Beowulf* was composed earlier than poems without such features – cannot help but seem tendentious. At all events, to a historical linguist any competing hypothesis would require some fairly good supporting evidence. A really defensible linguistic justification seems never to have been offered for such a competing hypothesis. Rather, it would appear, scholars who argue for a late date generally just ignore evidence about the archaic nature of the poem's language.

A particular archaism has earned a certain degree of attention in recent years, both for its intrinsic linguistic interest and for the relative particularity of its implications for the dating of the poem. This is the matter of resolution, whereby a light syllable plus another syllable is to be treated as a single metrical position. In *Beowulf* there is a remarkable restriction on resolution under secondary stress, whereby the second of the resolved syllables must have been a light syllable in prehistoric times. For example, the verse *frēawine folca*, with resolution of *-wine*, is acceptable, whereas a similar verse with the genitive plural *-wina* would not be acceptable, since the final syllable is etymologically heavy. *Beowulf*

---

[24] Cronan, "Poetic Meanings in the Old English Poetic Vocabulary," *English Studies* 84 (2003): 397–425; Russom, "Dating Criteria for Old English Poems," in *Studies in the History of the English Language: A Millennial Perspective*, ed. Donka Minkova and Robert P. Stockwell (Berlin: Mouton de Gruyter, 2002), 245–65. A survey of archaisms and supposed neologisms in the language of *Beowulf* is offered by R.D. Fulk, "Archaisms and Neologisms in the Language of *Beowulf*," in *Studies in the History of the English Language III: Managing Chaos: Strategies for Identifying Change in English*, ed. Christopher M. Cain and Geoffrey Russom (Berlin: Mouton de Gruyter, 2007), 267–87.

is the only poem that consistently observes this distinction; *Exodus* generally follows the rule, though not consistently, but in connection with compositions of sufficient length to demonstrate the point effectively, no other poet seems to have been aware of the rule at all. This is part of what is now referred to as Kaluza's law, with which George Clark's Chapter 12 in this volume also deals. Not all scholars who have examined the problem agree with the present author about how to explain the *Beowulf* poet's ability to distinguish heavy and light endings, but however it is explained, it is plain that the poet's linguistic knowledge is of a more archaic nature than other poets'.

But the topic is worth considering in greater detail, because it reveals some hard truths about the role of objectivity in scholarly handling of the linguistic evidence. Building on the work of Max Kaluza and A.J. Bliss, the present author argued in 1992 that because the *Beowulf* poet consistently distinguishes etymologically light and heavy endings in verses like *frēawine folca*, the poem must have been composed at least a generation before some of the light and heavy endings fell together as *-e* and so became indistinguishable – for example, in the light category, the nominative (see *Beowulf* 430a, 485a, 640a, etc.) and accusative (76a, 715a, 753a, etc.) singular of masculine *i*-stem nouns, and in the heavy category, the nominative plural of masculine *a*-stem adjectives (1641a, 1895a, 2476a) and the genitive singular of *ō*-stem nouns (2118a), whose endings are treated differently in the meter of *Beowulf* despite being spelt the same way in the manuscript.[25] If this is true, the poem must have been composed no later than about 725 if it is a Southumbrian composition, as seems most likely. Because of some mistaken beliefs about the chronology of the relevant sound changes,[26] Bliss supposed that the *Beowulf* poet's observance of Kaluza's law could not have been on the basis of a phonological distinction, but that the difference between originally heavy and light endings must have been morphologized in one of two ways, either on the basis of an analogical proportion (essentially, endings lost after heavy syllables but retained after light are metrically light, the rest metrically heavy) or on the basis of vowel quality (essentially, original high vowels are metrically light, the rest metrically heavy). Seiichi Suzuki subsequently attempted to refine Bliss's pair of explanations, clarifying Bliss's former solution considerably and combining the two,

---

[25] Max Kaluza, "Zur Betonungs- und Verslehre des Altenglischen," in *Festschrift zum siebzigsten Geburtstage Oskar Schade* (Königsberg: Hartung, 1896), 101–34; A.J. Bliss, *The Metre of* Beowulf, revised ed. (Oxford: Blackwell, 1967), 27–35, 118–21; Fulk, *A History of Old English Meter*, 153–68.

[26] See Fulk, *A History of Old English Meter*, 385–6, for an explanation.

though in a way that was not entirely successful.[27] The present writer has explained in some detail why neither explanation is feasible.[28] The chief difficulty with Bliss's former explanation is that the posited morphological proportions could not have persisted long enough to account for the adherence of *Beowulf* to the law in all the requisite inflectional categories.[29] The primary obstacle to Bliss's latter explanation is that there

---

[27] Suzuki, *The Metrical Organization of* Beowulf: *Prototype and Isomorphism* (Berlin: Mouton de Gruyter, 1996), 205–38.

[28] R.D. Fulk, "Secondary Stress Phenomena in the Meter of *Beowulf*," *Interdisciplinary Journal of Germanic Linguistics and Semiotic Analysis* 3 (1998): 279–304, at 290–8. Another explanation has recently been offered by Eric Weiskott, "A Semantic Replacement for Kaluza's Law in *Beowulf*," *English Studies* 93 (2012): 891–6. Weiskott's argument is that although the law was at one time phonologically motivated, its conditioning had been semanticized by the time *Beowulf* was composed. There are a number of implausibilities that attend this argument, one of which is that there is not, to the present writer's knowledge, a reasonable parallel to such a development in any natural language, and semanticization is not a commonly recognized linguistic process, like morphologization or grammaticalization. Moreover, the result of what Weiskott considers semanticization is a rule involving semantics, phonology, and morphology, and it is thus too complex to be plausible as a natural linguistic development. Although phonological rules are morphologized with great regularity, morphologization occurs because the conditioning of a phonological alternation has been obscured, and a non-phonological reason must therefore be found for the remaining phonological alternation if the alternation is to be maintained, as with the morphologization of the Old English phonological alternation in Modern English *thief ~ thieves*. Semanticizing Kaluza's law would be entirely unlike this: according to Weiskott, the original phonological basis for the law disappeared once the law was semanticized; yet without the phonological alternation in place, it is incredible that a poet should have perceived any remaining distinction of such salience that it required a captious ragbag of semantic, phonological, and morphological properties to maintain – and Weiskott must assume that it was maintained and transmitted from poet to poet for several generations if his hypothesis is to have any chance of allowing a dating of *Beowulf* long after ca. 725 at the latest, when the phonological distinction was lost. (The reader may have noted that, to a less obvious degree, the same general problem attends Bliss's morphological solutions.) By now it should be plain that some contributors to the literature on Kaluza's law have no interest in finding the most plausible linguistic explanation for the law but only in attempting to prove that it has no bearing on the date of *Beowulf*. But one need not even examine Weiskott's arguments to see that his aim is not to provide a better and more objective explanation for an acknowledged linguistic phenomenon, since everywhere in the article but in the title, deprecatory sanitizing quotation marks are used whenever Kaluza's "law" is referred to. A detailed refutation of Weiskott's argument by Leonard Neidorf and Rafael J. Pascual, "The Language of *Beowulf* and the Conditioning of Kaluza's Law," is forthcoming in *Neophilologus*.

[29] Unless, that is, *Beowulf* is to be dated very early – earlier than, it appears, any Anglo-Saxonist is now willing to suppose. For example, already by the end of the seventh century the heavy-stemmed masculine *i*-stems were on their way to completing their migration to the class of *a*-stems, so that there were no heavy-stemmed masculine *i*-stems to which light-stemmed nouns like *wine* might be compared. The only exception is a small class of heavy-stemmed *i*-stem nouns, mostly ethnic names like *Mierce*, which are irrelevant in the present context because -*e* is retained in them analogically,

are five verses in *Beowulf* in which this explanation can be tested, and in all five instances it makes the wrong prediction.[30] But even if this were not the case, and if this explanation were plausible, the consequences for the dating of *Beowulf* would be fairly negligible. The result would be simply that the poem could be dated to a time about a generation later than if the case were otherwise – that is, to about 750 at the latest if Southumbrian in origin. The reason is that south of the Humber the coalescence of high and low final unstressed vowels as -*e* had begun by the middle of the eighth century, at which point the *Beowulf* poet could have relied on neither vowel quantity nor vowel quality to conform to the law – conformity would simply have become impossible.

It is therefore surprising that Roberta Frank has adopted the former of the two explanations – that is, that only endings lost after heavy syllables but not light were regarded by the poet of *Beowulf* as resolvable under secondary stress – though the rule produces exceptions (see note 32), and at all events, no such morphological contrast could have remained in effect beyond the seventh century (see note 29). Nearly as surprising is that although she cites Bliss and Suzuki in her paper, she does not credit them with having devised the hypothesis she offers.[31] Neither does she discuss or even acknowledge any of the reasons already presented for viewing this explanation as untenable.[32] As for the manner in which she

---

and so they offered no contrast between light stems retaining -*e* and heavy stems losing it.

[30] See Fulk, "Secondary Stress," 293–4. See further about this in note 32.

[31] "A Scandal in Toronto," 860–1.

[32] There is, regrettably, a pattern in Frank's article of unreliable accounts of the scholarship. For example, one of the unfortunate consequences of Bliss's having mistaken the chronology of sound changes is that he was obliged to try to explain away the verses *mōdceare micle* (1778a) and *mōdceare mǣndon* (3149a), which are incompatible with both of his proposed explanations, by the remark that *mōdceare* "is suspicious; possibly it replaces an obsolete word of a different declension" (Bliss, *The Metre of* Beowulf, 119). Frank asserts that the present writer treats the ending -*e* on *mōdceare* as metrically light even though "other experts had concluded" that it "was probably historically long" (860). In actuality, the grammars of early Germanic are all in agreement that the vowel that developed to this -*e* was not circumflected in Proto-Germanic (and therefore it should result in a light ending under the law as formulated by Kaluza): see, e.g., Hans Krahe and W. Meid, *Germanische Sprachwissenschaft II: Formenlehre* (Berlin: de Gruyter, 1969), 22, and Alfred Bammesberger, *Die Morphologie des urgermanischen Nomens* (Heidelberg: Carl Winter, 1990), 103–4. Aside from Bliss himself, the only scholar, it appears, who has ever suggested that this -*e* is metrically heavy (and so necessarily an exception to Kaluza's law, by his own admission) is Suzuki (*Metrical Organization*, 210, 424 n. 29), and his analysis is as entirely *post hoc* as Bliss's, since they both classify the ending not according to whether the ending was circumflected in Proto-Germanic, as Kaluza had supposed when he formulated the law, but according to the very morphological explanation that Frank here espouses but does not attribute to Bliss and Suzuki. Naturally, it is entirely circular reasoning to classify the ending as "probably historically long" on such a basis.

chose to deliver her views, objective readers may form their own judgment of the matter.

A concerted focus on Kaluza's law, however, to the exclusion of the other linguistic evidence, is surely misguided. Kaluza's law does not offer incontrovertible proof that *Beowulf* was composed no later than the eighth century, although certainly it seems rather strong evidence. Those accustomed to assessing the weight of scientific arguments based on inductive reasoning agree that usually the cumulative effect of many different kinds of evidence is far more important to establishing the plausibility of a hypothesis than a lone, seemingly incontrovertible piece of evidence.[33] The testimony of Kaluza's law should be viewed in the context of the linguistic evidence as a whole, which, regarded objectively, makes arguments for a late date of composition seem willful.

The language of *Beowulf* would appear to suggest that the poem is at least a century older than the manuscript in which it is preserved. How credible is that suggestion? Eric Stanley has said more than once that the greater the distance in time assumed between the poem's first recording and the extant manuscript, the greater the element of conjecture.[34] That may well be true, though it may be said with equal justice that the longer the story is assumed to have circulated orally before being committed to parchment, the greater the element of conjecture, not simply because of the archaic nature of the language, but also considering that the poem appears to be set in the sixth century. The reason for this is that the *Beowulf* poet shows by his allusive style that he plainly expected his audience to have considerable knowledge of Scandinavian figures and events of that early era. Surely it is not to be expected that Anglo-Saxons of about the year 1000 should have been as familiar with such matters as were Anglo-Saxons of an earlier age.[35] It is therefore more conjectural to suppose that a poet of the tenth or eleventh century could have composed such a work (or expected his audience to understand it) than a poet of the earlier Anglo-Saxon period.

It is worth considering, then, whether the manuscripts of neighboring cultures have anything to reveal about whether it is very plausible to assume that *Beowulf* was composed long before the Cotton manuscript was made. The dating of eddic poetry in Old Norse is notoriously difficult, and it presents some of the same problems as the dating of Old English poetry, though most scholars are convinced that at least some of

---

[33] For references in the literature to this principle, see Fulk, *A History of Old English Meter*, 9–11.
[34] Stanley, "The Date of *Beowulf*," 200, 209.
[35] For evidence for this view, see Leonard Neidorf, "Germanic Legend, Scribal Errors, and Cultural Change," Chapter 2 in this volume.

the surviving eddic poems antedate the manuscripts in which they are preserved by several centuries.[36] But skaldic poetry is another matter, since most of it can be dated with a fair degree of precision. This is because the poems are mostly by known skalds who are to be associated with Norwegian kings and nobles of known, if sometimes approximate, dates. Aside from an Easter table, the earliest manuscripts in Old Norse are from after 1150; and aside from a hagiographic narrative about St. Eustace in skaldic form (*Plácitusdrápa*) from the late twelfth century, the earliest manuscripts containing skaldic verse are from the first half of the thirteenth century, though most skaldic verse is recorded in manuscripts later than this.[37] The earliest known skald, however, lived in the first half of the ninth century, and roughly half of the surviving skaldic verse is from before 1200. This is not a situation entirely analogous to what might be posited for *Beowulf*, since skaldic verse has a rigid form that is conducive to oral transmission over several centuries with relatively little corruption. But it is an example why the assumption ought not to be thought improbable that vernacular poems may be much older than the manuscripts in which they are preserved.

The situation in regard to Celtic literatures and manuscripts is more closely analogous. For example, the fifth-century Latin works ascribed to St. Patrick are preserved no earlier than in the ninth-century Book of Armagh, and the earliest manuscript of the *Amra Choluim Chille*, composed by Dallán Forgaill in the sixth century, is the twelfth-century Book of the Dun Cow (*Lebor na hUidre*). Likewise, although the medieval Welsh *Gododdin*'s date of composition is much debated, with dates proposed from the sixth century to the tenth, no one would date it within three centuries of the late thirteenth-century manuscript in which it is found.[38]

In Old English itself there is the example of *Guthlac A*, preserved only in the later tenth-century Exeter Book, though the poem must not have been composed much later than the mid-eighth century, if the narrator of the poem is to be credited. He asserts several times that the events of the saint's life occurred within the recall of living persons (including, it appears, himself), and it is known that Guthlac died in the year

---

[36] On the dating of eddic poetry, see Bjarne Fidjestøl, *The Dating of Eddic Poetry: A Historical Survey and Methodological Investigation* (Copenhagen: Reitzel, 1999). Roberta Frank is dismissive of evidence that even the very cautious Fidjestøl thinks probable: see her review of the book, *Speculum* 78 (2003): 165–7.

[37] See Hreinn Benediktsson, *Early Icelandic Script, as Illustrated in Vernacular Texts from the Twelfth and Thirteenth Centuries* (Reykjavík: The Manuscript Institute of Iceland, 1965), 13–18.

[38] On the controversy over the date of *Y Gododdin*, see David N. Dumville, "Early Welsh Poetry: Problems of Historicity," in *Early Welsh Poetry: Studies in the Book of Aneirin*, ed. B.F. Roberts (Aberystwyth: National Library of Wales, 1988), 1–16.

714.³⁹ More impressive a gulf between date of composition and of preservation is represented by the laws of King Æthelberht of Kent, which must have been recorded about the year 600, shortly after his conversion to Christianity, though they are preserved only in the twelfth-century *Textus Roffensis*. The language of Æthelberht's laws does contain some notable archaisms, showing that the text has indeed been transmitted from an early copy.⁴⁰

There is even greater historical distance between the composition of many classical texts and the earliest manuscripts in which they survive.⁴¹ For example, the earliest preserved manuscript of Tacitus's *Germania* is from the fifteenth century, copied from what must once have been a ninth-century manuscript, but which is now lost. One brief chapter of Petronius's *Satyricon*, probably composed during the reign of Nero, survives in a fragment of the ninth century; the earliest fragment of any significant length is from the fifteenth century. These are not unparalleled cases.

It is by no means improbable, then, that *Beowulf* should have been composed much earlier than the Cotton manuscript was made, especially since the conservative metrical features of *Beowulf* are similar to those found in *Guthlac A*, though *Beowulf* is somewhat more conservative in this respect. To the contrary, there is a distinct and by no means small probability of a relatively early date, given that so many different aspects of its language are more archaic than what is to be found in most Old English poetry. The same kind of probability does not attach to arguments that have been advanced for a late date.

Most of the information about linguistic archaisms in *Beowulf* summarized above has been known to scholars for many years. To anyone new to the debate about the dating of Old English poetry it might therefore seem more than a little surprising that while some scholars continue to argue for a late date for *Beowulf* and most literary researchers, at least, assert that no conclusions can be drawn, no attempt has been made (with

---

³⁹ See, for example, *Guthlac A* 153–9: *He gecostad wearð / in gemyndigra monna tidum, / ðara þe nu gena þurh gæstlicu / wundor hine weorðiað ond his wisdomes / hlisan healdað, þæt se halga þeow / elne geeode, þa he ana gesæt / dygle stowe* 'He was tempted within the times of people who remember, who now still for his sprirtual miracles revere him and retain the renown of his wisdom, what the holy servant accomplished by his bravery when he settled alone in a remote place'. (See also *Guthlac A* 401–3, and especially 752–9.) The poem is here cited from *The Exeter Book*, ed. George Philip Krapp and Elliott Van Kirk Dobbie, The Anglo-Saxon Poetic Records 3 (New York: Columbia University Press, 1936), 54.

⁴⁰ See Lisi Oliver, *The Beginnings of English Law* (Toronto: University of Toronto Press, 2002), 25–34.

⁴¹ Warmest thanks are due to George Clark, who suggested comparison to classical texts and proposed these examples.

a lone exception considered below) to examine the body of linguistic evidence methodically with the aim of demonstrating why it should not be regarded as convincing. Rather, scholarship that has the aim of persuading us that *Beowulf* is no early composition either simply does not take into account the linguistic evidence or chooses a lone linguistic argument to critique, while almost invariably treating the facts with some recklessness. Objectivity does not appear to be in equal supply on the two sides of the debate.

The one attempt to critique the linguistic evidence on a systematic basis was made by Ashley Crandell Amos, and although she found most of the evidence unconvincing, even she was obliged to concede that some linguistic criteria are reliable.[42] Although gratitude is owed to Amos for her contributions, it has subsequently been made plain that her study suffers, in places, from some unreliable reasoning, and, in general, from an inadequate grasp of A.J. Bliss's system of scansion and of the aspects of Old English language history and prehistory necessary to apply it accurately. In addition, she was concerned only to show that even such linguistic features as are of worth do not point reliably to any very definite date; she was not interested in gauging the cumulative effect of linguistic archaisms that suggest early composition without correlating in any very specific way to known dates in language history. That is, she was not interested in matters of probability – she in fact was self-reportedly in search of linguistic criteria she deemed "reliable, objective, and independent of the minds applying them" – though at least in regard to the larger question of dating Old English poetry, probability must for us be a matter of the first concern.[43] By now the wide array of archaic linguistic features in *Beowulf* is well enough established that any such systematic attempt to discredit them without taking into account the probabilistic force of their cumulative witness could only seem heavily biased. The alternative of chipping away at individual archaisms, like Kaluza's law, it should be apparent by now, is fraught with perils for those not genuinely interested in explaining linguistic phenomena but only in safeguarding the undatability, or a particular contrarian dating, of a single Old English poem. At all events, successfully discrediting this or that piece of evidence would leave intact the larger edifice – that is to say, the greater, cumulative implication of the variety of conservative linguistic features encountered.

Viewed from a linguistic perspective, the range of possible dates for the composition of *Beowulf* is not nearly as unconstrained as many

---

[42] See Amos, *Linguistics Means*, 167–70, for a summary of her views; also 8–12.
[43] Amos, *Linguistic Means*, 8. For a response to the position of Amos and others in regard to probability, see Fulk, *A History of Old English Meter*, 6–24.

literary scholars have acquired the habit of remarking as a matter of course. If *Beowulf* is not to be thought an early composition, advocates of a late date even now have before them the task of otherwise accounting for a considerable body of linguistic evidence in a manner that linguists might find persuasive.[44]

---

[44] Warm thanks are due to Leonard Neidorf for reading this chapter in draft and offering excellent advice.

2

Germanic Legend, Scribal Errors, and Cultural Change

Leonard Neidorf

The role of the *Beowulf* manuscript in scholarship dating the poem's composition has changed considerably in recent years. During the nineteenth and much of the twentieth century, discussions of the poem's date rarely embraced the manuscript as a source of relevant evidence.[1] The omission is not unreasonable, since the presence of transcription errors throughout the manuscript reveals that it is a copy of a copy, written out perhaps at a vast remove from the authorial original. The text transmitted in a copy might contain indications that it had been committed to parchment at a much earlier date, but there is no guarantee that such indications will be present. Accordingly, the previous disregard for the manuscript in dating studies was not an inexplicable oversight, though it suddenly seemed to be such in 1981, when Kevin S. Kiernan argued that his examination of the manuscript revealed it to contain an authorial draft of an eleventh-century poem.[2] Kiernan's hypothesis is rarely credited, and a series of subsequent studies have demonstrated that it is untenable,[3] but the notoriety of his argument has created the impression that manuscript studies might support a later dating. This impression is registered in Nicholas Howe's belief that "from the type of evidence offered, one can predict a scholar's dating of *Beowulf* ... the more closely one works with the language and metre, the more likely one is to date the poem early ...

---

[1] For an impression of the evidence and argumentation characteristic of early discussions of the dating of *Beowulf*, see the introduction to this volume. See also Robert E. Bjork and Anita Obermeier, "Date, Provenance, Author, Audiences," in *A Beowulf Handbook*, ed. Robert E. Bjork and John D. Niles (Lincoln: University of Nebraska Press, 1997), 13–34.

[2] Kevin S. Kiernan, Beowulf *and the* Beowulf *Manuscript* (New Brunswick: Rutgers University Press, 1981; reprinted with supplements 1996, Ann Arbor: University of Michigan Press).

[3] For a summary, see Johan Gerritsen, "*Beowulf* Revisited," *English Studies* 79 (1998): 82–6. See also David N. Dumville, "The *Beowulf* Manuscript and How Not to Date it," *Medieval English Student's Newsletter* 39 (1998): 21–7; and Ashley C. Amos, "An Eleventh-Century *Beowulf*?", *Review* (Charlottesville, VA) 4 (1982): 333–45.

the more closely one works with the manuscript, the more likely one is to date the poem late."[4] The second of Howe's two generalizations was not quite accurate when it was propounded, but it is certainly inaccurate at present.[5]

Manuscript-centered studies from Johan Gerritsen, Peter Clemoes, and Michael Lapidge have drawn attention to the dating implications of transliteration errors that must have entered into the transmitted text when it was copied from an earlier script into a later one.[6] Of these errors, the clearest chronological significance attaches to the confusion of **a** and **u**, which is exhibited, for example, in the manuscript readings *unhar* (for *anhar*, l. 357a), *wudu* (for *wadu*, l. 581a), *banū* (for *banan*, l. 158b), and *gumū* (for *guman*, l. 2821b). These **a/u** confusions were probably induced by the use of the open-headed **a** letterform in an earlier manuscript of the poem. This letterform is common in eighth-century manuscripts, such as the Épinal Glossary and the Moore MS of Bede's *Historia Ecclesiastica*, but it is rarely used after the ninth century; its latest documentary occurrence is in a charter of King Æthelwulf from 847.[7] Tenth-century scribes naturally would misread this obsolete letterform as an **u**. The conclusion plainly suggested by the presence of as many as fourteen **a/u** confusions in the text of *Beowulf* is that the poem had been committed to parchment at a time when the open-headed **a** remained in common use.[8] The dating implications of other scribal errors are not always so clear-cut. In a recent article, I assembled and analyzed upwards of fifty scribal errors pertaining to proper names in the *Beowulf* manuscript.[9] This chapter fleshes out

---

[4] Nicholas Howe, "Afterword: The Uses of Uncertainty: On the Dating of *Beowulf*," in *The Dating of* Beowulf, ed. Colin Chase (Toronto: University of Toronto Press, 1981; reprinted with Howe's afterword in 1997), 213–20, at 217 [Chase's collection is henceforth cited as *Dating*].

[5] To my knowledge, the only scholar who has ever concluded from an examination of the manuscript that *Beowulf* is a late composition is Kevin Kiernan. By the time of Howe's statement, two of the publications cited in the next footnote had already appeared and reached conclusions antithetical to Kiernan's.

[6] Johan Gerritsen, "Have with you to Lexington!: The *Beowulf* Manuscript and *Beowulf*," in *In Other Words: Transcultural Studies in Philology, Translation and Lexicography Presented to Hans Heinrich Meier*, ed. J. Lachlan Mackenzie and Richard Todd (Dordrecht: Foris, 1989), 15–34, at 24; Peter Clemoes, *Interactions of Thought and Language in Old English Poetry* (Cambridge: Cambridge University Press, 1995), 32–4; Michael Lapidge, "The Archetype of *Beowulf*," *Anglo-Saxon England* 29 (2000): 5–41.

[7] See Clemoes, *Interactions of Thought and Language*, 32, n. 77; and Lapidge, "The Archetype," 10–20.

[8] See *Klaeber's* Beowulf: *Fourth Edition*, ed. R.D. Fulk, Robert E. Bjork, and John D. Niles (Toronto: University of Toronto Press, 2008), 324–5 [henceforth *Klaeber IV*].

[9] Leonard Neidorf, "Scribal Errors of Proper Names in the *Beowulf* Manuscript," *Anglo-Saxon England* 42 (2013): 249–69.

the chronological significance of those errors by construing them as evidence for a larger process of cultural change.

For the purposes of the present essay, it is necessary only to provide a brief summary of the scribal errors of proper names that pervade the manuscript of *Beowulf*.[10] The names of heroes and peoples are frequently corrupted in ways that are suggestive of scribal unfamiliarity with the content of *Beowulf*. Eomer, son of Offa, appears in the manuscript as *geomor*, an adjective meaning 'mournful'. Beow, the Scylding scion, appears twice in the manuscript as *beowulf*, having been conflated with the Geatish protagonist. The Heaðobeard name is miswritten twice as *heaðobearn*, which turns the 'battle-beards' into 'battle-children'. Hreþric is corrupted into *hreþrinc*, which demotes this Dane from a proper name to a heroic epithet, since *-rinc* is not used in the Old English onomasticon. Jutes are converted into giants when the dative plural *Eotum* is corrupted twice into *eotenum* and monsters burst onto the battlefield at Finnsburh. Near the poem's end, the Swedish Scilfingas are corrupted into *scildingas*, and the long-absent Danes make an improbable return. When (*dryhten*) *Wedera* is miswritten as (*dryhten*) *wereda*, the lord of the Geats is converted into the lord of hosts (God?). The archaic genitive plural *Deniga* is corrupted into the curious *de ninga*. The names of Ongentheo, Finn, Hemming, the Heathoræmas, and the Merovingian are all spaced into units suggestive of incomprehension. Dozens of errors and oddities beyond those listed above confirm that these errors are not random or accidental, but are the consequences of a systematic problem affecting both scribes.

Just as the open-headed a was mistaken for u by scribes unfamiliar with this obsolete letterform, the names of heroes and peoples from Germanic heroic legend were corrupted into nouns and adjectives of similar appearance by scribes who were unfamiliar with the poem's archaic content. These errors cannot tell us when *Beowulf* was composed, but their presence plainly supports the hypothesis that the extant manuscript is a copy of a centuries-old poem, not of a recent composition. The knowledge that the *Beowulf* poet expected of his audience could not be expected of the two eleventh-century scribes, who either corrupted the text considerably or lacked the knowledge required to undo the corruptions of interceding copyists. Evidently, the heroic-legendary traditions essential for the comprehension and composition of *Beowulf* had fallen out of circulation and were no longer widely known by the end of the tenth century. Recognition of the proper name errors raises an important question: when were the heroes and peoples of Germanic legend known

---

[10] The errors cited in this paragraph are listed in the appendix of the article in fn. 9. Discussion of the issues surrounding these errors can be found in the body of that article.

in England, and when did this knowledge fall out of circulation? It is well known that the legends informing *Beowulf* had ceased to flourish by the time of the Middle English period, since no substantial knowledge of the old heroes is to be found there. Knowledge of Weland, Widia, and Wade persisted, but that is because they figured in independent folkloric traditions and were eventually incorporated into Arthurian legend.[11] The heroes belonging to legends of migration-era Geats, Swedes, Danes, Frisians, Goths, and Huns (*inter al.*), on the other hand, fell into obscurity, and may have fallen there long before the Norman Conquest.

The present essay examines four categories of evidence in its effort to track the circulation and cessation of Germanic heroic legend in England: Anglo-Latin testimonia, Old English poetry, the onomastic record, and the Anglo-Saxon royal genealogies. When examining these forms of evidence, it is necessary to be attentive to their precise implications about contemporary knowledge of heroic legend. One cannot assume, for example, that the mere existence of a heroic-legendary poem in a manuscript is a sign of flourishing knowledge. As the condition of the transmitted text in the *Beowulf* manuscript reminds us, the manual reproduction of a text can occur without contemporary knowledge of the traditions that informed its composition. Similar cautions are necessary when considering the attestation of heroic-legendary names or the reproduction of genealogical material. By reassessing the evidence for heroic legend in England, this essay reopens a longstanding debate in dating scholarship concerning the genesis and transmission of the legendary material in *Beowulf*. The prevailing view in earlier scholarship was that the traditions known to the *Beowulf* poet were orally transmitted to England by the Germanic settlers who migrated there during the fifth, sixth, and seventh centuries.[12] Several scholars have recently challenged this view, arguing that the legends in *Beowulf* were transmitted to England through Viking or Carolingian conduits during the ninth or tenth century.[13] The relative probability of these competing hypotheses

---

[11] The very few allusions to Germanic legend in Middle English texts are discussed in R.M. Wilson, *The Lost Literature of Medieval England* (London: Methuen & Co, Ltd., 1952), 1–23. Wilson's survey leads him to the view that Germanic legend "had disappeared long before the Conquest," 23.

[12] See, for example, R.W. Chambers, Beowulf: *An Introduction to the Study of the Poem with a Discussion of the Stories of Offa and Finn*, 3rd ed. with a supplement from C.L. Wrenn (Cambridge: Cambridge University Press, 1959; first published 1921), 98–104.

[13] Representative arguments include: John D. Niles, "On the Danish Origins of the *Beowulf* Story," in *Anglo-Saxon England and the Continent*, ed. Joanna Story and Hans Sauer (Tempe, AZ: ACMRS, 2011), 41–62; Roberta Frank, "Germanic Legend in Old English Literature," in *The Cambridge Companion to Old English Literature*, ed. Malcolm Godden and Michael Lapidge (Cambridge: Cambridge University Press, 1991), 88–106; Frank,

will be gauged as the evidence is sifted and its dating implications are enunciated.

Anglo-Latin Testimonia

Because Anglo-Latin sources tend to be more narrowly datable than those written in the vernacular, the evidence they provide must be accorded the greatest weight. As R.D. Fulk and Christopher M. Cain observe: "in constructing a history of Old English literature it is Anglo-Latin texts that must provide the framework into which undated vernacular works may be tentatively inserted."[14] Three Latin texts provide such a framework when examining the circulation of heroic-legendary knowledge in Anglo-Saxon England: the *Liber Monstrorum*, Felix of Crowland's *Vita Sancti Guthlaci*, and Alcuin's *Letter to Speratus*. References to *fabulae* and *citharistae*, common in Anglo-Latin regulatory literature, might hint at the circulation of heroic legend, but since they provide no specific indications, they are omitted from the present investigation.[15]

Paleographical and text-critical considerations enable the *Liber Monstrorum* to be "dated with some confidence to the century c. 650 x 750."[16] Within that century, Michael Lapidge has made a compelling case for attributing the composition of the *Liber Monstrorum* to a student or colleague of Aldhelm. The author of the *Liber Monstrorum* writes in what can be described as a Malmesbury "house style" and, besides Aldhelm, he is the only medieval author who possesses knowledge of Lucan's lost poem, *Orpheus*.[17] There are thus strong grounds for regarding the *Liber Monstrorum* as a Malmesbury text from ca. 700. Its significance for the history of Germanic legend in England resides in a passage that alludes to King Hygelac of the Geats:

> Et fiunt monstra mirae magnitudinis, ut rex Higlacus, qui imperavit Getis et a Francis occisus est, quem equus a duodecimo aetatis anno portare non potuit.

"Skaldic Verse and the Date of *Beowulf*," in *Dating*, 123–40; Walter Goffart, "*Hetware* and *Hugas*: Datable Anachronisms in *Beowulf*," in *Dating*, 83–100.

[14] R.D. Fulk and Christopher M. Cain, *A History of Old English Literature*, 2nd ed. (Chichester: John Wiley & Sons, 2013), 36.

[15] For a valuable discussion of the predominantly early references to *fabulae* and *citharistae*, where it is assumed that these words hint at the recitation of heroic poetry, see Patrick Wormald, "Bede, *Beowulf*, and the Conversion of the Anglo-Saxon Aristocracy," in *The Times of Bede: Studies in Early English Christian Society and its Historian*, ed. Stephen Baxter (Malden: Blackwell, 2006), 30–105, at 41–64.

[16] Michael Lapidge, "*Beowulf*, Aldhelm, the *Liber Monstrorum*, and Wessex," *Studi Medievali* 23 (1982): 151–92, at 165.

[17] Lapidge, "*Beowulf*, Aldhelm, the *Liber Monstrorum*," 168–75.

Cuius ossa in Rheni fluminis insula, ubi in Oceanum prorumpit, reservata sunt, et de longinquo venientibus pro miraculo ostenduntur.

(And there are monsters of an amazing size, like King Hygelac, who ruled the Geats and was killed by the Franks, whom no horse could carry from the age of twelve. His bones are preserved on an island in the river Rhine, where it breaks into the Ocean, and they are shown as a wonder to travellers from afar.)[18]

The allusion confirms that the story of Hygelac's disastrous raid in Merovingian territory, which the *Beowulf* poet considered significant enough to merit four allusions, was known in England before the middle of the eighth century.[19] The passage, moreover, contains two important signs that the legend of Hygelac was in current oral circulation, and that the author drew on an oral English account rather than a written Frankish source. The first is that Hygelac is presented here as a king of the Geats, in agreement with *Beowulf*, but in disagreement with the Frankish sources, where he is said to be a Dane. The second is that the author used the etymologically correct Old English form *Higlacus*, which could not plausibly have been reconstructed from written continental renderings such as *Chocilaicus*.[20] The value of the *Liber Monstrorum* as a witness to Germanic legend is thus considerable.

In the preface of the *Vita Sancti Guthlaci*, Felix of Crowland dedicated the life of this Mercian saint to Ælfwald, who ruled East Anglia from 713 to 749. On the basis of this and other internal considerations, Bertram Colgrave dated the composition of the *Vita Sancti Guthlaci* to ca. 730–40.[21] The text contains several indications that heroic legend flourished at the time it was composed. The Mercian nobleman Penwalh, father of Guthlac, is a descendent of the legendary Icel, whom the Anglian genealogies reveal to be descended from Eomer and Offa, migration-era rulers of Angeln.[22] Consequently, when Felix reports that Guthlac listened to songs of the deeds of his ancestors, it is reasonable to conclude that these songs derived from the same corpus of continental Anglian legendry known to

---

[18] For the text and translation, see *Pride and Prodigies: Studies in the Monsters of the* Beowulf *Manuscript*, ed. and trans. Andy Orchard (Cambridge: D.S. Brewer, 1995), 258–9.

[19] For the allusions to Hygelac's demise in *Beowulf*, see *Klaeber IV*, ll. 1202–14, 2354–79, 2501–9, and 2910–21.

[20] See Dorothy Whitelock, *The Audience of* Beowulf (Oxford: Clarendon Press, 1951), 47–8; Lapidge, "*Beowulf*, Aldhelm, the *Liber Monstrorum*," 176–8; for Gregory's account, see *Gregorii Episcopi Turonensis Historiarum Libri X*, 2nd ed., ed. Bruno Krusch, Monumenta Germaniae Historica, Scriptores rerum Merovingicarum 1.1 (Hanover: Hahnsche Buchhandlung, 1937), 99.

[21] See *Felix's Life of St. Guthlac*, ed. and trans. Bertram Colgrave (Cambridge: Cambridge University Press, 1956), 15–19.

[22] *Felix's Life of St. Guthlac*, 74–5; for the genealogies, see David N. Dumville, "The Anglian Collection of Royal Genealogies and Regnal Lists," *Anglo-Saxon England* 5 (1976): 23–50.

the *Beowulf* poet. Heroic legend is crucial to Guthlac's biography, since he decided to become a warband leader when "he remembered the valiant deeds of heroes of old" [*valida pristinorum heroum facta reminiscens*].[23] Conversely, later in life, Guthlac decided to cease raiding and become a hermit "when, with wakeful mind, he contemplated the wretched deaths and the shameful ends of the ancient kings of his race in the course of past ages ..." [*cum antiquorum regum stirpis suae per transacta retro saecula miserabiles exitus flagitioso vitae termino contemplaretur*].[24] This reference is particularly strong evidence for the circulation of migration-era legendry, since the narrative kernel of most of these legends was the tragic and often disastrous end of the hero's life.[25] The tales of Eormenric, Guðhere, Hygelac, Ælfwine, Hroðulf, Finn, Ætla, and Ingeld are aptly described as tales of the wretched deaths of ancient kings.

Perhaps the best-known reference to Germanic legend in early England is that which appears in a letter Alcuin wrote to a correspondent pseudonymously known as Speratus. Internal evidence dates the composition of this letter rather narrowly to "early/mid 797."[26] Donald A. Bullough has demonstrated that the Speratus to whom the letter is addressed should be identified as Bishop Unwona of Leicester.[27] Alcuin admonishes his friend to avoid drunkenness, dissipation, and ostentation, and then writes:

> Verba Dei legantur in sacerdotali convivio. Ibi decet lectorem audiri, non citharistam; sermones patrum, non carmina gentilium. Quid Hinieldus cum Christo? Angusta est domus; utrosque tenere non poterit. Non vult rex celestis cum paganis et perditis nominetenus regibus communionem habere; quia rex ille aeternus regnat in caelis, ille paganus perditus plangit in inferno.
>
> (Let God's words be read at the episcopal dinner-table. It is right that a reader should be heard, not a harpist, patristic discourse, not pagan song. What has Ingeld to do with Christ? The house is narrow and has no room for both. The Heavenly King does not wish to have communion with lost, pagan kings listed name by name: for the eternal King reigns in Heaven, while the lost, pagan king wails in Hell.)[28]

---

[23] *Felix's Life of St. Guthlac*, 80–81.
[24] *Felix's Life of St. Guthlac*, 82–3.
[25] For a discussion of this generic feature of heroic-legendary narrative, see Theodore M. Andersson, *A Preface to the Nibelungenlied* (Stanford: Stanford University Press, 1987), 1–27.
[26] Donald A. Bullough, "What has Ingeld to do with Lindisfarne?" *Anglo-Saxon England* 22 (1993): 93–125, 102.
[27] Bullough, "Ingeld," 115–22.
[28] *Epistolae Karolini Aevi II*, ed. Ernst Dümmler, Monumenta Germaniae Historica, Epistolae 4 (Berlin: Weidmann, 1895), 183. The translation follows Bullough, "Ingeld," 124.

The pagan king *Hinieldus* is unmistakably Ingeld, the Heaðobardic prince, who appears in *Beowulf, Widsið,* and several continental sources. Considering the details of his legend, it is easy to understand why Alcuin chose Ingeld to serve as a metonym for the songs of the pagans (*carmina gentilium*).[29] Embroiled in a feud between the Heaðobards and the Danes, Ingeld marries Freawaru, the daughter of Hroðgar, but the peace cannot last, as Ingeld's love for his wife wanes and his desire to avenge the murder of his father, Froda, waxes. Conflict erupts, Ingeld invades Heorot, and the hall is set on fire, but Hroðgar and Hroðulf prevail, killing Ingeld and his men. Alcuin did not select his representative from Germanic legend at random. The story of Ingeld's divided loyalties and tragic demise is a quintessential expression of the narrative content of Germanic heroic legend. Alcuin's allusion is a secure sign that legends of Ingeld circulated in eighth-century Mercia.

In sum, Anglo-Latin texts provide firm indications that legends known to the *Beowulf* poet involving migration-era Geats, Franks, Angles, Heaðobards, and Danes circulated in the earlier Anglo-Saxon period. The pertinent Anglo-Latin texts date to the beginning, middle, and end of the eighth century, and each is associated with the midland regions: the *Liber Monstrorum* belongs probably to Malmesbury, on the border of Wessex and Mercia; the *Vita Sancti Guthlaci* relates the life of a Mercian saint to an East Anglian king; and Alcuin addresses a Mercian bishop in a letter concerned with Mercian royal politics. It would be wrong to assign undue importance to details of localization, but since *Beowulf* itself has been dated to eighth-century Mercia on linguistic grounds, these details should not be neglected.

Old English Poetry

In addition to *Beowulf*, five Old English poems draw on the legends of heroes and peoples who flourished during the migration era: *Widsið, Waldere, Deor, Finnsburh,* and *Wulf and Eadwacer*. These poems are not narrowly datable, and with the exception of *Widsið*, they contain no conclusive signs of early or late composition. This is not a surprising state of affairs, considering the brevity of these poems. It may be reasonable, however, to regard the corpus of short heroic-legendary poems as relatively early or late depending on the distribution of independent forms of evidence for the circulation of Germanic legend in England. Fortunately,

---

[29] For a reconstruction of the Ingeld saga and a discussion of the pertinent sources, see Kemp Malone, "The Tale of Ingeld," in *Studies in Heroic Legend and Current Speech*, ed. Stefán Einarsson and Norman E. Eliason (Copenhagen: Rosenkilde and Bagger, 1959), 1–62.

Widsið, the poem that exhibits knowledge of the legends most pertinent to *Beowulf*, can be relatively dated with confidence.

Orthographic and lexical evidence provide the firmest indications that *Widsið* was composed in the earlier Anglo-Saxon period.[30] As Kemp Malone observed, the text of the poem transmitted in the Exeter Book contains certain spellings "explicable only on the theory that the poem was written down in the earliest period of English orthography."[31] These spellings include *Mearchealf* (with *ch* for *h*), *Moidum* (with *oi* for *æ*), *Amothingum* (with *th* for *þ*), *Rum* (for *Rom*), and *Eatule* (for *Italia*).[32] Complementing this evidence is the presence of several words indicative of archaic composition. The word *suhtor(ge)fædren* ("uncle-and-nephew") is a dvandva, or copulative compound, a formation that became unproductive in prehistoric Old English.[33] This compound is found only in *Widsið* and *Beowulf*, but the simplex *suhtriga* ("nephew") is equally rare, appearing only in *Genesis A* and in glosses generated during the seventh century.[34] The *Widsið* poet's language for the Romans also distinguishes him from later authors. The ethnonym *Rumwalas* ("Rome-foreigners") appears to have become obsolete at an early date, since it is found only in *Widsið*, glosses, and possibly the Franks Casket.[35] More remarkable, however, is the reference to the Roman Empire as the *Wala ric* ("kingdom of foreigners"). As the other reflexes of Proto-Germanic *walhaz* indicate, *wealh* must have been a standard term for "Roman" in prehistoric Old English.[36] After the migration to Britain, but as early as the Laws of Ine (c. 700), the word *wealh* underwent a semantic shift, in which it came exclusively to mean "a Celt" or "a slave."[37] The composition of *Widsið* would

---

[30] For a fuller discussion of evidence bearing on the dating of *Widsið*, see Leonard Neidorf, "The Dating of *Widsið* and the Study of Germanic Antiquity," *Neophilologus* 97 (2013): 165–83.

[31] *Widsith*, ed. Kemp Malone (Copenhagen: Rosenkilde and Bagger, 1962; rev. ed.), 114.

[32] See Fulk and Cain, *A History of Old English Literature*, 316; *Widsith*, ed. Malone, 114.

[33] See Charles T. Carr, *Nominal Compounds in Germanic* (London: H. Milford, 1939), 40–2. There are only three other Germanic copulative compounds recorded: OE *aþumsweoran* ('son-in-law and father-in-law,' *Beowulf* 84), OS *gisunfader* ('son and father,' *Heliand* 1176), and OHG *sunufatarungo* ('son and father', *Hildebrandslied* 4).

[34] See Dennis Cronan, "Poetic Words, Conservatism, and the Dating of Old English Poetry," *Anglo-Saxon England* 33 (2004): 23–50, 39.

[35] See *The Dictionary of Old English Corpus*, ed. Antonette diPaolo Healey (Ann Arbor: University of Michigan Press, 2004). On the Franks Casket, the names of Romulus and Remus are rendered *Romwalus* and *Reumwalus*. These forms might bear a punning or folk-etymological relation to the word *Romwealh*, but the similarity might be purely coincidental.

[36] See Leo Weisgerber, *Deutsch als Volksname: Ursprung und Bedeutung* (Stuttgart: W. Kohlhammer, 1953), 178–88.

[37] See David Pelteret, *Slavery in Early Medieval England: from the Reign of Alfred until the Twelfth Century* (Woodbridge: Boydell Press, 1995), 43; and Margaret L. Faull, "The Semantic Development of Old English *wealh*," *Leeds Studies in English* 8 (1975): 20–37.

appear to antedate the completion of this semantic shift. A narrow dating is not possible, but the confluence of archaic orthography, vocabulary, and semantics renders the hypothesis that *Widsið* was composed in the seventh or eighth century exceedingly probable.

The relative antiquity of *Widsið* is important, since the author of this poem clearly knew the majority of the legends known to the *Beowulf* poet. *Widsið* shares with *Beowulf* references to such heroes as Hroðgar, Hroðulf, Ingeld, Ongenþeo, Eormenric, Breca, Offa, Hama, Finn, and Hnæf, and to such peoples as the Danes, Swedes, Geats, Frisians, Hetware, Heaðobards, and Wulfings. *Widsið* is, in fact, the only extant text besides *Beowulf* where Breca is mentioned and where Heorot is the name of the Danish royal hall.[38] If *Widsið* is the early composition it appears to be, then arguments contending that material in *Beowulf* was unknown in England until the ninth or tenth century must be considered untenable. Regardless of when *Widsið* and the shorter heroic-legendary poems were composed, the etymologically correct Old English forms of the proper names in these poems demonstrate that they do not derive from oral Viking or written Carolingian sources. Like the *Beowulf* poet, the *Widsið* poet uses the forms Hroðgar and Hroðulf, which could not plausibly have been reconstructed from Scandinavian forms such as Roarr and Rolf. It is improbable that any poet possessed the philological abilities to convert Norse or Latin forms consistently into etymologically correct Old English forms, but it is exponentially more improbable that several authors of discrete poems possessed such abilities.[39] The forms of the proper names found in Old English heroic-legendary poetry indicate, rather, that these names circulated orally among the Anglo-Saxons early enough to undergo the earliest Old English sound changes.

The Franks Casket, a fusion of visual and literary art, contains runic inscriptions of Old English verse and is aptly considered here as a vernacular rendering of heroic-legendary narrative. Linguistic and art-historical evidence align in situating the construction of the casket in Northumbria around the year 700.[40] The casket is a valuable witness to

---

[38] The material shared between *Widsið* and *Beowulf* is discussed in *Klaeber IV*, clxxvii.
[39] See R.D. Fulk, "Review Article: Dating *Beowulf* to the Viking Age," *Philological Quarterly* 61 (1982): 341–59, at 343–4. As Fulk writes: "If we see the work of a linguist in *Beowulf* we must do the same for *Widsith*, *Deor*, *Waldere*, the Finnsburg fragment, and perhaps some others, and soon we shall be populating Alfred's England with Junggrammatiker," 344. This comment is a response to the suggestion that the *Beowulf* poet might have been exceptionally good at comparative Germanic philology; for this idea, see E.G. Stanley, "The Date of *Beowulf*: Some Doubts and No Conclusions," in *Dating*, 197–212, at 207.
[40] See the references compiled in Richard Abels, "What has Weland to do with Christ? The Franks Casket and the Acculturation of Christianity in Early Anglo-Saxon England," *Speculum* 84.3 (2009): 549–81, at 551, n. 7; see especially Arthur S. Napier,

the early circulation of heroic legend because its carvings reveal knowledge of the full legend of Weland, as it is recounted in *Völundarkviða* and alluded to in *Deor*.[41] The depiction of the smith at his anvil offering a skull-cup to a woman indicates that the artist behind the casket knew the story of Weland in all of its grim details. After being hamstrung by Niðhad, Weland takes revenge: he kills Niðhad's sons, makes cups of their skulls, and then drugs and rapes Beadohild, Niðhad's daughter. Weland then flies away in a device he constructed with the help of his brother, Egil, who is depicted on the lid of the Franks Casket under the inscription *ægili*. Later allusions to Weland in English sources convey no awareness of the gruesome revenge plot and represent him instead as a sanitized smith with magical powers.[42] The Franks Casket, like the corpus of short Old English heroic-legendary poems, is a product of oral traditions transmitted to England during the migration period, which flourished in subsequent centuries but were eventually forgotten.

Onomastic Evidence

The record of names borne by historical individuals who lived during the seventh, eighth, ninth, and tenth centuries provides significant evidence for the circulation and cessation of heroic-legendary knowledge in Anglo-Saxon England. Surveying the onomastic record, H.M. Chadwick observed that many names from Germanic heroic legend were used during the seventh and eighth centuries, but were no longer used during the ninth and tenth centuries.[43] Patrick Wormald's reassessment of the evidence reached the same conclusion and brought it explicitly to bear on the dating of *Beowulf* controversy.[44] Naturally, it is more probable that *Beowulf* was composed at a time when heroic legend flourished than a time when its cultural significance had lessened. The decline in heroic-legendary namegiving, like the corrupt proper names in the *Beowulf* manuscript, suggests that the traditions informing *Beowulf* were no longer productive or widely known in the later Anglo-Saxon period.

An additional layer of chronological significance attaches to the heroic-legendary names borne in early Anglo-Saxon England when it is

---

"The Franks Casket," in *An English Miscellany: Presented to Dr. Furnivall in Honour of his Seventy-fifth Birthday*, ed. W.P. Ker, A.S. Napier, and W.W. Skeat (Oxford: Clarendon Press, 1901), 362–81.

[41] See H.R. Ellis Davidson, "Weland the Smith," *Folklore* 69.3 (1958): 145–59.
[42] See footnotes 73–5 below.
[43] H.M. Chadwick, *The Heroic Age* (Cambridge: Cambridge University Press, 1912), 42–4, 64–6.
[44] Patrick Wormald, "*Beowulf*: The Redating Reassessed," in *The Times of Bede*, ed. Stephen Baxter (Malden: Blackwell, 2006), 71–81, 98–105.

recognized that many of these names contain elements that were foreign to or unproductive in the Old English onomasticon.[45] Because these names could not have been accidentally generated, it is highly probable that their use reflects awareness of heroic legend. The clearest example is the name Ætla (i.e., Attila), which derives from the diminutive form of the Gothic word *atta* ("father").[46] The name Widia (Jordanes' Vidigoia) is also of Gothic derivation.[47] Names such as Hroðulf, Beowulf, Ingeld, Theodric, Heremod, Widsið, and Wyrmhere contain elements (*hroð-, beow-, -geld, þeod-, -mod, -sið, wyrm-*) that were not commonly used to form new personal names in England. Monothematic names such as Breca, Froda, Hagena, Hama, Offa, Wada, and Witta likewise derive from elements that were never individually productive in English namegiving. It cannot be a coincidence that so many unusual names in the early onomasticon happen to be names borne by figures from Germanic legend. Although later bearers of these names might not be aware of their legendary namesakes, these names must have initially entered the Old English onomasticon due to familiarity with heroic legend. Instead of generating a name through the combination of productive Old English name-elements (such as *ælf, æðel, beorht, ead, frið, gar, mund, ræd, ric, stan, wine*, etc.), some parents chose to name their children after legendary heroes.[48] When these names contain elements foreign to or unproductive in Anglo-Saxon namegiving, their value as a witness to the circulation of heroic legend is especially strong.

Examined through the lens of these methodological considerations, the seventh-century monk named Beowulf (spelt *biuuulf*) becomes particularly interesting.[49] He is one of the 2819 people commemorated in the original core of the *Liber Vitae Dunelmensis* (*LVD*), the richest source

---

[45] See Leonard Neidorf, "Beowulf before *Beowulf*: Anglo-Saxon Anthroponymy and Heroic Legend," *Review of English Studies* 64 (2013): 553–73, where this observation is made at greater length and with much supporting data. For related methodological considerations, see Gustav Binz, "Zeugnisse zur germanischen Sage in England," *Beiträge zur Geschichte der deutschen Sprache und Literatur* 20 (1895): 141–223, at 143; F.M. Stenton, "Personal Names in Place-Names," in *Introduction to the Survey of English Place-Names: Part I*, ed. A. Mawer and F.M. Stenton (Cambridge: Cambridge University Press, 1924; reprinted 1980), 165–89, at 187–8; and Chadwick, *Heroic Age*, 42–3.
[46] See Moritz Schönfeld, *Wörterbuch der altgermanischen Personen- und Völkernamen* (Heidelberg: Carl Winter's Universitätsbuchhandlung, 1911), 275.
[47] See Schönfeld, *Wörterbuch*, 263.
[48] For data distinguishing productive name-elements from unproductive ones, see the appendices in Neidorf, "Beowulf before *Beowulf*."
[49] On the relative dating of Biuuulf and his contemporaries, see Chadwick, *Heroic Age*, 64–6. It is possible that Biuuulf was a man of the eighth century, but his early presence in the *nomina monachorum* list – in a section characterized by earlier spellings – makes it more probable that he flourished during the seventh century.

for Anglo-Saxon names from the seventh and eighth centuries.[50] Because the element *beow* is not used to form any of the other 2818 names in the *LVD*, the name Beowulf belongs to a group of heroic-legendary names, such as Ætla and Ingeld, which contain elements foreign to or unproductive in contemporary namegiving. The parents of Biuuulf could not have generated his name accidentally through the combination of productive name-elements, since *beow* was manifestly not productive at the time. It is therefore probable that Biuuulf the monk was named after the same legendary hero whom the *Beowulf* poet placed at the center of a long heroic-elegiac narrative. The use of this name in the seventh century suggests that legends involving Beowulf the Geat circulated in England at a very early date. This is not altogether surprising, since the *Liber Monstrorum* shows that legends involving Hygelac, Beowulf's uncle, were known before the middle of the eighth century. The value of the onomastic evidence, however, resides in its ability to confirm and augment the indications provided by the literary sources. Like *Widsið*, the record of heroic-legendary names borne by historical Anglo-Saxons is a testament to the circulation of a rich corpus of migration-era legends during the seventh and eighth centuries. The disuse of such names in subsequent centuries might indicate, in turn, that interest in heroic legend declined over time. As might be expected, traditions dating back to the migration period did not remain in perpetual circulation.

Anglo-Saxon Royal Genealogies

In the genealogies constructed for several Anglo-Saxon kings, figures from Germanic heroic legend are included among the king's distant ancestors. Eomer, Offa, and Wermund, the legendary Anglian dynasty, appear in the genealogy of King Æðelred of Mercia (r. 675–704). Finn, the legendary Frisian king, appears in the genealogy of King Aldfrið of Lindsey (r. 685–704/5). Hengest and Witta, leaders of Jutes and Swabians respectively, appear in the genealogy of King Æðelberht of Kent (r. 590–616). Hroðmund, the Scylding prince, appears in the genealogy of King Ælfwald of East Anglia (r. 713–49). Scealdwa, Scef, Beaw, and Heremod, figures drawn from Scylding legend, appear in the genealogy of King Æthelwulf of Wessex (r. 839–58). The first four genealogies, those of

---

[50] See *The Durham Liber Vitae: London, British Library, MS Cotton Domitian A.VII*, ed. David Rollason and Lynda Rollason. 3 vols. (London: British Library, 2007). See also David N. Dumville, "The Northumbrian Liber Vitae: London, British Library, MS. Cotton Domitian A.vii, Folios 15–24 & 25–45, the Original Text," *Anglo-Saxon Essays, 2001–2007* (Aberdeen: Centre for Anglo-Saxon Studies, 2007) 109–82. For further discussion of Biuuulf's context, see Neidorf, "Beowulf before *Beowulf*," 558–64.

Mercia, Lindsey, Kent, and East Anglia, are transmitted alongside several others in manuscripts containing the Anglian collection of genealogical material.[51] Æthelwulf's genealogy, on the other hand, is transmitted in manuscripts of the *Anglo-Saxon Chronicle* and in texts that translate or derive from *Chronicle* material.[52] In determining the significance of these five genealogies for the circulation of heroic legend, details of textual transmission are paramount. Above all, it is necessary to identify the period of the genealogy's construction, when heroic-legendary ancestors might have been politically significant, and to distinguish it from later periods of manual reproduction, when these ancestors might have been little more than (corrupted) names on a list.

The Anglian collection of royal genealogies has a complicated textual history, but its implications for the circulation of heroic legend are fairly straightforward. David N. Dumville has demonstrated that the extant manuscripts of the Anglian collection derive from a Mercian collection of genealogical material compiled between 787 and 796.[53] This Mercian collection, in turn, appears to derive from a Northumbrian collection that was put together between 765 and 779.[54] It is probable, however, that the genealogies themselves were constructed neither by the Northumbrian nor the Mercian compiler, but by royal genealogists operating during the reigns of the pertinent kings. The natural assumption that the genealogy of a king such as Ælfwald would have been composed during his reign has more than common sense behind it. When Bede provides the ancestry of king Rædwald in his *Historia Ecclesiastica* (c. 731), he betrays clear knowledge of an East Anglian royal genealogy.[55] Felix of Crowland, meanwhile, displays knowledge of Mercian genealogical tradition in the *Vita Sancti Guthlaci* (c. 730–40), when he claims that Penwalh descends from Icel.[56] Accordingly, although the textual history of the Anglian collection traces back to the second half of the eighth century, it is clear that the three Anglian genealogies (Mercia, Lindsey, East Anglia) containing identifiable figures from Germanic heroic legend were composed in the political climate of the first quarter of the eighth century. The Kentish genealogy is perhaps a century older than these. In any event, Bede's

---

[51] For the texts, see Dumville, "The Anglian Collection," 28–37.
[52] For a collation of the section of Æthelwulf's genealogy containing the Scylding names, see Kenneth Sisam, "Anglo-Saxon Royal Genealogies," *Proceedings of the British Academy* 39 (1953): 287–348, at 315.
[53] Dumville, "The Anglian Collection," 45.
[54] Dumville, "The Anglian Collection," 49.
[55] *Bede's Ecclesiastical History of the English People*, ed. Bertram Colgrave and R.A.B. Mynors, revised ed. (Oxford: Clarendon Press, 1991), 190–1; for discussion, see Sam Newton, *The Origins of* Beowulf *and the Pre-Viking Kingdom of East Anglia* (Cambridge: D.S. Brewer, 1993), 78.
[56] *Felix's Life of St. Guthlac*, 74–5; see Newton, *The Origins of* Beowulf, 62.

awareness of the Kentish genealogy confirms that it too existed during the first quarter of the eighth century.[57]

Scholars arguing for a later dating of *Beowulf* have frequently assumed that the genealogy of King Æthelwulf of Wessex was generated *ex nihilo* during the reign of his son, Alfred of Wessex (r. 871–99).[58] Linguistic and text-critical considerations render that assumption untenable and suggest that this genealogy was constructed during Æthelwulf's reign (i.e., 839–58) using written material of even greater antiquity. Divergent iterations of Æthelwulf's genealogy are preserved in the 855 annal of manuscripts of the *Anglo-Saxon Chronicle*, as well as in Asser's *Vita Alfredi* and Æthelweard's *Chronicon*, both of which derive from versions of the *Chronicle*.[59] Surveying the discrepancies and corruptions pervading the texts of this genealogy, Kenneth Sisam observed: "The variant forms of Æthelwulf's pedigree could not have arisen or survived if consistent legends about the heroes or gods in its remoter parts had been well known in the ninth century."[60] Indeed, there are signs that by the time of Alfred's reign, names that might have had momentary political significance during Æthelwulf's reign had lost their currency. In Asser's version of the genealogy, there is a comment conflating the mythical progenitor Geat (i.e., Woden) with Geta, a character from a comedy of Terence; in the same genealogy, Scef is corrupted into Seth.[61] Common

---

[57] *Bede's Ecclesiastical History of the English People*, 50–1, 150–1.

[58] Prominent examples include: Alexander C. Murray, "*Beowulf*, the Danish Invasion, and Royal Genealogy," in *Dating*, 101–11; Roberta Frank, "The *Beowulf* Poet's Sense of History," in *The Wisdom of Poetry: Essays in Early English Literature in Honor of Morton W. Bloomfield*, ed. Larry D. Benson and Siegfried Wenzel (Kalamazoo: Medieval Institute Publications, 1982), 53–65; Audrey L. Meaney, "Scyld Scefing and the Dating of Beowulf – Again," in *Textual and Material Culture in Anglo-Saxon England*, ed. Donald Scragg (Cambridge: D.S. Brewer, 2003), 23–74; Nicholas Jacobs, "Anglo-Danish Relations, Poetic Archaism, and the Date of *Beowulf*: A Reconsideration of the Evidence," *Poetica* (Tokyo) 8 (1977): 23–43.

[59] See Sisam, "Anglo-Saxon Royal Genealogies," 314–20; on the derivation of Æthelweard's *Chronicon* from an earlier version of the *Anglo-Saxon Chronicle*, see Audrey L. Meaney, "St Neots, Æthelweard, and the Compilation of the *Anglo-Saxon Chronicle*: a Survey," in *Studies in Earlier Old English Prose: Sixteen Original Contributions*, ed. Paul E. Szarmach (Albany, NY: State University of New York Press, 1986), 193–245.

[60] Sisam, "Anglo-Saxon Royal Genealogies," 346. Also pertinent are his observations: "Sometimes the stereotyped spellings of names tells against a living tradition. And there are instances of surprising carelessness," 346.

[61] See *Asser's Life of King Alfred*, ed. W.H. Stevenson, revised by Dorothy Whitelock (Oxford: Clarendon Press, 1959). In the notes to their translation of the *Vita Alfredi*, Simon Keynes and Michael Lapidge write: "Needless to say ... the character in Roman comedy has nothing whatsoever to do with the Geat of the genealogy." See *Alfred the Great: Asser's Life of King Alfred and Other Contemporary Sources*, ed. and trans. Simon Keynes and Michael Lapidge (New York: Penguin Books, 1983), 229. The comment reveals that a man in the king's personal circle had no understanding of the logic

to most versions of the genealogy is the name *Bedwig*, a corruption of the form *Beowi* and consequently a duplication of the figure listed elsewhere in the same genealogy as *Beaw*.[62] Furthermore, the earliest extant text of Æthelwulf's genealogy is preserved in a copy written out during Alfred's reign (in *Chronicle* MS A) and it already contains signs of corruption and extensive transmission.[63]

Like the genealogy of Offa of Mercia included in the 755 annal of the *Chronicle*, the genealogy of Æthelwulf must be regarded as an earlier record incorporated into the *Chronicle*, not a text that was freshly composed for dissemination therein.[64] Even when regarded as a product of the politics of Æthelwulf's reign, the genealogy cannot be imagined to be of entirely ninth-century composition. Sisam and Dumville have observed that some of the names in Æthelwulf's genealogy derive from a seventh-century Bernician genealogy.[65] The spellings of the names connected with *Beowulf* indicate that they too were drawn from an Anglian source of comparable antiquity.[66] The *-wa* suffix of *Scealdwa* (*Scyldwa*, *Scealdhwa*, *Sceldwea*) and *Tætwa* appears to be an archaic reflex of the *u*-formant of *u*-stem nouns. Similarly, the *-i* suffix of *Beowi* (preserved also in the corrupt *Bedwig*) appears to be an archaic reflex of the *j*-formant of *ja*-stem nouns.[67] Far from representing ninth-century genealogical innovations, the Scylding names (Scealdwa, Beaw, Scef, and Heremod) must have been part of a written genealogical tradition at a very early date. Sam Newton's hypothesis that these names were taken from an East Anglian genealogical source is plausible, since the Scylding prince Hroðmund, son of Hroðgar, is present in the extant East Anglian genealogy of Ælfwald.[68]

In sum, the Anglo-Saxon royal genealogies can provide evidence for the circulation of heroic legend only if careful attention is paid to

---

governing archaic sections of his genealogy. This should raise doubts as to whether Alfred was personally invested in promoting awareness of his father's genealogy.

[62] See Erik Björkman, "Bēow, Bēaw und Bēowulf," *English Studies* 52 (1918): 145–93, at 170.

[63] On the dating of the handwriting in this manuscript, see *The Anglo-Saxon Chronicle: MS A*, ed. Janet Bately (Cambridge: D.S. Brewer, 1986), xxiv–xxv. On the corruptions in this version, see Newton, *The Origins of* Beowulf, 71; see also Daniel Anlezark, "Sceaf, Japheth, and the Origins of the Anglo-Saxons," *Anglo-Saxon England* 31 (2002): 13–46, at 22–3; Sisam, "Anglo-Saxon Royal Genealogies," 315–16.

[64] See *The Anglo-Saxon Chronicle: MS A*, ed. Bately, 36–8.

[65] See Sisam, "Anglo-Saxon Royal Genealogies," 302–7; David N. Dumville, "Kingship, Genealogies and Regnal Lists," *Early Medieval Kingship*, ed. P.H. Sawyer and Ian N. Wood (Leeds: University of Leeds, 1977), 72–104, at 79–81.

[66] See Rudolf Kögel, "Beowulf," *Zeitschrift für deutsches Altertum* 37 (1893): 268–76.

[67] See R.D. Fulk, "The Etymology and Significance of Beowulf's Name," *Anglo-Saxon* 1 (2007): 109–36, at 128.

[68] See Newton, *The Origins of* Beowulf, 139–42.

philological details. These details indicate that various figures from Germanic heroic legend were incorporated into written genealogical records during the seventh and eighth centuries. The political currency of heroic legend extends perhaps into the first half of the ninth century, when a West-Saxon genealogist added Scylding names from a written source to Æthelwulf's pedigree. The corruptions and divergences characterizing the extant texts of Æthelwulf's genealogy suggest, however, that a living tradition did not accompany its subsequent textual transmission. By Alfred's time, the names *Scealdwa* and *Beowi* were merely fossils preserved in genealogical texts. Their names had become so obscure that they defied modernization and, to a large extent, Saxonization.[69] That these figures had lost their political currency is also suggested by the fact that Alfred and his heirs, in all of the voluminous documentation pertaining to them, never represent themselves as Scyldings.[70] The era of aggressively promoting the *Angelcynn* had begun; the era of proclaiming descent from migration-era heroes had evidently ended.[71]

Conclusion

The latest datable reference to a figure from Germanic heroic legend in an Anglo-Saxon text that could not have been copied or derived from an early composition occurs in the vernacular translation of Boethius' *De Consolatione Philosophiae*.[72] The author of this translation, operating during or after the reign of King Alfred, replaces Fabricius with Weland. He translates "Ubi nunc fidelis ossa Fabricii jacent?" as "[Hwær] sint nu þæs foremeran and þæs wisan goldsmiðes ban Welondes?" [Where are now the bones of the famous and wise goldsmith, Weland?].[73] It is significant that the sole allusion to a heroic-legendary character in a text of indisputably late authorship is an allusion to Weland, since knowledge of Weland persisted independent of migration-era legendry. Stories of

---

[69] See Sisam, "Anglo-Saxon Royal Genealogies," 345, where he writes: "For the man who introduced these names into Æthelwulf's pedigree this would be a scrap of antiquarian learning, to be copied exactly."

[70] For this observation, see Dennis Cronan's Chapter 6 in the present volume.

[71] See Sarah Foot, "The Making of the *Angelcynn*: English Identity before the Norman Conquest," *Transactions of the Royal Historical Society* 6 (1996): 25–49.

[72] On the date and authorship of this text, see *The Old English Boethius: An Edition of the Old English Versions of Boethius's De Consolatione Philosophiae*, ed. Malcolm Godden and Susan Irvine with a chapter on the Metres by Mark Griffith and contributions by Rohini Jayatilaka. 2 vols. (Oxford: Oxford University Press, 2009), vol.1, 140–6; see also M.R. Godden, "Did King Alfred Write Anything?" *Medium Ævum* 76 (2007): 1–23.

[73] For the allusions to Weland in the prose, see *The Old English Boethius*, vol. I, 283; for its versification in the Meters, see vol. I, 427; for the translation of the prose, see vol. II, 30; for the translation of the Meters, see vol. II, 125–6.

Weland were perpetuated not only in heroic legend, but also in toponymic folklore, and the Alfredian translator's emphasis on the location of the bones suggests that he has the toponymic tradition (rather than the legendary tradition) in mind.[74] The independent vitality of the toponymic tradition is confirmed by Weland's presence in Middle English literature, where he is one of the few figures from Germanic legend to be remembered.[75] The Middle English sources present Weland simply as a famous smith; they exhibit no knowledge of his revenge plot or his interactions with migration-era heroes. The Alfredian allusion plainly anticipates the superficial Middle English references. It provides no reliable indication of contemporary circulation of heroic legend.

Although the absence of evidence is not necessarily evidence of absence, it is worth noting that there is no firm evidence for the circulation of heroic legend in Anglo-Saxon texts of indisputably late authorship. Homilists of the tenth and eleventh centuries do not bemoan the recitation of tales of Ingeld. Learned compilers such as Byrhtferth of Ramsey do not think to impress readers with encyclopedic knowledge of migration-era rulers and peoples. Late vernacular poems contain no allusions to the old heroes. Families cease to name their children after migration-era heroes. Ambitious kings did not continue to add legendary figures to their genealogies. The absence of datably late evidence is remarkable because literary and documentary evidence survives in far greater quantity from the later period. For this same reason, the wealth of datably early evidence for the circulation of heroic legend is all the more compelling in its implications.

A chronological hypothesis that accommodates the evidence of Anglo-Latin testimonia, Old English poetry, the onomastic record, and the Anglo-Saxon royal genealogies is the following: that Germanic heroic-legendary traditions were orally transmitted to England by migrants during the fifth and sixth centuries; that these legendary traditions circulated vigorously during the seventh and eighth centuries, but declined in prominence during the ninth century and ceased to be widely known during the tenth century. The explanatory power of this hypothesis is considerable, because in addition to accommodating the four aforementioned corpora of evidence, it is capable of explaining a fifth: the scribal errors of proper names in the *Beowulf* manuscript. The generation or

---

[74] On the tradition of toponymic folklore involving Weland and the probable allusion to this folklore in the Boethius, see Ellis Davidson, "Weland the Smith," 149.

[75] The pertinent texts are discussed in Wilson, *Lost Literature*, 14–16. As Wilson writes: "the Middle English allusions show little knowledge of the actual story of Weland. In all probability it had already been forgotten by the time of the Conquest, his name and a vague memory of his skill as a smith being all that had survived," 14. The same can be said for the allusion in the Old English Boethius.

preservation of dozens of corrupt proper names in the transmitted text of *Beowulf* is here collaterally explained, and in being so explained, this body of evidence independently corroborates the adumbrated chronological framework. It is undeniable that extant sources represent a mere fraction of what was written and known, yet when five discrete varieties of evidence align in support of the same chronological hypothesis, it is improbable that their alignment is purely coincidental. Since heroic-legendary traditions are essential to the composition and comprehension of *Beowulf*, the chronology of their circulation and cessation plainly supports hypotheses dating *Beowulf* to the earlier Anglo-Saxon period.

Attending to the philological details inherent in the evidence for Germanic legend in England reveals that many alternative hypotheses concerning the genesis and transmission of the material in *Beowulf* cannot be credited. Late-dating arguments contending that *Beowulf* poet relied on oral Scandinavian sources or written Carolingian sources can seem tenable only if *Beowulf* is viewed as an isolated text of disputed date.[76] When datable evidence external to *Beowulf* is confronted, each of the pertinent corpora leads to the conclusion that theories of ninth-century transmission are implausible. The Anglo-Latin testimonia of the *Liber Monstrorum*, the *Vita Sancti Guthlaci*, and Alcuin's *Letter to Speratus* indicate that heroic legend circulated in England well before the ninth century, an indication corroborated by *Widsið* and the Franks Casket. The etymologically correct Old English forms of the proper names in the vernacular heroic-legendary poems, as well as the form *Higlacus* in the *Liber Monstrorum*, demonstrate that these names are drawn from ancient English oral tradition, not from late Scandinavian or Latin sources. The heroic-legendary names borne by historical Anglo-Saxons in the seventh century independently confirm that a rich corpus of legends had been orally transmitted to England during the migration period. The presence of foreign elements in names such as Ætla and Ingeld, moreover, ensures that these names entered the onomasticon due to the early circulation of heroic legend. Further evidence for such circulation appears in the Anglo-Saxon royal genealogies, where kings from the seventh century onwards advertised descent from legendary heroes.

The chronological implications are unmistakable. Each form of evidence demands a hypothesis of early Anglo-Saxon transmission and rules out a hypothesis of later Viking or Carolingian transmission. When it is recognized that heroic-legendary traditions were transmitted to England before the seventh century, it should come as no surprise to find that knowledge of these traditions waned before the tenth century. Literary culture tends not to exist in perfect stasis. New enthusiasms

---

[76] For these arguments, see the works cited in fn. 13.

supplant old ones: as the deeds of Alfred and Æthelstan came to occupy the imagination of the people, the deeds of Hygelac and Ingeld came to be forgotten. Anglo-Saxon England did not exist in cultural stasis for four centuries, though such stasis is implied whenever scholars adopt an agnostic position on the dating of *Beowulf* and suggest that early and late dates are equally probable.

Confronting evidence for diachronic change shatters this illusion of stasis and reveals that agnosticism is not an entirely defensible position. Just as evidence for language change dates *Beowulf* prior to the loss of etymological length distinctions that occurred in Mercia before ca. 725,[77] evidence for cultural change dates *Beowulf* prior to the loss of heroic-legendary traditions. As long as the dating of *Beowulf* connotes the effort to gauge the relative probability of competing chronological hypotheses, agnosticism is not a logical response.[78] When the evidence is examined, one hypothesis will be found to possess more explanatory power than others; its superior claims to probability must be acknowledged.

The hypothesis that *Beowulf* was composed in Mercia between 685 and 725, formulated to explain the poem's archaic linguistic features, appears rather natural in the light of the evidence reviewed in this essay. The chronology of the circulation and cessation of Germanic legend in England permits only the broad conclusion that *Beowulf* is relatively early rather than late, but the evidence surveyed fleshes out a rich literary-historical context for Mercian composition around the year 700. Felix of Crowland reports that Guthlac listened to heroic-legendary poetry in seventh-century Mercia. The contemporary author of the *Liber Monstrorum* alludes to the story of Hygelac's demise in a probable Southumbrian composition. Alcuin confirms that tales of Ingeld were popular in eighth-century Mercia. *Widsið* and the Franks Casket testify to the artistic vitality of heroic legend in early Anglian culture. In the first quarter of the eighth century, at least three Anglian kings were claiming descent from legendary heroes who appear in *Beowulf*, including Eomer, Offa, Finn, and Hroðmund. An even earlier Anglian king had probably listed Scyld (Scealdwa) and Beow (Beowi) among his ancestors. An early monk was named after Beowulf, and his contemporaries bore such names as Ingeld, Froda, Offa, Wiglaf, Hygelac, and Hroðulf. The allusive style of *Beowulf* indicates that it was composed for an audience deeply familiar with heroic-legendary traditions. If the *Beowulf* poet composed

---

[77] See R.D. Fulk, *A History of Old English Meter* (Philadelphia: University of Pennsylvania Press, 1992), 348–92; and Fulk, "Archaisms and Neologisms in the Language of *Beowulf*," in *Studies in the History of the English Language III*, ed. Christopher M. Cain and Geoffrey Russom (Berlin: Mouton de Gruyter, 2007), 267–87.

[78] For an elaboration of this point, see the introduction to this volume.

in Mercia around the year 700, it is probable that he would have readily found such an audience.

3

Names in *Beowulf* and Anglo-Saxon England

Tom Shippey

Passionate disputes over proper names in *Beowulf* began almost from the moment of its rediscovery and first publication in 1815. The poem's first editor, Grímur Jónsson Thorkelín, recognised the name of Scyld in line 4, translating *Scyld Scefing* as *Scyldus Scefides*. At line 26, however, perhaps thinking that verbal forms in barbarian vernaculars were too inconsistent to matter – an error of surprising longevity – he took *scyld* to be the past tense of *sculan*, and translated *Scyld gewat* as *Ubi discedendum erat*, "When it was time to leave." He went on to transform the boat-burial into a piratical expedition. One of the seven reviewers of the edition, N.F.S. Grundtvig, noticed the error, but Thorkelín refused to accept the correction, and the ensuing angry correspondence in *Nyeste Skilderie* was terminated only by the journal's editor.[1]

It could be said, though, that the problem began eight lines and eight hundred years earlier, for it is now generally accepted that the name *Beowulf* in line 18, and then line 53, is an error for *Beow*. The original manuscript's scribe A, coming upon the name, and knowing that the main hero of the poem he was about to copy was called Beowulf, seemingly assumed his copy-text was in error and "corrected" to the longer form.[2] And – though this is *not* generally accepted – that may not have been his first proper-name error. All editors since Thorkelín have recognised that the poem's second sentence ends bathetically, in line 6. We are told that Scyld Sceafing "took away the mead-benches from many tribes, from troops of enemies," all firmly in the plural, but then "struck fear into the [singular] noble," *egsode eorl*. Most editors have adopted the obvious solution of making the last word plural, *eorl[as]*.

---

[1] See Beowulf: *the Critical Heritage*, ed. T.A. Shippey and Andreas Haarder (London: Routledge, 1998), 21–3, 109, 114–15.

[2] See *Klaeber's* Beowulf: *Fourth Edition*, ed. R.D. Fulk, Robert E. Bjork and John D. Niles (Toronto: University of Toronto Press, 2008), 117.

But why would an Anglo-Saxon scribe fail to recognise a word as familiar as *eorlas*? A suggestion slowly arrived at is that the text Scribe A was copying read *eorle*, and that this is an i-stem tribal name in the accusative plural, of course written without a capital, and possibly corresponding to the (H)Eruli often mentioned by Roman and Byzantine historians. Scribe A, failing to recognise the proper name, as he would later with several other tribal names,[3] assumed this was a dative singular form of the common noun *eorl*, and "corrected" again to accusative singular *eorl*.[4] The emendation, the connection with the Heruli, and with eight inscriptions in Early Runic (all datable before 550), have been rejected on several grounds. The Early Runic forms **erilaR / irilaR** may indeed indicate a rank rather than a tribal name[5] (but a self-aggrandising tribal name is not unlikely). Sixth-century Byzantine comments about the notoriously savage Heruli are hard to interpret (though Jordanes' report that the Danes "drove the Heruli from their homes," *Herulos propriis sedibus expulerunt*, seems apposite).[6] And if the i-stem *Seaxe* could be shielded from front mutation by analogy with the weak form *Seaxan*[7] (as perhaps with the common noun *seaxas*), possibly the same could be true of *Eorle* by analogy with *eorlas*, to which the name is almost certainly related.[8] The attraction of the emendation, meanwhile, is that it transforms the poem's second sentence from a bathos to a proud and significant boast: that the Danes under Scyld struck fear into a people notoriously formidable, a major step in their rise to the local hegemony which the poet was evidently claiming for them.

Whatever one thinks of modern editorial decisions, there can in any case be no doubt now that both scribes of our original manuscript had great difficulty with proper names, personal, dynastic, and tribal. The natural conclusion, drawn in Neidorf's Chapter 3 in this volume, is that the poem's scribes were largely unaware of the heroic-legendary traditions constituting *Beowulf* because these traditions had to a great extent fallen out of cultural circulation by the time the manuscript was copied, if not before. Patrick Wormald has also confirmed H.M. Chadwick's old demonstration that heroic Beowulfian names are found in Anglo-Saxon

---

[3] See Leonard Neidorf, "Scribal Errors of Proper Names in the *Beowulf* Manuscript," *Anglo-Saxon England* 42 (2013): 249–69; and Neidorf, "Germanic Legend, Scribal Errors, and Cultural Change," Chapter 2 in this volume.
[4] This explanation is given in *Klaeber's* Beowulf, ed. Fulk *et al.*, 112.
[5] See Bernard Mees, "Runic erilaR," *North-western European Language Evolution* 42 (2003): 41–68.
[6] Jordanes, *De origine et actibus Getarum*, III: 23, in *Iordanis Romana et Getica*, ed. Theodor Mommsen, *Monumenta Germaniae Historica* (Auctores antiquissimi series, vol. 5:1) (Berlin: Weidmann, 1882), 59.
[7] As proposed in *Klaeber's* Beowulf, ed. Fulk *et al.*, 112.
[8] Mees, "Runic erilaR," 47.

records earlier rather than later.[9] But there is a further and negative finding that deserves attention.

Though the exact number is arguable, *Beowulf* contains some seventy Old English personal names.[10] The website for "Prosopography of Anglo-Saxon England" (PASE) (www.pase.ac.uk) by contrast lists some 4,500 names (or name-headwords) in Anglo-Saxon records. It is impossible to say how many individuals are represented by these names, as PASE's editors took the decision to process their data as little as possible: thus, for instance, "Herebeald 1, 2 and 3" are very likely the same man, a ninth-century Canterbury moneyer. Nevertheless the total of individuals must be many thousands. PASE does not list names from *Beowulf*, as being non-historical, but one can add to its listings some 800+ names from the original core of the *Durham Liber Vitae*, not integrated into PASE, which refer (by Lynda Rollason's count) to 2,819 individuals.[11]

PASE's extensive list contains no record of thirty of the seventy names in *Beowulf*. This may not be surprising in mythical or doubtful cases like Fitela, Hondscioh, Healgamen, but most of the thirty are normal-seeming dithematic Anglo-Saxon names, such as Ecgtheow, Hæthcyn, Hrethric, etc. Another twenty-seven appear rarely, between one and five times, and this count includes the doubtful cases of "Beulf" in Domesday Book (a form of Beowulf?) and the tenth-century moneyer Brece (a form of Breca?). Only thirteen of the seventy names are recorded at all commonly in PASE's extensive records, and this count again involves accepting the fairly frequent Wi(g)stans as a form of Weohstan.

Four of our unknown-to-PASE thirty appear, however, in *Widsith* (Folcwalda, Hnæf, Hoc, Withergyld), as do nine more of the remaining forty, including a Breca of the Brondings who is clearly the Beowulfian character. Meanwhile the original and pre–840 core of the *DLV* (helpfully labelled by Dumville as the *Northumbrian Liber Vitae*, or *NLV*)[12] knows nineteen of *Beowulf*'s overall seventy names, as opposed to PASE's generously scored forty, but from a sample no more than one-fifth the

---

[9] Patrick Wormald, "*Beowulf*: the Redating Reasessed" [appendix to "Bede, Beowulf and the Anglo-Saxon Aristocracy"], in *The Times of Bede: Studies in Early English Christian Society and its Historian*, ed. Stephen Baxter (Malden: Blackwell, 2006), 71–81, 98–100.

[10] In reaching this figure I have followed the editorial decisions about names in *Klaeber's Beowulf*, ed. Fulk *et al.*, 464–73, thus accepting the recent suggestions Fremu and Healgamen, and the emended forms Beow and Eomer. I have not counted Grendel, Abel or Cain.

[11] Lynda Rollason, "History and Codicology," in *The Durham Liber Vitae*, ed. David Rollason and Lynda Rollason, 3 vols. (London: British Library, 2007), 1: 5–42, at 7.

[12] David N. Dumville, "'The Northumbrian *Liber Vitae*': London, British Library, MS. Cotton Domitian A.vii, Folios 15–24 & 25–45, The Original Text," *Anglo-Saxon Essays, 2001–2007* (Aberdeen: Centre for Anglo-Saxon Studies, 2007), 109–82, at 112.

size.¹³ *NLV* also shows a suggestive concentration of Hrethling names: four Hyglacs,¹⁴ eight Herebealds, eleven Heardreds, and one Biuuulf, as opposed to PASE's count of, respectively, two, probably two (see comment on p. 60 above), three, and (doubtfully) one. Neidorf points out that *heard-* and *-red* are such common themes that the combination of them may be coincidence¹⁵ (as with *here-* and *-b(e)ald*), but the relative frequencies of *NLV* and PASE are markedly different. *NLV* also knows fifteen Ingilds and an Ingeld. Apart from the familiar reference in Alcuin's angry letter, PASE lists two Northumbrian nobles and an abbot, all early to middle eighth-century, with no further occurrences till *Domesday Book*, which has seven mentions, variously spelled, from three different counties. (As said above, one cannot be sure how many individuals these represent.) One may sum up by saying that the onomastics of *Beowulf* fit PASE's historical listings, predominantly from the later Anglo-Saxon centuries, surprisingly badly; *NLV*'s mostly seventh- and eighth-century list rather better; while there is obvious overlap with *Widsith*, the early date of which has been recently reaffirmed.¹⁶

There are then a number of questions to be asked about the proper names in the poem. Why are there so many of them? So unevenly distributed? Are they historical, or legendary, or even fictional (that is to say, invented by the poet)? Why, given the presence of so many apparently redundant details about kin-relationships, are important characters (Hrothulf, Wiglaf) left unidentified? And what, if anything, can we deduce from the lack of "fit" between the poem's onomastics and those of real-life Anglo-Saxon England?

Behind these questions, furthermore – as behind the question of *eorl[as]* / *Eorl[e]* – lies another issue not commonly faced. Ever since Tolkien in 1936 it has been an axiom in *Beowulf* scholarship (for which see further below) that the poem has no value as history, that its "illusion of historical perspective ... is largely a product of art" and that seekers after historical fact must beware of "the glamour of Poesis."¹⁷ As Michael Drout points out in Chapter 8 of this volume, this is what critics in the modern world wanted to hear, for it gave their imaginations free

---

¹³ Heroic-legendary names in the *NLV* are discussed in Leonard Neidorf, "Beowulf before *Beowulf*: Anglo-Saxon Anthroponymy and Heroic Legend," *Review of English Studies* 64 (2013): 553–73; there is a list of pertinent names in its appendix. I am much obliged to the author for allowing me to read a copy of this prior to publication.

¹⁴ Hyglac was probably the poet's form of the name now conventionally written Hygelac, see *Klaeber's* Beowulf, ed. Fulk *et al.*, 470.

¹⁵ Neidorf, "Beowulf before *Beowulf*," 557–8.

¹⁶ Leonard Neidorf, "The Dating of *Widsið* and the Study of Germanic Antiquity," *Neophilologus* 97 (2013): 165–83.

¹⁷ J.R.R. Tolkien, "*Beowulf*: The Monsters and the Critics," *Proceedings of the British Academy* 32 (1936): 245–95, at 247–8.

rein. Their tacit assumption seems to have been that the poem's many unexplained names were part of what Roland Barthes has called "the reality effect": the unnecessary details which novelists have learned to put in, and which form "the basis of that unavowed verisimilitude which forms the aesthetic of all the standard works of modernity."[18] One might sum up by saying that, for Flaubert and his many successors, "redundancy creates truth." But can that assumption be read backwards into far older works?

Tolkien, after all, did not back up his statements about "art" and "glamour" by argument of any kind. One thing we can now be absolutely sure of is that his plea for the autonomy of fantasy had a strong, undeclared personal motive. What he did, indeed, was to present the *Beowulf* poet as a kind of proto-Tolkien, creating a personal fantasy-world from antiquarian materials. It is also perfectly clear[19] that when he was not trying to score a point, he took the poem as history very seriously indeed. But the question of whether the poem's many names are a "product of art," or a knowledgeable record, deserves to be probed more deeply. We should ask, with Barthes, "What is ... the significance of [their frequent] insignificance?"[20]

The Yrmenlaf Problem: Redundant Names?

The poem's narrative core, the "three great fights," could hardly be more economical with names and characters than it is. On one side there are the three monsters, only one of them named. On the other are Beowulf, his sidekick Wiglaf, and the unnamed *þeow* or *þeof* whose theft provokes the dragon. To these one could add the names of the two human casualties, Hondscioh and Æschere. Outside this narrative core, however, in the human world in which the fights are embedded, there are some sixty-six further named men and women, and a further five whose names could be deduced from *–ingas* forms.[21] One needs to ask what some of these contribute to the poem.

I remarked many years ago that of all the lines in the poem, none is more apparently redundant than line 1324.[22] After the surprise attack on

---

[18] Roland Barthes, "The Reality Effect," *The Rustle of Language*, trans. Richard Howard (Berkeley and Los Angeles: University of California Press, 1989), 141–8, at 148.
[19] From his posthumously published study *Finn and Hengest: the Fragment and the Episode*, ed. A.J. Bliss (London: Allen & Unwin, 1982).
[20] Barthes, "The Reality Effect," 143.
[21] Nine or ten more characters remain nameless, including the coastguard, the Messenger, Beowulf's mother, Hygelac's daughter.
[22] T.A. Shippey, *Beowulf* (Arnold's Studies in English Literature) (London: Edward Arnold, 1978), 24–5. See further the section "Allusion and Reality," 24–7.

Heorot by Grendel's mother, Beowulf appears and asks Hrothgar if he has had a pleasant night. Hrothgar replies, "Do not speak of pleasure! Grief is renewed to the Danish people. Æschere is dead, *Yrmenlafes yldra broþor*. He was my confidant and my counsellor, my right-hand man ... " The eulogy of Æschere could easily run straight on from the fact that he is dead. If line 1324 had somehow dropped out of the poem, not even the most *scharfsinnig* of nineteenth-century editors would ever have supposed a lacuna. One might say that there was something to be gained by giving Grendel's mother's victim a name and a touch of characterisation: it makes Hrothgar's grief more personal. But what is gained by saying that he had a younger brother, who plays no further part in the poem?

Before looking for an answer, one should note that while Yrmenlaf might be the most redundant character in the poem, he has strong competition. There are eight other names in the poem which appear only once; only in the genitive; and with a noun of relationship as their headword. Breca is *sunu Beanstanes* (524); Hildeburh is *Hoces dohtor* (1076); Finn is *Folcwaldan sunu* (1089); Eomer is *nefa Garmundes* (1962); Hygelac is *nefa Swertinges* (1203); Ingeld is *Frodan sunu* (2025); Heardred is *nefan Hererices* (2206); Wiglaf is *mæg Ælfheres* (2604). To these eight once-only pairs one might add Hygd, named twice as *Hæreþes dohtor* (1929, 1981), Offa and Eomer, both named as *Hemminges mæg* (1944, 1961), and Wulf, who is *sunu Wonredes* (2971), as also *Wonreding* (2965). Unferth's father Ecglaf is named five times, but always in the genitive and always connected with his son. And at line 1910 the Danes collectively are labelled as *eaforum Ecgwelan*. The roles of Breca, Hildeburh, Finn, etc. are obvious. But what is gained by adding in the names of, for instance, Beanstan, Hereric, Hæreth, Ælfhere or Ecgwela, of whom no more is known than of Yrmenlaf?

One suggestion, made by Rolf Bremmer, is that such names fulfilled a powerful "anchoring" function for Anglo-Saxons. "Such a [kin-group] identification of a man's – and occasionally a woman's – position appears to be indispensable for their *raison d'être* within the fabric of the early medieval heroic society."[23] If, then, a character needed to be invented – as for instance Æschere – it might make sense to invent another name, just to make the invented character seem more normal and more solid. In this view, both Æschere and Yrmenlaf might be taken as fictional, the

---

[23] Rolf H. Bremmer, Jr., "The Minor Entries in Beowulf's Who's Who: The Personalities behind the Unidentifiable Names," unpublished paper read at session 109 of the International Medieval Congress, Kalamazoo, MI, May 6th, 2004.

poet's own invention, and along with them Beanstan, Ælfhere,[24] Hereric, Hæreth, etc.

However, as Bremmer also notes, what is striking from the list above is that several of the "singleton-genitive" names are very definitely *not* the poet's own invention, but are presented in exactly the same casual way as the others. Ingeld's father Froda is mentioned repeatedly in later Scandinavian legend. Even more significantly, Hygd's father Hoc might have been dismissed as an uncorroborated invention if it were not for a fleeting mention in *Widsith* line 29, and the recent demonstration, by Carl Hammer, that his is one of the names used by a Bavarian noble family with the consistent habit of naming themselves after characters associated with Danish royal dynasties.[25] Of the fourteen names-in-the-genitive listed above, eight are unknowns. Six, however – Hoc, Folcwalda, Garmund,[26] Swerting, Froda and Hemming – figure prominently or vestigially elsewhere, in *Widsith*, in genealogies, in Scandinavian legend. In our limited state of knowledge, it would be rash in the extreme to declare that anyone of whom we have no other record can never have existed even in legend.[27]

Returning to Yrmenlaf, one possibility is indeed that he is a fictional invention by the poet. The other possibility is that at one time he had a role of some kind in the Scylding story. One might compare him, for instance, with a minor character from the Arthurian cycle, such as Mador de la Porte. There was never a romance about Mador de la Porte, but any follower of Arthurian legend would recognise the name. He appears in nine or ten French and English romances; is known as being exceptionally tall and strong; has a *contretemps* with Sir Tristram; and in Malory's version, which has French antecedents, accuses Guinevere of poisoning an apple meant for Gawain, for which he is challenged by Lancelot. He may have had Celtic antecedents as well, and was perhaps at one time a "porter," in the sense of one who guards the door, an often important role in heroic story.[28] One might remember here Hrothgar's door-ward, Wulfgar, identified firmly as *Wendla leod*, with the approving addition

---

[24] There is no reason to connect the Ælfhere of *Beowulf* with the Aquitanian Ælfhere, father of Waldere, mentioned twice in the Old English *Waldere* fragments, and in *Waltharius*.

[25] Carl Hammer, "Hoc and Hnaef in Bavaria? Early Medieval Prosopography and Heroic Poetry," *Medieval Prosopography* 26 (2009 for 2005): 13–50.

[26] This rests on the assumption, generally accepted, that Garmund in line 1962 is yet another scribal error for Wærmund, like *geomor* for Eomer two lines above. Wærmund is linked with Offa several times in legend, and with Offa and Eomer in the Mercian royal genealogy. PASE has five further eighth- and five ninth-century Wærmunds, but only one later record. There are three Wærmunds in the *NLV*.

[27] Neidorf forcefully argues this point in "Beowulf before *Beowulf*," 566–8.

[28] See further http://kingarthur.wikia.com/wiki/Mador.

that "his character was known to many, his valor and wisdom." Is this also fiction? Or an appeal to previous knowledge, meant to be recognised?

The main argument against the former possibility – though this seems to be what Tolkien hinted at as the "product of art" – is that corroboration / non-corroboration are so randomly distributed. Are we to think that the poet built in a handful of names he knew would be recognised, just so he could sprinkle in a further handful of names he had made up himself? How could he know which names would be recognised and which would not? Is it at all likely that his original audience would have been in exactly the same state of (very patchy) knowledge that we are? It seems an unusually self-conscious procedure: also one requiring a lot of care and thought, for little effect. After all, Yrmenlaf has meant nothing to a modern audience, and would have meant as little to an original audience that had never heard of him.

The Dæghrefn Problem: Invented Names?

If one is, nevertheless, to continue looking for pure fiction, made up by the poet, with no previous basis in legend, then the central figure of Beowulf is the obvious place to start. Suspicion might well be aroused by the different ways in which Beowulf himself and his uncle Hygelac are introduced. Hygelac is named at line 194 well before Beowulf is (343), and is then mentioned repeatedly, in ways which suggest that Beowulf is emotionally dependent on him. Yet for more than a thousand lines we are never told who Hygelac is, and when we do find out (1485), the information seems to slip out rather than be foregrounded: Hygelac is *sunu Hrædles*, which means he is Beowulf's mother's brother, thus explaining the emotional dependence.

By contrast, Beowulf's ancestry is explained carefully early on. Hrothgar says that his father was Ecgtheow, his mother the only daughter of Hrethel (373–5). Hrothgar adds further detail at lines 459–72: Ecgtheow killed one Heatholaf *mid Wilfingum*, was forced into exile from the Geats, and took service with Hrothgar, who composed the feud for him. The easiest way to graft a fictional character into a family known in legend must be to make him the son of a nameless daughter, as is the case with Beowulf. But does it follow that Ecgtheow, Heatholaf, and the Wilfings are all fictional too, invented to give Beowulf some background and also – a point often made in the past – to save Hrothgar's face by making Beowulf indebted to him?

Three facts about Ecgtheow are, first, his name is unknown elsewhere in Anglo-Saxon records. There is no Ecgtheow in PASE, or in *NLV*. On the other hand, the name was known in Scandinavia, for its exact cognate,

Eggthér, is given to a giant in the Eddic poem *Völuspá*, st. 10. Finally, Ecgtheo(w) is a name archaic in form, as R.D. Fulk explains.[29] Heatholaf is likewise a name which figures nowhere in the PASE lists. So if the poet was inventing the whole story, he must have said to himself something like: "I need a name for the hero's father; it has to be an unusual name; but one current in Scandinavia (because after all the whole story takes place there); I need an archaic name too; and another unknown, but not impossible name for the victim; and to tie everything in, I need to mention a known tribal or sub-tribal group, like the Wilfings" – who, according to *Widsith* 29 were ruled by Helm, another name marginally present in *Beowulf*. (Hnæf and Hoc are in the same *Widsith* line.) Referring to Tolkien again, this would be art indeed.

Another place in Beowulf's biography where one might suspect invention is the climactic battle against the Franks. This, of course, is the one part of the poem where we have very strong evidence of historical fact. Nevertheless, Beowulf's own role in the disaster looks like fiction. He had to survive, or the story would stop too soon. The swimming home with thirty suits of armor can be nothing but a "moral victory" story, of the sort commonly manufactured after national defeat. But then there is his extended boast, as he psyches himself up for the dragon-fight, that he was the death of Dæghrefn, *Huga cempan*, standard-bearer to the Frisian king (though in this battle the poet seems to regard Franks and Frisians as interchangeable). It has long been noted that Dæghrefn is "a Frankish, non-A[nglo]-S[axon] name (*Dag-hraban*),"[30] recorded elsewhere in Continental Europe as *Dagaramnus, Daigramnus*.[31] One might go further and say that it is a *characteristically* Frankish name. The prototheme Dago- was familiar from the Frankish royal dynasty, with its three Dagoberts; the *MGH* volume cited below has twenty-four more Dagnames in its "Index Nominum." "Raven" was also popular in Frankish circles as prototheme, deuterotheme, and simplex form; see respectively Gregory's *Chramnesindus*, the Frankish St Wulfhramn, and Hrabanus Maurus, abbot of Fulda. Dæg- names are not uncommon in Old English. Wormald counts twenty-four, twenty-two of them from before 840, and sixteen of these from *NLV*. PASE finds two or three more both before and after 840. "Raven" names, however, are almost unknown in Old English. PASE's approximately fifteen cases include some definite Franks, like the abbot of Fulda above and Alcuin's pupil *Waldramnus*, and three more

---

[29] See R.D. Fulk, "*Beowulf* and Language History," Chapter 1 in this volume.
[30] *Klaeber's* Beowulf, ed. Fulk *et al.*, 248.
[31] In two south German fraternity books, see *Libri confraternitatum Sancti Galli, Augiensis, Fabariensis*, ed. Paul Piper (*MGH* Antiquitatum series 2, Necrologia Germaniae, vol. 2 Supplementband) (Berlin: Weidmann, 1884), 208, 215.

Frankish forms, like the seventh-century Kentish charter-witness *Raban* and the "Hramnwulf" boldly reconstructed from a coin-inscription *RANNL*. Others are read as Old Norse names, like the "Hrafnsvart" and "Hrafnketil" believed to be represented by various spellings in *Domesday Book*. The only identifiable Anglo-Saxon "raven" name, oddly, is "Wælhræfn," found once in *NLV*, as *Walrafan*, three times in *Domesday Book*, and four times as the name of an eleventh-century Lincoln moneyer. One can say that "raven" names were uncommon in Anglo-Saxon onomastics, while the Dæg- prefix became so. Only *Beowulf* and the Continental examples combine the two elements.

Did the poet, then, deliberately make this name up, to add local color? It is not impossible, given the unlikelihood of the story of Beowulf "bear-hugging" his adversary to death. But if so, it is odd that the poet makes no more of what would have been a considerable feat of narrative imagination – just the kind of "realism effect" pointed to by Barthes. The name, moreover, while culturally consistent with its Frankish setting, is in perfect Anglo-Saxon form, with no trace of having been "transposed" from some (non-extant) written Frankish source. A straightforward explanation is that "Dayraven" was a Frankish champion once well-enough known for his death to be remembered; and that his name passed into legend in the sixth century, acquiring its purely Old English form, like the names of so many known and unknown heroes in *Widsith*, by the natural processes of philological development. In this it would parallel the place-name *Scedenigge*, derived from Early Germanic *Skaðin-awjo* by regular change, while in Scandinavia itself different linguistic processes led to its borrowing into Alfredian Old English as *Sconeg*.[32]

A third potentially fictitious character must be Weohstan, father of Wiglaf. Wiglaf's presence in the poem is obviously essential, and as with others it might be natural to give him a patronymic as soon as he appears: *Wiglaf wæs haten, Weoxstanes sunu* (2602). Wiglaf is, however, then given three more authenticating details in quick succession, as many as Hygelac: he is *leod Scylfinga, mæg Ælfheres*, and his ancestral possession is the estate of the "Wægmundings," Wægmund being then presumably his grandfather or a more remote ancestor. One might feel that there is then something to be gained, Flaubert-style, by the stress on the sword Wiglaf has inherited from his father Weohstan (2610–30). It is a kind of guarantee of his nobility and valor, and therefore worth inventing. But what is gained by making the sword *Eanmundes laf*, and attaching to it a story full of complexities? They are complexities of a kind (civil war,

---

[32] As demonstrated by R.D. Fulk, "Review Article: Dating *Beowulf* to the Viking Age," *Philological Quarterly* 61 (1982): 341–59, at 343–4.

change of allegiance, divided families) which notoriously happen in reality. But why raise so many unanswered questions in fiction?

A likelier possibility is that as with Yrmenlaf, Ecgtheow and Dæghrefn, Weohstan was someone who had a prior existence in legend, or even history, and had done something which was remembered. Klaeber suggested that he might be identified with the hero Vésteinn who rode to battle with the Swedish king Áli in the Old Norse poem *Kálfsvísa*;[33] Áli is indeed (if opaquely) cognate with *Beowulf*'s Onela, though *Kálfsvísa* ascribes Vésteinn to a battle later on in the Swedish civil war. The *Beowulf* poet might then have been unable to invent freely with regard to Weohstan. As for the ancestral Wægmund, if he was pure invention, the poet multiplied his invention by creating a name which, like Yrmenlaf, is otherwise unknown in the records of Anglo-Saxon England: there are eight Wiglafs in PASE (with one more in *NLV*), and ten Wihstans, but no Wægmund, and only three cases of Weg(e) as simplex or prototheme.

The Heorogar Problem: Dynastic Names?

Of the poem's seventy personal names, only seven belong to *dramatis personae*, i.e., people who do something or (like Wulfgar the door-ward) at least speak. To this count one could add the names of the two casualties in Heorot. The largest group of names, by contrast, comes from the poem's many tales and allusions, twenty-seven of them: eight from the Finnsburh story including its teller Healgamen, three from the Fremu story, and so on. Names in this group belong to characters as important as Breca and Hengest, as mythical or fleeting as Weland or Withergyld. Fourteen more function as "authenticators," as listed on p. 63 above, to which one could add Wægmund and Helm from outside the seventy. The remaining group are dynastic names: ten Scyldings apart from Hrothgar and Wealhtheow, five Scylfings, five Hrethlings apart from Hygelac. These give the best opportunity to consider the question: historical, legendary, or fictional?

There is no doubt about the legendary character of the Scyldings, for they appear in a dozen medieval Scandinavian texts, in what is now once more known collectively – thanks to unexpected and still continuing archaeological discoveries – as "the legend of Lejre."[34] Its central character is King Hrólfr, regularly identified with the Hrothulf mentioned in *Beowulf* as present in Heorot (1017, 1181), though silent and passive.

---

[33] Klaeber's original point is still included in *Klaeber's* Beowulf, ed. Fulk *et al.*, lxiii, n.3.
[34] See Marijane Osborn, "Legends of Lejre, Home of Kings," in Beowulf *and Lejre*, ed. John D. Niles (Tempe, AZ: ACMRS, 2007), 235–54. (Osborn also gives introductions to some of the texts involved, 295–387.)

There should also be no doubt that the poet expected his audience to know some version of the legend, from the fact that – as with Wiglaf, as very nearly with Hygelac and with Ingeld – the poet never bothers to say who Hrothulf is. The "legend of Lejre," however, consistently identifies him as the son of Helgi son of Hálvdan, taken by all to be identical with the Halga son of Healfdene of line 61, and therefore Hrothgar's nephew. The main discrepancy between *Beowulf* and the "legend of Lejre" collectively is, however, that the latter knows of only seven Skjöldungs, at most, while the former names twelve Scyldings. The shared characters are, in their Old English forms, Scyld, Healfdene, Hrothgar, Halga, Hrothulf, Hrethric, and Heoroweard, the ones known only to *Beowulf* being Beow, Heorogar, Wealhtheow, Hrothmund and Freawaru. Beow can be discounted, as a mythical figure who has crept into a genealogy. The most immediately interesting of the four "unknowns" is Heorogar.

He is mentioned three times in the poem, once at line 61, with his two brothers, once at lines 467–9, when Hrothgar says that Heorogar was his elder brother, adding "he was better than I," and once at line 2158, when Beowulf hands over armor to Hygelac, noting that it had belonged to Heorogar who had not wished it to go to his own son Heoroweard. The "legend of Lejre" is meanwhile consistent in stating, in five different texts, that the man responsible for the death of King Hrólfr was one Hiörvarthr, Hiorvardus, Hiartwarus or Hiarwarthus, though four of these five versions ascribe blame also to Hiörvarthr's consort Skuld.[35] We therefore have two traditions. In the later Scandinavian one King Hrólfr is killed by one Hiörvarthr, no relation to him, egged on by his consort Skuld; in *Hrólfs saga* she is Hrólf's half-sister, product of a liaison between Halga and an elf-woman. In *Beowulf* nothing is said about the death of Hrothulf, but a powerful motive for hostility to him is set up by the revelation that he has a cousin, who has been effectively disinherited. Since in the Scandinavian tradition Hrólfr and Hiörvarthr are not related, Hiörvarthr's father *Hiörgeirr does not appear there. If one has to choose between the two stories, it is obvious which is the more plausible in real-world terms. Heoroweard is in exactly the same situation as the Wessex prince Æthelwold, who rebelled when put aside in favor of his cousin Edward on the death of his uncle Alfred in 899.

There is no doubt, then, that Heoroweard played a role in the Scylding legend, and a strong case for declaring Heorogar to be *a fortiori* likewise traditional, if not historical: although, note, we have no corroboration for him whatsoever. The alternative is to declare that the *Beowulf*

---

[35] See discussion in Tom Shippey, "*Hrólfs saga kraka* and the Legend of Lejre," in *Making History: Studies in the Fornaldarsögur*, ed. Martin Arnold and Alison Finlay (London: Viking Society, 2011), 17–32, at 24–5.

poet invented a relationship between the proto-Hiörvarthr and the proto-Hrólfr, and supplied them with an invented father/uncle to match, his name, once again (while entirely plausible) found nowhere else in Anglo-Saxon records. Indeed, there is no clear case of any Heoro- proto-theme in PASE or in *NLV*.

What then of Hrothmund? Like so many, he appears to have no function at all in the poem. He is mentioned once with his brother Hrethric, at line 1189, but while Hrethric finds a somewhat confusing place in the "legend of Lejre," Hrothmund is, like Heorogar, unknown to Scandinavian tradition. He might just be a doubling of his brother, added for reasons of increased pathos. But if an invention, he is quite a pointless one, and quite a difficult one: the name Hrothmund appears only twice in PASE, one of them a dubious Rodmundus from *Domesday Book*, the other (as Sam Newton noted)[36] an ancestor of the East Anglian kings. Hrothmund might well be accepted, like Heorogar, as non-fictional, part of an extended "legend of Heorot" fuller and more convincing than the "legend of Lejre," and one which the *Beowulf* poet expected his audience to know without being told.

One could meanwhile make out a case for seeing both female Scyldings, Wealhtheow and Freawaru, as fictional, the poet's invention. There is no legendary corroboration for either, but both have a significant, even pivotal role in the poem's narrative. Who better to indicate trouble brewing in Heorot, as the poet clearly intends, than an anxious mother? As for Freawaru, Ingeld's revenge was one of the most popular legendary stories of the Northern world – as shown by *NLV*'s sixteen men called Ingild / Ingeld, some perhaps the same as the three eighth-century Northumbrian notables listed by PASE: the name then vanishes till *Domesday Book*. Only *Widsith*, however, locates his fateful wedding *æt Heorote* (45–9), though *Beowulf* 83–5 appears to agree. If there were a shared story and a shared location, it would make sense to focus on the bride. Both female names are, again, unknown elsewhere, and the Frea- prototheme is especially rare, occurring three times in PASE, all three occurrences male, two of them from very early stages in royal genealogies and the third from a fake ninth-century charter. If the poet were inventing both characters, once again he took extra trouble over both names, for no clear gain.

The situation with the Scylfings is not dissimilar. They too are prominent in later Scandinavian tradition. *Beowulf* lists five of them, a grandfather-figure, Ongentheow, his two sons, Onela and Ohthere, and two sons of the latter, Eadgils and Eanmund. The three in the middle

---

[36] Sam Newton, *The Origins of* Beowulf *and the Pre-Viking Kingdom of East Anglia* (Cambridge: D.S. Brewer, 1993), 78, 103–4.

appear in the ninth-century poem *Ynglingatal*, extensively used in Snorri's later *Ynglinga saga*, as respectively Áli, Óttarr, Athils. The names correspond etymologically, the relationship between Óttarr and Athils corresponds exactly, and the clash between Áli and Athils, mentioned in *Beowulf*, was remembered also in Arngrímur Jónsson's sixteenth-century epitome of the lost *Skjöldunga saga* and in the poem *Kálfsvísa* already mentioned. The grandfather Ongentheow seems to have been better remembered in England than in Scandinavia, for according to *Widsith* line 31 he "ruled the Swedes."

The interesting case, however – as with Heorogar and Hrothmund – is the character who appears nowhere outside *Beowulf*, Eanmund, mentioned in the poem only once (2611). Should he be taken as complete invention? If so, the purpose of the invention is utterly obscure. The story of his sword, taken by Wiglaf's father Weohstan to be passed on to Wiglaf and used so prominently in the dragon-fight, creates, as already stated, apparently unnecessary complications which have never been explained. Could the poet not have called the sword **Ohtheres laf*, and placed Weohstan on the same side in the Swedish civil war as his relative Beowulf? Not if his invention was curbed by continuing memory of Eanmund and Weohstan, lost to later Scandinavian tradition.

Finally, the Hrethlings are represented once again by a grandfather, Hrethel, three sons, Herebeald, Hæthcyn and Hygelac, the latter's wife Hygd, and son Heardred (as well as Beowulf himself). We have no corroborating information for any of these except Hygelac, and the whole dynasty might well be regarded as fictional – if it were not for the surprising fact that Hygelac (not quite completely forgotten in Scandinavian tradition)[37] is better confirmed as not even a legendary but a historical character than anyone else in the poem. Did the poet then, on the basis of one known figure, invent the rest of his detailed stories about the deaths of the other four Hrethlings? If he did, he once again showed remarkable narrative art in interweaving those stories with the legendary accounts of the Scylfings; in turn interweaving these with the legendary accounts of the Scyldings; presenting those interweavings in both marginal and remarkably non-chronological fashion; and doing so without emphasis or self-contradiction. If one were to believe Tolkien, this would be a case of *ars est celare artem* on a unique scale. It is a feat he himself could not always manage.[38]

---

[37] Though the memory seems to have been no more than the name, from which a story was concocted by false analysis of the *-lac* / *-leikr* deuterotheme, see F.C. Robinson, "The Significance of Names in Old English Literature," *Anglia* 86 (1968): 14–58, at 50–7.

[38] In *The Hobbit*, different dates are given at the end of Chapter 3 and the start of Chapter 4 for the narratively vital "Durin's Day." The discrepancy was not corrected for almost sixty years.

Interweavings of an even more marginal kind could be seen in the poem, if one cared to take its personal names seriously. As mentioned above, we are told that Wealhtheow is *ides Helminga* (620); Helm, according to *Widsith* 29, ruled the Wulfings, and Beowulf's father Ecgtheow was involved in the feud with the Wilfings settled by Hrothgar (461, 471). Should this indicate that Wealhtheow has a familial as well as an immediate reason for distrusting and trying to placate Beowulf, which latter she clearly does? Heremod is mentioned twice in the poem, both times used to make a very clear contrast with Beowulf himself, but the poet does not bother to say who he was or give him an "authenticating" relative, as he does with many others. One might, however, readily infer that it was the overthrow and exile of Heremod which created the Danish interregnum mentioned at the start of the poem (14–16), and allowed the rise of the Scyldings.

Some Conclusions and a Hypothesis

The gist of what has been said so far is that the *Beowulf* poet was not only well aware of legendary tradition in places where it can be corroborated, but very likely so in places where our limited knowledge offers no corroboration. Names like Yrmenlaf, Hereric, and Ælfhere probably did mean something to the well-informed. Characters like Ecgtheow or Dæghrefn are unlikely to be pure invention. The dynastic names missing from later Scandinavian legend like Heorogar, Hrothmund, Eanmund, create a fuller and more plausible story than those later legends, without substantially contradicting them. It is not that the poet was incapable of invention. All his place-names, for instance (other than well-known national territories) look as if they have been created according to a simple formula: animal-name in genitive plus familiar word for natural feature, so *Earna Naes, Hrefnes Holt* and three more, plus *Biowulfes Biorh*.[39]

But the personal names are different. To repeat a point made above: it is surprising, first that the "singleton" names, appearing once only, and so the likeliest to be invented, are corroborated about as often as not. Conversely, relatively prominent characters in the poem, like Unferth and Ecgtheow, may be completely unknown elsewhere. There is little or no correlation between frequency of appearance in the poem and record in legend. The simple explanation is that the poet was embedded in early Germanic legend to a degree beyond that of any other writer we know, and drew freely on his knowledge. The alternative explanation,

---

[39] As noted by R.D. Fulk, "The Etymology and Significance of Beowulf's Name," *Anglo-Saxon* 1 (2007): 109–36, at 113.

the one hinted at by Tolkien, is that the many names scattered through the poem are a cunning creation of Barthes's "realist effect"; so that the poet deliberately modelled (e.g.) Heardred nephew of Hereric, both complete unknowns, on Ingeld son of Froda, both extremely famous; and furthermore covered his invention by presenting all four in the same matter-of-course way. Once this explanation is framed rather than hinted, it looks unlikely.

It should be noted also that this argument does not apply only to names. In the aftermath of the rejection of the old composite-authorship theories, critics found it easy and rewarding to show that the many "digressions" in the poem were not digressions at all, but had a function which demonstrated the poet's artistic skill and the poem's much-desired organic unity. What this critical industry obscured was the number of cases where the poet hints at something which never comes into focus at all, and seems to have no evident point. Among the queries arising from the poem's many "lost tales" one might list: why were the Danes and Geats on bad terms some time in the past (1855–8)? What did the Geats do to the Swedish king Ongentheow's wife (2930–32)? What did "Hemming's kinsman" Offa do to change the character of Queen Fremu, long thought to be Queen Modthrytho (1944–54)? What started the Danish / Heathobeardan conflict, when Withergyld was killed (2047–52)? His name appears also in *Widsith* line 124, though without further details.

Closer to the poem's core, what happened to all the Wægmundings, Beowulf's own family (2813–16)? For that matter, how is Wiglaf son of Weohstan related to Beowulf? Once again, the poet never says who this vitally important character actually is, and this time we have no source to tell us from outside the poem.[40] Perhaps most tantalizing is the tale of how Unferth, Hrothgar's counsellor, killed his brothers. Beowulf accuses him of this (lines 587–9), and the accusation is confirmed by lines 1167–8. One wonders how a fratricide can continue to be held in honor in a heroic court, while recognizing that fights between family members are a standard part of the heroic repertoire. But we are left to speculate.

Are we to think that there never was an answer, the story (like all those other unnecessary stories) being there just as a teaser? Exactly as with the names, there are similarly veiled allusions where, by chance, we have an idea how to fill in the gap, as at lines 82–5, the burning down

---

[40] Rolf H. Bremmer Jr. suggests, in "The Importance of Kinship: Uncle and Nephew in *Beowulf*," *Amsterdamer Beiträge zur älteren Germanistik* 15 (1980): 21–38, at 35–6, that Wiglaf would make sense as Beowulf's nephew by an unnamed sister, so being in the same relationship to Beowulf as Beowulf to Hygelac and Heardred to Hereric. But why is it never stated?

of Heorot, or at line 62, Healfdene's missing child. But as with the characters whom the poet never bothers to identify (Hrothulf, Wiglaf), or where identification slips out almost by accident (Hygelac, Ingeld), on a narrative level the modern reader is surprisingly often left twisting in the wind: though this fact has been obscured by the efforts of editors, with their helpful notes and family-trees.

Coming finally to the issue central to this volume, what are the implications of the above for dating the poem's composition? One name has a direct bearing on that question, and since it has been a matter of controversy I return to it. In 2005, I put forward the argument that the poem's *Merewioing[e]s* is the only philologically accurate form recorded for the dynasty normally called "Merovingian"; that this form could only with implausible difficulty have been reconstructed from any of the written texts proposed as sources; that the name was accordingly probably still in oral circulation at the time of the poem's composition; while familiar oral use probably dwindled soon after the Carolingian takeover.[41] At the end of his Thorkelín-like reply to this in 2007, Walter Goffart declared himself unable to comment on the philological question.[42] But this is to ignore the whole of the argument. A continuing literary tradition of references to the Merovingians tells us nothing about the uniquely accurate form of the name found in *Beowulf*; while the fact that the name meant nothing to the poem's scribe B (just as many Continental scribes produced only garbled forms of it) backs up the case for oral unfamiliarity. As for the idea of *damnatio memoriae*, to which Goffart takes such exception, Carolingian attempts to erase traces of their predecessors' rule are mentioned by several eminent historians.[43] Goffart's parting shot is an appeal to authority, in the form of E.G. Stanley, and this is especially unfortunate, given that Stanley's surely facetious dismissal of a similar philological argument was patiently reduced *ad absurdum* thirty years

---

[41] Tom Shippey, "The Merow(ich)ingian Again: *damnatio memoriae* and the *usus scholarum*," in *Latin Learning and English Lore: Studies in Anglo-Saxon Literature for Michael Lapidge*, ed. Katherine O'Brien O'Keeffe and Andy Orchard, 2 vols. (Toronto: University of Toronto Press, 2005), 1: 389–406.

[42] Walter Goffart, "The Name Merovingian and the Dating of *Beowulf*," *Anglo-Saxon England* 36 (2007): 93–9.

[43] J.M. Wallace-Hadrill, *The Long-Haired Kings* (Toronto: University of Toronto Press, 1982), 231; Ian Wood, *The Merovingian Kingdoms 450–751* (New York: Longmans, 1994), 324; and Rosamond McKitterick, *History and Memory in the Carolingian World* (Cambridge: Cambridge University Press, 2004), see "Index" under "Merovingian kings ... belittling of." Especially notable, from the last, is "the complete absence of the Merovingian rulers in the section [of the *Annales regni francorum*] before 751," 113.

ago by R.D. Fulk.⁴⁴ Goffart's claim to hear "the ring of truth" in Stanley's unsupported assertion does not even pretend to objectivity. Once again, the simple explanation is that the poet knew the name, in its etymologically correct rather than its conventional literary form, because it was still familiar; and he called the ruler of the Franks "the Merovingian," without historical explanation, because at the time of writing, as at the time of the event being mentioned, he was.

Meanwhile, and independent of the above, one may well feel that the poet's deep knowledge of legend implies a time of composition significantly earlier than that of our other, later, scattered and unsatisfactory records; as does the striking lack of fit between the poem's extensive onomastics and the mostly later records of Anglo-Saxon England as recorded in PASE. The remarkable correspondences between the poem's onomastics and those of the original core of the *Durham Liber Vitae* are also suggestive; and that original core must be earlier than the 840s, most of it much earlier: its identifiable names go back as far into the seventh century as King Edwin (died 633). All these points indicate a date of original composition no later than the mid-eighth century.

This raises one final issue, and one further challenge to the post-Tolkien consensus. Since Tolkien it has been accepted almost without debate that *Beowulf* cannot be regarded as a guide to history. The editors of *Klaeber's Beowulf* declare, "the poem does not offer reliable historical fact,"⁴⁵ and in doing so summarize a conviction repeatedly stated. One finds it again in the volume Beowulf *and Lejre*, though this whole collective enterprise was stimulated by archaeological discoveries which overturned previous disbelief in "the legend of Lejre," if not "the legend of Heorot."⁴⁶ In his outstanding Ph.D. thesis of 1999, Carl Edlund Anderson makes the obligatory denial of *Beowulf* as history; but this immediately follows his observation that details of the poem "fit neatly into the pattern of Scandinavian history" as revealed by archaeology. Anderson later describes the critical situation as "fossilised."⁴⁷ The *Klaeber IV* editors similarly concede, on the same page as their dismissal, that the poem does "present an air of reality and truth" – which takes us back to Tolkien's "product of art" and "glamour of Poesis." It is surely time to challenge Tolkien.

---

⁴⁴ See respectively Goffart, "The Name Merovingian," 99; E.G. Stanley, "The Date of *Beowulf*: Some Doubts and No Conclusions," in *The Dating of* Beowulf, ed. Colin Chase (Toronto: University of Toronto Press, 1981), 197–212, at 207; Fulk, "Review Article," 344.
⁴⁵ *Klaeber's* Beowulf, ed. Fulk *et al.*, li.
⁴⁶ See Beowulf *and Lejre*, ed. Niles, 82, 225.
⁴⁷ Carl Edlund Anderson, "Formation and Resolution of Ideological Contrast in the Early History of Scandinavia" (Ph.D. diss, Cambridge University, 1999), 56, 100.

The questions which then arise are, how far can oral memory be expected to stretch? And how far can it be trusted? Personal experience indicates that accounts of dramatic events – in my case, the 1914 bombardment of Hartlepool by German battle-cruisers – can readily be passed, grandfather to grandson, for a hundred years; though the same experience, checked against documentary history, indicates that such accounts are likely to be "airbrushed" in detail into a form acceptable to the teller. This latter point is corroborated by parts of Gísli Sigurðsson's careful study of the well-evidenced Icelandic saga tradition. Gísli's overall conclusion, however, is that Icelandic sagas may well be based on oral accounts of events two centuries or more older than the sagas as eventually written down, and may equally well preserve memory of real events, if adapted, distorted or self-serving.[48] Why are we so sure that the same could not be true of *Beowulf*?

Returning now to the poem's first few lines, discussed at the start of this chapter: its comment about "[taking] away the mead-benches from many tribes" is unparalleled in our records, but has been readily understood. Since mead-halls are centers for communal drinking and displays of authority, as they obviously are in *Beowulf*, taking away tribal mead-benches means removing local autonomy, imposing central authority, beginning the process of state-formation. That this was actually happening in Scandinavia in the "Early Germanic" period is strongly suggested by archaeology.[49] The Uppsala archaeologist Frands Herschend indeed considers the increasing evidence for smashed and burned halls in pre-Viking Scandinavia and concludes, very appositely, "The struggle for power among the leading families was to a certain degree a matter of fighting each other with the purpose of destroying each others' halls. Smashing rather than plundering was the keynote of this kind of political rather than economic warfare":[50] pretty much what the poem says.

Meanwhile the image given in the poem, of Scandinavian royal dynasties fighting each other and themselves into a state of near-extinction, harmonises well with several indications of serious trouble in southern Scandinavia around the start of the Vendel Period, i.e., mid-sixth century: "an abrupt end to the supply of precious metals in Scandinavia"; new construction of Swedish hill-forts; in Östergötland, the home of the

---

[48] Gísli Sigurðsson, *The Medieval Icelandic Saga and Oral Tradition: A Discourse on Method*, trans. Nicholas Jones (Cambridge, MA: Harvard University Press, 2004). See especially pp. 247–9, and (with analogy to the Scylding / Skjöldung discrepancies), 309–20.
[49] See Lotte Hedeager, *Iron-Age Societies: from Tribe to State in Northern Europe, 500 BC to AD 700*, trans. John Hines (Oxford: Blackwell, 1992), 239–55.
[50] Frands Herschend, *The Idea of the Good in Late Iron Age Society* (Occasional papers in archaeology 15) (Uppsala: Institutionen för arkeologi och antikens historia, Uppsala Universitet, 1998), 37.

Geats, a mid-century breach in cultural continuity.[51] In their 1985 reconsiderations of the old thesis of a "migration period crisis," Scandinavian archaeologists pointed out that while there was evidence for significant change, it could have had several causes besides, though not excluding, "inre maktkamp" or domestic power-struggles;[52] and since then others have been added, including the strong evidence for a "Fimbulwinter" in the 530s caused by a far-off asteroid strike or volcanic explosion.[53] Herschend's dramatic formulation is that "in the middle of the [first] millennium" the region went "down to hell."[54] Martin Rundkvist more moderately suggests it was "a highly stressful time," adding that the mid-sixth-century transfer of power in Östergötland is unlikely to have taken place "in an undramatic fashion":[55] once again, pretty much what the poem says. One especially pertinent suggestion by Rundkvist is that trouble was exacerbated by sixth-century Merovingian control over the transfer of gold, as gifts or payments to the north.[56] Though Rundkvist does not say this, such a development might in the first place have triggered Hygelac's fatal and historical raid, while it makes unexpectedly literal sense of the poem's lines 2920–1, "ever since the favor of the Merovingian has not been granted us." This would then not indicate an (implausible) threat of military reprisal, of the sort expected from the Swedes, but simply what it says: the Geats were entirely cut out of any form of gift exchange, as the archaeological evidence suggests.

Without dates and documentary confirmation, some say, there can be no history, and since *Beowulf* has neither (Hygelac apart), in a sense it cannot be historical. That is not to say that it may not, nevertheless, preserve memories, no doubt partly false, "airbrushed" or otherwise *parti*

---

[51] Respectively, Martin Rundkvist, *Mead-halls of the Eastern Geats: Elite Settlements and Political Geography AD 375–1000 in Östergötland, Sweden* (Stockholm: KVHAA, Royal Swedish Academy, 2012), 40; Michael Olausson, "När aristokratin flyttade upp på höjderna [When the aristocracy moved uphill]," *Historisk Tidskrift* 56 (2008): 24–40; Rundkvist, *Mead-halls*, 46.

[52] Näsman, Ulf, "Den folkvandringstida ?krisen i Sydskandinavien," in idem and Jørgen Lund, eds., *Folkevandringstiden i Norden: En krisetid mellem ældre og yngre jernalder* (Aarhus: Aarhus Universitetsforlag, 1988), 227–55, at 249–50.

[53] Bo Gräslund, "Fimbulvintern, Ragnarök och klimatkrisen år 536–537 e. Kr.," *Saga och Sed* (2007): 93–123.

[54] Quoted in Giorgio Ausenda, "Current Issues and Future Directions in the Study of the Scandinavians: Summary of Participants' Discussions and Comments," in *The Scandinavians from the Vendel Period to the Tenth Century: An Ethnographic Perspective*, ed. Judith Jesch (Woodbridge: Boydell Press, 2002), 321–52, at 333.

[55] Rundkvist, *Mead-halls*, 39, 46.

[56] Rundkvist, "Post festum. Solid gold among the Swedes from the end of the Migration Period solidi import to the beginning of the Viking raids," unpublished paper read to the Medieval Academy of America, Minneapolis, 12 April 2003, accessible at http://www.algonet.se/~arador/postfestum.html, accessed 16th May 2012.

pris, of genuine events: events moreover deeply traumatic for those who survived them, and who perhaps – like Hengest (mentioned in *Beowulf*, name recorded once in PASE as the immigrant conqueror of Kent);[57] or Hrothmund (mentioned in *Beowulf*, name securely recorded in PASE once, as an immigrant ancestor of East Anglian kings);[58] or the remnants of the Hrethlings (whose names survive in unusual concentration in the *Northumbrian Liber Vitae*) – made their defeated way across the sea to England, to tell their own version of events, so strikingly dissimilar from the stories of the winners they left behind, but preserved, most probably, from a time before later traumas had overlaid them.

---

[57] Tolkien's view of the story behind this character is hard to extract from his increasingly clotted presentation in *Finn and Hengest*, but appears clearly in a work of children's fiction by Jill Paton Walsh, *Hengest's Tale* (London: Macmillan, 1966). Ms Walsh was an undergraduate at Oxford in the 1950s, and could have heard (about?) Tolkien's lectures on the subject, on which his 1982 book was based. Her maiden name was Bliss: I do not know whether there is a family connection with the editor of *Finn and Hengest*, A.J. Bliss.

[58] See Newton, *Origins of* Beowulf, 103–4.

4

The Limits of Conservative Composition in Old English Poetry

Megan E. Hartman

As the introduction to this collection makes clear, the various forms of linguistic and metrical evidence bearing on the dating of *Beowulf* point to a date of composition fairly early in the Anglo-Saxon period. In his article for *The Dating of Beowulf* in 1980, Thomas Cable proposed a rough guide to the metrical dating of poems using the incidence of type C, D, and E verses, which decline in frequency over the Anglo-Saxon period.[1] Cable's criterion places *Beowulf* toward the beginning of a relative chronology. Since then, much additional metrical and linguistic evidence has been gathered that places *Beowulf* in the early to mid-eighth century. R.D. Fulk's *A History of Old English Meter* is the most substantial work of this kind, for it examines the presence of archaic metrical features throughout the corpus of Old English poetry and finds that *Beowulf* is by far the most archaic poem.[2] Since that work, other scholars have written articles on individual metrical or linguistic features of the poetic corpus, which have corroborated the conclusions that Fulk so carefully reached.[3]

Some scholars, however, remain dubious about the reliability of this type of evidence. At this point, the force of linguistic scholarship is too formidable to be undermined by the doubts raised by E.G. Stanley, who urged that the poem should not be dated by means of sundry linguistic oddities that could well be scribal error or just a few bad lines.[4] The

---

[1] Thomas Cable, "Metrical Style as Evidence for the Date of *Beowulf*," in *The Dating of Beowulf*, ed Colin Chase (Toronto: University of Toronto Press, 1981; reprinted with an afterword by Nicholas Howe, 1997), 77–82.

[2] R.D. Fulk, *A History of Old English Meter* (Philadelphia: University of Pennsylvania Press, 1992) [henceforth *HOEM*].

[3] See, for example, Geoffrey Russom, "Dating Criteria for Old English Poems," in *Studies in the History of the English Language: A Millennial Perspective*, ed. Donka Minkova and Robert P. Stockwell (Berlin: Mouton de Gruyter, 2002), 245–65; and Dennis Cronan, "Poetic Words, Conservatism, and the Dating of Old English Poetry," *Anglo-Saxon England* 33 (2004): 23–50.

[4] E.G. Stanley, "The Date of *Beowulf*: Some Doubts and No Conclusions," in *The Dating of* Beowulf, ed. Chase, 208–9.

linguistic and metrical evidence spans too great a range of features to dismiss its combined weight; while a few instances of these features could be the result of scribal errors or compositional anomalies, it is enormously improbable that they all are. The main argument against relying on linguistic and metrical evidence, therefore, is the possibility that the archaic features could be the result of the poet's writing in a self-consciously archaizing style. Scholars who argue for a later date must believe that the *Beowulf* poet was trying to create an archaic text and used his own linguistic knowledge to recreate the linguistic and metrical forms of the past.[5]

Certainly such an argument is not out of the realm of possibility; poetry tends to use conservative language, and many modern poets have employed vocabulary and stress patterns from an older era when trying to sound archaic. Yet to make the argument that all of the early features in *Beowulf* could be explained this way, we must explore to just what extent an Anglo-Saxon poet might have been able to employ such archaic features consistently and meticulously. While a poet might use some vocabulary and metrical values from an earlier time, the idea that he could perfectly replicate all of those features seems more problematic. The *Beowulf* poet was, after all, a poet, not a philologist; while he no doubt had an ear for language and a knowledge of the poetic tradition that would have allowed him to approximate archaic diction, the idea that he could have known all the vowel lengths and obsolete words of an earlier age and managed to reproduce them perfectly is difficult to credit.

To investigate the possibility of that sort of mastery, this chapter performs a three-way comparison, examining the metrical features of particularly conservative poems that can be reliably dated to the tenth century and analyzing both to what degree they differ from other late poems and how well they are able to match the conservative features of *Beowulf*. For a typical poem of this period, I use *The Battle of Maldon* as a representative example because it was composed in 991 or later and is often cited as illustrating the distinguishing features that are characteristic of late Old English poems.[6] Metrically, late poems such as *Maldon* can be characterized a few ways. First, they tend to employ secondary stress less frequently, thereby shifting the balance of verse types to the alternating stress patterns of type A and B verses rather than the clashing or

---

[5] See for example Nicholas Jacobs, "Anglo-Danish Relations, Poetic Archaism, and the Date of *Beowulf*: A Reconsideration of the Evidence," *Poetica* 8 (1977): 23–43; and Roberta Frank, "A Scandal in Toronto: *The Dating of Beowulf* a Quarter Century On," *Speculum* 82 (2007): 843–64.

[6] See *The Battle of Maldon*, ed. D.G. Scragg (Manchester: Manchester University Press, 1981), 28–35; and *HOEM*, 251–7.

falling stress patterns of types C, D, and E. They also have longer drops, which more frequently consist of multiple syllables and several separate words. These differences are largely due to linguistic changes that were influencing the language near the end of the Old English period.[7]

In contrast to *Maldon*, the poems that best fit the criteria for metrically conservative late poems are *The Battle of Brunanburh* and *Judith*. *Brunanburh* is known to be a tenth-century poem since it must have been composed in or after 937. *Judith* cannot be dated as definitively, but most scholars agree that it is probably a tenth-century poem as well.[8] In spite of their late date, *Brunanburh* and *Judith* tend towards shorter drops and more secondary stress, distinguishing them from *Maldon*. Russom singles these poems out as conservative more methodically in his article "Dating Criteria for Old English Poems," using a set of tests that investigates how strictly the poets follow standard compositional patterns and how often they revert to verse patterns that are easy to construct.[9] According to this test, *Judith* and *Brunanburh* rate "best" on the scale of "best, good, so-so, and bad"; as such, they are the only "best" poems of the "late" (on a scale of "early, middle, and late") period and should contrast sharply with *Maldon*, which rates as "bad" on Russom's scale.[10] Thus, if late poets could compose poetry as conservatively as *Beowulf*, the poets of these two poems should be able to do so.

For this investigation, I focus on the metrical structure of the poems to show how the poets try to recreate the sound of a past era for their audience. To do so, I examine specific metrical features that other scholars have previously isolated in an attempt to date *Beowulf* and, using their methodology, compare their findings to the features of *Brunanburh* and

---

[7] At the end of the tenth century, stress on non-root syllables was beginning to decrease and Old English was beginning to develop more analytic features. As a result, secondary stress was not employed as frequently and auxiliary words, which would have been unstressed in poetry, were becoming more prominent. For a more detailed explanation of these linguistic changes and the effect they had on the meter, see *HOEM*, 251–68; Thomas Cable, *The English Alliterative Tradition* (Philadelphia: University of Pennsylvania Press, 1991), 41–65; Thomas Bredehoft, "Ælfric and Late Old English Verse," *Anglo-Saxon England* 33 (2004): 77–107, and *Early English Metre* (Toronto: University of Toronto Press, 2005), 70–98; and Megan E. Hartman, "Poetic Attitudes and Adaptations in Late Old English Verse," *Leeds Studies in English* 43 (2012): 73–91.

[8] See *HOEM*, 3, 196; Cable, "Metrical Style," 80; and John C. Pope, "On the Date of Composition of *Beowulf*," in *The Dating of Beowulf*, ed. Chase, 189.

[9] In particular, Russom looks at how often the poets use A3 verses (× × × $\perp$ ×), which impose very few constraints on the verse, and to what degree type-A verses are displaced from the on-verse in order to create room for particularly complex or unusual verses. Russom, "Dating Criteria," 248–53.

[10] Russom's term "bad" means that the poem does not follow the classical forms of verse composition as closely as the others. I do not believe that this means it is badly written, just that it is not metrically conservative.

Judith. Ultimately, my research shows that these two poets do successfully maintain a number of conservative features that distinguish their poems from contemporary poems such as *Maldon* in a way that would have been noticeable to the audience. However, although the conservative features that they maintain can sometimes equal *Beowulf* in quantity, they tend not to do so in quality. Where *Brunanburh* and *Judith* exhibit conservative poetics, they tend to be superficial in some ways, giving the poem an archaic feel without necessarily recreating archaic diction in the details. *Beowulf*, in contrast, maintains more natural and complete archaic features, suggesting that the poet was in fact composing in a genuinely archaic style rather than trying to imitate an earlier one.

One particularly important and prominent metrical feature that can help to date poetry is the distribution of the verse types. For my metrical analysis, I am following Sievers's system, which uses the following five types: A: $\acute{-} \times \acute{-} \times$, B: $\times \acute{-} \times \acute{-}$, C: $\times \acute{-} \acute{-} \times$, D: $\acute{-} \acute{-} \acute{-} \times$, E: $\acute{-} \acute{-} \times \acute{-}$.[11] In each of these types, the stressed position consists of a single stressed syllable, while the drops can be expanded to multiple syllables, though only the verse-initial drops of types B and C tend to be particularly long. Cable first noticed a shift in distribution of these five types in relation to verses with two distinct levels of stress: C, D, and E. Type D and E verses both contain a half stress, which can take the form of secondary stress on a compound, as in *fromum feohgiftum* (D1: $\smile \times \acute{-} \acute{-} \times$) 'with splendid dispensing of treasure' (*Beowulf* 21a), or tertiary stress on a trisyllabic simplex word, as in *flotan ēowerne* (D1: $\smile \times \acute{-} \acute{-} \times$) 'your ship' (*Beowulf* 186a). According to Sievers's system, a type C has two equal stresses, but because they clash, Cable argues that the first metrically stressed position receives a greater degree of phonological stress than the second.

In terms of the distribution of verse types, Cable demonstrates that the presence of these three verse types distinguishes Old English verse forms from the newer forms that arise in the Middle English period, and he ultimately shows that the Old English period can be characterized by a gradual decline in these types. This argument places *Brunanburh* and *Judith* later in the chronology than *Beowulf*: they contain an incidence of 34.1% and 35.3% of these verses respectively, as opposed to *Beowulf*, which uses the types at an incidence of 38.3%. As Cable points out, the difference between *Beowulf* and the two late poems is not immense, but given that the poems show little variation in these distributions overall, Cable argues that the numbers do seem significant. In this regard, then, *Brunanburh* and *Judith* are more conservative than *Maldon*, which uses the verses at only an incidence of 24.5%, but they do not match the conservatism of *Beowulf*.

---

[11] Eduard Sievers, *Altgermanische metrik* (Halle: Max Niemeyer, 1893).

As Fulk shows, however, this tool is a relatively blunt one; while Cable is no doubt correct that the Old English period shows a general decline in the incidence of these verses, some variation is to be expected.[12] In particular, poems that rely heavily on heroic vocabulary would naturally be expected to have more of these types of verses than those that do not because heroic poems are more apt to contain a large number of poetic compounds, which in turn engender more verses with secondary stress. While compounds probably did decrease in later times due to linguistic changes, a lower incidence of compounds might also be expected in religious poetry, so the variation is not exclusively a result of the date of composition. With this distinction in mind, Russom argues that taking a closer look at the details of the distribution of verse types could provide a finer tool for dating poems.

Russom limits his data to only those verses that have a simplex word in the position with a half-stress, such as *weras wæccende* (D1: ⏑ × ⏑́ ⏑́ ×) 'waking men' (*Judith* 142a) or *scyppendes mægð* (E: ⏑́ ⏑́ × ⏑́) 'creator's maiden' (*Judith* 78a), as opposed to verses with a compound in those positions, such as *hæleð higerōfe* (D1: ⏑× ⏑× ⏑́ ×) 'brave-minded heroes' (*Judith* 302a) and *glēawhȳdig wīf* (E: ⏑́ ⏑́ × ⏑́) 'prudent woman' (*Judith* 148a).[13] Focusing on these so-called simplex verses allows him to make comparisons across the corpus without skewing the data by comparing poems that rely heavily on compounds to those that contain very few.

Furthermore, Russom also compares the incidence of these verses to each other instead of comparing them to type A and B verses. He argues that type D verses are the most metrically conservative of the three. Both type D and type E have two words with a stressed root syllable, one of which is longer than the other. Because it is more unusual to have the longer word come first, type D should appear more frequently than type E in a metrically conservative poem. Type C, in contrast, has two stressed positions on a single word; because the metrical ideal is to have two separate stressed words per verse, Russom argues this type of verse should also appear less frequently in a conservative verse. Both type E

---

[12] Fulk in fact shows that 34.5% of the first hundred lines of *Beowulf* are one of these three types, while 41% of the second hundred are. He acknowledges that his smaller data set might not be as statistically reliable, but the evidence does still suggest that more variation can be expected than what Cable initially thought. *HOEM*, 255–6.

[13] With the exception of *Beowulf*, all references to Old English poems refer to *The Anglo-Saxon Poetic Records*, ed. George P. Krapp and Elliott Van Kirk Dobbie, 6 vols. (New York: Columbia University Press, 1931–53) (henceforth *ASPR*). The *ASPR* does not include marks of vowel length in the text, but because they are useful for metrical studies, I have added them here. References to *Beowulf* come from *Klaeber's* Beowulf: *Fourth Edition*, eds. R.D. Fulk, Robert E. Bjork, and John D. Niles (Toronto: University of Toronto Press, 2008). Translations are mine.

and type C verses, however, have reason to appear more frequently in later verses. When they contain no compounds, type D verses will often have a noun followed by an inflected adjective, as in the example above, *weras wæccende*. This archaic word order that relies on the inflectional ending would be less natural, especially in later poetry. A type E verse would therefore contain the more natural word order when using a simplex word, as in *glēawhȳdig wīf*, where the adjective precedes the noun. A type C verse can also allow for more natural composition, especially in later verse. Because the verse-initial drop of type C verses can often be quite long, poets can include multiple function words in these verses, as in *in ðām fæstenne* (C1: × × ́- ́- ×) 'in the stronghold' (*Judith* 143a). In later Old English poetry, when the syntax was just beginning to include more analytic features and require more function words, such verses could be quite useful, even though they are metrically less conservative. Thus, Russom argues, not only would more conservative poems use verse types that contain secondary stress, they would do so with a greater incidence of type D verses than either of the other two types; poems that are composed later or to less exacting standards would reverse this tendency. According to this test, *Beowulf* is one of the most conservative poems in the corpus. It contains a large number of all of these simplex types, and the type D verses outnumber the verses of both type E and type C. In fact, with the exception of *Brunanburh*, the type D verses dominate more than in any other poem.[14]

Brunanburh adheres to the model Russom suggests as much as the test can apply to the short poem. It does contain a type D verse with only simplex words whereas it does not contain such a verse as either a type C or a type E, so it employs the D verses more frequently. While noteworthy, this evidence can hardly be considered conclusive, since it consists of just the one verse. What is telling in the context of Russom's argument is how the balance of these three verse types compares overall. Russom limits his findings to the simplex verses so that he can compare a large number of poems, many of which do not contain many compounds. Yet *Brunanburh* does not show a lack of compounds; the poet uses a very large number of them for so short a poem. An analysis of the poem that includes verses with compounds can therefore give a clearer picture of how the poet is constructing his verses.

While Cable is correct that *Brunanburh* has a lower incidence of C, D, and E verses than *Beowulf* overall, not all of the types have a lower incidence; *Brunanburh* in fact has a larger proportion of type D verses. The incidence of the three verse types in the two poems is shown in Table 4.1:

---

[14] Russom, "Dating Criteria," 253–5.

Table 4.1. Incidence of Type C, D, and E verses in *The Battle of Brunanburh* and *Beowulf*.

	Type C	Type D	Type E
Brunanburh	15.07%	17.12%	4.11%
Beowulf	18.30%	10.60%	8.80%

The decrease in the verses in question overall results largely from the radical drop in type E verses, but the number of verses with a half-stress remains relatively high. What is more, the type of verse that the *Brunanburh* poet relies upon to create these verses with half-stress is the type that Russom argues is the most metrically conservative.

This distribution of types therefore suggests an effort on the *Brunanburh* poet's part to add gravity to his poem and give it a more traditional sound. The heavy types, especially types D and E, which typically have two separate words and are particularly heavy with their falling stress patterns, slow the poem down while adding to the variety of the verse types. In the context of other late poems, which have a smaller number of such heavy verses, *Brunanburh* would have stood out both for its solemnity and its variety. The poet's choice to use a large number of compound words to create this effect only adds to the traditional sound of the poem, since such compounds are part of the poetic diction that was also being lost. Thus, the poet made choices that would have been obvious and audible to his audience, giving prominence to the traditional features. Significantly, the poet chooses to use the verse type that, according to Russom, would have been the most conservative and therefore the most natural to add this type of weight to the poem. Perhaps the poet did so because this verse type was most readily associated with the traditional sound that he wanted. Or perhaps it was the verse type that the poet heard most often in such positions in the formulae that he learned. Either way, it was probably a type that he associated with the conservatism that he was striving for.

Also significant, though, is that the use of compounds cuts down on one of the obstacles to using these type D verses. Russom shows that type E often has a more natural word order when a trisyllabic simplex word is employed, since the poet would not need to invert a monosyllabic noun and an inflected adjective, which are frequently the words that construct such verses. When the poet uses a compound rather than a simplex, however, the compound is often the noun, so no inversion is needed, as in *heardes handplegan* (D*2: $\acute{-} \times \acute{-} \smile \times$) 'hard hand-play' (*Brunanburh* 25a). Of the twenty-five type D verses in *Brunanburh*, only four have an inverted word order. The verse distribution in the poem therefore creates a pattern that the audience would have recognized as heavier and more conservative than that of poems such as *Maldon*, but also one that is created through attention to the most obvious features rather than to the smaller details. Because the poem matches *Beowulf* in the quantity of type D verses, it looks and sounds similar to *Beowulf*, but it fails to match the overall quality of the conservative verse distribution, since the *Brunanburh* poet is relying more heavily on a type of verse that is easier to compose. In contrast, the *Beowulf* poet's style appears less self-consciously conservative because he frequently uses type D verses formed of both compounds and simplex words, and he readily employs the inverted word order next to the standard word order.

Judith similarly shows a mix of conservative and late features in verse distribution. As far as Russom's test of the relative frequency of the simplex variants of C, D, and E verses, *Judith* is not particularly conservative: it contains five simplex E verses and eleven simplex C, as compared to three simplex D verses. Russom attributes the less standard frequency to the late date of composition. Like *Brunanburh*, though, *Judith* also has a very large number of compound words and therefore a large number of verses with secondary stress on compounds. Still, the *Judith* poet does not focus on creating multiple verses with falling stress patterns the way that the *Brunanburh* poet seems to; instead, the number of verses with secondary stress stands between *Beowulf* and the less conservative *Maldon*, as the following table indicates:

Table 4.2. Incidence of Type C, D, and E verses in *Judith*, *The Battle of Maldon* and *Beowulf*.

	Type C	Type D	Type E
Judith	18.47%	10.28%	3.66%
The Battle of Maldon	15.25%	6.16%	5.08%
Beowulf	18.30%	10.60%	8.80%

Table 4.2 shows that *Judith* is relatively consistent with *Beowulf* as far as type C and D verses go, but that it has far fewer type E verses, making the overall incidence of verses with a half stress lower. While these data indicate that the poet perhaps did not focus on constructing heavy verses the same way that the *Brunanburh* poet did, the contrast between *Judith* and *Maldon* is still striking: the *Maldon* poet uses all of these verse types

less often than the *Beowulf* poet does, while the *Judith* poet uses all but type E similarly. Clearly the *Judith* poet maintained verses with secondary stress to a greater degree than his near contemporary, but he still composed fewer such verses than the *Beowulf* poet did.

Where the *Judith* poet does stand out in terms of conservative verse distribution is in his use of hypermetric verses. Hypermetric meter is a variant on normal alliterative meter that is half again as long and that, in strictly regular poetry, only appears in extended groups of verses. The verses each consist of a normal verse preceded by a two-position onset. In the on-verse, the onset is typically formed by a stressed plus an unstressed position, as in *fēran, folces rǣswan* (HA1: $\acute{-} \times \acute{-} \times \acute{-} \times$) 'to go to the leader of the people' (*Judith* 12a). In the off-verse, the onset is an extended unstressed position, as in *þæt hē hīe wið þæs hēhstan brōgan* (hA1: $\times \times \times \times \times \acute{-} \times \acute{-} \times$) 'so that he [protected] her against the high danger' (*Judith* 4b). Several scholars have noted that hypermetric verses are not prominent in late poetry.[15] One other late poem, *the Meters of Boethius*, does use hypermetric verse, but it is not as rule-bound. It uses twenty-one hypermetric verses, most of which are in single hypermetric lines. The longest hypermetric sections, of which there are two, are pairs of lines together. Furthermore, many of the lines have two verses that open with a long drop instead of the more traditional distinction between a heavy onset with an additional lift in the on-verse and a light onset with a long drop in the off-verse. Regular hypermetric verse, therefore, is quite rare in late poems.

While the lack of hypermetric verses in *Brunanburh* cannot be a definitive marker of anything, since many poems do not employ the unusual meter, the presence of such verses in *Judith* is a clear choice to break from contemporary compositional patterns. The choice is particularly evident because the hypermetric lines in *Judith*, though not perfectly regular, look much more traditional than those in *Meters*: the poem has two short sections, one lone line and one pair of lines, but other than that, all the hypermetric verses come in longer groupings; two normal verses occur in the middle of a hypermetric passage, but aside from those two, the lines are perfectly regular; and one pair of verses opens with two light

---

[15] Russom argues that hypermetric verse had become exceptional at the end of the Old English period, which is why Middle English verse develops exclusively from normal verse patterns (see "The Evolution of Middle English Alliterative Meter," in *Studies in the History of the English Language II: Unfolding Conversations*, ed. Anne Curzan and Kimberly Emmons (Berlin: Mouton de Gruyter, 2004), 279–304; and "Some Unnoticed Constraints on the A-Verse in *Sir Gawain and the Green Knight*," in *Approaches to the Metres of Alliterative Verse*, ed. Judith Jefferson and Ad Putter (Leeds: Leeds Texts and Monographs, 2009), 41–58). Bredehoft goes so far as to say that hypermetric meter is "no longer available" to late poets (*Early English Meter*, 91).

onsets, but the rest contain the traditional pairing of a heavy onset with a light onset. In addition, the *Judith* poet employs quite a large number of hypermetric verses. With 133 hypermetric verses in a 349-line poem, *Judith* has a higher incidence of hypermetric lines than any Old English poem except *Maxims I*. The hypermetric verses are therefore a very unusual feature of the poem, and one that the poet uses very carefully.

These lines could very well serve a purpose similar to the many type D verses in *Brunanburh*. Poets seem to switch into hypermetric meter for many different reasons, such as to give a scene emphasis, to add gravity to a particular moment, to speed up the narrative progress, or to create a more straightforward syntax. In *Judith*, the hypermetric lines tend to create particularly descriptive narrative that slows down the pace of the story, thereby adding weight to the most important scenes.[16] By using hypermetric lines this way, the poet composes large sections of the poem that are simultaneously very formal and strictly traditional. Furthermore, since hypermetric lines stand out so impressively from normal verse, the audience would easily notice the shift in meter that created these effects. At the same time, though, the tool is a very blunt one; it creates heavy, traditional sections without needing to produce the more subtle metrical patterns found in *Beowulf*.

Both *Judith* and *Brunanburh* therefore show some clearly identifiable conservative features of verse distribution that set them apart from contemporary poetry such as *Maldon*. Nevertheless, neither poem matches *Beowulf* or other presumably early poems in terms of the fine details of distribution patterns described by Russom. Instead, these poets seem to be painting a conservative picture in broad brush strokes; the major features are evident, but the finer details are not. In this way, their technique creates a recognizably conservative sound, but it does not match conservative metrical patterns exactly. This distinction is not at all surprising, since many of the precise metrical patterns described by modern metrists may very well have been composed below the level of consciousness; they were metrical patterns that occurred naturally in the course of composition rather than rules that the poets were specifically trying to follow. Later poets trying to match that conservative sound therefore would not have replicated the resulting patterns exactly, but rather they would have imitated only the most distinctive and distinguishable features. Because *Beowulf* does in fact contain the more exacting patterns, it stands apart from these later poems.

---

[16] See Megan E. Hartman, "A Drawn-Out Beheading: Style, Theme, and Hypermetrics in the Old English *Judith*," *The Journal of English and Germanic Philology* 110.4 (2011): 421–40.

A second compositional feature that modern scholars have used to measure the conservatism of poetry and that Old English poets could well have used to give an archaic ring to their text is poetic diction. As far as poetic diction is concerned, *Judith* and *Brunanburh* follow a similar pattern of adhering generally to conservative features but not replicating the traditional vocabulary of poems such as *Beowulf* entirely. Overall, conservative diction can take three forms. First, poets can use simplex words from the poetic *koiné*; doing so both adds formality to the poem by distinguishing the vocabulary from normal prose and also aligns the poem with older works that likewise rely on this established and traditional vocabulary. Secondly, poets can create compounds and kennings that include these poetic words, a practice that reinforces the traditional diction while also creating the heavier verses discussed above. Finally, poets can also employ compounds that are not exclusively used in poetry. While these non-poetic compounds do not necessarily stand out as much as the poetic ones, heavy use of compounds still gives a poem an older feel because as stress decreased in the tenth century, compounding in general was employed less often.[17]

Both *Judith* and *Brunanburh* employ these three types of words frequently, especially as compared to *Maldon*. Table 4.3 shows the incidence of the different types of words in the three poems as well as in a representative sample from *Beowulf* that consists of three fifty-verse sections.

Table 4.3. Use of traditional diction in *Judith*, the *Battle of Brunanburh*, the *Battle of Maldon*, and *Beowulf*.

	Poetic Simplexes		Poetic Compounds		Non-poetic Compounds	
	Number	Percent	Number	Percent	Number	Percent
Judith	107	18.64	108	18.84	61	10.63
Brunanburh	27	18.49	16	10.96	19	13.01
Maldon	91	14.02	30	4.62	30	4.62
Beowulf (sample)	29	19.33	21	14.0	7	4.67

---

[17] See *HOEM*, 252–6.

The percentages in Table 4.3 represent the percent, on average, of verses that contain a poetic word. The table shows that late poetry such as *Maldon* does not use poetic diction and compounds as often as *Beowulf* does, and that *Judith* and *Brunanburh* look more similar to *Beowulf* than to *Maldon* in this regard. While *Maldon* does contain a relatively large number of poetic simplexes, it does not use nearly as many compounds as any of the other poems. Furthermore, the variety of individual simplexes that *Maldon* employs is relatively limited. Although it has ninety-one instances of a poetic word, eighteen words occur at least twice and some of the more common words are used even more frequently. For example, *gar* 'spear' and *guð* 'battle' are used six times each and *beorn* 'warrior' is used twelve times. The *Judith* poet does this to a degree, using common terms such as *maegð* 'maiden' and *ides* 'virgin' to refer to Judith multiple times, eleven and eight times respectively, but he also uses a greater proportion of the poetic words just once. The *Brunanburh* poet uses even more variety, repeating no single poetic word more than twice. By varying their vocabulary more and using a larger number of poetic and compound words overall, the *Judith* and *Brunanburh* poets compose similarly to *Beowulf*.

Yet while it may be similar, the diction is hardly identical. One major difference that stands out is the use of poetic versus non-poetic compounds. Although *Brunanburh* contains a greater incidence of compounds than *Beowulf* overall, a much larger number of these compounds are non-poetic. *Judith* makes extensive use of poetic compounds, surpassing *Beowulf* in terms of quantity, but a close look at these compounds shows yet again that they differ in quality from those in *Beowulf*. In *Beowulf*, more often than not, when the poet constructs a poetic compound, at least one of the constituent words is also poetic. For example he takes the poetic word *hild* 'battle' and makes compounds such as *hildeblac* 'battle-pale' and *hildedēor* 'brave in battle.' When using two non-poetic words, often the compounds are clearly kennings, as when he uses the terms *bēaggyfa* 'king (ring-giver)' and *bēaghord* 'treasure (ring-hoard).' Occasionally he will create descriptive compounds from non-poetic words, such as *merewif* 'mere-woman' and *merefisc* 'mere-fish,' but these are the exception rather than the rule. Such compounds are considered poetic because they are never used in prose, but the vocabulary is not unusual. The poetic compounds used by the *Judith* poet take on this more descriptive quality much more frequently. For instance, the terms *ælfscinu* 'bright as an elf' and *wundenlocc* 'with braided hair' combine two relatively common words to produce a creative description of Judith. The poet is particularly fond of using present participles to create new compounds that he then uses substantively, often using two non-poetic words, as in *bencsittend* 'bench-sitting ones,' *byrnwīggend* 'byrnie-wearing ones' and *woruldbūend* 'world-dwelling ones.' These compounds show a particularly creative facility with language on the part of the *Judith* poet, greater than that of the *Brunanburh* poet, since he is able either to use or to create combinations of words that are not commonly found in prose. They also indicate that the *Judith* poet clearly desired to use such creative and poetic vocabulary, since he so often turns to these compounds. Nevertheless, his method of compounding does not show an overwhelming knowledge of traditional vocabulary, since he does not work with individual terms from the poetic *koiné* as frequently as the *Beowulf* poet does.

One possible explanation for the different methods of compounding used in *Beowulf*, as opposed to the two late poems, is that the *Beowulf* poet was more comfortable using the traditional diction than the other poets, and he could therefore be more creative with it than they were. Another explanation is that the late poets were more interested in making the compounds in order to create the variation in verse patterns and less interested in the diction itself. Either of these differences could point to a difference in style or a difference in skill on the parts of the poets. Another rationale for the differences, however, would be that the *Beowulf* poet was more familiar with a wider range of older words, having composed his poem earlier.

The latter possibility becomes more probable in light of the poetic simplexes that the different poets use. Dennis Cronan shows how attention to particular aspects of poetic diction can be used as a tool to help date poetry. He focuses on poetic simplexes, arguing that simplexes are more traditional than compounds: since creating new compounds requires a certain degree of creativity on the part of the poets and far more *hapax legomena* are compounds than simplexes, compounds can be at least partially the invention of an individual poet, whereas simplexes tend not to be. Simplexes often appear in a large number of poems, an average of eight poems each. Some poetic simplexes, however, are limited to three or fewer poems. In some cases, poets might have chosen these symplexes because no good synonyms were available to them, and other poets might have not used them because they had no need for that word in their poems. In other cases, where these words have synonyms that the poet could have chosen and other poems use some of those synonyms in preference to the simplex in question, the use of that simplex illustrates another distinctive choice on the part of the poet.[18]

Cronan mainly interprets the significance of that choice by looking at the associations they create between poems. *Beowulf* in particular has a

---

[18] Cronan, "Poetic Words," 24–7; vocabulary restricted to metrically archaic poems receives further examination in Leonard Neidorf, "Lexical Evidence for the Relative Chronology of Old English Poetry," *SELIM* 20 (2013): 7–48.

number of simplexes that also appear only in *Genesis A*, which is another poem characterized by metrically and linguistically conservative features. The poem that *Beowulf* bears the next closest affinity to is *Maxims I*, which contains very traditional diction, since it is mostly made up of aphoristic statements that had presumably been passed down for some time. In addition to these, *Beowulf* also contains one or more simplexes that otherwise appear only in *Daniel*, *Exodus*, and *Guthlac A*, which are also linguistically very conservative poems.[19] Certainly not every pair of poems that share a simplex word with each other and no other poems are closely related. *Beowulf* also shares a word with *Maldon*, and the two poems are quite different in style and diction. Overall, though, the group of poems with which *Beowulf* shares multiple poetic words does create a pattern: most of them are likewise very conservative, suggesting that these poems should be grouped together as older poems. *Judith* and *Brunanburh*, in contrast, do not share a large amount of diction with these poems. *Judith* has one poetic word, *bælc* 'pride,' that appears otherwise only in *Genesis A*, but apart from that, these two poems do not have a strong lexical connection to the group of particularly conservative poems.[20]

In addition to looking at this sort of relative dating, Cronan also attempts to verify the older provenience of *Beowulf* and the other poems it is associated with by examining the character of the words involved. Some words under consideration, such as *fær* 'ship,' *missere* 'half year,' and *þengel* 'lord,' are common Germanic words with synonyms in numerous other cognate languages. Since they were inherited from Germanic but ultimately fell out of use, they must have been used primarily early on in the Old English period. Similarly, a few words were used in particular kennings in both *Beowulf* and *Genesis A* or *Maxims I*, but not elsewhere: *dyhtig* in *ecgum dyhtig* 'strong in edges' for sword and *eodor* in various kennings such as *eodor æþelinga* 'protector of men' to mean lord.[21] Cronan argues that these phrases appear to have been fossilized in these particular kennings, but that eventually, the word in question was lost in favor of a synonym (in the case of *dyhtig*) or yielded to a more common meaning (in the case of *eodor*). Thus, the few poems that employ the words in their early meanings show particularly conservative features. Significantly, with the possible exception of *missere*, both *Judith* and *Brunanburh* could have employed many of these archaic simplexes, but they do not. Unlike *Beowulf*, they contain more current synonyms.

---

[19] See *HOEM, passim.*
[20] Cronan, "Poetic Words," 44–5.
[21] Cronan, "Poetic Words," 29–30, 32–3.

One particularly illustrative word that Cronan finds is the term *heoru* 'sword.' It occurs as a simplex only in *Beowulf* and *Maxims I*; however, it appears quite frequently as the first element in a compound. Sometimes, as in *Beowulf*, it is used in its literal sense in compounds, but more frequently it is used either as an intensifier or in the sense 'war, battle.' Presumably, then, it went through a process of generalization over the Old English period and the older meaning became obsolete. *Judith* does use the element *heoru-* in a compound in *heardum heoruwǣpnum* (D*1: ´ × ⌣× ´ ×) 'hard battle-weapons' (*Judith* 263a), and in this case the word must possess its generalized meaning.[22] It is hardly surprising that the *Judith* poet would choose this meaning; the obsolete one would very likely have confused his audience. Yet it does create another point of contrast between *Judith* and *Beowulf*, inasmuch as the *Beowulf* poet uses not only archaic diction, but also older meanings of words that were still in use in the tenth century, whereas the *Judith* poet sticks to the contemporary meanings of those words.

The idea that the *Judith* poet would prefer more contemporary terms is reinforced by other vocabulary found in the poem. Several scholars have noted the use of *hopian* 'to hope' in *Judith*, which is a word that does not appear in early texts and seems to be newly coined at this time.[23] Stanley further argues that some additional terms, *beæftan* 'behind,' *binnan* 'within,' *ofdune* down,' and *ufan* 'from above' are further examples of neologisms in the text.[24] These terms suggest that the *Judith* poet relied on his contemporary lexicon quite a bit. The *Beowulf* poet, in contrast, includes no such neologisms. Instead, his work is characterized by a wide range of subtle archaisms, such as using older inflectional endings and employing a dative object for verbs that later take accusative objects – traits not found in tenth-century poems.[25]

These examples of shifting words and meanings point to a reason why the tenth-century poets would probably have avoided using a preponderance of archaic and obsolete terms, if they even knew such terms to begin with: their audiences would not have understood them. This conclusion could also explain the heavier reliance that the poets

---

[22] Cronan, "Poetic Words," 31–2.
[23] In poetry, the word only otherwise appears in *The Meters of Boethius*. In prose it occurs a few times in Alfredian texts, but occurs much more often in later texts. For a discussion of this word as a neologism, see Ashley Crandell Amos, *Linguistic Means of Determining the Dates of Old English Literary Texts* (Cambridge, Mass.: Medieval Academy of America, 1980), 149; and *HOEM*, 337–8.
[24] Stanley, "The Date of *Beowulf*," 198.
[25] For a summary of the archaic features of *Beowulf*, see R.D. Fulk, "Archaisms and Neologisms in the Language of *Beowulf*," in *Studies in the History of the English Language III: Managing Chaos: Strategies for Identifying Change in English*, ed. Christopher M. Cain and Geoffrey Russom (Berlin: Mouton de Gruyter, 2007), 267–87.

behind *Judith* and *Brunanburh* have on non-poetic compounds or poetic compounds formed from non-poetic words. Compounds can create an archaic sound, since compounds were becoming less prominent in late poetry. At the same time, however, these particular compounds are self-explanatory and formed from common vocabulary, so an abundance of such compounds would not present any difficulties for the audience. Thus, these two poets create conservative-sounding diction by employing poetic words that were still in use and supplementing that vocabulary with a heavy reliance on compounding. This strategy gives their poems a number of traditional features that distinguish them from works such as *Maldon*, but it also puts them in contrast to *Beowulf*, which is far richer in the subtle range of archaic vocabulary and poetic compounds it contains.

The major trend that stands out for the composition of tenth-century poems is that while they may give the overall impression of conservative metrical and lexical choices, they do not necessarily contain particularly conservative features. This combination is hardly surprising for late Old English poets. There were no handbooks of alliterative verse that explained metrical patterns or archaic diction; instead poets learned their trade from the evolving oral tradition. At the same time, the tradition was quite conservative, and some older poems were preserved in manuscript form for literate poets to read, giving them access to works with traditional features. But as certain vocabulary became obsolete and ceased to be used in formulaic systems, later poets might not have learned the older definitions. Furthermore, the common metrical patterns depended very much on speech patterns; as the language changed, causing metrical patterns to shift, poets might no longer have had access to the earlier patterns. It would take a sophisticated linguist indeed to reproduce earlier forms of a word and also understand how those earlier forms would affect the way the line is composed. While the formulaic nature of Old English poetry slows such changes and allows poetic compositions to remain more archaic than contemporary speech, it cannot stop language change entirely. These tenth-century poets, therefore, seem to have been able to replicate the more salient patterns of conservative composition, but their ability to recreate the details is not evident.

Furthermore, the two poets might not have had the goal of forming perfectly archaic verse in mind when they wrote these conservative poems. The compositional features they do use would give the impression of traditional poetry to their audiences. The extensive use of poetic diction, the larger number of compound words, and the reliance on the metrical patterns in type D or hypermetric verses must have created a sound that was distinct from poems such as *Maldon*, which tend to contain verses with longer drops, more alternating stress patterns, and fewer poetic words. Audience members would have picked up on that sound, recognized that these are particularly conservative poems, and associated them with other older compositions. Although the features do not match conservative composition perfectly, they ultimately do not need to because they mirror the features most clearly associated with conservative composition in a way that audiences would have appreciated.

In this way, the archaic features in these poems are similar to the dialectal features in the eye dialects of medieval authors such as Chaucer and the author of the *Second Shepherd's Play*, as well as later authors such as Shakespeare and Twain. When Chaucer replicated the northern dialect for *The Reeve's Tale*, he did not recreate a particular dialect perfectly; instead, he relied on the most obvious and recognizable features of northern speech and played those up as much as possible.[26] Whether or not Chaucer had the ability to write in perfect dialect is irrelevant, because ultimately perfect accuracy is not as important as the audience's ability to recognize the dialect; without that, the audience would not get the joke or understand how they should regard the speakers with the unusual dialects. The conservative features in *Brunanburh* and *Judith* appear quite similar. The poets focus on the more salient features, which allow them to give a clear impression of conservatism to the audience and to set the tone they desired. They did not necessarily have a reason to create any more conservative features; if anything, the desire to remain clear by avoiding obsolete vocabulary and archaic sentence structure might have prevented them from doing so.

The choices that the poets of *Judith* and *Brunanburh* made, then, did an impressive job of creating poems in the tenth century in a conservative style, yet the results of those choices also illustrate the limits of conservative poetic composition. Either through an inability to match the details perfectly, a lack of a desire to do so, or both, the tenth-century poets only went so far in their efforts to recreate archaic poetic technique. According to several independent criteria, *Beowulf* differs markedly from late conservative poetry. Whereas the tenth-century poets used traditional diction that would nevertheless have been available to their audience, the *Beowulf* poet used genuinely archaic diction. Whereas the tenth-century poets chose a limited set of metrically heavy verses to increase the gravity of their poems, the *Beowulf* poet used the diverse range of heavy verses that we should expect to find in an early composition. In the light of the evidence analyzed here, the hypothesis that the *Beowulf* poet could have

---

[26] For accounts of eye dialect and how they approximate their target dialect, see Seth Lerer, "I Is as Ille a Millere as Are Ye: Middle English Dialects" and "Antses in the Sugar: Dialect and Regionalism in American English" in his *Inventing English: A Portable History of the English Language* (New York: Columbia University Press, 2007), 85–100 and 192–206.

been a late poet who created an archaizing style can be seen to demand credence in two ancillary propositions. One is that the *Beowulf* poet was extraordinarily more skilled at archaizing than the poets of *Judith* and *Brunanburh*, who cannot be accused of being incompetent in their efforts. The other is that the *Beowulf* poet saturated his work with subtle archaic features without any clear motivation, since the techniques employed in *Judith* and *Brunanburh* suggest that late audiences would have recognized the significance of conservative features rendered more broadly. Since the only two late poems that aimed to affect a conservative style resemble each other so closely yet stand in such stark contrast to *Beowulf*, another explanation must be found for the conservative features that pervade *Beowulf*. The simplest and most logical explanation is that *Beowulf* is in fact a much earlier composition.

5

The Date of Composition of *Beowulf* and the Evidence of Metrical Evolution

Thomas A. Bredehoft

Since the date of the *Beowulf* manuscript is widely agreed upon, the very question which prompts this volume (and the conference it derives from, and even the 1980 conference with its 1981 proceedings volume) must assume that the date of the poem may not be the same as the date of the manuscript.[1] It is certain that there must have been a moment of first inscription for the poem, and that the time and place of that moment remains a central point of interest for students of the poem. In this essay, I will bring new evidence to bear on this venerable question, and my argument shall be that *Beowulf* is metrically conservative according to a variety of independent metrical criteria. Further, I will suggest that that conservatism is so varied and consistent as to strongly indicate that the original version of *Beowulf* must be placed among the very earliest of the longer narrative Old English poems that survive, probably in the eighth century.

Of course, it remains true, I believe, that the moment of inscription is only one of the moments of interest which might engage modern scholars of the poem. As I argued in *Authors, Audiences, and Old English Verse*,[2] our focus on authorship (and on moments of authorship) may sometimes cause us to lose sight of what can be gained by also considering audience, and I proposed there two later audiences for *Beowulf*, one located

---

[1] *The Dating of* Beowulf, ed. Colin Chase (Toronto: University of Toronto Press, 1981; reprinted with an afterword in 1997). I take the date of the *Beowulf* manuscript as lying not more than a couple of decades from 1000 or 1010; although Ker, Kiernan, and Dumville differ in the precision or narrowness of their own expressions of the date, their conclusions all center on this time period. See N.R. Ker, *A Catalogue of Manuscripts Containing Anglo-Saxon* (Oxford: Clarendon, 1957), 281; Kevin Kiernan, Beowulf *and the* Beowulf *Manuscript*, rev. ed. (Ann Arbor: University of Michigan Press, 1996); and David Dumville, "*Beowulf* Come Lately: Some Notes on the Palaeography of the Nowell Codex," *Archiv für das Studium der neueren Sprachen und Literaturen* 225 (1998): 49–63.

[2] *Authors, Audiences, and Old English Verse* (Toronto: University of Toronto Press, 2009).

at Alfred's Wessex court in the late ninth century, and another, sometime around the turn of the eleventh century, perhaps in Canterbury, represented most clearly by the author of *Maldon*. My previous book, then, argued for a date of composition for the poem that must have preceded the Alfredian period; in that sense, the new data I bring to the question here supports my earlier arguments, as well as supporting the linguistic arguments of R.D. Fulk. To understand *Beowulf*'s place in Anglo-Saxon England, we must attend to its date of composition, but it seems important to also recall that these later moments, when we have some evidence that the poem was being read, are also important dates for the poem, including the date of the manuscript.

But when we do turn our attention fully to the date of composition, I believe that metrical evidence, previously unrecognized or underappreciated, offers a powerful new argument for an early date of composition. Specifically, although the Old English verse system has long been held to have been extraordinarily conservative and virtually unchanging, the tradition of Old English verse was indeed a living tradition during much of the Anglo-Saxon period, constantly evolving. A consideration of innovative metrical strategies and structures across the tradition allows us to conclude that *Beowulf* is clearly the most metrically conservative of the longer Old English poems. And while being conservative does not necessarily prove it is early, the range and nature of the evidence suggests that *Beowulf* is unlikely indeed to have been produced at any late point within the changing tradition.

Metrical Evolution and Old English Verse

Key to any assessment of metrical innovation in Old English verse must be an assessment of what the most archaic form of Old English verse must have been like. In this, we are incredibly fortunate to have the testimony of Old Saxon, a sister tradition within the West Germanic language family. Like the languages with which they are associated, Old English and Old Saxon meters must have begun to evolve separately in the prehistoric period, and afterwards, the two traditions developed in relative isolation. Significantly, neither tradition remained static: various metrical changes applied to each, and the record of Old English verse in particular is both extensive enough and diverse enough to attempt to trace the evolutionary changes that occurred within it.

In order to trace such changes, it is necessary of course to adopt some sort of descriptive metrical formalism; I will use the metrical system I have employed elsewhere for Old English and Old Saxon, as presented or summarized in *Early English Metre* and in "Old Saxon Influence."[3] One reason for this choice is that Old Saxon meter in particular is very poorly served by a Sievers-based formalism, which cannot account for many particular features of Old Saxon verse: supposed examples of anacrusis, five- and six-position verse types, and the like. But as will be seen, the actual metrical criteria to be addressed here rarely make specific reference to such an analysis and involve metrical patterns that should be acceptable and observable in virtually any formalism; where possible, in the following presentation of data, I will rely on published accounts as well as on my own collection of evidence.

First I will describe the metrical features identifiable as most traditional, and likely inherited from the West Germanic ancestor tradition, and then identify those poems which can be dated with some security.

The Inherited Tradition

Features shared in Old English and Old Saxon are likely to be inherited, and we can simply list the most obvious shared features:

- Both traditions use alliteration to join verses into lines; the first S positions (roughly, fully stressed syllables) in the two verses in a single line must alliterate with one another, and if there are two S positions in the a-line, double alliteration is required in all verse types except Sx/Sx. Verses with proper names, full-verse compounds, semantic doublets, or rhyme may be excluded from the double alliteration requirement.
- All vowels alliterate with one another in both traditions, and the initial clusters *sp*, *st*, and *sc/sk* count as separate alliterators. In general, primary alliteration may not fall on any S or s position after the alliterating position of the b-line (although it is acceptable

---

[3] Thomas A. Bredehoft, *Early English Metre* (Toronto: University of Toronto Press, 2005) and "Old Saxon Influence on Old English Verse: Four New Cases," in *Anglo-Saxon England and the Continent*, ed. Hans Sauer and Joanna Story, with the assistance of Gaby Waxenberger. Medieval and Renaissance Texts and Studies 394 (Tempe, AZ: ACMRS, 2011), 83–112. In what follows, 'S' should be taken as representing a fully stressed syllable (or the resolved equivalent), usually filled by a lexical noun, adjective, adverb, or non-finite verb, but occasionally filled by another type of word or syllable given metrical full stress. Note that this formalism, then, does not insist upon a one-to-one relationship between linguistic stress and metrical stress. Lower-case 's' will represent morphemes with secondary stress, words receiving secondary metrical stress, or the stressed core of a metrical foot dominated by a finite verb other than *wesan* or *weorðan*. Lower-case 'x' represents an unstressed syllable.

on a preceding s position, and cross alliteration may involve S or s positions after the b-line alliterator).
- Both traditions originally allow hypermetric lines in clusters only; Type 1 hypermetric rules (in which a-lines must be sSS or SSS, and b-lines must be sSS or xSS) are the most traditional.
- Both traditions use formulaic rhyme (within the half-line), including some shared rhyming formulas; as indicated above, both allow formulaic rhyme as an occasional substitute for double alliteration. The oldest rhyme in both traditions is so-called hending rhyme, in which only root-syllables are involved, regardless of subsequent syllables.

Evidence for Relative and Absolute Chronology

What can be established with certainty about absolute and relative chronology must also be briefly summarized. First, all poems must date from a time at or before the time of their oldest surviving manuscript witness, and where authors are known, such poems must date from the authors' lifetimes. The manuscript appearances of the *Chronicle* poems and the Exeter, Junius, Vercelli, and Nowell poems are well established, and I will not rehearse the evidence for them here.[4] But a few other less obvious points must be noted, although I do not believe there is really much room for debate about most of these issues: the largely classical *Pastoral Care* poems and *Meters of Boethius* must cluster around or after 890, and Katherine O'Brien O'Keeffe has shown that *Riddle 40* was probably translated in the tenth century.[5] Examples of late Old English verse are attested starting in the middle tenth century, with the *Water Elf* charm being no later than the recording of *Brunanburh*, and *Exhortation to Christian Living* pre-dating the Vercelli manuscript.[6] *The Menologium* quotes from *The Metrical Psalms*, and the dates of *Maldon*, Ælfric's alliterative works and

---

[4] Ker, *Catalogue*, 153 and 460 dates the Exeter Book and the Vercelli Book to the second half of the tenth century; at 406 Ker dates the Junius manuscript to the turn of the eleventh century; but see Leslie Lockett, "An Integrated Re-examination of the Dating of Oxford, Bodleian Library, Junius 11," *Anglo-Saxon England* 31 (2002): 141–73. The dates of the *Chronicle* poems must be after the events in each case, beginning with *Brunanburh* sometime after that battle in 937.

[5] Katherine O'Brien O'Keeffe, "The Text of Aldhelm's *Enigma* no. c in Oxford, Bodleian Library, Rawlinson C. 697, and Exeter Riddle 40," *Anglo-Saxon England* 14 (1985): 61–73.

[6] The *Water-Elf* charm is written into London, British Library, Royal 12. D. xvii, by Scribe 3 of the Parker Chronicle, who records *Brunanburh* and *The Capture of the Five Boroughs*; a passage from *Exhortation* is recycled in Vercelli XXI.

the Sutton Brooch cluster around 1000.[7] Firm dates are not really available for *The Menologium* and the *Metrical Psalms*, but I date the *Psalms* to the middle tenth century on the basis of their late Old English forms, and I hope this one bit of dating by argument can be tolerated.[8] I believe the data to be presented here will support the date.

Catalogue of Metrical Innovations

Numerous metrical innovations have long been recognized, especially those relating to late Old English verse. In summarizing what we know about such innovations, it makes sense to begin with what appear to be the latest innovations and work backwards.

1. Alliteration patterns. Some poems treat *s* clusters and *g* in innovative ways. In regards to *g*, some poems distinguish between palatal and velar *g* as separate alliterators.

    A. Innovation in *s* cluster alliteration
        i. *Capture of the Five Boroughs*, l. 8 (*sn* and *st* alliterate; after about 950)[9]
        ii. *Metrical Psalms* (*s* and *sc* alliterate)[10]
        iii. *Maldon* (after 991)[11]
        iv. Ælfric (after ca. 995)[12]
    B. Palatal and velar *g* as separate alliterators[13]
        i. *Brunanburh* (probably) after ca. 950
        ii. *Menologium* (probably 970s, but after *Metrical Psalms*)
        iii. *Maldon* (after 991)

---

[7] For the argument that the parallel between the *Psalms* and *The Menologium* is a borrowing or quotation in the latter, see Bredehoft, *Authors, Audiences*, 113–14. *Maldon*, of course, concerns events in 991; the Sutton Brooch can be found in Elisabeth Okasha, *Hand-List of Anglo-Saxon Non-Runic Inscriptions* (Cambridge: Cambridge University Press, 1971), 116–17.

[8] Bredehoft, *Early English Metre*, 70–80.

[9] References to specific Old English poems will generally be to *The Anglo-Saxon Poetic Records*, ed. George Philip Krapp and E.V.K. Dobbie, 6 vols. (New York: Columbia University Press, 1931–53).

[10] Briefly noted by R.D. Fulk, *A History of Old English Meter* (Philadelphia: University of Pennsylvania Press, 1992), 414.

[11] See discussion of *s* alliteration in *The Battle of Maldon*, ed. D.G. Scragg (Manchester: Manchester University Press, 1981), 29 and note 136.

[12] *Homilies of Ælfric: A Supplementary Collection*, ed. J.C. Pope, 2 vols. Early English Text Soxiety o.s. 259–60 (London: Early English Text Society, 1967–1968), I, 128–9.

[13] Ashley Crandell Amos, *Linguistic Means of Determining the Dates of Old English Literary Texts* (Cambridge, Mass.: The Medieval Academy, 1980), 100; Fulk, *History*, 258–9; *Homilies of Ælfric*, ed. Pope, I, 130–1; Bredehoft, *Authors, Audiences*, 123–4.

iv. Ælfric (after ca. 995)
v. *Judgment Day II* and *Judith* (undated)[14]

In the case of s clusters, some poems treat one or more clusters as alliterating with s; *Maldon* treats all s clusters as separate alliterators. First appearing datably in *Brunanburh* and *Capture*, one or both of these innovations affect *all* the other datable later poems under consideration here: *Psalms, Menologium, Maldon,* Ælfric. How we date *Judith* may affect when we date the allowability of these innovations, but they seem widespread after the middle tenth century.

2. *Late Old English Verse Forms.* I include here a whole suite of innovative forms as discussed in *Early English Metre*: final-stress alliteration, lack of resolution, four-position verse feet, verse rhyme substituting for primary alliteration, and so on.[15]
   A. Late Old English Verse
      i. *For the Water Elf Disease* (at or before middle tenth century)
      ii. *Exhortation* (before Vercelli book)
      iii. *Metrical Psalms* (before *Menologium*)
      iv. *Chronicle* poems (middle tenth century and after)
      v. Ælfric (after about 995)
      vi. Sutton Brooch (about 1000)
      vii. *Durham* (after 1103)
      viii. *Judgment Day II, Instructions for Christians,* various Metrical Charms (undated)

This innovation seems most plausibly dated to the middle tenth century, and it is important to note that the lists under my points 1 and 2 include *all* of the poems that are securely dated after about 950: *Maldon* and some *Chronicle* poems may have a fairly classical feel, but they all have scattered late features, and the classicism of the *Menologium* is undermined by its quotation of one late Old English feature in the passage it borrows from the *Psalms* as well as its treatment of *g* alliteration.

3. *Influence from Old Saxon.* For reasons of space, here I shall simply summarize work I have presented in *Authors, Audiences, and Old English Verse* and in my essay on "Old Saxon Influence."[16] Old Saxon influence is variously lexical, formulaic, and metrical, and it affects, in

---

[14] The testimony of *Judith* is ambiguous here, sometimes seeming to indicate the sounds do alliterate, sometimes indicating the opposite; see *Judith*, ed. Mark Griffith (Exeter: University of Exeter Press, 1997), 25–6.
[15] Bredehoft, *Early English Metre*, 70–80.
[16] Bredehoft, *Authors, Audiences*, 68–80, and Bredehoft, "Old Saxon Influence."

different ways, most of the identifiably Alfredian poems (excepting only the *Metrical Epilogue to the Pastoral Care*, really).

A. Lexical and formulaic Old Saxon influence

  i. *Meters of Boethius* (lexical and formulaic) (after about 890)

  ii. *Metrical Epilogue to the Pastoral Care* (formulaic) (about 890)

  iii. *Metrical Psalms* (lexical) (before *Menologium*)

  iv. *Maldon* (lexical) (after 991)

  v. *Genesis B* (lexical and formulaic) and *Solomon and Saturn* (formulaic) (undated but probably Alfredian)

  vi. *Instructions* (lexical), *Dream of the Rood* (formulaic), *Vainglory* (lexical), *Christ III*[17] (undated)

B. Metrical Old Saxon influence

  i. *Metrical Preface to Gregory's Dialogues* (Alfredian or post-Alfredian)

  ii. Scattered examples in *Meters of Boethius* (after about 890)

  iii. *Genesis B* and *Solomon and Saturn* (undated, but probably Alfredian)

  iv. *Dream of the Rood* and *Finnsburh* (undated)

As discussed in "Old Saxon Influence," contextual evidence supports the likelihood that both *Genesis B* and *Solomon and Saturn* are Alfredian in origin, and the likelihood is thus that these Old Saxon innovations date from the end of the ninth century, and no earlier, because of the powerful association between certainly Alfredian poems, probably Alfredian poems, and Old Saxon influence.

4. Use of Verse Rhyme. In verse rhyme, rhyme on the final stressed positions of the two verses links the a-line to the b-line. Generally, examples considered here must affect three consecutive verses or two consecutive lines to be counted as functional and non-random, although I include an example from *The Meters of Boethius* where verse rhyme appears to substitute for alliteration.

A. Examples of Verse Rhyme

  i. *Meters of Boethius* 20.103 (no alliteration present) (after about 890)

  ii. *Solomon and Saturn* 79–80, 83 (undated but probably Alfredian)

  iii. *Death of Edgar II* and other late *Chronicle* poems (after 975)

  iv. Sutton Brooch 2–3 (about 1000).

  v. *Judgment Day II* (undated but late Old English verse)

  vi. *Riming Poem* (passim); *Christ II* 591–6; *Phoenix* 15–16, 53–55; *Maxims I* 120–1; *Elene* 114–15; *Judith* (no two consecutive lines, but

---

[17] For *Christ III*, see Roland Zanni, *Heliand, Genesis, und das Altenglische* (Berlin: Walter de Gruyter, 1980), 73–9.

frequent and probably not just random); *Andreas* 867–70; Cynewulf (signature passage: *Elene* 1236–50) (undated)

Note that I treat the coherence of the Cynewulf group agnostically, splitting off the signature passages from the bodies of the four poems: as shall be seen, there is not complete coherence among the five groups that result, supporting the possibility that the signature passages may indeed have sometimes been added to pre-existing compositions.[18]

5. *Innovations in Hypermetric Rules.* Three types of innovations affect hypermetric rules: the allowing of Type 2 and Type 3 rules, and the allowing of single, unclustered hypermetric lines.

   A. Type 2 (SSS or sSS or xSS a-line + sSS or xSS b-line)
      i. *Meters of Boethius* (after about 890)
      ii. *Daniel, Andreas, Christ II, Guthlac A, Fortunes of Men, Riming Poem, Riddle 16, Against a Dwarf* (undated)
   B. Type 3 (SSS or sSS or xSS a-line + sSS or xSS or SSS b-line)
      i. *Solomon and Saturn* (undated but probably Alfredian)
      ii. Cynewulf (signature passage: *Fates* 97, 102); *Maxims I, Maxims II, Christ III* (undated)
   C. Hypermetric lines unclustered
      i. *Meters of Boethius* (after about 890)
      ii. *Solomon and Saturn* (undated but probably Alfredian)
      iii. *Genesis A, Andreas, Dream of the Rood, Christ II, Christ III, Guthlac A, Guthlac B, Phoenix, Riming Poem, Psalm 50,* Cynewulf (signature passage: *Fates* 102) (undated)

6. *Single alliteration allowed in specific SS types.* To be counted here, a poem must exhibit at least two examples, making up at least one-third of the a-line examples of the verse type.

   A. Single alliteration in Type E: Ssx/S
      i. *Meters of Boethius* (after about 890)
      ii. *Brunanburh* (after about 950)
      iii. *Metrical Psalms*
      iv. *Menologium* (after *Metrical Psalms*)
      v. *Maldon* (after 991)[19]
      vi. *Genesis A, Exodus, Daniel, Christ and Satan, Dream of the Rood,*

---

[18] On the suggestion that Cynewulf may have added signature passages to pre-existing works, see Daniel Donoghue, *Style in Old English Poetry: The Test of the Auxiliary* (New Haven: Yale University Press, 1987), 115–16.

[19] In *Maldon*, I count two Ssx/S verses with single alliteration, four with double alliteration, nine with proper names, one with cross alliteration, and two with Ss alliteration; if we exclude verses with substitutes for double alliteration entirely, then the "one-third" criterion is met; if, instead, we count proper names, cross alliteration, and Ss alliteration as meeting the double alliteration requirement, then *Maldon* would not belong on this list.

Elene, Christ I, Christ III, Juliana, Widsith, Maxims I, Order of the World, Deor, Judith, Instructions, Judgment Day II (undated)
B. Single alliteration in Type D: S/Sxx
  i. *Guthlac A, Guthlac B, Gifts of Men, Beowulf* (undated)

I leave out of consideration from point 6B all verses with 'maðelode' as this verb's usual appearance with proper names allows it to appear in Ss/Sxx and Sx/Sxx a-lines with single alliteration. Note also that other types (such as Ss/Sx or Sx/(x)Sx) which might yield useful data are passed over here.

7. *Preference for expanded Type D* verses over Type D*. Most metrical theories (e.g., Sievers, Russom) take the four-position verse as basic, and the five-position verse as a more complex and thus rarer or harder-to-process alternative.[20] Thus, Type D (S/Ssx in Russom-esque scanning, or / | / \ x in Sievers-style scansion) is treated as more fundamental than 'Expanded Type D' (D*: Sx/Ssx or / x | / \ x). But actually most Old English poems (as noted below) prefer expanded D to unexpanded D, often quite substantially. I hypothesize that a preference for unexpanded Type D is original, preference for expanded Type D is innovative.[21]

A. Frequency of S/Ssx and Sx/Ssx verses

Poem	Ratio of S/Ssx: Sx/Ssx verses	% of S/Ssx
Beowulf	153:95	62%
Exodus	26:19	57%
Genesis A	71:53	57%
Judith	12:10	54%
Christ and Satan	15:16	48%
Cynewulf (sig passages)	4:5	44%
Solomon and Saturn	8:12	40%
Heliand (Old Saxon)	86:132	39%
Daniel	14:22	39%
Guthlac B	26:40	39%
Christ I	12:20	38%

---

[20] See Eduard Sievers, *Altgermanische Metrik* (Halle: Max Niemeyer, 1893) and Geoffrey Russom, *Old English Meter and Linguistic Theory* (Cambridge: Cambridge University Press, 1987).

[21] Because separate constraints limit the appearance of both D types in the b-line, the data presented here will concern only a-line frequencies.

Elene	26:45	37%
Menologium	5:9	36%
Metrical Psalms	23:50	32%
Christ III	20:42	32%
Juliana	13:29	31%
Andreas	47:111	30%
Christ II	12:31	28%
Phoenix	17:46	27%
Fates	2:6	25%
Meters of Boethius	7:25	22%
Guthlac A	7:35	17%

Clearly, we cannot use this lone criterion as the basis for a firm relative chronology, as it places *The Meters of Boethius* lower on the chart than *The Menologium* and the *Metrical Psalms*, but for poems with forty or fifty or more examples of type D verses, where a small change in the raw numbers would have little effect on the percentages, the numbers do suggest the possibility of a real change over time, with *Beowulf*, *Exodus*, and *Genesis A* being the most conservative.

The implications of all the data presented under points 1–7 are significant, and it is also useful to re-present some of this data in tabular form, as I have attempted to do in Table 5.1. But some explicit commentary is also in order.

First, we can observe once again that *all* Old English poems that are certainly datable to after about 950 show one or more late features: alliterative innovations involving *g* and *s* clusters, or general employment of late Old English forms. At the same time, *no* poem certainly datable to after about 950 uses hypermetric rules of any sort. Taken together, I believe it is reasonable to hypothesize that both the use of classical Old English metrical forms and all use of hypermetric rules essentially ceased across the tradition by about 950. I realize that this claim is worded quite strongly; my point is simply that there is no concrete evidence to support the hypothesis of continued classical composition after 950: the poems with the most classical feel (*The Menologium*, *Maldon*, and the *Chronicle* poems) exhibit no hypermetric verses and they all either have innovations involving *s* or *g*, or else they have scattered but significant use of late Old English metrical forms. Further, most of the lengthier poems in this category also show the persistence of earlier innovations, except for those relating to hypermetric verses. *Judith* is the only poem with an alliterative

Table 5.1. Proposed Sequence for Metrical Innovations: Innovations Plotted Against Chronology

Innovative/Date Feature		Undated		About 890–900	After ca. 950
1A in Ssx/S	Exodus Christ1	GenA	Maxims1, Elene	**Meters** Christ3	Brun, Maldon PPs, Instr JDay2, Men
Unclustered Hypermetric		GenA, GuthB	Daniel		
Hypermetric Types 2 and 3			GuthA	**Meters, S&S** Christ3	
Verse Rhyme			Daniel, GuthA, Max2	**Meters, S&S** Christ3	
Old Saxon			Cynewulf(sig) Christ2, Phoenix, Riming, Andreas	**Meters, S&S** Christ3	
Late OE Forms			Cynewulf(sig) Christ2, Maxims1, Riming, Andreas		DEdg2, JDay2, Sutton, Judith
Alliterative w/ s, g			Cynewulf(sig) Elene, Phoenix Maxims1, Christ2 Riming, Andreas	**CPPref, GDPref GenB, Meters** Christ3, **S&S**	PPs, Maldon Instr
					PPs, DEdg2 Exhort, JDay2 Ælfric, Durh Sutton, Instr
					Men, Brun, PPs, Maldon, Ælfric, JDay2

Boldfaced titles = Alfredian-era compositions. Italicized titles = Poems datable to after ca. 950

innovation to use hypermetric verses, and *Judith*'s ambiguous problems with *g* may thus suggest a date in the first half of the tenth century.[22]

Second, the close conjunction of Old Saxon features and demonstrably Alfredian-era poems indicates that Old Saxon influence was allowed in or by the Alfredian period. Thus we can see that Types 2 and 3 hypermetric rules are also allowed by the Alfredian period, as are verse rhyme and unclustered hypermetrics, since these innovations frequently also appear in poems showing Old Saxon influence. Since these other innovative strategies also appear in a variety of poems that show no influence from Old Saxon, we may hypothesize that verse rhyme and the innovative hypermetric strategies probably pre-date the Alfredian period. Again, it is important to note that virtually every substantial poem that can be dated reliably to the Alfredian period shows some or all of the Old Saxon innovation features *and* many of the presumed earlier innovations.

Third, single alliteration in type E is very widespread, and thus very likely to be an early innovation, due to the distribution. Further, *Beowulf*'s lone innovative feature found here, single alliteration in Type D without secondary stress, occurs in too few poems to be of much use in chronology, and the similarity of these verses to the 'maðelode' verses also raises the possibility that this verse type is not very revealing.

Finally, although Table 5.1 offers a tentative sequence for innovations before Alfred's time, verse rhyme may have been avoided on stylistic grounds by some poets, and it does not necessarily need to be placed chronologically after changes to hypermetric rules. Likewise, it may be the case that the authorization of Type 2 and 3 hypermetric rules happened simultaneously with the authorization of unclustered hypermetrics. This section of the chart necessarily remains fairly tentative. And while I have not been able to place data on Table 5.1 regarding the preference for expanded or unexpanded D verses, as addressed in point 7 above, that data would seem to place *Beowulf*, *Exodus*, and *Genesis A* on the left side of the chart and other poems further to the right.

But worrying too much about the details of sequencing in the pre-Alfredian section of Table 5.1 misses the important point, which is that the table shows quite clearly a tradition in more or less constant transition, in which innovations happen, and that, when they do, later compositions almost always show evidence of at least some of the earlier innovations. No single innovation can serve to tell the whole story, but the larger pattern is unmistakable, and it is especially clear in the most reliably datable components of Table 5.1, those poems in bold or italic type, in which category I include *Solomon & Saturn* and *Genesis B*

---

[22] Compare *Judith*, ed. Griffith, 47: "late ninth or early tenth century," and Fulk, *History*, 197: "*Judith* belongs with the *Meters* and *Maldon* in the latter part of the chronology."

as Alfredian, and *The Metrical Psalms* and *Menologium* as after about 950. The Alfredian moment and the mid-tenth-century moment (whether we associate it with the Benedictine Reform or not) show up on Table 5.1 as watershed moments in the evolution of Old English verse, but the table also makes clear that Old English verse had already evolved substantially from its West Germanic origins by the end of the ninth century, allowing a variety of hypermetric structures, verse rhyme, and single alliteration in Type E, and as point 7 above again makes clear, also allowing a preference for expanded type D.

To return to the central question of the date of *Beowulf*, all we need note is that *Beowulf* features *none* of the innovative forms under discussion: its hypermetric verses are Type 1, and they are always clustered. Verse rhyme appears not to be used. Double alliteration is heavily favored in Type E. *Beowulf* shows the greatest preference for unexpanded type D. In short, *Beowulf* is so thoroughly conservative in relation to all these features that it is practically impossible to place it anywhere other than on the far left side of the chart.

This result is important. Scholars wishing to assign a late date of composition to *Beowulf* have long made use of the implicit claim or belief that the Old English verse tradition was highly stable and that the conservative nature of *Beowulf*ian meter could be explained perfectly by invoking the supposed stability of the metrical system. The evidence I have presented here, I believe, makes that claim untenable: the Old English metrical tradition was not stable, but constantly evolving, as all living traditions tend to be. From my perspective, anyone arguing for a late date for *Beowulf*'s composition—whether in the era of Alfred or of Ælfric—must clearly explain the degree to which *Beowulf* is very much atypical of the verse of those times, the degree to which *Beowulf*, indeed, departs radically from the nature of the Old English verse tradition as it appears to exist from the late ninth century onwards. It is especially important to note that, if *Beowulf* was written after 950, it differs very widely indeed from every poem for which a similar date can be proved: if *Beowulf* was written after 950, it does not fit well at all into its tradition, unless we claim (on the basis of no evidence at all that I can find) that an alternative, less innovative tradition somehow survived alongside the one I have traced in this essay. I cannot find it in myself to believe in the existence of such an invisible tradition, and thus I am forced to conclude that *Beowulf* cannot be both late and traditional.

Given the innovations identified on Table 5.1 that are likely to have occurred before Alfred's time, I would have no difficulty in hypothesizing a date for *Beowulf* in the eighth century or, possibly, the beginning of the ninth; the difference depends upon how quickly we imagine the various innovations occurred and spread. In its metrical forms, on a number of seemingly independent criteria, *Beowulf* is closer to the archaic metrical tradition that a comparison with *The Heliand* allows us to reconstruct than is any other substantial Old English poem. That this conclusion meshes so well with the linguistic conclusions drawn by R.D. Fulk, conclusions that are based on criteria that appear to be independent from the criteria I have used, adds important supporting weight to Fulk's linguistic conclusion.

Conclusions

If *Beowulf* is, indeed, as early as the eighth or early ninth century, it must have passed through at least one later transcription, and very possibly two or more. These transcriptions undoubtedly brought changes: to orthography, at the least, and possibly also other changes affecting issues of both dialect and meter. To take just one familiar example, in the fourth edition of *Klaeber's Beowulf*, the editors both print and under-dot the troublesome article "þara" from line 9b, which appears in the manuscript as "þara ymbsittendra."[23] The underdotting is intended to indicate a "probable scribal insertion," and the note on the verse in the Commentary section justifies the printing of the word by suggesting that "as emendation solely on the basis of meter is now largely avoided, the word is perhaps best allowed to stand."[24] Elsewhere, the verse is identified as having unusual, even unmetrical, disyllabic anacrusis before Type D.[25] The metrical form of "þara ymbsittendra," however, would not be problematic at all in a late Old English verse composition dating from the beginning of the eleventh century; in *The Metrical Psalms*, for example, four-syllable words like "mildheortnesse" and "soðfæstnesse" are frequently preceded by one, two, or three initial unstressed syllables. In short, there was no metrical problem at all with "þara ymbsittendra" at the time the manuscript was written, unless we presume or assert that the meter of the poem must be thoroughly self-consistent—and even then, we seem to commit ourselves to a leap from "very rare" to "unmetrical" that is at least potentially troublesome. Such uncertainties or inconsistencies regarding metrical form are unavoidable in a study of this sort: yet the surprising consistency with which *Beowulf* prefers conservative forms to innovative ones—on all the criteria considered here—must give us confidence that the manuscript or manuscripts were not affected by wholesale metrical changes: "þara ymbsittendra" and the

---

[23] *Klaeber's* Beowulf: *Fourth Edition*, ed. R.D. Fulk, Robert E. Bjork, and John D. Niles (Toronto: University of Toronto Press, 2008) [henceforth *Klaeber IV*].
[24] *Klaeber IV*, 2 and 112.
[25] *Klaeber IV*, 333.

like are occasional changes, but not frequent enough, apparently, to alter the overall metrical statistics characteristic of the poem. The other poems considered in this essay must likewise have remained fairly consistent in meter—at least those whose manuscript dates would place them at moments when the tradition has moved beyond the metrical forms they exhibit.

The relative chronology offered in my Table 5.1, then, helps us assess not only *Beowulf*'s date of composition, but likely dates (or ranges of dates) of composition for many other Old English poems. To the degree that the conclusions reached here are in general agreement with the linguistic conclusions reached in R.D. Fulk's *A History of Old English Meter*, and with the formula-based conclusions of Andy Orchard,[26] we now have a remarkable series of independent chronologies (metrical, linguistic, and formulaic) for the dates of composition for Old English poems that are largely in agreement about matters of date. Much important work remains to be done, but our understanding of the history of Old English verse may itself have reached a watershed moment.

---

[26] Andy Orchard, "Both Style and Substance: The Case for Cynewulf," in *Anglo-Saxon Styles*, ed. Catherine E. Karkov and George Hardin Brown (Albany, NY: State University of New York Press, 2003), 271–305, and "Computing Cynewulf: The Judith-Connection," in *The Text in the Community: Essays on Medieval Works, Manuscripts, Authors, and Readers*, ed. Jill Mann and Maura Nolan (South Bend, IN: University of Notre Dame Press, 2006), 75–106.

6

Beowulf and the Containment of Scyld in the West Saxon Royal Genealogy

Dennis Cronan

The correspondences between the names in the Scylding genealogy at the beginning of *Beowulf* and three names in the upper reaches of the genealogy of Æthelwulf in the *Anglo-Saxon Chronicle*, Beaw, Sceldwa and Sceaf, frequently appear in arguments for a late dating of *Beowulf*. But these arguments overlook many aspects of Æthelwulf's genealogy that disrupt their case for a late dating. As H. Munro Chadwick pointed out over a century ago, the forms *Sceldwa* and *Beaw* found in the *Chronicle* for *Scyld* and *Beow* are not West Saxon spellings, and the *-wa* suffix of *Sceldwa* and *Tætwa* suggests that these forms may be archaic.[1] Thus spelling alone indicates that these names were probably copied from an older, non-West Saxon text. Furthermore, the very presence of these names in the royal pedigree is puzzling. On one level the presence of Scyld is easy to explain: Scyld and the Scyldings were famous in heroic legend, and his inclusion in Æthelwulf's pedigree provides reflected glory for the West Saxon dynasty and implies genealogical, political and cultural connections between the West Saxons and the Danes that could be useful for Alfred and his heirs to foster. But on another level his inclusion is rather surprising: according to genealogical conventions, the presence of Scyld implies that the West Saxon royal family is a cadet branch of the Scylding dynasty, and is thus potentially subordinate to Scandinavian rulers in England claiming direct descent from Scyld. This potential subordination suggests that the ninth-century extension of the West Saxon royal pedigree is not as simple and transparent a sequence as has commonly been assumed. A thorough examination of this extension demonstrates that the case for a connection between the pedigree and *Beowulf* is extremely weak – far too weak to provide any evidence for the dating of the poem.

Everyone who has studied and discussed the West Saxon pedigree over the last three decades has relied, to a greater or lesser extent, upon

---

[1] H. Munro Chadwick, *The Origin of the English Nation* (Cambridge: Cambridge University Press, 1907), 272.

the work of Kenneth Sisam. But my arguments here depend more upon the work of David Dumville, who has significantly extended the work of Sisam and, more importantly for the issues discussed here, introduced to the field of Old English the study of the political and social ramifications of the construction and manipulation of genealogies.[2] Drawing upon Celtic studies where there is an abundance of genealogical texts, especially among the Irish, and also upon anthropological work among African peoples, Dumville has demonstrated how genealogies in the British Isles can function as "charters" that explain social groupings and institutions, and can also be attempts to shape society in the future by modeling desired social relationships.[3] Although the inclusion of Scyld in the West Saxon pedigree has been regarded as a straightforward attempt by this dynasty to support their claim to political authority over the Danes, an analysis of this pedigree reveals just how problematic, even quixotic, this attempt was, since it works against a genealogical convention.

Dumville discusses the example of the Dál Cáis, the dynasty which produced the most famous of early Irish kings, Brian Bóruma. After seizing the kingship of Munster in the tenth century they set about "legitimizing" their control. An essential component of their strategy was to present themselves and the previous rulers of the province, the Éoganacht, as members of the same dynasty with equal claims to the kingship. To this end they invented an ancestor, Ailill Ólom, who was identified as the founder of both lines, the Éoganacht and the Dál Cáis. To this fabrication they added the (equally false) claims that the Éoganacht and the Dál Cáis had shared the kingship in prehistoric times, and that there were two Dál Cáis kings during the early historic period.[4] It is worth stressing that their genealogists did not manufacture their claim by deriving the Dál Cáis from a key Éoganacht ancestor, a move that would have been similar to the inclusion of Scyld in the West Saxon pedigree, and would have made them a junior or cadet branch of the Éoganacht. Although such a move would have legitimized their possession of the throne, their goal

---

[2] Kenneth Sisam, "Anglo-Saxon Royal Genealogies," *Proceedings of the British Academy* 29 (1953): 287–348; David N. Dumville, "Kingship, Genealogies and Regnal Lists," in *Early Medieval Kingship*, ed. P.H. Sawyer and I.N. Wood (Leeds: The University of Leeds, 1977), 72–104.

[3] Dumville, "Kingship," 83–5. On p. 85 n. 70, he cites L. Bohannan, "A Genealogical Charter," *Africa: The Journal of the International African Institute* 22 (1952): 301–15, for the use of 'charter' to describe genealogies.

[4] Dumville, "Kingship," 82–93. Donnchadh Ó Corráin, "Irish Regnal Succession: A Reappraisal," *Studia Hibernica* 11 (1971): 7–39, at 38–9. For the historical background, see John V. Kelleher, "The Rise of the Dál Cáis," in *Selected Writings of John V. Kelleher on Ireland and Irish America*, ed. Charles Fanning (Carbondale, Illinois: Southern Illinois University Press, 2002), 173–86.

was apparently more than simple legitimization: they wished to present themselves as a dynasty that was the equal of the Éoganacht, yet entirely independent.

A different sort of manipulation can be seen in the genealogy of Clann Chólman, the branch of the Southern Uí Néill who shared the kingship of Tara with the Cenél nÉogain of the Northern Uí Néill. Like the Dál Cáis, Clann Chólman was somewhat of an upstart dynasty, although there apparently was never any doubt about their descent from Niall Noígiallach, the founder of the Uí Néill dynasties. Instead of manufacturing a genealogy that justified their eligibility for the kingship, which was not in question, they set out to adjust their pedigree so it could distinguish their claim for the kingship from the equally legitimate claims of others. One of their manipulations created a distinction between the line of Domnall Midi and that of Folloman, king of Meath. Domnall Midi ruled as king of Tara for two decades in the middle of the eighth century, the first member of Clann Chólman to hold the overkingship of the northern half of Ireland. Six other members of his dynasty held the kingship in alternation with Cenél nÉogain over the next two and a half centuries. During Domnall's reign Folloman, who was a member of a junior branch of Domnall's dynasty, became king of Meath. Although the genealogies present Clann Cholmáin as the descendants of Colmáin *Már* son of Díarmait, and the line of Folloman as descendants of Colmáin *Becc* son of Díarmait, Ailbhe Mac Shamráin has argued convincingly that there was only one son of Díarmait named Colmáin who was the ancestor of both Domnall Midi and Folloman. The genealogists duplicated Colmáin into Colmáin *Már* 'the great' from whom came the 'greater' line of Domnall, which supplied kings of Tara, and Colmáin *Becc*, 'the small,' from whom came the 'lesser' line of the kings of Meath.[5]

Eighth-century Leinster genealogies reflected the political, as opposed to the biological, relationships of the *tuatha* in the province. Nearly all the Leinster peoples were presented as descendants of a common ancestor, Sétnae Síthbacc, although many of these *tuatha* were unlikely to be related in any way whatsoever. Alfred Smyth cites the example of the Uí Dróna and the Uí Dega who were presented as distant relations of the dominant Uí Cheinnselaig in order to explain their subordinate position. Although the individual tribal segments of the genealogies probably contain genuine historical information, Smyth judges that the inter-tribal

---

[5] Ailbhe Mac Shamráin, "*Nebulae discutiuntur*? The Emergence of Clann Cholmáin, Sixth–Eighth Centuries," in *Seanchas: Studies in Early and Medieval Irish Archaeology, History, and Literature in Honour of Francis J. Byrne* (Dublin: Four Courts Press, 1999), 83–97, esp. 95–7. See Table I, 96, for the genealogy he reconstructs. Francis John Byrne, *Irish Kings and High-Kings* (New York: St. Martins Press, 1973) presents the traditional genealogy, with the two Colmáins, in Tables 1 and 2, at 280–1.

framework has little or no historical validity. Despite its fictional nature, this framework is nonetheless useful for the historian because it presents "the social, political and even geographical position of each tribe within Leinster."[6]

Dumville argues that similar manipulations probably lie behind some Old English genealogies. It is commonly assumed that Old English written genealogies were extended in three stages. The first stage ended in Woden, as can be seen in the Kentish pedigrees in Bede.[7] These relatively brief pedigrees presumably resemble the oral genealogies that were cultivated before the conversion, although with a combined total of eight generations from Æthelberht to Woden they are perhaps a bit longer, since one of the earliest impacts of literacy upon Old English genealogies appears to have been the expansion of the number of generations counting back to Woden, who is presented as the founding father of many royal dynasties. When the Anglian collection was assembled in the late eighth century, the pedigrees typically included fourteen generations from the most recent king listed back to Woden.[8] By this time all the pedigrees had been extended again, a further four generations from Woden back to Geat.[9] The final extension, back to Scyld, Sceaf, and the Old Testament via Noah, is found only in the ninth-century West Saxon pedigree. The genealogies of all the Anglian royal families are distinct until they join in Woden. But the conclusion of the first stage of the West Saxon pedigree in the copy of the Anglian collection in MS CCCC 183, which runs *Aluca–Giwis–Brand–Bældæg–Woden*, closely resembles

---

[6] Alfred P. Smyth, *Celtic Leinster: Towards an Historical Geography of Early Irish Civilization, A.D. 500–1600* (Blackrock, County Dublin: Irish Academic Press, 1982), 13–15. For more information on Irish genealogies, see John V. Kelleher, "The Pre-Norman Genealogies," *Irish Historical Studies* 16 (1968): 138–53.

[7] *Bede's Ecclesiastical History of the English People*, ed. Bertram Colgrave and R.A.B. Mynors (Oxford: Oxford University Press, 1969), I, 15 and II, 5. The genealogy of Æthelwulf in the West Saxon Regnal List also ends in Woden. David N. Dumville, "The West Saxon Genealogical Regnal List: Manuscripts and Texts," *Anglia* 104 (1986): 1–32, at 21.

[8] Sisam, "Anglo-Saxon Royal Genealogies," 326–8. There are some minor variations in this number. These genealogies are published in David N. Dumville, "The Anglian Collection of Royal Genealogies and Regnal Lists," *Anglo-Saxon England* 5 (1976): 23–50, at 30–7. Both Sisam and Dumville are sceptical that extensive oral genealogies ever existed among the English. Sisam, "Anglo-Saxon Royal Genealogies," 322, remarks that oral genealogies may have extended back to great-grandfathers; this would allow for four generations from a reigning king back to Woden. Dumville, "Kingship," 96, suspects that the Church may have been behind the cultivation of long genealogies, but still allows for the existence of oral pedigrees in the seventh century; see also 85.

[9] Although the manuscripts present this extension as belonging only to the rulers of the kingdom of Lindsey, Dumville, "Kingship," 90, has convincingly argued that this placement is a mistake caused by manuscript layout, and this extension belonged to all the pedigrees.

the Bernician sequence *Alusa–Ingebrand–Wægbrand–Beornic–Bældæg–Woden*.[10] The final two names, *Bældæg* and *Woden*, are identical in both pedigrees. Furthermore, just as *Beornic* is the eponym of the Bernicians, so too *Giwis* is an eponym of the West Saxons, who were known as the *Gewisse* in the seventh century. The West Saxon name *Brand* is identical to the second element of the two Bernician compound names, *Ingibrand* and *Wegbrand*, while *Aluca* and *Alusa* are very similar.[11] Sisam assumed these similarities resulted from a copying error, but Dumville argues that the transfer was intentional.[12] Noting that *Giwis* is a seventh-century spelling, he suggests that the West Saxon pedigree may have been remodeled after the marriage of King Oswald of Bernicia with the daughter of Cynigils, king of the West Saxons, in 635. This marriage was coupled with the conversion of Cynigils, with Oswald standing as godfather when his father-in-law was baptized. The remodeled West Saxon pedigree would thus be a reflection of the new relationship between the kingdoms. According to Bede, Oswald was the most powerful Anglo-Saxon king of the time. Given Oswald's wide sovereignty and influence, the adoption of names from the Bernician into the West Saxon pedigree (and not vice-versa) appears to reflect the subordinate position of the West Saxon king. Indeed, Bede tells us that both kings (*ambo reges*) gave the city of Dorchester to Bishop Birinus as his see, a detail that presents Cynigils as an underking acting with his overlord Oswald's approval.[13] Dumville also discusses a similar remodeling of the Kentish genealogy on that of the kings of Deira, identifying the marriage of Edwin of Deira to Athilberg, the sister of Eadbald of Kent, as the only political occasion that could have prompted the grafting of the Kentish pedigree on to the

---

[10] These names are cited from Dumville's edition of the pedigrees in CCCC 183, "The Anglian Collection," 32–4.

[11] The similarity is even more pronounced in the pedigree of Ida of Bernicia presented under the year 547 (549 in MS C) of the *Chronicle*, which runs *Brand–Bældæg–Woden*, the same sequence as in the West Saxon pedigree. *The Anglo-Saxon Chronicle. A Collaborative Edition*, vol. 3: *MS A*, ed. Janet M. Bately (Cambridge: D.S. Brewer, 1986). As Dumville, "Kingship," 79, observes, we have no information about the stage above Cerdic in the West Saxon pedigree before it was remodeled. If such a stage existed, it is possible that it concluded in Woden, but as Dumville suggests, descent from Woden seems to express belief in an Anglian origin or a political link between a non-Anglian people and an Anglian kingdom. It is possible that the West Saxons may originally have derived their kings from Seaxnet, as the East Saxons did. For the East Saxon pedigree, see Dumville, "The West Saxon Genealogical Regnal List," 31–2.

[12] Sisam, "Anglo-Saxon Royal Genealogies," 303; Dumville, "Kingship," 79–81.

[13] Bede, II.5 and III.7. Dumville, "Kingship," 81, suggests that another possible occasion for the remodeling of the West Saxon genealogy on the Bernician could be the marriage of King Aldfrith of Northumbria (685–704) to the sister of King Ine of Wessex. Although the political implications are less clear in this case, he speculates that the marriage may have sealed an alliance against Æthelred of Mercia.

Deiran stem. As in the case of Oswald, Bede credits Edwin with wide sovereignty over other kingdoms, and the adoption of names from the Deiran pedigree into the Kentish appears to imply a subordinate position for the kings of Kent.[14]

Craig Davis plausibly suggests that the settlement of the Danelaw, coupled with the baptism of Guthrum in 878, is the most likely occasion for the West Saxon royal family to incorporate Scyld in their pedigree.[15] The degree to which the inclusion of Scyld in the West Saxon royal pedigree departs from genealogical convention can be clearly seen if we compare the context of Guthrum's baptism with that of Cynigils. In the latter case Oswald, overlord of all the English kingdoms, stood sponsor to his father-in-law Cynigils when he was baptized. There is no doubt that Cynigils was subordinate to Oswald, and we can read this subordination in the incorporation of names from the Bernician pedigree into that of the West Saxons. We can, moreover, conclude that if an alliance such as this one is reflected in genealogy, then the pedigree of the subordinate kingdom may become a branch of that of the more powerful kingdom.

When Alfred stood sponsor to Guthrum, the Danes were not conquered, but they were defeated. By accepting baptism, Guthrum was presumably also accepting Alfred as his overlord and signaling his willingness to rule within the Christian world.[16] Eric John's observation that the baptism in 943 of Sihtric, the Norse king of York, with Edmund of Wessex standing as his godfather, "implied a real if undefined subordination" may be a good description of the implications here as well,[17] although we can also read the ceremony as merely placing Alfred in a symbolic position of

---

[14] Dumville, "Kingship," 79–80. Bede, II.5. As Dumville notes, Bede states that Edwin had sovereignty over all Britain, except for Kent. Although Eadbald was not his underking, there would presumably have been some degree of subordination involved in the marriage alliance.

[15] Craig R. Davis, "An Ethnic Dating of *Beowulf*," *Anglo-Saxon England* 35 (2006): 111–29, at 119. Roberta Frank, "Skaldic Verse and the Date of *Beowulf*," in *The Dating of Beowulf*, ed. Colin Chase (Toronto: University of Toronto Press, 1981), 123–39, at 128, agrees that the expansion of the genealogy is unlikely to have occurred before Guthrum's baptism at Wedmore.

[16] David N. Dumville, *Wessex and England from Alfred to Edgar: Six Essays on Political, Cultural, and Ecclesiastical Revival* (Woodbridge: The Boydell Press, 1992), 1, views Guthrum as the first of the kings of southern Britain to accept Alfred's overlordship. Guthrum's willingness to join the Christian European world can also be seen in the coins he issued while he was king of East Anglia, which bear his baptismal name Æthelstan. See Mark Blackburn, "Currency under the Vikings. Part I: Guthrum and the Earliest Danelaw Coinages," *The British Numismatic Journal* 75 (2005): 18–43, at 26.

[17] Eric John, *Reassessing Anglo-Saxon England* (Manchester: Manchester University Press, 1996), 94.

superiority over his new godson.[18] In either case, Guthrum's position vis-à-vis Alfred was analogous to that of Cynigils vis-à-vis Oswald in 635. But the addition of Scyld to the royal pedigree does not demonstrate the superiority of the West Saxon king. If we read this addition according to the conventions governing the earlier remodeling of the West Saxon pedigree, then the presence of Scyld in Æthelwulf's pedigree appears to transform it into a subordinate branch of the Danish royal family.

There is no need to stress that this subordination was not the purpose behind the inclusion of Scyld. Nonetheless, the presence of Scyld suggests that the West Saxon genealogists either had a poor grasp of genealogical conventions, or, as I argue here, they were willing to risk working against these conventions. If the West Saxons were determined to use genealogy as a tool to achieve a shared community with the Danes, they had no choice but to modify their own pedigree. Unlike the Dál Cáis, they could not simply invent or import a new ancestor from whom both the West Saxon and Danish kings descended, since such an ancestor would mean nothing to the Danes. The West Saxons had to incorporate a figure who already had prestige and resonance among both the Danes and the English, and they had to alter their own royal genealogy to accommodate this figure.

Given the decision to proceed with the inclusion of Scyld despite the potential implications of this inclusion, the West Saxon royal family and/or their genealogists presumably had enough confidence in the context and presentation of their claim to proceed with it. Indeed, it is the contexts of this claim, in both the affairs of men and in the constructed genealogies, which make it a political strategy that was at least worth trying. The most immediate external context was the prestige of the dynasty. Alfred's family had a long history behind it by the end of the ninth century. By this time it was one of the longest established and most prestigious dynasties in Europe. As Eric John points out, the house of Cerdic claimed to be contemporaries of the Merovingians, and it provided distinguished royal pedigrees to various continental ruling families through the marriage of daughters during the tenth century – five of Edward's daughters were given in such marriages between 916 and 930.[19] Murray's comparison of the West Saxon dynasty to the "petty and disunited Scandinavian kings and earls of northern England"[20] is certainly relevant here, although it overlooks the claims of Scylding descent

---

[18] Clare Downham, *Viking Kings of Britain and Ireland: The Dynasty of Ívarr to A.D. 1014* (Edinburgh: Dunedin Academic Press, 2007), 111.

[19] John, *Reassessing*, 86–7.

[20] Alexander Callander Murray, "*Beowulf*, the Danish Invasions, and Royal Genealogy," in *The Dating of* Beowulf, ed. Colin Chase (Toronto: University of Toronto Press, 1981), 101–11, at 105.

that were apparently made by Halfdan, Inwær and their descendants: the eleventh-century *Historia de sancto Cuthberto* twice refers to the Danes as *Scaldingi* and names the Halfdan who allowed his army to settle in southern Northumbria as 'king of the Danes' (*rex Danorum*). Both Halfdan and his brother Inwær (ON Ívarr) were dead before 878, but there is evidence that their dynasty continued to control the kingdom of York for most of the period from the death of Halfdan until the kingdom was absorbed by Alfred's descendants.[21] But even this Scandinavian dynasty appears parvenu in comparison, and it must have needed every source of legitimation it could muster. Thus, however problematic the inclusion of Scyld in the West Saxon royal pedigree was, it was balanced to some extent by the greater prestige of Alfred's dynasty.

Nonetheless, it is telling that the genealogists were not content to add Scyld alone to this pedigree: they also provided a biblical extension, and they included a number of other names from Germanic legend, the most important of which are Sceaf and Beow (apparently included twice). The inability of the additional Germanic names to advance directly the dynasty's claims of authority over the Danish settlers can be seen most clearly in the case of Sceaf and Beow. The connections between Scyld and his father/ancestor Sceaf and his son Beow are found only in England. Neither of these names appear in Danish genealogies, and their presence in Icelandic texts is derived from England.[22] If, as is generally assumed, the purpose of the inclusion of Scyld in this pedigree was to encourage a sense of community between the English and the recent Scandinavian settlers, and to give the West Saxons kings a claim to authority over these settlers, then one of the central questions we face as we attempt to unravel the strategy of the West Saxon genealogists is why they incorporated all three of these names instead of simply including *Skjǫldr* (or the anglicized *Scyld*) alone. Furthermore, since these three names appear to have been adopted and incorporated as a unit, then the separation of Scyld and Sceaf by five generations poses yet another question: if these names constitute a set, as everyone seems to agree they do, why was this set

---

[21] *Historia de sancto Cuthberto*, ed. Ted Johnson South (Cambridge: D.S. Brewer, 2002), Chapters 11 and 12. On Halfdan's division of Northumbria among his men, see the entry for 876 in MS A of the *Chronicle*. Although the *Historia* was long believed to stem from the mid-tenth century, South has argued for a date in the eleventh, at least a century and a half after the death of Halfdan. David N. Dumville, "Old Dubliners and New Dubliners in Ireland and Britain: A Viking-Age Story," *Medieval Dublin* 6 (2004): 78–93, at 87–9, argues convincingly that the king of York named Guthred/Guthfrid who died in 895 was a member of Halfdan and Inwær's family. Downham, *Viking Kings of Britain and Ireland*, 253–5, lists six different Viking leaders with this name (Irish *Gofraid*) in her "Prosopography of Viking-leaders."

[22] Alexander M. Bruce, *Scyld and Sceaf: Expanding the Analogues* (New York: Routledge, 2002), 55, 58.

broken up in the *Chronicle* genealogy? And finally, why is Æthelwulf's pedigree in the *Chronicle* extended through Noah to Adam and God? And given this extension, why is Sceaf presented as an extra-biblical fourth son of Noah, when he could just as easily have been connected to Noah through Japheth?

Once we recognize the implication of subordination generated by the presence of Scyld, we can see that the genealogists attempted to play a double game in order to balance this implication. Although they apparently had little control over the choice of Scyld as the ancestor connecting the West Saxon and Danish royal lines, they could control the pedigree in which he was embedded, presenting it as a thoroughly West Saxon and Christian pedigree. Perhaps a comparison to a nuclear reactor would be useful here: the construction of the surrounding pedigree is designed as a containment field that encloses the problematic implications of the presence of Scyld, attempting to trap and neutralize these implications while permitting the pedigree as a whole to draw upon the positive cultural and political energy that Scyld represents.

Because the sequence of this stage of the pedigree in the *Chronicle* and Asser differs so much from that in Æthelweard, it is necessary to examine each sequence separately, beginning with the one in the *Chronicle*. Unfortunately the scribe of MS A (Corpus Christi College, Cambridge, MS 173) omitted from the entry for 855 some of the names that are the most important for our purposes here, so the passage from the entry for 856 in MS C (British Library, Cotton Tiberius B. i) will serve as the representative of this version, with the text edited to present one generation per line for clarity:

> Geatt Tætwaing,
> Tætwa Beawing,
> Beaw Scealdwaing,
> Scealdwa Heremoding,
> Heremod Itermoning,
> Itermon Haðraing,
> Haþra Hwalaing,
> Hwala Bedwiging,
> Bedwig Sceafing,
> id est filius Noe
> se wæs geboren on þære earce Noes,
> Lamech,
> Matusalem,
> Enoh,
> Iared,
> Malalehel,

Camon,[23]
Enos,
Seth,
Adam primus homo
et pater noster id est Cristus.[24]

From our perspective today, the "containment field" or "shielding" of Scyld appears to consist of a five-fold strategy:

1) The spelling *Sceldwa* is non-West Saxon, and perhaps a corruption of an archaic form. As both H.M. Chadwick and Kenneth Sisam have noted, the stem vowels of most of the spellings of the name of Scyld in the copies of the Chronicle and Asser – *Sceldwea*, MS A; *Sceldwea*, Asser; *Scyldwa*, MS B (British Library MS Cotton Tiberius A.vi); *Scealdwa* MS C; *Scealdhwa* MS D (British Library MS Cotton Tiberius B.iv) – and *Beaw* are non-West Saxon. The obvious inference, which both Chadwick and Sisam go on to make, is that these name-forms were borrowed from a non-West Saxon text.[25] Sisam identifies the forms *Sceldwea*, *Sceldwaing* of MS A as the spelling of the *Chronicle* archetype on the basis of the agreement of these forms with the form *Sceldwea* in Asser and the patronymic *Sceldweaing* in MS B.[26] The –*e*- of the root syllable of *Sceldwea* is either Anglian or Kentish, while the –*ea*- of the other manuscripts appears to stem from carelessness and/or a misunderstanding of the name. Only MS B has the expected West Saxon –*y*- in *Scyldwa*, although it has –*e*- in the patronymic *Sceldweaing*. The -*ea*- of *Beaw*, on the other hand, is apparently a copying error, although there is a slight possibility that it could be

---

[23] The error *Camon* for New Testament *Cainan* (Luke 3:37) is found in all the copies of the *Chronicle* that include this genealogy.

[24] Text cited from *The Anglo-Saxon Chronicle. A Collaborative Edition*, vol. 5: *MS C*, ed. Katherine O'Brien O'Keefe (Cambridge: D.S. Brewer, 2000), 57. The genealogy from MS C is also presented in *Klaeber's* Beowulf: *Fourth Edition*, ed. R.D. Fulk, Robert E. Bjork and John Niles (Toronto: University of Toronto Press, 2008), in Appendix A, 291. R.W. Chambers, Beowulf: *An Introduction*, 3rd ed. with a Supplement by C.L. Wrenn (Cambridge: Cambridge University Press, 1959), 202–3, presents the stages from Noah to Sceaf in a variety of manuscripts, and Bruce, *Scyld and Sceaf*, 96–9, 101–3 presents the entire genealogy from MS A and Asser, and the stages from Geat to Sceaf from manuscripts B, C, and D.

[25] Chadwick, *The Origin of the English Nation*, 272, suggests a genealogy in Latin; Sisam, "Anglo-Saxon Royal Genealogies," 344, observes "So it may be inferred that, at that time, the names did not belong to West Saxon tradition, but were imported into Æthelwulf's pedigree from a non-West Saxon source; and, on the analogy of forms like *Creoda*, from a written, not from an oral source." See also 318.

[26] Sisam, "Anglo-Saxon Royal Genealogies," 316 n. 1. Bately, *MS A*, lxxv, gives priority to MS A, arguing that it "is therefore an independent witness for the textual history of the *Chronicle*, representing an earlier stage in the evolution of the *Chronicle* than do the other surviving vernacular manuscripts and sometimes presenting 'better' readings."

a Northumbrian or Kentish spelling.[27] Sisam's observation and conclusion, which have been ignored in discussions that present this pedigree as evidence for a late dating of *Beowulf*,[28] could have been even stronger. However, unlike Chadwick, he separated the issue of the vocalism of the stem vowels in these names from the even more problematic issue of the *–w(e)a* suffix in *Tætwa* and *Sceldwa*. Although Sisam believed that there was no satisfactory explanation for this ending, he did venture a couple of carefully qualified hypotheses, neither of which he seemed to take very seriously.[29] R.D. Fulk, following a suggestion of Rudolf Kögel's, has suggested that the *w* in this *–wa* suffix probably represents the old nominative ending of the *u*-stem. Although the noun *scyld* is inflected as an *a*-stem in the surviving Old English texts, it was originally a *u*-stem, as can be seen from cognates such as Old Icelandic *skjǫldr* and Gothic *skildus*. Fulk's approach has the virtue of consistency, since it seeks to explain the suffix of both *Tætwa* and *Sceldwa*, and he argues that *Beowi*, which occurs in manuscript D of the *Chronicle*, and appears to be another form with a prehistoric final vowel, underlies the form *Bedwig* in Asser and manuscripts B and C of the *Chronicle*. The corruption of *Beowi* to *Bedwig* is fairly straightforward given the similarity of the letters *o* and *d* in some forms of Insular script and the regular substitution of *–ig-*for

[27] According to A. Campbell, *Old English Grammar* (Oxford: Oxford University Press, 1959), §278–80, the diphthong *ēo* is unrounded to *ēa* in the Northumbrian of the glosses to the *Lindisfarne Gospels* and the *Rituale Ecclesiae Dunelmensis*, and also in the Kentish charters of the ninth century. But this unrounding does not generally occur before *w*, although Campbell lists a few exceptions in §279 n. 1. In these dialects a form **bēa* could arise in the nominative and accusative singular after loss of the final *w*; Campbell §584 cites *ðēa* for *ðēo* in both the *Lindisfarne* and *Rituale* glosses. Restoration of the final *w* by analogy could then produce the *Bēaw* of the pedigree, but we are then left with the question of why the *w* would be restored but not the rounded vowel. Further complicating the issue are the uncertainties surrounding the etymologies of *bēow* 'barley' and the name *Bēow* in the pedigree, which may well belong to different noun classes. As R.D. Fulk, "The Etymology and Significance of Beowulf's Name," *Anglo-Saxon* 1 (2007): 109–36, at 129, points out, a Germanic **bewwa-* explains the vowels in Old English *bēow* 'barley' and Old Saxon *beuuo* (g. pl.) 'crops' and *beuuod* 'crop', but not Old Icelandic *bygg* 'barley.' Furthermore, if a form like *Beowi* in MS D underlies the *Bedwig* of manuscripts B and C, then the name appears to be an *–i* stem, and would give *Bīuw/Bīow* in Northumbrian, which distinguished *īu/īo* from *ēu/ēo* dipthongs throughout the Old English period, unlike the other dialects where these diphthongs merged (Campbell, *Old English Grammar*, §293–7). Such a form would not produce the *Beaw* of the pedigree. Given the manifold uncertainties here, no conclusions can be reached. See Fulk's entire discussion, "The Etymology" (at 126–36) for the complexities involved in the question.

[28] So, for example, the discussions of Murray, "*Beowulf*, the Danish Invasions"; Frank, "Skaldic Verse," 128–29; Audrey Meaney, "Scyld Scefing and the Dating of *Beowulf* – Again," *Bulletin of the John Rylands University Library of Manchester* 71 (1989): 7–40; John Niles, "Locating *Beowulf* in Literary History," *Exemplaria* 5 (1993): 79–109, at 95.

[29] Sisam, "Anglo-Saxon Royal Genealogies," 341 and n. 3.

-i- in West Saxon spelling. There are thus three names in the nine-name sequence from *Tætwa* to *Sceaf* which can be explained as reflexes of archaic forms.[30] Whatever explanations we adopt (or don't adopt) for this suffix, its presence, together with the non-West Saxon stem vowels in *Beaw* and *Sceldwa*, indicate a complex and perhaps long textual history behind these names, with possibly archaic forms underlying the names ending in the *-wa* suffix. The spellings of these names and the textual history these spellings imply greatly diminish the possibility that this extension of the West Saxon royal pedigree influenced the opening of *Beowulf*, since these spellings demonstrate that these names occurred in texts well before the end of the ninth century.

This odd spelling of *Scyld* as *Sceldwa* would have been retained only if it had some value or served some purpose for the genealogists. The most likely explanation for this retention is that it was an attempt to give the presence of this name, and the pedigree as a whole, an air of antiquity, an attempt to imply that the genealogical flow of generations receding into the past is matched by a similar span of generations during which this name has been an integral part of the royal pedigree. The use of this spelling can be read as an implicit claim that the upper reaches of the pedigree are extremely old.

2) *Sceldwa* is presented in a completely English context. None of the names in this stretch of the pedigree are found in later Danish genealogies. The issue of whether these figures belonged exclusively to English legend or to wider Germanic legend is irrelevant.[31] Inasmuch as these names were adopted from stories, they were adopted from narratives presented in England to English audiences. Heremod is perhaps the most telling example here. Although he appears in both English and Norse poetry, he is identified as a king of the Danes and a predecessor of Scyld only in *Beowulf*, and as an ancestor of Scyld only in this genealogy.

3) The presentation of Sceldwa in the company of Beaw and Sceaf, as part of a group, intensifies this English context. Neither Beaw nor Sceaf would have been included here if they were merely agricultural figures whose significance was limited to the meaning and obvious symbolism of their names. As David Dumville observes, this extension was intended "to establish for the dynasty a commanding position within the world

---

[30] Fulk, "The Etymology," 126–8. See also R. Kögel, "*Beowulf*," *Zeitschrift für deutsches Altertum* 37 (1893): 268–76, at 271, n. 1.

[31] See, for example, Chambers, Beowulf: *An Introduction*, 73, where he insists that *Sceaf* was not essentially an English hero. He may well be correct in this, but the important distinction here is not between exclusively English heroes and those shared with other Germanic peoples, but between those found in English texts and those found, or not found, in Danish texts.

of Germanic heroic legend, and then to anchor it firmly in universal history and a Christian context."[32] Names associated only with agricultural folklore could make no contribution to this commanding position. Nor could such names balance the unwanted implications of Sceldwa. The presentation of Sceldwa as an integral member of a group provides a fuller context for this figure and implies that he is one part of a greater whole. As a result, only the English genealogical tradition can claim to preserve the entire genealogy. Thus this tradition is potentially more authoritative than the Danish tradition, and implies that the rulers of Wessex had a vital, living connection with Sceldwa and his ancestors that Danish claimants lacked. As Craig Davis observes in a different but related context, "It is the claimed reliability of the pedigree, the clarity and completeness of the tradition, which is as important as its putative antiquity."[33] The presence of Beaw and Sceaf would provide no balance or context if these names were derived directly from agricultural folklore, devoid of heroic and royal associations – associations most likely gained in heroic verse. If Scyld, Sceaf and Beow were figures in heroic poetry before they were adopted in this pedigree, there is no case for the influence of the pedigree on *Beowulf*.

Although the *Chronicle* genealogy separates Sceldwa from Sceaf, there are good grounds for regarding this sequence as an expansion that is derived from the original trio. Although the argument that these three names were presented without this expansion in an early version of the *Chronicle* is much weaker than it has been assumed to be (see below, p. 129f), it is likely that the three figures were adopted as a unit. As we have seen, the spellings *Sceldwa* and *Beaw* indicate a possibly archaic, non-West Saxon text as the immediate source. The doubling of Beow and the presentation of him as a son of both Sceldwa and Sceaf suggests that the genealogists may have combined two sources for these names: heroic poetry with the sequence *Beow–Sceldwa–Sceaf* that we encounter in *Beowulf,* and another source, presumably some sort of folklore narrative, in which Beow was the son of Sceaf. Given the significant role that both Sceldwa and Sceaf play in this pedigree, they could not be doubled, although Beow could be and was. This doubling compensates somewhat for the separation of Sceldwa and Sceaf, implying a connection or an underlying similarity between them, and retaining the presentation of Sceldwa as an integral part of a larger whole.

4) But even while an implied connection is maintained between these two, they are distinguished in a manner that is far more consequential:

---

[32] Dumville, "Kingship," 95.
[33] Craig R. Davis, "Cultural Assimilation in the Anglo-Saxon Royal Genealogies," *Anglo-Saxon England* 21 (1992): 23–36, at 31.

the story of the arrival of a foundling in a boat is attributed to Sceaf, not Scyld as in *Beowulf*. Although the *Chronicle* does not include this story, it is implied by the birth of Sceaf in the ark, and presented explicitly in Æthelweard's *Chronicon*. Thus, in contrast to the presentation in *Beowulf*, Sceldwa is not an originary, apical ancestor, but is merely a descendant of the originary Sceaf. The five generations between these two figures provide historical depth, but more importantly they diminish Sceldwa by separating him from the ultimate Germanic ancestor Sceaf, presenting him as one descendant of Sceaf among others. The presence of either version of Sceaf's sea-borne arrival strengthens the contextualization of Sceldwa. Thus, as important as he is to the origins of the Scyldings and to the implied claims of the West Saxon dynasty, Sceldwa is shown to be merely a part of a wider, more significant story of origins – the origin of all Germanic kingship. The contrast with *Beowulf* could not be sharper. Not only is Scyld presented as the originary royal ancestor in the poem, his story is the first episode a listener or reader encounters, and it thus receives a special emphasis. The presentation of Scyld in the poem contradicts the strategy of the genealogy so clearly and directly that it is difficult to believe that the poem could be a product of the strategy that produced the royal pedigree, or that it reflects or serves this strategy in any way. The poem thus appears to be the product of a different time and a different cultural situation.

5) The story of the arrival of the foundling Sceaf is supplanted by the brief account of his birth in the ark, thus connecting the native Germanic pedigree to the Old Testament via Noe (Noah), and deriving this pedigree through Adam, the first man (*primus homo*), from God himself: *et pater noster id est Christus* "and our father, that is Christ."[34] This connection demonstrates the divine source of the authority of the royal family,[35] an authority which could not be claimed by pagan Scandinavian rulers in England at the end of the ninth century. Even when Guthrum agreed to convert and be baptized, he received his baptism through the agency of King Alfred, who stood as his sponsor. His Christianity was as much of a gift from Alfred as was the *feo* 'treasure' that the king presented to him on this occasion.[36] The Christianity of Guthrum is mediated through Alfred, whose claim to divine authority for his rule could not

---

[34] *MS A, anno* 855. As Davis, "Cultural Assimilation," 30, observes, the conclusion of this genealogy is based on the genealogy of Christ in the Gospel of Luke, where Adam is presented as the son of God (Luke 3:38). Davis cites in this connection Francis P. Magoun, "King Æthelwulf's Biblical Ancestors," *Modern Language Review* 46 (1951): 249–50. Sisam, "Anglo-Saxon Royal Genealogies," 320, notes that the source of these names in Luke was first recognized by William of Malmesbury.

[35] Davis, "Cultural Assimilation," 33.

[36] *MS A, anno* 878.

be surpassed, although it could be imitated by Scandinavian rulers who convert.

Given the earlier Anglo-Saxon custom of grounding their royal pedigrees in divine figures, deriving their kings first from Woden and then later from Geat, this derivation of a royal pedigree from a genealogy in the Old Testament in order to achieve a divine authorization does not seem surprising. From our perspective today, it appears to be a natural strategy to pursue after the conversion. But it apparently did not seem natural to the Anglo-Saxons themselves. Although the conversion of the kings and other nobles was completed by the last quarter of the seventh century, it is not until two full centuries later, in the last quarter of the ninth century, that a genealogical connection to the Old Testament is first made. These two intervening centuries are evidence that the derivation of their royal pedigrees from an Old Testament genealogy did not strike the Anglo-Saxons as either natural or necessary. As Daniel Anlezark observes, "The shift back to the world's early history through the ark-born son is not a cultural development associated with the conversion but rather with the ideological programme of the reign of Alfred ..."[37] Thus the connection with Noah that we see here in the West Saxon pedigree is a highly unusual move. It is, in fact, unprecedented among the English, and like the inclusion of Beow and Sceaf, it is most likely to have been done in order to offset the problematic implications of the presence of Sceldwa, a task it accomplishes extremely well, since it bestows ultimate royal authority on those descendants of Sceaf – the West Saxon dynasty – who can recognize and articulate their descent from God via Adam and Noah, and who are able to understand and accept the responsibilities and privileges of this descent thanks to their Christian faith.

The presentation of Sceaf as a son of Noah is even more extraordinary. Sceaf could have been unobtrusively connected to Noah simply by making him a son of one of Noah's sons. Such a descent would also have been compatible with a birth in the ark, preserving Sceaf's water-borne arrival, and it would have been able to pass as more or less orthodox. Regardless of whether we read this presentation of Sceaf as a fourth son of Noah as a claim of a separate descent from Noah only for the West Saxon royal lineage, as Thomas Hill has suggested, or as a descent for all the Germanic kings and their peoples, as Davis argues,[38] by assigning Sceaf such a privileged position this genealogical connection places

---

[37] Daniel Anlezark, "Sceaf, Japheth and the Origins of the Anglo-Saxons," *Anglo-Saxon England* 31 (2002): 13–46, at 32.

[38] Thomas D. Hill, "The Myth of the Ark-Born Son of Noe and the West-Saxon Royal Genealogical Tables," *Harvard Theological Review* 80 (1987): 379–83, at 379–80; Davis, "Cultural Assimilation," 30–1. Even if the significance of this descent is limited to the royal lineage, the presence in this pedigree of Scyld, Geat, and Woden, who are

even more emphasis on him as *the* originary ancestor. By elevating and glorifying Sceaf, this connection places Scyld a bit more in his ancestor's shadow, presenting him as a slightly diminished and less significant figure.

There is some evidence that this genealogy may have been constructed in two stages, and that the identification of Sceaf as a fourth son of Noah may have resulted from a discomfort or dissatisfaction with an earlier, more ambiguous version that merely presented him as a child who is born and conveyed on the ark. The transition between the Germanic and the biblical portions of the pedigree is awkward, and may well have been made at a late date in the development of the pedigree. This awkwardness has produced a seam in the genealogy which makes it possible for us to distinguish what may have been two stages in the compilation of the pedigree. It will be useful to present this portion of the genealogy, again from MS C, with the passage relineated for clarification:

> Bedwig Sceafing.
> Id est filius Noe,
> se wæs geboren on þære earce Noes,
> Lamech,
> Matusalem,
> Enoh,
> Iared,
> Malalehel,
> Camon,
> Enos,
> Seth,
> Adam, primus homo
> et pater noster id est Cristus.[39]

An examination of the text of MS A, where a number of names have been omitted at the beginning of this sequence, is also useful:

> Itermon Hraþraing
> se wæs geboren in þære earce,
> Noe
> Lamach,
> Matusalem,
> Enoh,
> Iaered,
> Maleel,
> Camon,
> Enos,

---

claimed as royal ancestors by the kings of many Germanic peoples, means that this special descent cannot belong to the West Saxon kings alone.

[39] MS C, *anno* 856.

Sed,
adã prim3 homo
&tpafnr̃÷xp̃sam̃:.⁴⁰

The very form of the pedigree at this point demonstrates how artificial it is: the dropping of the patronymics and the reduction of the names to a mere list suggests an indifference to the style and coherence of the overall genealogy. Although the first Latin clause has been omitted in MS A, the second is presented with an extraordinary density of abbreviation. Thomas Bredehoft observes that we encounter here a "range of abbreviation and the use of forms unique to, or at least unusual in, this manuscript."[41] Since abbreviations are usually adopted to save space and to reduce the amount of text to be copied, it is unlikely that these abbreviations originated with the scribe of MS A, who had no apparent need to save space in the entry for 855. This Latin phrase was probably abbreviated in this manner because it originated as a gloss to the text of an earlier manuscript, and was then incorporated into the text itself by a copyist. The origin of the biblical extension in a marginal gloss would explain not only this use of dense abbreviations, but also the reduction of the pedigree to a list of names, and the macaronic juxtaposition of Latin and English at the transition to the biblical names. Bredehoft also views this portion of the genealogy as a single unit which was added to an earlier, shorter version of the pedigree, although he does not identify this addition with a marginal gloss.[42]

If the biblical names were a later extension, the original pedigree could have concluded with *Bedwig Sceafing*. But given the brief narrative that Æthelweard supplies for Scef in his *Chronicon*, and given the arguments presented above for the advantages of the strategy of elevating Sceaf in contrast to Scyld, it seems more likely that a shorter pedigree would have concluded with *Bedwig Sceafing, se wæs geboren on þære earce Noes*. In this context the verb phrase *wæs geboren* would possess a double meaning, both 'was born' and 'was carried,' thus including the meaning of *aduectus est* 'brought hither, carried to' in Æthelweard's account of Scef. But the potential ambiguity of this phrase is resolved in favor of 'was born' in the surviving pedigree because it follows *Id est filius Noe*. In

---

[40] MS A, anno 855. I have altered Bately's rendition of the concluding Latin phrases to represent the abbreviations on folio 13a of the manuscript. See the reproduction of this folio in *The Parker Chronicle and Laws: (Corpus Christi College, Cambridge, MS. 173) A Facsimile*, ed. Robin Flower and A.H. Smith, EETS o.s. 208 (Oxford: Early English Text Society, 1941).

[41] Thomas A. Bredehoft, *Textual Histories: Readings in the* Anglo-Saxon Chronicle (Toronto: University of Toronto Press, 2001), 123. It was through Professor Bredehoft's discussion that I first learned of these abbreviations.

[42] Bredehoft, *Textual Histories*, 205, n. 14.

the absence of this Latin phrase and the list of Noah's ancestors, a pedigree that ended with *Sceafing, se wæs geboren on þære earce Noes* would have had several advantages: it would be a Christianized version of the arrival of Sceaf, placing him in an epochal moment of world history, and it would have connected, through implication, the figure of Sceaf with the Old Testament pedigree stretching back from Noah to Adam, but without specifying Sceaf's father. In its own way, this conclusion would have manifested a strategy similar to the double game that can be seen in the rest of the ninth-century extension of the royal pedigree. But instead of the simultaneous promotion and deprecation of Scyld seen elsewhere, this conclusion would have connected the apical Germanic ancestor of the royal family to the Old Testament with little overt manipulation of the Old Testament account in Genesis: Sceaf is presented as being carried and presumably born in the ark. If he is born there, he must be a member of Noah's family, and thus a direct descendant of Noah and Adam, yet his father is not named.

But the surviving pedigree does identify Sceaf's father, and generates the problematic assertion of a fourth son of Noah. Daniel Anlezark has suggested that Ælfric's repeated emphasis in his writings on the number of people saved in the ark – eight – and on the descent of northern peoples, including the Anglo-Saxons, from Noah's son Japheth may have been a reaction against this presentation of Sceaf as the fourth son of Noah who is born in the ark.[43] If so, this reaction in itself does not necessarily imply that the connection of the royal pedigree with the Old Testament was either unusual or unacceptable: it is merely a response to the unorthodox manner in which it was accomplished. But Æthelweard's presentation in his *Chronicon* of Sceaf as the final and apical ancestor in the royal pedigree does imply that the extension of this pedigree through Noah was an unusual measure for an extraordinary time, a time which had passed when Æthelweard composed his work. As a direct descendant of Alfred's older brother Æthelred, Æthelweard was in an excellent position to learn about the genealogy of the royal family, which was his genealogy as well. Given his position, the genealogy he presents deserves to be considered as the production of a man who probably knew his family's pedigree and understood the implications of both the structure and sequence of this pedigree. Indeed, the departures from the *Chronicle* genealogy in his version make considerable sense as a response to the changed political situation.

Æthelweard's willingness to shorten this pedigree implies, first of all, that by his time the version in the *Chronicle* was not part of the identity of the royal family and possessed neither currency nor prestige, and

---

[43] Anlezark, "Sceaf, Japheth and the Origins of the Anglo-Saxons," 36ff.

secondly, that he did not take the extension of the pedigree through Noah very seriously. Audrey Meaney has argued that Æthelweard was dependent here on an earlier version of the *Chronicle* where Æthelwulf's pedigree had not yet been connected to the Old Testament. Her argument is based in part on the observation that written pedigrees tend to develop by growing longer, not shorter.[44] But as she herself has shown, Æthelweard demonstrates an independence from his genealogical sources, as when he substitutes the name of the Norse god *Balder* for the English *Bældæg*, and spells *Woden* as *Vuothen*.[45] We see an analogous process in the *Beo–Scyld–Scef* sequence, where he drops the *Chronicle* forms *Beaw, Sceldwa,* and *Sceaf*, replacing them with spellings that represent his own pronunciation.[46] Given this evidence of his readiness to alter his source(s) in small details, we should accept the possibility that he introduced more substantial changes as well.

Meaney's argument maintains that the pedigree in Æthelweard's source ended with Sceaf and that Æthelweard did not know the longer version concluding with Adam.[47] But as Meaney herself emphasizes, the royal pedigree is also Æthelweard's pedigree. He is very knowledgeable about his wider family; indeed, he composed his *Chronicon* for his cousin Mathilda in Germany. In the prologue he not only explains how he and Mathilda are related, he also outlines the marriages between the royal family and members of the continental aristocracy. There is no known textual source for this material, and no reason for us not to accept his testimony that he learned this information from his parents.[48] If Æthelweard, a powerful and influential ealdorman closely related to the royal family who was very knowledgeable about family marriages

---

[44] Both Meaney, "Scyld Scefing," 13, and R.D. Fulk, "An Eddic Analogue to the Scyld Scefing Story," *Review of English Studies* 40 (1989): 312–2, at 321, agree that written genealogies such as this one are shortened only through accidental omission.

[45] A. Campbell, ed., *The Chronicle of Æthelweard* (London: Thomas Nelson and Sons, 1962), 33; Meaney, "Scyld Scefing," 14, n. 31. Initial [w] appears to have been lost before back vowels in Old Norse before the tenth century; see Adolf Noreen, *Altnordische Grammatik, I, Altisländische und altnorwegische Grammatik (Laut- und Flexionslehre) unter Berücksichtigung des Urnordischen*, 4th ed. (Tübingen: Niemeyer, 1923; repr. University of Alabama Press, 1970), § 235, where he cites, among other evidence, examples from Danish runic inscriptions.

[46] If Æthelweard's source actually was an earlier version of the *Chronicle,* the spelling of *Beaw* and *Sceldwa* in this source would have been more or less the same as the other *Chronicle* manuscripts, since otherwise there would be no explanation for the odd spellings that these manuscripts contain. Meaney, "Scyld Scefing," 19, appears to assume that Æthelweard's *Chronicle* exemplar included a usual West Saxon form like his own *Scyld*, which would then have been revised to the more opaque *Sceldwea* in the exemplar of the other versions of the text.

[47] Meaney, "Scyld Scefing," 18.

[48] Campbell, *The Chronicle of Æthelweard*, xvii, 1–2.

and descent, did not know of the longer version of the royal pedigree, as Meaney argues, then it probably did not function as a component of the effort to unite the English and the Danes, and it probably did not influence *Beowulf*.

Indeed, no matter how we view Æthelweard's version of this pedigree, its very existence argues against the wide dissemination or influence of either version. In his work we encounter the judgment of someone who felt free to alter the royal pedigree and to present a version that was based on his understanding of genealogical conventions and the political situation, with perhaps a touch of antiquarianism as well. When he was writing in the 970s or the 980s, the last independent Scandinavian rulers had been gone for decades, the Scandinavian settlers had been converted and were now Christian and the entire country was ruled by the West Saxon kings.[49] Since this kingdom embraced both English and Danish subjects, the presence of Scyld was still a potential asset for the royal house. Yet at this point, after the unification of the country and before the resumption of steady Scandinavian attacks,[50] the problematic implications of the inclusion of Scyld in this pedigree were greatly reduced. The conclusion of the pedigree in Æthelweard can be read as a response to these changed conditions:

> … quintus decimus Geat, sextus decimus Tetuua, septimus decimus Beo, octauus decimus Scyld, nonus decimus Scef. Ipse Scef cum uno dromone aduectus est in insula oceani que dicitur Scani, armis circundatus, eratque ualde recens puer, et ab incolis terræ ignotus. Attamen ab eis suscipitur, et ut familiarem diligenti animo eum custodierunt, et post regem eligunt; de cuius prosapia ordinem trahit Aðulf rex.

> (… his fifteenth Geat, his sixteenth Tetwa, his seventeenth Beow, his eighteenth Scyld, his nineteenth Sceaf. And this Sceaf arrived with one light ship in the island of the ocean which is called Skaney, with arms all round him. He was a very young boy, and unknown to the people of that land, but he was received by them, and they guarded him with diligent attention as one who belonged to them, and elected him king. From his family King Æthelwulf derived his descent.)[51]

---

[49] Campbell, *The Chronicle of Æthelweard*, xiii, n. 2 places the composition of the *Chronicon* between 978–88, probably later rather than earlier. Wojtek Jezierski, "Æthelweard Redivivus," *Early Medieval Europe* 13 (2005): 159–78, at 160, suggests composition after 982, the year Mathilda's brother, Duke Otto of Swabia and Bavaria, died.

[50] Viking attacks resumed in 980, but they were on a small scale and appear to have been rather sporadic – there were no attacks recorded from 982 to 988. Large attacks, on the scale of an organized army, did not begin until 991. See Frank Stenton, *Anglo-Saxon England*, 3rd ed. (Oxford: Oxford University Press, 1971), 374–77.

[51] Text and translation from Campbell, *The Chronicle of Æthelweard*, 33.

The connection with the Old Testament is gone. In the altered political and cultural circumstances, descent from God through Adam and Noah apparently no longer seemed necessary in order to balance the presence of Scyld. Æthelweard's understanding of genealogical implications can be seen most clearly in the brief paragraph he includes to explain the origins of Scef and thus the entire lineage: Scef arrives in a boat upon an island as a very young boy surrounded by weapons. By identifying this island as *Scani*, a name which refers to the southernmost part of Scandinavia, Æthelweard is presenting a version of the Scandinavian origin myth which is found elsewhere as an explanation of the pre-migratory origins of a number of Germanic peoples. But here we encounter an unusual version of this myth, one that emphasizes not the origins of a people, but the origins of Germanic kingship.

We have no way of knowing whether Æthelweard edited the pedigree himself or whether he simply reverted to an earlier version. But it would be rash to dismiss the knowledge and understanding of this man who was much more than a translator of the *Chronicle*, and we should not assume that he was simply following a single textual source and did not know the biblical extension in the *Chronicle* manuscripts. Whatever the source(s) of his version may be, we need to accept the possibility that Æthelweard knew and understood the materials he was working with – there was, after all, no other person working with these materials who was in a better position to understand their nature and implications.

The West Saxon dynasty, especially the portion of this dynasty beginning with Ecgbyrht, is at the very center of Æthelweard's concerns throughout his work. As Wotjek Jezierski has observed, only six out of thirty-two chapter titles in books two, three and four address topics other than the reigns of kings and their deeds, and only three of these do not include the name of a king.[52] Jezierski also points out that the accession of Ecgbyrht in 800 receives an extraordinary emphasis through the way Æthelweard connects this moment to the most important events in Anglo-Saxon and world history: the creation, the birth of Christ, the arrival of Hengest and Horsa, the reign of Cerdic and the beginning of the conversion of the Anglo-Saxons with the arrival of Augustine. Even Æthelwulf's genealogy, at the end of book three, concludes with the observation that at the death of Æthelwulf fifty-five years had passed since Ecgbyrht began to reign.[53] Book four is then introduced as the book in which "the origin of those descended from our family is indicated

---

[52] Jezierski, "Æthelweard Redivivus," 177.
[53] Campbell, *The Chronicle of Æthelweard*, 28 and 33; Jezierski, "Æthelweard Redivivus," 172.

more clearly" (*origo prosapiæ generis nostri indicatur apertius*).[54] The deliberate emphasis on family, dynasty, and genealogy can be perceived in the structure, the chronology, and the purpose of the *Chronicon*. The work as a whole gives us every reason to assume a similar deliberation in the structure and the purpose of Æthelweard's version of the West Saxon pedigree. Even the smaller changes that we can attribute to Æthelweard with confidence elsewhere in the genealogy, such as the replacement of *Bældæg*, the name of the son of Woden in the *Chronicle* pedigree, with the Scandinavian *Balder*, and the spelling of the name of Woden as *Vuothen*, demonstrate, in their modest way, an interest in emphasizing the shared past of the English and Scandinavian peoples, and it is not surprising to see this emphasis emerge more overtly in the conclusion of the royal pedigree.

Most discussions of the longer royal pedigree assume that the written version reflects dynastic claims that the West Saxons were spreading among both the native English and the Danish settlers. But if this were the case, no trace of these claims survives other than the genealogy itself. It seems unlikely that this unwieldy and unfinished genealogy would have had much oral currency. If the Scylding lineage of the West Saxon kings was presented to the populace at large, it probably would have been through intermediary oral forms: perhaps shortened versions of the pedigree, or the use of epithets such as "Ælfred Scyldinga," or perhaps through poetry. It is this latter possibility that has fueled arguments that *Beowulf* borrowed its opening genealogy from the West Saxon pedigree, and that the poem served to promote this pedigree and the political and cultural union of the English and the Danes. But if these genealogical claims are reflected in *Beowulf*, why are they absent from tenth-century chronicle poems such as the *Battle of Brunanburh* and *The Capture of the Five Boroughs*, poems that praise the deeds of the very royal dynasty claiming descent from Scyld? *Brunanburh*, after all, celebrates an English victory at a time when this dynasty was ruling Danes as well as Saxons and Mercians. The opportunity for a reference to royal descent from Scyld is even stronger in *The Capture of the Five Boroughs*, a poem that presents Edmund as a *wiggendra hleo* 'protector of warriors' (l. 12) who has rescued the Danes from the oppression of the heathen Northmen.[55] The epithet *eodor Scyldinga* 'protector of the Scyldings' would have fitted naturally into either of these poems.

---

[54] Campbell, *The Chronicle of Æthelweard*, 34. Jezierski, "Æthelweard Redivivus," 170.
[55] *The Capture of the Five Boroughs* is cited from *The Anglo-Saxon Minor Poems*, ed. Elliot van Kirk Dobbie, vol. 6 of *The Anglo-Saxon Poetic Records* (New York: Columbia University Press, 1942), 20–1.

A comparison of this claim of descent from Scyld with the West Saxon dynasty's claim to rule over Angles as well as Saxons strongly suggests that this genealogical claim was probably stillborn, and had no historical or literary influence. At some point by the mid-880s, Alfred became the ruler of western Mercia.[56] This expansion of power is reflected in the titles attributed to him in written sources. In charters he is titled *rex Anglorum et Saxonum* or the like, in the entry for 900 in the *Chronicle* that records his death he is described as "cyning ofer eall Ongelcyn," and in Asser he is repeatedly presented as *Angul-Saxonum rex*.[57] It is also possible that similar titles were included on coins: one surviving coin styles him as *rex SM*, presumably an abbreviation for *rex Saxonum et Merciorum*, and another presents him as *rex Anglo*, perhaps standing for *rex Anglorum*.[58] The use of such titles was continued by Alfred's son Edward the Elder, especially in his charters.[59] Moreover, this claim is reflected elsewhere, even when it is not presented explicitly. The treaty between Alfred and Guthrum establishes a peace not only between these two rulers but also between "ealles Angelcynnes witan 7 eal seo ðeod ðe on Eastænglum beoð."[60] In the Preface to his law code Alfred claims that he drew not only on the laws of his predecessor Ine, but also on the codes of Æthelbryht the king of Kent and of Offa king of Mercia, a claim designed to provide his laws with legitimacy over his entire realm.[61]

When it was first presented in the *Chronicle*, the claim of descent from Scyld was entirely prospective, a claim made in the hopes that it would one day help legitimize West Saxon rule over the Danish settlers. This rule was achieved, of course, during the reigns of Edward, Æthelstan and Edmund.[62] The English absorption of the Danelaw is analogous to the extension of Alfred's authority over western Mercia. In both cases there was a recent expansion of rule that needed to be reinforced and supported by any available means. The variety of sources that present or

[56] Simon Keynes, "King Alfred and the Mercians," in *Kings, Currency and Alliances: History and Coinage of Southern England in the Ninth Century*, ed. Mark A.S. Blackburn and David N. Dumville (Woodbridge: The Boydell Press, 1998), 1–45, at 12–13, argues on the basis of the five years assigned to Ceolwulf in the Mercian regnal list that Ceolwulf ruled until 879.

[57] Keynes, "King Alfred and the Mercians," 25–6; Simon Keynes and Michael Lapidge, trans., *Alfred the Great: Asser's* Life of King Alfred *and Other Contemporary Sources* (New York: Penguin Books, 1983), 38–41 and 227, n. 1.

[58] Keynes, "King Alfred and the Mercians," 18, 16.

[59] Simon Keynes, "The West Saxon Charters of King Æthelwulf and His Sons," *The English Historical Review* 109 (1994): 1109–49. See p. 1148 n. 4 for a list of the charters of Edward in which he is presented in this style.

[60] Keynes, "King Alfred and the Mercians," 31. The treaty is cited from F. Liebermann, *Die Gesetze der Angelsachsen*, vol. 1 (Halle: Niemeyer, 1903–16), 126–8.

[61] Keynes, "King Alfred and the Mercians," 40.

[62] Stenton, *Anglo-Saxon England*, 320–63.

reflect Alfred's claim to be king of the Angles as well as the Saxons illustrates the range of resources that were available to the dynasty for the promulgation of their political claims. Yet apart from Æthelwulf's pedigree in the *Chronicle* and those texts directly derived from this pedigree we do not encounter any references to Scyld as an ancestor of the West Saxon dynasty: there is nothing in poetry, nor in charters, in the laws, on coins, nor even in other entries of the *Chronicle* itself.

Given the potentially unwelcome implications of the inclusion of Scyld in Æthelwulf's pedigree, the absence of any references to the dynasty's descent from Scyld in the surviving texts apart from copies of the genealogy itself is not surprising. During the 870s and 880s, when the very survival of Wessex at times appeared to hang in the balance, this rather quixotic attempt to connect Alfred and his family to the eponymous ancestor of the Scyldings apparently seemed worth trying. But the surviving evidence suggests that it was a project that never gained traction and was ultimately abandoned. There is, first of all, the lack of finish, the incompletion of the biblical section. Then there is the rather striking restriction of this expanded royal pedigree to the entry for 855 within the *Chronicle* itself. If this genealogy reflected an active dynastic policy we would expect to see the expansions it includes added onto Cerdic's pedigree in the entries for 554 and 597 and in the West Saxon Genealogical Regnal List. Although the West Saxon Regnal List was probably edited during the reign of Alfred, and the copies of this list that appeared in conjunction with the *Chronicle* were altered to agree with some aspects of the *Chronicle* genealogies,[63] Cerdic's pedigree in this list concludes with Woden, as it does in the entries for 554 and 597. We would also expect to find some echo of this longer genealogy elsewhere, and the absence of this echo is quite telling. Further evidence for the abandonment of this genealogy as a political tool lies in Æthelweard's revision and reduction of the pedigree. We encounter here a clear exception to the observation that literary genealogies are rarely shortened after they have been expanded. If Æthelwulf's pedigree was an integral and useful part of the identity of the royal dynasty, it is highly unlikely that Æthelweard would have altered it as freely as he did.

The concluding stage of the West Saxon pedigree was constructed in an attempt to balance and contain the potential subordination implied by Scyld's presence while activating the cultural energy he represents. It is unlikely that this containment would have been attempted if Scyld,

---

[63] Dumville, "The West Saxon Genealogical Regnal List," 17: "However, none of these witnesses gives an absolutely complete copy of this text which probably originated, in its present form, in the reign of King Alfred; it concludes in the most primitive surviving version with a notice of his accession."

Beow and Sceaf were not already familiar to the genealogists from heroic poetry as well as from folklore. The Christianization of the arrival of the infant Sceaf from across the water by placing him in Noah's ark was a brilliant stroke that also framed and contained Scyld, simultaneously presenting him as a descendant of the apical Germanic ancestor Sceaf and deriving the lineage and authority of the West Saxon kings from the Old Testament. But as we have seen, the opening presentation of Scyld in *Beowulf* as the originary, apical ancestor of the Danes and the reduction of Sceaf to an epithet completely contradicts the central strategy of the royal pedigree, which presents Sceaf as the originary ancestor, reducing Scyld to one ancestor among others: an important, heroic, and illustrious ancestor, to be sure, and one shared by both the West Saxons and the Danes, but hardly the most important figure in the genealogy. This difference in strategy reflects the more significant underlying difference in purpose. Scyld and Sceaf are included in the royal pedigree in order to glorify the West Saxon dynasty and to advance the political and cultural agenda of this dynasty. In contrast, the introduction of Scyld Scefing at the beginning of the poem glorifies the Scylding dynasty and the expansion of the Danish kingdom under Scyld and his descendants. There is no reflected lustre here for Alfred and his family, no appropriation of Danish glory for West Saxon purposes. Indeed, as Craig Davis has argued, the poem as a whole, not just the beginning, presents a fairly consistent Danish perspective on the relations among northern peoples.[64] There is nothing that even remotely resembles an English perspective in the poem. The passage that praises the Offa (1944–62) whom the Mercian royal genealogy presents as an Anglian ancestor of the Mercian kings[65] has at most an oblique, entirely understated connection to England: the praise of the continental Offa can serve as indirect praise for Offa the eighth-century King of Mercia and/or his dynasty. But this Anglian Offa is an uncontested figure, and his role in the poem does not substantially differ from his role in the Mercian pedigree, where the antiquity and legitimacy of the ruling family is demonstrated through the inclusion of ancestors who ruled the Anglian homeland.

In contrast, the West Saxon claim of Scyld as a royal ancestor transformed him into a highly contested figure. As a result his adoption into the West Saxon royal pedigree generated a genealogy that needed to contain him as well as include him. Everything in this stretch of the pedigree, especially the presence of Beow and Sceaf, and the identification of Sceaf as the originary royal ancestor who was born in the ark or who arrived alone in a boat from over the sea, contributes to the carefully

---

[64] Davis, "Ethnic Dating," 127.
[65] Dumville, "The Anglian Collection," 30, 33, 36.

constructed containment of Scyld. The praise of Scyld at the beginning of *Beowulf* could not double as oblique praise for an Anglo-Saxon king the way the praise of Offa does because the Scyld portrayed in the poem is in many respects the opposite of the figure presented in the West Saxon royal pedigree. This Scyld is uncontained in every way: he possesses the glory that is assigned to Sceaf in the pedigree as the dynastic founder, and he is thus both the apical ancestor of a dynasty of strong, effective kings and the founder who through his own vigorous actions establishes the continuing pattern of Danish expansion and the conquest of neighboring peoples. It is easy to imagine this portrayal receiving a favorable response in the Danelaw, but it would not be a response that would advance the political goals of Alfred or his descendants. The Scylding genealogy at the beginning of *Beowulf* and the inclusion of Sceldwa, Sceaf, and Beaw in the West Saxon royal pedigree are the products of different historical and cultural periods. The opening fitt was not designed to serve any West Saxon political purpose, nor was it derived from the royal pedigree.

7

History and Fiction in the Frisian Raid[1]

Frederick M. Biggs

Beowulf is a remarkable poem to have been written at any time. Around 3,200 lines of linguistically and metrically sophisticated poetry that sets "two moments in a great life," in J.R.R. Tolkien's phrase,[2] into a distant past and conveys a profound respect for the hero's actions while at the same time expressing a sense of the loss and futility of that world, is a remarkable achievement. A poem not of an age, but for all time. Which is not to say that it is undatable or that its date does not matter. Even without external evidence such as manuscripts and editions, we would recognize that well-known accounts of the deeds of three northern European heroes from around the year 500 – Beowulf, Arthur, and Hamlet – were written by their authors – our poet, Malory, and Shakespeare – at very different times, and recognizing their historical contexts is essential to any real appreciation of them. The reverse is also true. In the absence of precise evidence for a particular date of composition, understanding the meaning of the poem can help us to locate its likely place in history. My claim is that succession, or more precisely a change in the rules of succession brought about by the conversion of the Anglo-Saxons to Christianity, is a major theme in *Beowulf*.[3] The poet explores a shift from an older "Germanic" system in which many members of a kin-group are eligible for the throne to a newer "Christian" one, which limits the

---

[1] I would like to thank Lindy Brady and Brandon Hawk for improving this essay.
[2] Tolkien, "*Beowulf*: The Monsters and the Critics," *Proceedings of the British Academy* 22 (1936): 245–95; repr. in Beowulf: *A Verse Translation*, Norton Critical Edition, trans. Seamus Heaney, ed. Daniel Donoghue (New York: W.W. Norton, 2002), 103–30, at 124.
[3] For a recent study, which addresses this theme and reviews previous scholarship on the poem's use of historical material, see Francis Leneghan, "The Poetic Purpose of the Offa Digression in *Beowulf*," *Review of English Studies* ns 60 (2009): 538–60. While I agree with much of Leneghan's discussion, I would argue not that the poet uses historical material to comment on the hero's life, but that he uses both this material and Beowulf's deeds to reflect on the theme of succession.

contenders and favors the succession of sons.[4] While this change could have been addressed at any point following the arrival of Christianity, it would have been more relevant and so more likely to be treated as its effects were felt early in the Anglo-Saxon period.

The *Beowulf* poet, as I have argued elsewhere,[5] explores this shift in a number of his fictions including Ecgþeow, Breca, Hondschioh, Æschere, Weohstan, Wiglaf, and the female Geatish mourner; let me summarize these arguments by mentioning only Grendel, Grendel's mother, and the dragon. As apt images for kin-violence, the first two express the conflicts likely to occur when there are too many successors for the throne. Although in defeating them Beowulf appears to cleanse Heorot, by involving him in the Danish succession through the gifts Hroðgar gives him, the poet aligns him with the problem: Beowulf is yet one more contender to succeed Hroðgar in a court where there are already too many. Similarly, the dragon, hoarder of treasure, articulates the end of a royal line where there is no heir to the kingdom. In dying without a son, Beowulf embodies this problem as well. In these fictions, then, the poet not only presents the life of a hero, but also examines two dangers that can confront a people when a king dies: internal strife seems all but inevitable when many members of a kin group vie for power, or foreign enemies appear likely to attack if there is no clear successor.

This same theme, I would like to argue here, controls the poet's use of the most certain historical event discussed in *Beowulf*, Hygelac's death in a raid in Frisia. This moment, as R.W. Chambers suggested long ago,[6] marks, at least for the poet,[7] the historical end of the Geatish line and so

---

[4] For a discussion of historical evidence that supports this claim, see my "The Politics of Succession in *Beowulf* and Anglo-Saxon England," *Speculum* 80 (2005): 709–41, at 712–19.

[5] In addition to the article cited in the previous note, see also my "The *Dream of the Rood* and *Guthlac B* as a Literary Context for the Monsters in *Beowulf*," in *Text, Image, Interpretation: Studies in Anglo-Saxon Literature and its Insular Context in Honour of Éamonn Ó Carragáin*, ed. Alastair Minnis and Jane Roberts (Turnhout: Brepols, 2007), 289–301; "Hondscioh and Æschere in *Beowulf*," *Neophilologus* 87 (2003): 635–52; "Beowulf and some Fictions of the Geatish Succession," *Anglo-Saxon England* 32 (2003): 55–77; "Beowulf's Fight with the Nine Nicors," *Review of English Studies* ns 53 (2002): 311–28; and "The Naming of Beowulf and Ecgtheow's Feud," *Philological Quarterly* 80 (2001): 95–112.

[6] R.W. Chambers, Beowulf: *An Introduction to the Study of the Poem with a Discussion of the Stories of Offa and Finn*, 2nd ed. (Cambridge: University Press, 1932), 13.

[7] Unlike the vivid portrayal of three generations of Geatish kings in *Beowulf*, the historical record about these people remains obscure; in addition to Chambers, *Introduction*, 1–13, see Robert T. Farrell, Beowulf: *Swedes and Geats* (London: Viking Society for Northern Research, University College London, 1972) and the assessment in *Klaeber's* Beowulf: *Fourth Edition*, ed. R.D. Fulk, Robert E. Bjork, and John D. Niles (Toronto: University of Toronto Press, 2008) [henceforth *Klaeber's* Beowulf], lix–lxvii. Even assuming, as most do, that the Geats correspond to the Scandinavian Gautar, it is

parallels Beowulf's death in the fictional conclusion of the work: both kings die without an heir capable of assuming power since Heardred lacks experience and Beowulf has no son. Yet his decision to carry the story of the Geats past the Frisian raid where he depicts their history as ending, while focusing on the raid as that end, causes the poet a narrative problem,[8] which he solves by recounting this event differently at five separate points in the work. In doing so he is able both to emphasize that the raid is a devastating historical failure for the Geats and to introduce the fictional details, especially Beowulf's survival, that allow him to continue his story and explore its significance. In itself, Hygelac's death presents a dramatic end to the other presumably historical events in the Geatish past: Herebeald's accidental slaying of his brother Hæðcyn, Hreðel's death from grief over this tragedy, and Hæðcyn's own death in the Swedish conflicts. Although other sources do not allow us to confirm these details as historical, they appear to be as much a part of the poet's knowledge of the past as the raid itself, raising the possibility that he has selected not just the raid but the larger historical setting for its metaphoric potential. An old story of a royal line that dwindles and finally dies out when a son is not ready to follow his father to the throne allows the poet to explore a weakness that he sees in a political change happening in his own day.

The Sources of the Frisian Raid

As Augustine Thompson has argued,[9] there are three largely independent sources for Hygelac's death in Frisia: Gregory of Tours' *Historia*

---

not clear when they would have lost their distinct political identity. Yet it seems more likely to me that the *Beowulf* poet thought that Hygelac's death marked a significant point in that process than that he would invoke their history so prominently to misrepresent it.

[8] In contrast, the historical problems that confront the Danes, Hroðulf's likely killing of Hreðric and Hroðmund as he assumes power following Hroðgar's death and violence surrounding Freawaru's failed marriage to Ingeld, both lie in the future. For other views on this matter, see the note on ll. 1017–19 in *Klaeber's* Beowulf, and my "Politics," 710 n. 4.

[9] Thompson, "Rethinking Hygelac's Raid," *ELN* 38 (2001): 9–16. In proposing three sources for the event, Thompson effectively challenges the two-source theory of Francis P. Magoun, "Beowulf and Hygelac in the Netherlands," *English Studies* 35 (1954): 193–204. Yet, while mentioning Walter Goffart's "*Hetware* and *Hugas*: Datable Anachronisms in *Beowulf*" (in *The Dating of* Beowulf, ed. Colin Chase (Toronto: University of Toronto Press, 1981), 83–100), he does not address its claims that the Old English poem draws specifically on the *Liber Historiae Francorum* for its account of the Frisian raid and that the tribal name "Hugas" mentioned in connection with it is best explained by the control of Neustria in the late ninth century by Hugh the Abbot and in the second quarter of the tenth century by Hugh the Great. For a refutation of the

Francorum, which in turn underlies the *Liber Historiae Francorum*; Frisian oral tradition, which is represented by the *Liber Monstrorum*, but which also influenced the *Historiae Francorum*; and English oral tradition represented by *Beowulf*. (Unlike earlier critics, particularly Francis P. Magoun, Thompson discounts any direct influence of the Old English poem on the *Liber Monstrorum*).[10] While containing one major inaccuracy, the identification of the raiders as Danes rather than Geats,[11] the *Historia Francorum*, written some fifty years after the event of around 520,[12] provides the most historically accurate account:

> His ita gestis, Dani cum rege suo nomen Chlochilaichum evectu navale per mare Gallias appetunt. Egressique ad terras, pagum unum de regno Theudorici devastant atque captivant, oneratisque navibus tam de captivis quam de reliquis spoliis, reverti ad patriam cupiunt; sed rex eorum in litus resedebat, donec navis alto mare conpraehenderent, ipse deinceps secuturus. Quod cum Theudorico nuntiatum fuisset, quod scilicet regio eius fuerit ab extraneis devastata, Theudobertum, filium suum, in illis partibus cum valido exercitu ac magno armorum apparatu direxit. Qui, interfectu rege, hostibus navali proelio superatis oppraemit omnemque rapinam terrae restituit.[13]

(When these things had thus transpired, the Danes, along with their king, by the name of Chlochilaichus, approached Gaul over the sea with naval transport. Upon disembarking, they laid waste a district of the kingdom of Theudoricus, and with their ships freighted equally with captives and other spoils, they desired to return to their own country. But their king remained ashore until the ships should reach the high seas, whereupon he would follow. When this was reported to Theudoricus, i.e. that his kingdom had been devastated by invaders, he directed his son to the area with a powerful and well-equipped

---

first claim, see Tom Shippey, "The Merov(ich)ingian Again: *damnatio memoria* and the *usus scholarum*," in *Latin Learning and English Lore: Studies in Anglo-Saxon Literature for Michael Lapidge*, 2 vols., ed. Katherine O'Brien O'Keeffe and Andy Orchard (Toronto: University of Toronto Press, 2005), 1: 388–404. While not impossible, the second seems less likely than the traditional, if doubted, connection of the Hugas with the ancient Chauci; for further references, see *Klaeber's* Beowulf, lx. In my view, Thompson's approach, which allows for oral traditions, is more plausible than Goffart's, which stresses written sources, since poems like *Deor* and *Widsið*, in addition to *Beowulf*, suggest that this material circulated orally, as does the correspondences of names such as Chlochilaichus/Hygelac and even Attoarii/Hetware.

[10] See also Andy Orchard, *Pride and Prodigies: Studies in the Monsters of the* Beowulf-*Manuscript* (Cambridge: D.S. Brewer, 2003), 86–115.
[11] Thompson attributes this mistake to Gregory's lack of information about events in the north and "the assimilation of the Geats into the Swedes in the mid-sixth century"; "Rethinking," 12.
[12] This approximate date is inferred from Gregory's chronology.
[13] *Gregorii Episcopi Turonensis Historiarum Libri X*, 2nd ed., ed. Bruno Krusch, Monumenta Germaniae Historica, Scriptores rerum Merovingicarum 1.1 (Hanover: Hahnsche Buchhandlung, 1937), 99.

army. Once he had killed the king, Theudobertus crushed the overwhelmed enemy in a naval battle and restored all that had been taken from the land.)[14]

The *Liber Historiae Francorum* (ca. 725) derives from Gregory's account but adds one detail, identifying Hygelac as King of the Geats (although this name has been marked for deletion), that corrects the *Historia Francorum* and another, specifying one of his opponents as the Attoarii, that appears to improve it by representing more accurate local tradition:

> In illo tempore Dani cum rege suo [rege Gotorum (*expunct. et superscr. sec. m.* suo) nomine] nomine Chochilaico cum navale hoste per alto mare Gallias appetent, Theuderico paygo Attoarios vel alios devastantes atque captivantes, plenas naves de captivis alto mare intrantes, rex eorum ad litus maris resedens. Quod cum Theuderico nuntiatum fuisset, Theudobertum, filium suum, cum magno exercitu in illis partibus dirigens. Qui consequens eos, pugnavit cum eis caede magna atque prostravit, regem eorum interficit, preda tullit et in terra sua restituit.[15]

> (At that time the Danes with their king (*var.* king of the Goti), whose name was Chochilaic, attacked Gaul by sea with a naval force, ravaging the land of Theuderic, of the Attoarii, and others, and taking prisoners, the ships full of prisoners entering the high sea, their king remaining ashore. When this was reported to Theuderic, he sent his son Theudebert with a large force into those parts. Pursuing them, the latter fought with them with much slaughter and overwhelmed (them), killing their king, took (back) the booty and returned (it) to his country.)[16]

Finally, the *Liber Monstrorum*, which Thompson dates to around 700 and, following Michael Lapidge, considers of English origin, perhaps from Malmesbury,[17] provides a striking confirmation of the raid since it mentions Hygelac's death in a different context, a record of king's monstrous size:

> Et fiunt monstra mirae magnitudinis, ut rex Higlacus, qui imperauit Getis et a Francis occisus est, quem equus a duodecimo aetatis anno portare non potuit. Cuius ossa in Rheni fluminis insula, ubi in Oceanum prorumpit, reseruata sunt, et de longinquo uenientibus pro miraculo ostenduntur.

> (And there are monsters of prodigious size, such as King Higlacus, who ruled the Getae and was killed by the Franks, whom, once he reached the age of twelve, no horse was able to bear. His bones are preserved on an island in the

---

[14] The translation is from *Klaeber's* Beowulf, 310.
[15] *Fredegarii et aliorum chronica. Vitae Sanctorum*, ed. Bruno Krusch, Monumenta Germaniae Historica, Scriptores rerum Merovingicarum 2 (Hanover: Hahnsche Buchhandlung, 1888), 274–5.
[16] G. Storms, "The Significance of Hygelac's Raid," *Nottingham Mediaeval Studies* 14 (1970): 3–26, at 8.
[17] Michael Lapidge, "*Beowulf*, Aldhelm, the *Liber Monstrorum*, and Wessex," *Studi medievali* 3rd ser., 23 (1982): 151–92. Lapidge dates the work to "*c.* 650 x *c.* 750" (164–5).

river Rhine where it empties into the sea, and they are shown to visitors from afar as a wonder.)[18]

To this surprisingly detailed and largely consistent information may be added other possible references to Hygelac. Perhaps most relevant for my argument since it points to conflicts between the Geats and Swedes is Saxo Grammaticus's brief mention of a Danish king, Huglek, "qui Hømothum et Høgrimum Suetię tyrannos maritimo fertur oppressisse conflictu"[19] ("who crushed the Swedish despots, Omoth and Øgrim in a sea-skirmish").[20] Drawing on this background, Thompson proposes that "Hygelac's raid probably passed into Frankish history" and, one might add, into the more general knowledge of early medieval northern Europe "because of the stature of its leader, its size, and that for once the Frankish host could boast of defeating one of those elusive parties of Northmen."[21]

Yet, while I accept Thompson's conclusion that *Beowulf* is an independent source of information for the raid, he gives, in my opinion, a false impression of its historical reliability when he claims that the poet's use of tribal names "suggests a clear knowledge of the course of the fighting;"[22] instead, I would argue that taken together they convey the impression of a powerful enemy. As Thompson presents it, the poet,

> uses "Frisian" for the area the Geats attack and sack (*Beowulf* 1207a and 2915b) and for the site of the battle (l. 2357b). He uses "Hugas," an epic title, for the whole of Hygelac's foes (ll. 1220a and 2914b). Haettware appear only in his description of the victorious Frankish host (ll. 1216a, 2364a).[23]

From this he concludes: "This use of names would be logical if the Geats initially attacked the Frisian coast, reached Frankish-Haettware territory on the journey inland, encountered resistance, and headed to the coast with a Frankish-Haettware host in hot pursuit."[24] At the beginning of his speech, however, the horseman, who announces Beowulf's death to the Geats and predicts their destruction, uses Frisian not as a place name but as a people comparable to the Franks:

---

[18] Orchard, *Pride*, 258–9.
[19] Saxo Grammaticus, *Gesta Danorum: Danmarkshistorien*, 2 vols., ed. Karsten Friis-Jensen, trans. Peter Zeeberg (Copenhagen: Det Danske Sprog- og Litteraturselskab, Gad, 2005), 1.270.
[20] *The History of the Danes*, trans. Peter Fisher, ed. Hilda Ellis Davidson, 2 vols. (Cambridge: D.S. Brewer, 1979–80), 1.110. The note asserts that the identification with Hygelac "is by no means certain" and provides references to the other possible references to him; 2.70, n. 41. See also *Klaeber's* Beowulf, lxi.
[21] Thompson, "Rethinking," 11.
[22] Thompson, "Rethinking," 13.
[23] Thompson, "Rethinking," 13.
[24] Thompson, "Rethinking," 13.

>   Nu ys leodum wen
> orleghwile,   syððan underne
> Froncum ond Frysum   fyll cyninges
> wide weorðeð. (2911b–14a)[25]
>
> (Now this folk may expect
> a time of trouble, when this is manifest
> to the Franks and Frisians, and the fall of our king
> becomes widespread news.)[26]

Moreover, earlier in the poem Beowulf suggests a more complicated relationship among these tribes when he identifies Dæghrefn (itself a Frankish name) as a "Huga cempan" (2502b; "a champion of the Hugas"), who is unable to bring the spoils, including the neck-ring to which I will return later, he has won by defeating Hyglac not to his own king but to the Frisan ruler:

> nalles he ða frætwe   Frescyninge,
> breostweorðunge   bringan moste … (2503–4).
>
> (He could not carry off to the Frisian king
> that battle-armor and that breast-adornment …)

Finally, there is a fifth name, Merewioing,[27] not considered by Thompson but used by the horseman to conclude his comment about the Raid: "Us wæs a syððan // Merewioingas milts ungyfeðe" (2920b–1; "Ever after that the Merovingians have not shown mercy to us"). The dynastic name underlines the point of this litotes – the Geats' destruction at the time of Hygelac's death was complete and will be again – as it absorbs all of the tribes into one threatening force. These names, then, provide a first indication that the poet does not intend to present a historically accurate account of the encounter, which might encourage us to accept all of his details as true, but rather that he uses a general knowledge of it for his own purpose.

Before turning specifically to *Beowulf*, let me summarize what I would view as the three main points for my argument to be taken from the historical record. In this conflict, Hygelac, king of the Geats, dies; his company is destroyed; and the goods he had plundered remain with the victors. While there may be other details that the poet has taken from history, these are the basic facts to which he was drawn for their metaphoric potential and into which he wove his fiction of Beowulf's survival.

---

[25] Quotations of the poem are from *Klaeber's* Beowulf; diacritics and indications of editorial intervention have been removed.

[26] Translations are from Beowulf: *A New Verse Translation*, trans. R. M. Liuzza (Peterborough, Ont.: Broadview Press, 2000).

[27] See Shippey, "Merov(ich)ingian."

Beowulf's Frisian Raids

The poet varies the details he presents in the five passages in *Beowulf* that refer to the Frisian raid so he can distinguish the historical core of the event from his fictional elaborations and so he can connect both the history and his fictions to the theme of succession.[28] In the first, which occurs surprisingly in the Danish section of the poem, he both emphasizes its main historical facts by focusing on Hygelac and prepares for his later fictional elaborations by introducing it in the context of Wealhþeow's gift of a spectacular neck-ring to the hero. This passage is most obviously in striking contrast to later accounts since it contains no mention of Beowulf:

> Þone hring hæfde   Higelac Geata,
> nefa Swertinges   nyhstan siðe,
> siðþan he under segne   sinc ealgode,
> wælreaf werede;   hyne wyrd fornam
> syþðan he for wlenco   wean ahsode,
> fæhðe to Frysum.   He þa frætwe wæg,
> eorclanstanas   ofer yða ful,
> rice þeoden;   he under rande gecranc.
> Gehwearf þa in Francna fæþme   feorh cyninges,
> breostgewædu,   ond se beah somod.
> Wyrsan wigfrecan   wæl reafeden
> æfter guðsceare;   Geata leode
> hreawic heoldon.   (1202–14a)

> (Hygelac the Geat on his last journey
> had that neck-ring, nephew of Swerting,
> when under the banner he defended his booty,
> the spoils of slaughter. Fate struck him down
> when in his pride he went looking for woe,
> a feud with the Frisians. He wore that finery,
> those precious stones, over the cup of the sea,
> that powerful lord, and collapsed under his shield.
> Into Frankish hands came the life of that king,
> his breast garments, and the great collar too;
> a lesser warrior looted the corpses
> mown down in battle; Geatish men
> held that killing field.)

The focus here is on Hygelac's death: this is his last journey, fate struck him down, he collapsed under his shield, his life came into Frankish hands, and his corpse is looted. Yet the last clause extends his tragedy to his people more generally. While "Geata leode hreawic heoldon"

---

[28] He uses a similar strategy in the two versions of the Breca story; see my "Beowulf's Fight."

seems momentarily to mean that the Geats won ("they held the place of slaughter"), a more grim reality is quickly apparent: "their bodies covered the battlefield."[29] Finally, the passage notes the Geats' loss of their treasure as Hygelac dies defending his "booty, the spoils of slaughter." Aside from the neck-ring, this passage fits easily into the historical tradition of the *Historia Francorum*, the *Liber Historiae Francorum*, and the *Liber Monstrorum*.

Yet even as the poet establishes a historical baseline for the Frisian raid, he includes what I would argue is a fictional detail, the neck-ring, to allow the audience to distinguish between history and his own elaborations of it since he will provide two contradictory accounts of its fate. Indeed, he alerts us to this strategy by comparing the jewel itself to a famous gem from the Germanic past, the Brosinga mene:

> Nænigne ic under swegle   selran hyrde
> hordmaððum hæleþa   syþðan Hama ætwæg
> to þære byrhtan byrig   Brosinga mene,
> sigle ond sincfæat –   searoniðas fleah
> Eormenrices,   geceas ecne ræd. (ll. 1197–1201)
>
> (Under heaven I have not heard tell of a better
> hoard-treasure of heroes, since Hama carried off
> to the bright city the Brosinga necklace,
> the gem and its treasures; he fled the treachery
> of Eormanric, chose eternal counsel.)

This passage is obscure, yet seems to combine the medieval depiction of the historical Eormenric, the late fourth-century king of the East Goths, as a cruel and avaricious tyrant and the mythical story of Freyja's necklace.[30] If so, the poet alerts the audience to the roles that fictional objects may play in historical narratives. In any case, this allusion should encourage us to follow carefully the fate of Wealhþeow's gift, which here is unambiguously said to pass into Frankish hands at Hygelac's death.

Finally, the context of this first passage about the Frisian raid is significant for my larger argument since it links the event to the theme of succession. Wealhþeow gives her gift to Beowulf during the feast following the defeat of Grendel, where her own speeches, which have attracted much attention,[31] appear to speak to the impending crisis in the Danish succession when Hroðulf treats Hreðric and Hroðmund poorly on his way to the throne. By alluding here to Hygelac's death, which of course

---

[29] This is the gloss offered in the note on 1213b–14a in *Klaeber's* Beowulf, which discusses similar passages and another interpretation of this clause.
[30] See the note on 1197–1201 in *Klaeber's* Beowulf.
[31] See the note on 1169 ff in *Klaeber's* Beowulf.

has no bearing on the Danish succession and indeed no relevance for this part of the poem, the poet prepares us to see it as related to a crisis in the Geatish succession.

The next mention of the Frisian raid is only a phrase, and so often overlooked in discussions on this topic; yet the passage in which it occurs deserves attention since it provides a first seemingly factual account of Beowulf's becoming king. As I have argued in more detail elsewhere,[32] the context is significant: immediately before it, Beowulf gives the Danish treasure he has received from Hroðgar to Hygelac and Wealhþeow's neck-ring to Hygd, receiving in return Hreðel's sword, seven thousand hides of land, and a throne; and the passage itself leads into the first mention of the dragon's ravages, which of course bring Beowulf's reign to an end. The lines themselves, however, appear simply factual:

> Eft þæt geiode   ufaran dogrum
> hildehlæmmum,   syððan Hygelac læg,
> ond Heardrede   hildemeceas
> under bordhreoðan   to bonan wurdon,
> ða hyne gesohtan   on sigeþeode
> hearde hildefrecan,   Heaðo-Scilfingas,
> niða genægdan   nefan Hererices:
> syððan Beowulfe   brade rice
> on hand gehwearf ... (ll. 2200–2208a)

> (Then it came to pass amid the crash of battle
> in later days, after Hygelac lay dead
> and for Heardred the swords of battle held
> deadly slaughter under the shield-wall,
> when the Battle-Scylfings sought him out,
> those hardy soldiers, and savagely struck down
> the nephew of Hereric in his victorious nation –
> then came the broad kingdom
> into Beowulf's hands ...)

This passage repeats the basic historical fact of the Frisian raid: Hygelac dies. Yet it also connects his death with Heardred's, which occurs when the Swedes attack him, and both of these with Beowulf's ascension to the throne. Indeed, since it is so short, the passage implies that all three events take place at the same time and so offers a plausible explanation of Beowulf's rise to power – one that the poet then complicates in his next discussion of the raid.

In the third retelling of the Frisian raid the poet's fictional elaborations appear prominently, indeed so prominently that they raise the

---

[32] See my "Politics" for the argument that the poet presents Beowulf's coming to the throne first as a joint-king with Hroðgar and then, in the passage discussed here, following Heardred's death.

possibility that the following account of the deeds of the Swedish princes Eanmund and Eadgils, which complicates the issue of when Heardred actually dies, is his own creation rather than part of the historical record as he knew it. The passages that lead up to this retelling shift toward the fabulous. Beowulf learns that the dragon has burned his hall, wonders momentarily (and uncharacteristically) if he has angered God, and orders an iron-shield made to protect him (ll. 2323–42); the poet informs us that Beowulf scorns the thought of bringing a host to this conflict with the dragon and does not fear it since he had survived the fight with Grendel. It is against these fights with monsters that the Frisian raid is introduced:

> No þæt læsest wæs
> hondgemota   þær mon Hygelac sloh,
> syððan Geata cyning   guðe ræsum,
> freawine folca   Freslondum on,
> Hreðles eafora   hiorodryncum swealt,
> bille gebeaten.   Þonan Biowulf com
> sylfes cræfte,   sundnytte dreah;
> hæfde him on earme   ealra þritig
> hildegeatwa   þa he to holme þrong.
> Nealles Hetware   hremge þorfton
> feðewiges,   þe him foran ongean
> linde bæron;   lyt eft becwom
> fram þam hildfrecan   hames niosan.
> Oferswam ða sioleða bigong   sunu Ecgðeowes,
> earm anhaga   eft to leodum …   (ll. 2354b–68)

(It was not the least
of hand-to-hand combats when Hygelac was slain,
when the king of the Geats, in the chaos of battle,
the lord of his people, in the land of the Frisians,
the son of Hrethel, died sword-drunk,
beaten by blades. Beowulf escaped from there
through his own strength, took a long swim;
he had in his arms the battle-armor
of thirty men, when he climbed to the cliffs.
By no means did the Hetware need to exult
in that fight, when they marched on foot to him,
bore their linden shields; few came back
from that brave soldier to seek their homes.
The son of Ecgtheow crossed the vast sea,
wretched, solitary, returned to his people …)

Although some scholars have tried to minimize the fabulous nature of Beowulf's actions here, the editors of *Klaeber's Beowulf* assert that "the unmarked meaning of *swimman*" (l. 2367b; translated by Roy Liuzza as "crossed") is "swim:"[33] Beowulf returns alone from Frisia to the land of the Geats with thirty suits of armor not by boat but in the water. Moreover, the emphasis here is more equally on the Frisian/Frankish slaughter since "few" of them returned to their homes. While this detail may resolve one of the "disturbing questions" – why does Beowulf not avenge Hygelac's death? – that John McNamara sees as arising from this account,[34] the answer – he does since he kills all of the enemy – is so implausible that it too calls attention to itself as fiction. This account, then, jars with what we already know about the raid and focuses our attention on Beowulf's role in these events.

In the following passages, the poet carries his fiction beyond the historical end of the Geats, turning specifically to the issue of succession. In the first, I would argue, he examines the Christian model of selecting kings, which favors the sons, stressing the weakness of the Geats following Hygelac's death by having Hygd offer Beowulf the throne:

> … þær him Hygd gebead   hord ond rice,
> beagas ond bregostol;   bearne ne truwode,
> þæt he wið ælfylcum   eþelstolas
> healdan cuðe,   ða wæs Hygelac dead.
> No ðy ær feasceafte   findan meahton
> æt ðam æðelinge   ænige ðinga
> þæt he Heardrede   hlaford wære,
> oððe þone cynedom   ciosan wolde;
> hwæðre he him on folce   freondlarum heold,
> estum mid are,   oð ðæt he yldra wearð,
> Weder-Geatum weold.   (ll. 2369–79a)

> (… where Hygd offered him the hoard and kingdom,
> rings and royal throne; she did not trust
> that her son could hold the ancestral seat
> against foreign hosts, now that Hygelac was dead.
> But despite their misery, by no means
> could they prevail upon that prince at all
> that he should become lord over Heardred,
> or choose to rule the kingdom.
> Yet he upheld him in the folk with friendly counsel,
> good will and honors, until he was older,
> and ruled the Weder-Geats.)

---

[33] See the note on 2367 in *Klaeber's* Beowulf.
[34] J. McNamara, "Beowulf and Hygelac: Problems for Fiction in History," *Rice University Studies* 62.2 (1976): 55–63, at 57. Since McNamara works from the assumption that "it is, of course, inconceivable that Beowulf was anything less than heroic during the Frisian raid" (57), he reaches a very different conclusion than the one argued here.

In context of both the role of women elsewhere in the poem and traditions governing succession in the early Middle Ages,[35] it is surprising that Hygd, Hygelac's widow, makes this offer. Initially contrasting her action to Wealhþeow's speeches on behalf of her sons' succession in the Danish court, Stacy S. Klein suggests that the Geatish queen "seems to endorse *comitatus* values, namely the succession of the strongest man."[36] Yet the poet, I would argue, places as much if not more emphasis on Beowulf's refusal of the kingship in support of Heardred, Hygelac's son and so an appropriate heir in the Christian model. Hygd disappears from the poem, unless of course she is, as some believe, the unnamed female mourner at Beowulf's pyre,[37] her power, if not always just poetic exaggeration, momentary. Indeed, that it is a woman who offers the throne may simply indicate the weakness of the Geats following Hygelac's death: other than Heardred, there appears to be no one else. Similarly, Hygd's own reason for not trusting her son to rule is that he is too young to defend his country, an idea the poet repeats in the comment that Beowulf "upheld" ("heold") him "until he became older" ("oð ðæt he yldra wearð"). Geatish history continues through the fictions of Beowulf's spectacular swim and magnanimous gesture; yet even these actions call attention to the Geats' vulnerability following Hygelac's death.

By providing apparently historical details about Heardred's reign, the immediately following passage challenges the claim that the poet uses the Frisian raid to mark the historical end of the Geats. Here we learn that Heardred (the "hyne" of the opening line) harbors two Swedish princes, Eanmund and Eadgils, fleeing from their uncle, Onela, who has seized the throne from their father, Ohthere:

> Hyne wræcmæcgas
> ofer sæ sohtan, suna Ohteres;
> hæfdon hy forhealden helm Scylfinga,
> þone selestan sæcyninga
> þara ðe in Swiorice sinc brytnade,
> mærne þeoden. Him þæt to mearce wearð:

---

[35] For a survey of scholarship on the role of women in the poem, see Alexandra Hennessey Olsen, "Gender Roles," in *A Beowulf Handbook*, ed. Robert E. Bjork and John D. Niles (Lincoln: University of Nebraska Press, 1997), 311–24. The note on this passage in *Klaeber's* Beowulf (ll. 2369 ff), refers to Tilman Westphalen, Beowulf *3150–55: Textkritik und Editionsgeschichte* (Munich: Fink, 1967), 300 ff for "Germanic parallels to a queen's deciding the succession upon her husband's death." The examples offered here are few and do not prove that this was common practice.

[36] Stacy S. Klein, *Ruling Women: Queenship and Gender in Anglo-Saxon Literature* (Notre Dame: University of Notre Dame Press, 2006), 117. Klein goes on to note similarities between the two queens.

[37] See my "Beowulf and Some Fictions," 69–70.

> he þær for feorme   feorhwunde hleat,
> sweordes swengum,   sunu Hygelaces,
> ond him eft gewat   Ongenðioes bearn
> hames niosan   syððan Heardred læg,
> let ðone bregostol   Biwulf healdan,
> Geatum wealdan;   þæt wæs god cyning.
> XXXIIII Se ðæs leodhryres   lean gemunde
> uferan dogrum,   Eadgilse wearð
> feasceaftum freond;   folce gestepte
> ofer sæ side   sunu Ohteres,
> wigum ond wæpnum;   he gewræc syððan
> cealdum cearsiðum,   cyning ealdre bineat.   (ll. 2379b–96)[38]
>
> (the sons of Ohtere, sought him out across the seas;
> they had rebelled against the Scylfing ruler,
> the best of all the sea-kings
> who dispensed treasure in the Swedish lands,
> a famous king. That cost him his life:
> for his hospitality he took a mortal hurt
> with the stroke of a sword, that son of Hygelac;
> and the son of Ongentheow afterwards went
> to seek out his home, once Heardred lay dead,
> and let Beowulf hold the high throne
> and rule the Geats – that was a good king.
> XXXIIII In later days he did not forget
> that prince's fall, and befriended Eadgils
> the wretched exile; across the open sea
> he gave support to the son of Ohtere
> with warriors and weapons. He wreaked his revenge
> with cold sad journeys, and took the king's life.)

Rather than being caused simply by his unreadiness to rule when his father dies in Frisia, here Heardred's death is a result of his own political miscalculation. While one might argue that the poet sees his action as related to the raid – Heardred makes an unwise political decision because he lacks experience – and so roughly contemporary with it, I would like to suggest that the poet is instead manipulating what he knows about this history.[39] Both Ohthere (Óttarr) and Eadgils (Aðils) are well represented in Scandinavian sources, which identify them as father and son; and *Ynglinga Saga* records a famous battle between Aðils and

---

[38] The fitt division here is one of those that R.D. Fulk questions; see "The Origin of the Numbered Sections in *Beowulf* and in other Old English Poems," *Anglo-Saxon England* 35 (2006): 91–109, at 101. By dividing the material at this point, however, the poet may emphasize the surprising revelation that Onela allows Beowulf to rule.

[39] For what can be constructed about this history from other sources, see *Klaeber's Beowulf*, lxi–lxiv.

the Norwegian king Áli (corresponding to Onela), although he is obviously not Óttarr's brother:

> Aðils konungr átti deilur miklar við konung þann, er Áli hét inn upplenzki. Hann var ór Nóregi. Þeir áttu orrostu á Vænis ísi. Þar fell Áli konungr, en Aðils hafði sigr. Frá þessi orrostu er langt sagt í Skjǫldunga sǫgu ...[40]

> (King Aðils had mighty dealings with that king who was called Áli the Opplander. He was from Norway. They joined battle on the ice of Lake Väner. There King Áli fell, and Aðils won the day. This battle is described extensively in *Skjǫldunga saga*.)[41]

These details affirm that the poet must have had historical traditions from which to work even though we cannot know exactly what they were. Yet given his use of the Frisian raid throughout the poem, here I would suggest that he either used a variant tradition of Geatish history that included the story of Heardred's fatal harboring of Eanmund and Eadgils or that he created it to blur Hygelac's historical death into Beowulf's fictional survival.[42] In any case, the story itself calls attention to Beowulf's problematic place in the Geatish succession. Here, just as he had failed to aid or then avenge Hygelac on the Frisian raid, Beowulf is unable to protect Heardred and only assists in avenging him (ll. 2391–96). Yet even this aid is difficult to explain since the poet also tells us that it is Onela who has allowed Beowulf to rule (l. 2389). These contradictions identify the details as fictional and suggest that a major advantage of restricting the succession to sons of a king is that it decreases the likelihood of competing liabilities between successive generations.[43] In this passage, then, Heardred and history itself blur into fiction.

The penultimate passage concerning the Frisian raid establishes the fictional nature of the poet's elaborations by returning to the neck-ring, contradicting the earlier statement that the treasure passed into the control of the Geats' enemies. It occurs, appropriately, in Beowulf's lengthy recounting of his life prior to fighting the dragon (ll. 2426–09). Directly following a brief account of the high point in Hygelac's career that the poet will return to after the final discussion of the Frisian raid, his victory over Ongenþeow at Ravenswood, Beowulf asserts that he repaid all of the gifts his lord had given him by supporting him in battle:

---

[40] Snorri Sturluson, *Heimskringla*, 2 vols., ed. Bjarni Aðalbjarnarson (Reykjavik: Hið Íslenzka Fornritafélga, 1941–45), I:57.
[41] The translation is from *Klaeber's Beowulf*, 298.
[42] This story also allows the poet to identify Wiglaf as the owner of Eadmund's weapons (ll. 2602–25a), which would provide further reason for a Swedish attack especially were he to succeed Beowulf.
[43] For Wiglaf's place in this theme, see my "Beowulf and Some Fictions," 71–4.

> Ic him þa maðmas   þe he me sealde
> geald æt guðe,   swa me gifeðe wæs
> leohtan sweorde;   he me lond forgeaf,
> eard eðelwyn.   Næs him ænig þearf
> þæt he to Gifðum   oððe to Gar-Denum
> oððe in Swiorice   secean þurfe
> wyrsan wigfrecan,   weorðe gecypan;
> symle ic him on feðan   beforan wolde,
> ana on orde,   ond swa to aldre sceall
> sæcce fremman,   þenden þis sweord þolað
> þæt mec ær ond sið   oft gelæste,
> syððan ic for dugeðum   Dæghrefne wearð
> to handbonan,   Huga cempan –
> nalles he ða frætwe   Frescyninge,
> breostweorðunge   bringan moste,
> ac in campe gecrong   cumbles hyrde,
> æþeling on elne;   ne wæs ecg bona,
> ac him hildegrap   heortan wylmas,
> banhus gebræc.   (ll. 2490–2508a)
>
> (I have paid in battle for the precious treasures
> he gave me, as was granted to me,
> with a gleaming sword; he gave me land,
> a joyous home. He had no need
> to have to go seeking among the Gifthas
> or the Spear-Danes or the Swedes
> for a worse warrior, or buy one with his wealth;
> always on foot I would go before him,
> alone in the front line – and all my life
> I will wage war, while this sword endures,
> which before and since has served me well,
> since I slew Dæghrefn, champion of the Hugas,
> with my bare hands in front of the whole army.
> He could not carry off to the Frisian king
> that battle-armor and that breast-adornment,
> but there in the field the standard-bearer fell,
> a nobleman in his strength; no blade was his slayer,
> but my warlike grip broke his beating heart,
> cracked his bone-house.)

If the "breostweorðung" is, as most agree,[44] the "healsbeag" that Wealhþeow gave to Beowulf, then this passage contradicts the earlier suggestion that Hygelac lost the gem at his defeat in Frisia.[45] Moreover, Beowulf's way of slaying Dæghrefn, not with a sword but by crushing him to death, recalls his fight with Grendel, contributing to the fictional

---

[44] See the note on 2501 ff, in *Klaeber's* Beowulf.
[45] On Beowulf's later gift of this neck-ring to Wiglaf, see my "Politics," 738–9.

quality of the passage. Taken together, then, this and the previous passage present a radically different image of the end of the raid, not as the slaughter of the Geats but rather as the triumphant deeds of Beowulf.

The poet returns to the historical version of the raid in his final retelling of it by the horseman who announces Beowulf's death to the waiting Geats. This speech, often referred to as the Messenger's Prophecy, again focuses on the basic historical fact of Hygelac's death, making its significance clear for the Geats as a whole:

> "Nu ys leodum wen
> orleghwile,   syððan underne
> Froncum ond Frysum   fyll cyninges
> wide weorðeð.   Wæs sio wroht scepen
> heard wið Hugas   syððan Higelac cwom
> faran flotherge   on Fresna land,
> þær hyne Hetware   hilde genægdon,
> elne geeodon   mid ofermægene,
> þæt se byrnwiga   bugan sceolde,
> feoll on feðan;   nalles frætwe geaf
> ealdor dugoðe.   Us wæs a syððan
> Merewioingas   milts ungyfeðe." (ll. 2911b–21)

("Now this folk may expect
a time of trouble, when this is manifest
to the Franks and Frisians, and the fall of our king
becomes widespread news. The strife was begun
hard with the Hugas, after Hygelac came
travelling with his ships to the shores of Frisia,
where the Hetware attacked him in war,
advanced with valor and a vaster force,
so that the warrior in his byrnie had to bow down,
and fell amid the infantry; not at all did that lord
give treasure to his troops. Ever after that
the Merovingians have not shown mercy to us.")

As in the first description of the raid, there is no mention of Beowulf; instead the subject is Hygelac's death, "the fall of our king," who "had to bow down and fell amid the infantry." While there is less emphasis on the scale of the disaster for Hygelac's accompanying force or indeed on their loss of their booty, both are alluded to in the grim comment that "not at all did that lord give treasure to his troops." Moreover, these themes are picked up in the horseman's larger claim that Beowulf's death will lead to a time of trouble for the Geats as a whole ("Now this folk may expect a time of trouble"), which pervades his speech and provides his closing image of slaughter:

> Forðon sceall gar wesan
> monig morgenceald   mundum bewunden,
> hæfen on handa,   nalles hearpan sweg
> wigend weccean,   ac se wonna hrefn
> fus ofer fægum   fela reordian,
> earne secgan   hu him æt æte speow,
> þenden he wið wulf   wæl reafode."   (ll. 3021b–7)

("Thus many a cold morning
shall the spear be grasped in frozen fingers,
hefted by hands, nor shall the sound of the harp
rouse the warriors, but the dark raven,
greedy for carrion, shall speak a great deal,
ask the eagle how he fared at his feast
when he plundered corpses with the wolf.")

Although the tone of this last description of the raid is carefully controlled, its devastating import for the Geats could not be clearer.

Moreover, the poet then sets off the short, factual nature of this last account of the raid by having the horseman turn next to a much longer description of the battle at Ravenswood from the Swedish-Geatish wars. The explicit link between the two is that, like the Frisians and Franks, the Swedes will attack the Geats as soon as they learn of Beowulf's death. Yet their connection is more profound, again focusing attention on the theme of succession. While the Frisian raid ends in Hygelac's disastrous defeat, the battle at Ravenswood marks his successful coming to power, when he is able to save the Geatish band, which has been left lordless ("hlafordlease"; l. 2935b) after the death of his brother, Hæðcyn, and subjected to a night of threats from the Swedish king, Ongenþeow (ll. 2928–45). Without an effective transfer of power, the Geats would be in the same position as they are following Beowulf's death. Moreover, the poet recalls his fictional elaborations on the Frisian raid by recounting Ongenþeow's death at the hands of the fictional brothers Wulf and Eofor (ll. 2961–81), whose mutual aid echoes that of Hæðcyn and Hygelac. Indeed this description ends with Hygelac rewarding Wulf and Eofor by giving them land and wealth, and Eofor by allowing him to marry his only daughter (ll. 2989–98).[46] This marriage, which recalls that of Ecgþeow, Beowulf's father, to Hreðel's only daughter (ll. 372–5a), calls attention to Eofor's absence and the absence of any child from his marriage at the end of the poem. Although the account of the Frisian raid itself remains free of fictional elaboration, the poet has again linked it to the Swedish-Geatish wars in a way that allows him to focus on succession.

---

[46] For another interpretation of this passage, see Alaric Hall, "Hygelac's Only Daughter: A Present, a Potentate and a Peaceweaver in *Beowulf*," *Studia Neophilologica* 78 (2006): 81–7.

Conclusion

When considered first separately in their own contexts and then as they work together, the five accounts of the Frisian raid reveal a poet who blends history and fiction to explore what must have been a fraught moment in the political lives of many kingdoms in early medieval Europe, the transition of power following the death of a king. He controls this material carefully, beginning and ending with more historical versions of the story that establish the raid as a decisive defeat for the Geats. Between these, he offers accounts with fictional details – the crushing of Dæghrefn, the recovery of the neck-ring, the swim home, Hygd's offering of the throne, and perhaps even the harboring of Eanmund and Eadgils – that allow him to continue his narrative and to reflect on the theme of succession. These fictions fit in with others in the poem that focus on Beowulf as not only an extraordinary hero but also someone who embodies the problems of the kingdoms he seeks to aid since they invite us to ponder his inability to help either his lord, Hygelac, or his lord's young son, Heardred. When there is no appropriate heir to the throne, doom seems inevitable. Yet while the Frisian raid is the only event from Geatish history that other sources confirm, it appears to be one of several that the poet considered historical. As we have seen, he associates it twice with Hygelac's victory at Ravenswood, and he presents the background to this battle, Hreðel's death from sorrow caused by the accidental killing of Herebeald by Hæðcyn, in a way that may even allow us to glimpse an older myth, Baldr's death,[47] behind his history. These matters take us well beyond the scope of this chapter, and yet the Frisian raid provides a first indication that the poet has chosen to place his fictions in this historical setting because it compliments the theme in the final third of his work, the danger of a royal line that dies out.

In discussing the Frisian raid, this chapter provides further evidence of a contrast between Germanic and Christian models of succession, which I have argued elsewhere is a major theme in the poem. Here the emphasis is on a danger in the Christian system, the lack of a suitable heir, that is less likely to have occurred in the older Germanic way of selecting kings. Does this insight date *Beowulf*? Not precisely. And yet, it seems to fit into the early period of Anglo-Saxon England when a poet could look back to the Germanic tradition and see its faults, the horror of kin-violence, but also respect the strong bonds that held that world together. For all time, yet tied to a particular historical moment.

---

[47] See the discussion in *Klaeber's* Beowulf, xlvii–xlviii.

8

"Give the People What They Want": Historiography and Rhetorical History of the Dating of *Beowulf* Controversy

Michael D.C. Drout with Emily Bowman and Phoebe Boyd[1]

In 1958, the movie mogul Harry Cohn died. Seeing the huge crowds that turned out for the funeral, one actor expressed his bewilderment: "But everyone in Hollywood *hated* Harry!" he exclaimed. "Why are all these people here?" In 1981, after a conference in Toronto and the publication of a proceedings volume, a no-less-surprising throng began to gather, in books, journals and conferences, for the scholarly funeral of a dateable *Beowulf*. We have no record of anyone exclaiming in surprise: "But the evidence for an early date of *Beowulf* is relatively consistent, convincing and well-established! Why would people be *happy* to replace it with speculation and uncertainty?" But the words of the comedian Red Skelton, who had worked for Cohn, explain both seeming paradoxes: "Give the people what they want and they'll turn out for it."[2]

Even when I was a graduate student at my first significant Anglo-Saxon conference, ISAS 1995 at Stanford, I heard the rumors about that Toronto conference. Sometimes they were *sotto voce*, sometimes louder (especially when there was an open bar), but always they said a version of the same thing: the famous Dating of *Beowulf* conference at Toronto and the subsequent proceedings volume[3] were not entirely on the level.

---

[1] The authors performed the historiographical research and analysis as a team. The "I" of the present chapter is Drout, and responsibility for the tone and rhetoric lies with him alone. The authors are grateful to Leah Smith, Simone Hartwell-Ishikawa, Rose Berger, Namiko Hitotsubashi, Paula Smith-Macdonald, Yvette Kisor, Paul Szarmach, Joseph Harris, John Hill, Leonard Neidorf, and Wheaton College Provost Linda Eisenmann. The research that underlies this paper was made possible by the generosity of the Mars family through their support of a Mars Summer Research Fellowship in 2011.

[2] The story is widespread both in print and online, and I have conflated several slight variations, including one told to me by Paul Szarmach at the Harvard conference. For documentation of the remark and the context, see Bob Thomas, *King Cohn: The Life and Times of Harry Cohn* (New York: G.P. Putnam, 1967), xvii.

[3] *The Dating of* Beowulf, ed. Colin Chase (Toronto: University of Toronto Press, 1981) [henceforth cited as *Dating*].

Not that the individual papers at the conference or in the volume were insincere, but *as a whole* the enterprise was not the disinterested and even-handed reconsideration of the evidence that it purported to be.

To a certain extent this controversy did not bother me. On my way to Stanford I had read James Earl's *Thinking About Beowulf* and found his conclusions about an un-dateable *Beowulf* congenial to my dissertation research.[4] Also, the old-school dating arguments about language, historical references, and meter were so *difficult* that the path of least resistance was to try to smile knowingly and discount the criticisms as academic griping and sour grapes. But something about the whole situation nagged at me. From my early training as a journalist I recognized a pattern in the stories of dissenters being silently excluded, marginalized not because they had lost an intellectual debate on the merits, but through the application of institutional and personal power. It was politics rather than intellectualism, power rather than truth. I did not (and still do not) want the profession to work that way.

But were the stories true? The introduction to the volume says what it says.[5] Many of the individuals who criticized the conference in social gatherings never put their thoughts in print, and even if they had, as I now understand from much painful experience of editing, what from the outside seems conspiratorial, or at least planned, can in truth be merely the result of stumbling from one forced move to another in the chaotic process of organizing a conference or producing a volume. Professional motives are hopelessly entangled with intellectual convictions, and we can never know the minds of various actors.

But even though an unbiased behind-the-scenes history has not been (and is not likely to be) written,[6] we need not despair completely. As medievalists we are used to dealing with a fragmentary record in which often over-determined motives need to be ferreted out, rhetoric recognized, silences parsed. Therefore in this essay I will rely on neither the testimony of the participants[7] nor the plaints of the marginalized, but instead use the documentary record to investigate whether or not the papers selected for *The Dating of Beowulf* volume represent the range and relative

---

[4] James W. Earl, *Thinking About* Beowulf (Stanford: Stanford University Press, 1994).
[5] Colin Chase, "Editor's Preface," in *Dating*, vii.
[6] Ullica Segerstråle's examination of the "evolution wars" surrounding E.O. Wilson's 1975 *Sociobiology* could provide a useful model for such a sociological and political-science approach to what seems like a technical debate within a field. Ullica Segerstråle, *Defenders of the Truth: The Battle for Science in the Sociobiology Debate and Beyond* (Oxford: Oxford University Press, 2000).
[7] The most detailed discussion by any of the participants of which I am aware is Roberta Frank's piece in *Speculum*. Roberta Frank, "A Scandal in Toronto: *The Dating of* Beowulf a Quarter Century On," *Speculum* 82 (2007): 843–64.

proportion of scholarly opinions in the years leading up to 1980. This evidence, it turns out, is consistent with an interpretation that the conference and the volume were an effort to construct an illusory consensus of a late date for the poem.[8] But although the subsequent development of *Beowulf* scholarship shows that there was indeed a post-Toronto change in the field's overall perception of the poem's likely date, it was not the change to a late date that the conference organizers had worked to establish. Instead, a general belief arose among Anglo-Saxonists that the poem was essentially un-dateable and therefore could be interpreted within the context of any historical period before the date of the manuscript – or in no historical period at all.[9] This consensus cannot be a logical result of the papers in the proceedings volume or of influential subsequent arguments about the date, but it has nevertheless become established almost as dogma: to the overall detriment of the field.[10]

This is not the first time in the history of *Beowulf* studies that a rhetorically effective argument had unintentionally given the people what they wanted, that what was wanted was not exactly what was intended by the promulgator of that rhetorically effective argument, and that the resulting consensus view of the poem was not entirely consistent with the argument that had been so influential. J.R.R. Tolkien's "*Beowulf*: The Monsters and the Critics" triggered an even larger tectonic shift in *Beowulf* studies, moving the poem firmly from the category of "documentary evidence" into that of "literature" and enabling interpretations that did not have to view *Beowulf* as fundamentally flawed and obviously inferior to Classical texts.[11] But Tolkien's actual interpretation of the poem, which grounded it firmly in what he called "the named lands of the North" and in a detailed historical, political, and philosophical

---

[8] I use the word "illusory" to refer to the consensus itself, not the arguments for a late date. Why specifically a late date was desired is beyond the scope of this paper, but see Bryan Ward-Perkins' discussion of the ideological underpinnings of recent historical analysis of the fall of Rome and the early medieval period. Bryan Ward-Perkins, *The Fall of Rome and the End of Civilization* (Oxford: Oxford University Press, 2005).

[9] Some evidence for this assertion is assembled by Leonard Neidorf in the introduction to this collection. Neidorf cites several of the same scholars I had noted in the original draft of this paper, including James W. Earl and Nicholas Howe. Earl, *Thinking About Beowulf*; Nicholas Howe, "The Uses of Uncertainty," in *The Dating of* Beowulf, ed. Colin Chase (Toronto: University of Toronto Press, 1997), 213–20.

[10] This is not to say that the effects of the Toronto conference and volume were completely negative. Re-examining fossilized and uncritically accepted dogmas is valuable for any field. Replacing them with less accurate dogmas, however, is not.

[11] J.R.R. Tolkien, "*Beowulf*: The Monsters and the Critics," *Proceedings of the British Academy* 22 (1936): 245–95. Reprinted many times. The version cited here is J.R.R. Tolkien, "*Beowulf*: The Monsters and the Critics," in *The Monsters and the Critics and Other Essays*, ed. Christopher Tolkien (London: HarperCollins, 1997 [1983]), 5–48. Hereafter, "Monsters."

context (of the post-conversion eighth century), was far less influential than his freeing of the poem from the strictures of previous scholarly consensus. Comparing these two major shifts in *Beowulf* criticism, we can see that giving the people what they want can be both critically successful – especially in the short term – and bad for the long-term intellectual health of a field.

The crowds at Cohn's funeral and the reaction to the Toronto volume revealed preferences that had been widespread but mostly unspoken. In both cases the people wanted freedom: from an oppressive bully who abused actors, directors and anyone else who ended up in his path, or from the demands of more than a century of philological, linguistic and historical scholarship. But, ironically, in both cases the result was not the intent of the organizers. The arrangers of Cohn's funeral presumably wanted to commemorate his life; instead they got a celebration of his leaving of it. The organizers of the Toronto conference appear to have wanted to replace the eighth-century consensus with a late-date hegemony, but instead it produced an un-dateable *Beowulf*, a poem that could now be interpreted without historical constraint.

Manufacturing a Problem, Proffering Its Solution

In his "Editor's Preface" to *The Dating of* Beowulf, Colin Chase explains that the book is the result "of a scholarly dialogue which took place between the autumn of 1978 and the spring of 1981, [which began] when contributors were asked to compose brief statements describing the evidence they intended to investigate and the methodology each planned to adopt." Participants circulated these statements, and then their finished papers, before the April 1980 conference. They had six months to revise them "in light of what had been heard at the conference."[12] There is no mention of how the contributors were selected, either for this process or for the eventual proceedings volume, and it is hard to think of what evidence would allow us to determine if the "dialogue" was an unbiased reconsideration or, as Tom Shippey has called it, "really more of a party rally."[13] As noted, it is difficult to untangle personal ambition, deeply held intellectual belief, and politics (both academic and more general): decisions are over-determined, memories fallible and subject to retrospective reconstruction. Maybe, as Chase in his preface and Roberta Frank in her 2007 defense assert, there really was just a remarkable confluence of

---

[12] Chase, "Editor's Preface," vii.
[13] Tom Shippey, "Tolkien's Two Views of *Beowulf*: One Hailed, One Ignored. But did we get this Right?" http://www.lotrplaza.com/forum/forum_posts.asp?TID=238598, July 25th, 2010. Accessed July 15th, 2012.

opinion in Toronto at the end of the 1970s that an eighth-century date of composition for *Beowulf* was no longer probable.

To see if this confluence was shared only among the participants in the conference or was more widespread throughout Anglo-Saxon studies, our research team read every English-language article published on *Beowulf* from 1970–80, a corpus which, when printed double-sided, fills three enormous binders.[14] To gather these texts, we used the Old English Newsletter on-line bibliography,[15] Greenfield and Robinson's *A Bibliography of Publications on Old English Literature to the End of 1972*,[16] and various databases, including the MLA Bibliography.[17] For each article we recorded the range of dates that the author accepted for the composition of the poem. These results we then divided into three categories: (1) articles directly concerned with the date; (2) articles that did not mention a date at all and in which a date could not be contextually reconstructed; and (3) articles that were not making an argument about the date, but which accept some particular date range. The first category, articles directly concerned with the date, is problematic because only one such article appeared between 1972 and 1978, and only three more between then and the publication of *The Dating of* Beowulf. Either the data were faulty and there were many more articles about the date of *Beowulf* than are picked up in the bibliographical references, or for some reason in the 1970s arguments about the date were relegated almost entirely to sections of monographs (that we somehow missed) rather than being in articles or essays, or the field was not particularly interested in the date of *Beowulf* in the 1970s, treating it as a settled or uninteresting question. The last explanation seems most likely.

Category 2, the many articles that did not mention the date at all, is not particularly relevant to our argument, although reading through all of these papers was certainly an education. The final category, the papers that did not make an explicit argument for a date but simply accept some particular dating, are, for present purposes, the most interesting. These articles are evidence of what scholars in the field were thinking when they were not grinding any particular dated-related axes. It is this sub-corpus from which the data in Figure 8.1 is drawn.

---

[14] We also tried to find references to the date of the poem in monographs, but it is likely that we have missed some, particularly in books not primarily focused on *Beowulf*.
[15] http://www.oenewsletter.org/OENDB/index.php. Accessed June 28th, 2012.
[16] Stanley B. Greenfield and Fred C. Robinson, *A Bibliography of Publications on Old English Literature to the End of 1972* (Toronto: University of Toronto Press, 1980).
[17] http://mla.org/bibliography. Accessed June 28th, 2012.

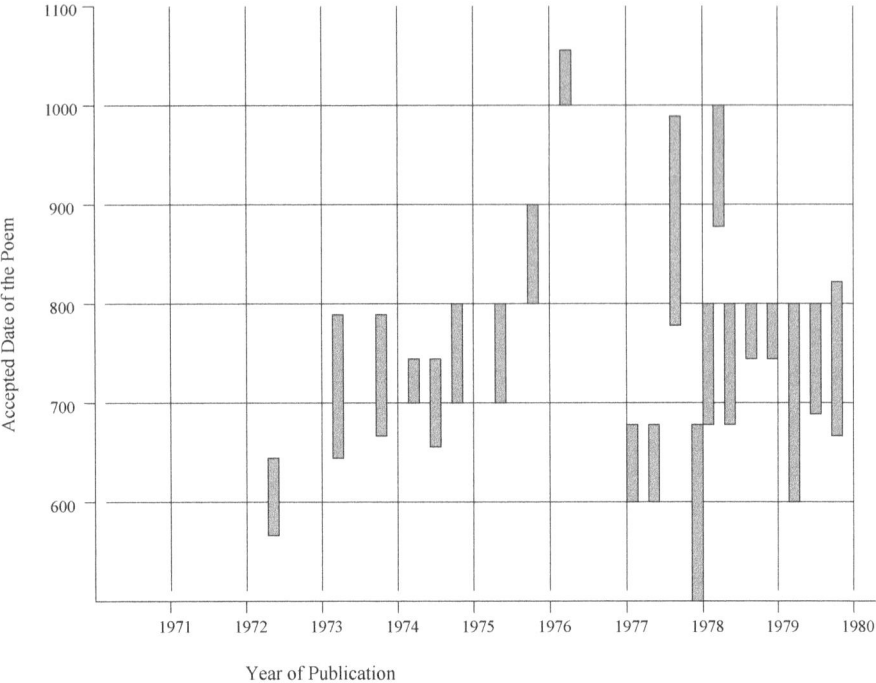

Figure 8.1. Date Ranges for *Beowulf* in Articles not Directly Concerned with the Date of the Poem, 1970–80.

Each box in Figure 8.1 represents an article, with the upper and lower termini indicating the range of dates accepted by the author. From simple visual inspection we can see that nearly every date-range stays below the 800 line,[18] leading to the conclusion that for Anglo-Saxonists who did not have a direct stake in dating arguments, the consensus of the field between 1970 and 1980 was that the poem had a date before 800. The documentary record does not show widespread dissatisfaction with an eighth-century date, nor many Anglo-Saxonists even questioning the consensus opinion.

---

[18] We have tried to be as fair as possible in constructing this diagram and indeed worry that we may have gone too far in the other direction. Two of the five papers that argue for dates later than 800 could be special-pleaded away. Jeff Opland's 1976 paper gives a date range of 1000–99, although he states several times that he is merely dating the manuscript and that the poem itself *cannot* be dated. Likewise in her 1977 book, Jane-Marie Luecke focuses on the manuscript date of the poem (taking it as tenth-century), but accepts that the poem would have existed orally before that time. Jeff Opland, "*Beowulf* on the Poet," *Mediaeval Studies* 28 (1976): 442–67; Jane-Marie Luecke, *Measuring Old English Rhythm: An Application of the Principles of Gregorian Chant Rhythm to the Meter of* Beowulf (Madison: University of Wisconsin Press, 1978), 56, 96.

Chase admits as much in his survey, "Opinions on the Date of *Beowulf*, 1815–1980," which broadly summarizes the history of debates over the date and provenance of the poem from Thorkelin's 1815 *edito princeps* to 1978.[19] In the twentieth century, according to Chase,[20] between Levin Schücking's 1917 argument for a late ninth- or early tenth-century date[21] and Dorothy Whitelock's 1951 *The Audience of Beowulf*, which argued for the court of Offa of Mercia in the later eighth century,[22] the consensus of the field was for a date from approximately the late seventh to the early eighth century. But "since 1951 several studies have appeared investigating a possible ninth- or tenth-century date for the poem – an idea that seemed to have died after Schücking's article of 1917."[23] The implication in this sentence and through the rest of Chase's paper is that seemingly dead ideas were now, in the second half of the twentieth century, being re-animated in light of new arguments and re-consideration of evidence. However, of the several studies Chase cites to support this contention, only the least influential would move the date later than 800, while the two most significant, by C.L. Wrenn and Kenneth Sisam, although allowing the poem to be composed after 750, keep it in the eighth century.[24] Thus Chase's use of these examples to suggest a groundswell of reconsideration is not entirely consistent with the wider, long-term currents of the field.

The rhetoric of Chase's article comes to full flower on its final page, where the minority view[25] of a late date for the poem is set up as if it has

---

[19] Colin Chase, "Opinions on the Date of *Beowulf*, 1815–1980," in *Dating*, 3–8. For a much more detailed discussion that goes well beyond the dating of the poem and which puts Chase's examples in context, see Beowulf: *The Critical Heritage*, Tom Shippey and Andreas Haarder, eds. (New York: Routledge, 1998).

[20] Chase, "Opinions," 6–7.

[21] He is referring to Levin Schücking, "Wann entstand der *Beowulf*? Glossen, Zweifel, und Fragen," *Beiträge zur Geschichte der deutschen Sprache und Literatur* 42 (1917): 347–410.

[22] Dorothy Whitelock, *The Audience of* Beowulf (Oxford: Oxford University Press, 1951).

[23] Chase, "Opinions," 7.

[24] C.L. Wrenn, "Sutton Hoo and *Beowulf*," in *An Anthology of* Beowulf *Criticism*, ed. Lewis E. Nicholson (South Bend: University of Notre Dame Press, 1959), 311–30; Kenneth Sisam, "Dialect Origins of the Earlier Old English Verse" in his *Studies in the History of Old English Literature* (Oxford: Oxford University Press, 1953), 119–39.

[25] Some of the papers Chase cites are not precisely mainstream, detailed discussions of the full range of evidence. R.L. Reynolds' note on the links between *Beowulf*, *The Wonders of the East* and political and social history is only three pages long. Gösta Langenfelt's suggestion that Carolingian missionaries are the source of the Scandinavian elements in the poem has not found much favor with subsequent critics. R.L. Reynolds, "Note on *Beowulf's* Date and Economic Social History," *Studi in onore di Armondo Sapori*, 2 vols. (Milan: Instituto editoriale cisalpino, 1957), I, 175–8; Gösta Langenfelt, "Beowulf och Fornsverige: Ett forsook till datering av den fornengelska hjältedikten 1," *Ortnamnssällskapets i Uppsala Årsskrift* (1961): 35–55, "Tillägg," 37–8;

now, in 1980, become the mainstream opinion: "*This is not to say, however, that more traditional positions on the question have been abandoned*" (my emphasis). Here, what at first seems like a standard scholarly "on the other hand" is so constructed as to imply that readers were likely to think that the eighth-century date had been abandoned (and in fact the three scholars that Chase here cites – Patrick Wormald, W.F. Bolton, and Eric John – would numerically balance the three he previously noted who were in favor of a later date). "*Further*," Chase continues, "a survey of more than 80 percent of the editions and translations since 1815 fails to turn up any editor or commentator since Thorkelin who firmly commits himself to a date outside the range 650–800."[26] This "further" implies that the evidence of the editions (why 80%?) is equivalent to that of the studies, which it is not, because studies are the work of single individuals and, although they have to be peer-reviewed, by their nature they do not reflect as broad a consensus as editions and translations, which must appeal to a wider scholarly audience if they are to be adopted. More significantly, the remarkable consistency of the editions and translations is made rhetorically equivalent to the previous evidence of "several" studies (i.e., it is merely "further" evidence for a point that is already set up as a contrast) instead of being used as devastatingly effective evidence of consensus. "*Nevertheless*," Chase adds, "some commentators reach an extreme limit of skepticism, as when Bruce Mitchell said in 1968 that 'examination of the language can do little more than confirm the possibility that the poem was composed between c. 680 and 800 (or perhaps later).'"[27] This final sentence is misleading, as Mitchell is arguing about the *language* of the poem and not the full range of evidence, and so it is not logically clear what the sentence is doing in this paragraph. Rhetorically, however, the sentence works to add a gloss of reasonableness to the argument. Mitchell may be at the "extreme limit" of skepticism,[28] but, by implication, the contributors to the volume are not. The overall effect of the paragraph is to suggest that for many years *Beowulf* criticism was stuck with a seventh-century date but that now such a consensus no longer holds even though a few hold-outs still believe in an early date for the poem: the majority and minority positions have been flipped. When Chase then concludes by stating that "the date of *Beowulf's* composition is sufficiently ambiguous to make the subject seem ready for

---

Gösta Langenfelt, "till Beowulf och Fornsverige: Ett forsook till datering av den fornengelska hjältedikten 2," *Ortnamnssällskapets i Uppsala Årsskrift* (1962): 23–36.

[26] Chase, "Opinions," 8.

[27] Chase, "Opinions," 8; my emphasis.

[28] If Mitchell is at the "extreme limit," then being even the slightest bit more skeptical would, presumably, be intellectually indefensible.

reexamination,"[29] he has created the appearance of a widespread dissatisfaction with the seventh-century date, a scholarly discontent that does not seem to have existed in the published record. This paragraph displays the dominant rhetorical mode of the volume as a whole: it implies that there is some kind of problem with an eighth-century date, exaggerates the degree of dissent within the field, and then asserts that the volume is just "a reexamination" brought about by a "sufficiently ambiguous" date when both that ambiguity and the field's dissatisfaction with it have been rhetorically constructed.

Figure 8.2 is a visual representation of the date ranges given in the papers published in the conference volume.

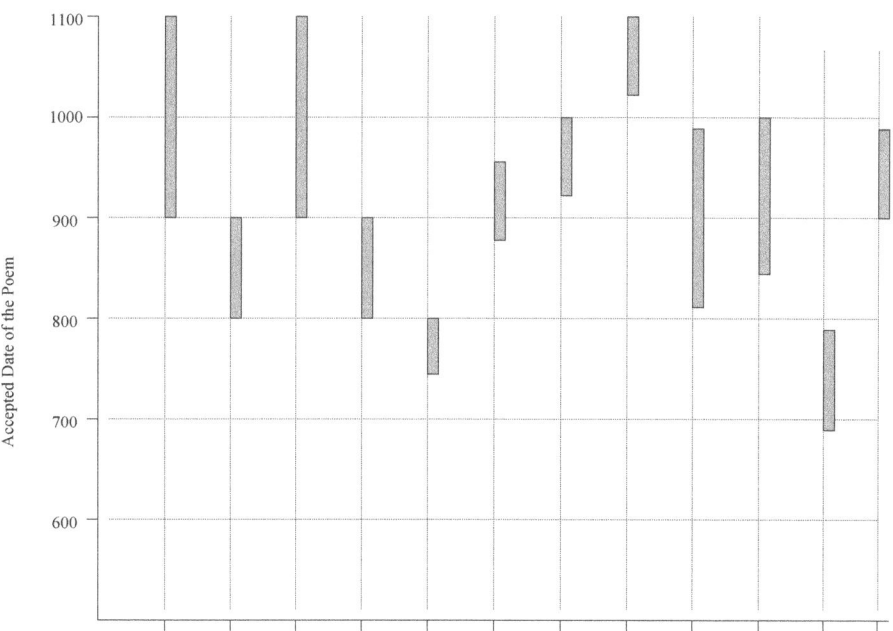

Figure 8.2. Date Ranges for *Beowulf* in Essays in *The Dating of* Beowulf Proceedings Volume.

---

[29] This sentence is mildly difficult to parse. I do not think that Chase means that the date itself of *Beowulf* is "ambiguous" (the way it would be if the poem were a composite, for example) but that the *evidence* for the date is ambiguous. This imprecision in language is probably just an unfortunate lapse (though similar imprecisions occur elsewhere in the essay), but it is easy to see here the transformation of questions about the significance of particular pieces of evidence into the idea – so influential among self-identified post-modernist scholars – that the date of the poem is itself ambiguous.

If we compare the date ranges in the papers in the decade before the conference (Figure 8.1) with the papers contained in the proceedings volume, we note a striking difference: Although the field as a whole in the years leading up to 1981 consistently accepted a date for the composition of *Beowulf* before 800 and only a very few papers suggesting later dates were published, nearly all the Toronto papers support a date *after* 800 or consider such a date to be equally or more likely than an earlier date. This disjunction does not by itself prove that the Toronto conference brought about a controversy and then provided a solution for the problem so created, but it is not the ratio we might expect if the conference represented an unbiased debate in which representative opinions from the field as a whole were welcomed.

Before concluding that the distribution of date ranges is due to bias, however, we should weigh the evidence and perhaps adjust the data. For example, two papers presented at the conference that were not included in the published volume, those by Michael Lapidge and David Dumville, supported an early date,[30] so the total distribution of date ranges in the conference presentations was less biased towards a late date than the papers in *The Dating of Beowulf*. Secondly, some authors, although they accept a late date in their essays, go on to equivocate to various degrees.[31] Perhaps these papers should count as less than full data-points. Third, the particular kinds of evidence considered in each essay might have been an important part of the selection criteria for the volume, and early dating might not be relevant to some of those criteria (i.e., a paper on the possible influence of Skaldic verse on *Beowulf* could not be balanced with an early dating paper that used the same type of evidence). Finally, it is possible, even probable, that all variables are not independent. That is, if the poem really dates from the late ninth or tenth centuries, then anachronism, audience analysis, language and the influence of Saints' Lives (among other factors) would all support the same dating and therefore would not end up being balanced with contradictory papers.

But even modifying the data to take into account Lapidge's and Dumville's papers and discounting hedged or equivocated date claims does not fully balance either the conference or the volume. Although it might be impossible to write a paper using potential evidence of Skaldic influence to support an eighth-century date, certainly any given combination of evidence and interpretation presented in the volume could

---

[30] These were discussed at the 2011 Harvard conference in which this paper was first presented.

[31] Although at least one, Eric Stanley, starts off as if he is equivocating but then comes down rather strongly on the side of a late date. Eric G. Stanley, "The Date of *Beowulf*: Some Doubts and No Conclusions," in *Dating*, 197–212.

be – and probably has been – argued against; otherwise the field would have adopted that particular unassailable argument. And although it is possible that the different strands of evidence all coalesced to support a late date in contradistinction to the generally shared opinion of the rest of the field, the volume as a whole does not – and can not – hang together in this way, with each paper supporting the other, because the arguments of some of the late-date papers are incompatible with each other.

Most significant among these is Kevin Kiernan's essay, which is given pride of place at the front of the collection, but whose argument is not only inconsistent with but contradictory to most of the other late dates proposed in the poem.[32] Detailed analysis of Kiernan's specific claims is beyond the scope of this paper, but it is sufficient to note that if his argument about the eleventh-century origin of *Beowulf* is correct, then arguments for a ninth- or tenth-century poem are just as wrong as those for a seventh- or eighth-century poem, as it is not logically possible to take Kiernan's argument as merely refuting the earlier datings. A strong argument *for* the eleventh century is not necessarily an argument *against* the eighth century *unless the eleventh-century argument is correct*. But if it is, then *all* the other earlier dates, seventh- through tenth-century, are also wrong. In fact, an eleventh-century date is more exclusionary than an eighth-century one, because an earlier poem could as least have been received or adapted in the ninth, tenth and eleventh centuries, while an eleventh-century composition could not. Since the other papers in the volume do not accept Kiernan's eleventh-century dating, it is hard to see how different approaches to the poem would find their confluence in a late – but not quite as late as the eleventh-century – date, so even this explanation fails to explain fully the significant difference between the dates supported in the volume and those accepted by the wider field.

When we combine this evidence with Chase's rhetoric, the sub rosa oral history of the field and the comments of scholars like Shippey, we are on reasonably firm ground in concluding that rather than representing the wide currents of *Beowulf* criticism at the time, the Toronto Conference was a deliberate, thesis-driven intervention into the debate. There is nothing existentially wrong with making such an intervention, and the organizers deserve some admiration for being so successful at calling into question conclusions that had been (perhaps) taken on faith for too long. But it is also fair to criticize rhetoric, both that which is embedded in the structure of the volume as a whole and that used by Chase in his preface and survey article. Having Kiernan's paper open the volume has the effect of making the other, earlier-but-late dates appear

---

[32] Kevin S. Kiernan, "The Eleventh-Century Origin of *Beowulf* and the *Beowulf* Manuscript," in *Dating*, 9–21.

more reasonable, so that ninth- or tenth-century datings therefore seem like they are merely and judiciously splitting the difference between old and new opinions (even if such a procedure is illogical and not in the slightest supported by Kiernan's argument). It seems evident that the organizers of the conference did not believe that Kiernan's dating was correct but nevertheless used his paper to advance their agenda of a late date for the poem. *The Dating of Beowulf*, therefore, is, at least in part, an exercise in creating the impression that an eighth-century date was a problem and that the solution was a new consensus built around a later (but not eleventh-century) date for the poem.

However, although the conference was certainly successful in calling into question the early dating of the poem, its preferred solution of a ninth- or tenth-century date does not appear to have been rapidly adopted. Figure 8.3 shows the distribution of date ranges in those relatively few papers that are focused on the date of the poem from 1980–90 (exclusive of the articles in the Toronto proceedings).

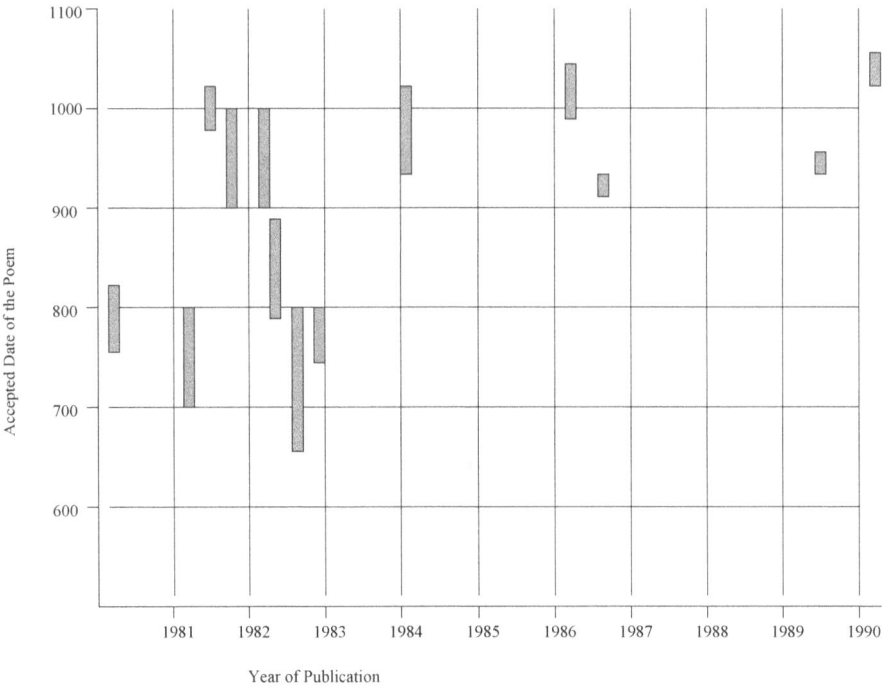

Figure 8.3. Date Ranges for *Beowulf* in Articles not Directly Concerned with the Date of the Poem, 1980–90.

The eighth-century date range does practically disappear, but, much more strikingly, even though the number of articles published on *Beowulf* increases substantially in this time period, the number of articles that even mention a date shrinks significantly when compared to 1970–80. Unfortunately for our task of reconstructive intellectual history, there are multiple ways to interpret this data. That there was not any substantial pushback to the claims made in *The Dating of Beowulf* could be due to the overwhelming logical and rhetorical force of its arguments: suddenly the previous consensus of an early date was replaced throughout the field. Or, scholars may have just been tired of dating arguments (although my experience suggests that any avoidance of the topic during the 1980s had worn off by 1995, it is possible that Anglo-Saxonists were just sick of the dating of *Beowulf* for the decade or so after the Toronto conference). Or, the institutional and personal prestige of the conference participants may have shifted the critical ground. It is difficult to say. We note that throughout the 1980s few scholars published papers about the date of the poem, and of these, very few supported the previous consensus position of the early date, although the specific later dates favored by the conference participants were not widely adopted, either.

This evidence supports Neidorf's contention that one of the most significant effects of the Toronto Conference was not to make a late date the consensus view in *Beowulf* studies but rather to produce a state of "dogmatic agnosticism" (a phrase taken from the Patrick Wormald) about the date.[33] Although it is hard to see how one concludes from the papers in *The Dating of Beowulf* that the poem is un-dateable, that appears to be just what scholars did. James Earl, for example, states that after the "unexpected and unwished-for gift of Kevin Kiernan," he now considers it "axiomatic that the problem of the poem's date is insoluble."[34] The Toronto volume gave the people what they wanted: a *Beowulf* that was no longer confined to the "Age of Bede" but could be interpreted in any historical segment of the Anglo-Saxon period from the migration to the Norman Conquest.

---

[33] Neidorf, "Introduction." The quotation from Wormald is from Patrick Wormald, "*Beowulf*: the Redating Reassessed," in *The Times of Bede: Studies in Early English Christian Society and Its Historian*, ed. Stephen Baxter (Malden: Wiley-Blackwell, 2006), 71–81 at 80.

[34] Earl, *Thinking About* Beowulf, 16–17. I think this is a slightly incorrect use of "axiomatic," a term which implies that a particular premise is a starting point for reasoning. One could assert the insolubility of the date problem as an axiom, but if it were so, then there would be no need to preface the statement with the experience of reading *The Dating of* Beowulf, Kevin Kiernan's book, and articles by Michael Lapidge and David Dumville. Generally, axioms are not disputed premises.

Previously, When the People Got What They Wanted

The aftermath of the *Dating of Beowulf* volume was not the first time in the poem's critical history that Anglo-Saxon studies broke free from historical strictures against which, we can see in hindsight, scholars had been quietly chafing. The most famous essay ever written about *Beowulf*, J.R.R. Tolkien's "*Beowulf*: The Monsters and the Critics," similarly triggered a "preference cascade"[35] that forever changed the critical landscape of the poem. Although Tolkien's argument carried the day, the received triumphal version of the critical history of *Beowulf* studies,[36] in which all Anglo-Saxonists immediately recognized the truth of Tolkien's contentions and at once set to reading the poem in his terms, is not entirely accurate.[37] The field did not in fact uncritically accept all of Tolkien's arguments. Friedrich Klaeber, for example, was politely but strongly critical of several important points,[38] and for at least ten years after the 1936 lecture much *Beowulf* criticism continued on paths continuous with those of other late nineteenth- and early twentieth-century scholars.[39]

Tolkien's essay was also not as complete a break with all that had gone before as the received critical history may suggest. Much of his argument, as he acknowledges,[40] is built on the work of R.W. Chambers, who made several of Tolkien's major points but in a less forceful rhetorical style.[41] Chambers had argued that *Beowulf* should be judged on its own

---

[35] Sushil Bikhchandani, David Hirshleifer and Ivo Welch, "A Theory of Fads, Fashion, Custom, and Cultural Change as Informational Cascades," *Journal of Political Economy* 100 (1992): 992–1026. See also Daniel B. Neill, "Cascade Effects in Heterogeneous Populations," *Rationality and Society* 17.2 (2005): 191–241.

[36] See *An Anthology of* Beowulf *Criticism*, ed. Lewis E. Nicholson (Notre Dame: University of Notre Dame Press, 1963).

[37] I, unfortunately, contributed to this misconception in the introduction to J.R.R. Tolkien, Beowulf and the Critics, rev. ed., ed Michael D.C. Drout (Tempe: Arizona Medieval and Renaissance Texts and Studies, 2011), 2–5. For a more accurate critical history of Tolkien's essay's reception, see Michael D.C. Drout, "'*Beowulf*: The Monsters and the Critics' Seventy-Five Years Later," *Mythlore* 30: 1/2; 115/116 (2011): 5–22.

[38] Friedrich Klaeber, "Review: J.R.R. Tolkien, "*Beowulf*: The Monsters and the Critics," *Beiblatt zur Anglia* 48 (1937): 323.

[39] Compare the citations in Greenfield and Robinson under the headings "Cultural and Historical / Authorship and Date" for the time period 1930–40 and 1940–50 with the entries under "Literary Interpretations" for the same period. The influence of "Monsters" was by no means immediate, even if we account for normal publication delays.

[40] Tolkien, "Monsters," 12; For more praise of Chambers by Tolkien, see the Oxford lectures that eventually evolved into "Monsters." Tolkien, *Beowulf and the Critics*, 75, 88–9.

[41] R.W. Chambers, "*Beowulf* and the Heroic Age," in Beowulf *Translated into Modern English Rhyming Verse*, ed. and trans. Archibald Strong (London: Constable, 1925), vii–xxxii.

aesthetic terms and not merely in comparison to Homer and Vergil, and although he de-emphasized and even apologized for the monsters, he did at least establish that the portrayal of sorrows and tragedy in the Anglo-Saxon poem's "world of humans" – to use the well-turned phrase from the fourth edition of Klaeber's *Beowulf* [42] – could reasonably be compared to tragedy in Classical texts. It may well be that Chambers was restrained by filial piety from criticizing W.P. Ker, his honored and admired teacher,[43] and so let lie the stronger argument for the value of the monsters that Tolkien then so successfully developed, but it is quite possible that Tolkien's essay would have found a less receptive audience had not Chambers laid the groundwork for it.[44]

Building on Chambers' foundation, Tolkien argued for the artistry of *Beowulf* – including a strangely compelling but never-justified assertion that the macro-structure of the poem mirroring the micro-structure of the line is an aesthetic success[45] – and so allowed scholars to find intellectually acceptable the possibility that a Germanic epic might be a successful work of art. But Tolkien took this argument further than his predecessor and so gave Anglo-Saxonists a reason to stop apologizing for and instead celebrate the aesthetic value of the monsters. Ironically, in light of Tolkien's argument and the later critical history of the poem, Chambers had built upon Ker's work to argue for the significance and aesthetic accomplishment of a Germanic *type* of tragedy typified by the story of Ingeld (as it was reconstructed, for no single text gives us the entire story). Tolkien contended that the interaction of the hero with

---

[42] Frederick Klaeber, *Klaeber's* Beowulf: *Fourth Edition*, ed. R. D. Fulk, Robert E. Bjork and John D. Niles (Toronto: University of Toronto Press, 2008), li–lxvii.

[43] See R.W. Chambers, *Man's Unconquerable Mind: Studies of English Writers from Bede to A. E. Housman and W.P. Ker* (London: Jonathan Cape, 1939). Chambers also wrote Ker's entry in the *Dictionary of National Biography*; R.W. Chambers, "William Paton Ker," in *Dictionary of National Biography 1922–1930* (London: Oxford University Press, 1937), 467–9.

[44] Michael D.C. Drout, "The Rhetorical Evolution of '*Beowulf*: The Monsters and the Critics'," in *The Lord of the Rings, 1954–2004: Scholarship in Honor of Richard E. Blackwelder*, ed. Wayne Hammond and Christina Scull (Milwaukee: Marquette University Press, 2005), 183–215.

[45] Tolkien claimed that the poem divided into two large sections, 1–2199 and 2200–3182. These portions, "different in matter, manner, and length," produce a "static" structure that is the same as that of the poetic line (i.e., the B-verse in usually short and only includes one alliterating element, while the A-verse can have two such), "more like masonry than music." Tolkien, "Monsters," 28–30. See, among many others, R.D. Fulk, who notes that Tolkien's "explanation of the poem's larger structure, though frequently disputed, has never been bettered, and the methodology inherent in his practice of basing claims about the macrostructural level on patterns everyone discerns in the microstructure remains a model for emulation," R.D. Fulk, "Preface," in *Interpretations of* Beowulf: *A Critical Anthology*, ed. R.D. Fulk (Bloomington: Indiana University Press, 1991), ix–xix.

the monsters further advanced such themes and in fact developed them more effectively than events in the world of humans could alone.

In order to make this case, however, Tolkien had to demolish what he called the "historical document fallacy," the notion that the intellectually respectable reason for studying *Beowulf* was to quarry the poem for information about the lost history of the Germanic north.[46] Treating the poem as a historical or quasi-historical document allowed it onto the syllabus. *Beowulf* was old and full of history and thus, in the words of the chorus in Tolkien's allegory of the voices, "worth studying"[47] even if, pre-Tolkien, scholars had not developed successful arguments to assert the poem's aesthetic merit in comparison to Homer and Vergil.[48] The poem might remain aesthetically and literarily marginalized, but it would at least be taught and studied.[49] However, in order to advance his main arguments about the literary merits of *Beowulf*, Tolkien had to extricate the poem from the long-fossilized matrix of this compromise. *Beowulf* needed to be interpreted within the category of literature rather than history.

Unfortunately, as the critical history of the poem shows, there was collateral damage. Tolkien never meant to kill historical research (any more than the Toronto conference participants, I think, intended to create a dateless *Beowulf*); although he only mentions the date of the poem once in "The Monsters and the Critics," he was an "Age of Bede" dater himself.[50] And if we look beyond the British Academy lecture to Tolkien's

---

[46] Tolkien, "Monsters," 6–9, 27. Tolkien attacks the "historical document fallacy" in much greater detail in Beowulf *and the Critics*, 117–22.

[47] Tolkien, "Monsters," 9. For explication of the different voices in the Babel, see Michael D.C. Drout, "'The Babel of Voices' and the Structural Evolution of '*Beowulf*: The Monsters and the Critics,'" in Tolkien, Beowulf *and the Critics*, 29–41.

[48] Exemplified by Ker's evaluations. Although *The Dark Ages* was the proximate source for Tolkien's argument – see Beowulf *and the Critics*, xxiii–xxv – Tolkien also engages with the arguments in Ker's *English Literature: Medieval* and *Epic and Romance*. The comparison to Homer and Vergil (with *Beowulf* coming off much the worse for the engagement) occurred throughout the nineteenth century, but Ker is likely reacting to its most acidic proponent, Arthur Quiller-Couch, whose aspersions Chambers also tentatively challenges. W.P. Ker, *The Dark Ages* (London: Blackwood and Sons, 1904), 26; Ker, *English Literature: Medieval* (London: Williams and Norgate, 1912), 30–4; Ker, *Epic and Romance: Essays on Medieval Literature* (London: Macmillan and Co., 1897; Repr. New York: Dover, 1958), 269–76. Arthur Quiller-Couch, "On the Lineage of English Literature," *Cambridge Lectures* (London: J.M. Dent and Sons, 1943), 21–5. R.W. Chambers, "*Beowulf* and the Heroic Age," vii–xxxii.

[49] This compromise is with us still, with *Beowulf*'s age keeping it both in the syllabus and safely marginalized.

[50] "I accept without argument throughout the attribution of Beowulf to the 'age of Bede' – one of the firmer conclusions of a department of research most clearly serviceable to criticism: inquiry into the probable date of the effective composition of the poem as we have it. So regarded *Beowulf* is, of course, an historical document of the first order for the study of the mood and thought of the period and one perhaps too little used

other work, particularly the posthumously published *Finn and Hengest*[51] and the material on *Beowulf* that Christopher Tolkien published in *Sigurd and Gudrún*,[52] it becomes evident that when Tolkien says that we have in *Beowulf* a hero "walking the *named lands of the North*,"[53] he is not just making a fine rhetorical flourish. Tolkien thought the *Beowulf* poet knew his history and geography, that he had a great deal of mostly accurate information about the migrations of peoples and the relationships between tribes, families and kings. Most importantly, Tolkien believed that the historical detail gave greater resonance to the more mythological fights against the monsters. Beowulf defeats Grendel, but feud and war among named families and peoples destroys Heorot. The hero is killed by a dragon's venom, but his people are prophesied to be destroyed by their neighbors. The monsters are symbols but not specific allegories (Grendel does not equal Heathobards; the dragon does not equal Swedes) exactly because the rest of the poem is historically and politically specific. But in rescuing *Beowulf* from the condescension of Arthur Quiller-Couch, the criticism of Ker and even the apologies of Chambers, Tolkien unintentionally gave the wider field too much of what it wanted: a chance to escape from the seeming oppression of the (mostly German) philologists and cultural historians who not only seemed to care little for the poem's literary merits but had entangled the text in a web of technical scholarship. This freedom from dead dogma had positive results, but it also had in the long run the negative effect of marginalizing much historically grounded research about the poem – a development that appears to have been not un-congenial to many scholars over the next three quarters of a century.[54]

> for the purpose by professed historians. But it is the mood of the author, the essential cast of his imaginative apprehension of the world, that is my concern, not history for its own sake; I am interested in that time of fusion only as it may help us to understand the poem. And in the poem I think we may observe not confusion, a half-hearted or a muddled business, but a fusion that has occurred at a given point of contact between old and new, a product of thought and deep emotion," "Monsters," 20. In the Oxford lectures that evolved into "Monsters," Tolkien elaborates a bit more on the presumed mindset, religiosity and historical knowledge of an author in the seventh or eighth century; Tolkien, Beowulf and the Critics, 98, 138.

51 J.R.R. Tolkien, *Finn and Hengest: The Fragment and Episode*, ed. Alan Bliss (Boston: Houghton Mifflin, 1981).
52 J.R.R. Tolkien, *The Legend of Sigurd and Gudrún*, ed. Christopher Tolkien (Boston: Houghton Mifflin; London: Harcourt, 2009), 311–34, 337–63
53 "Monsters," 17, my emphasis.
54 This is not to say that "historical" interpretation cannot run off the rails, particularly when it becomes political allegory elaborated to the point where is resembles modern conspiracy theories. See, for example, what Tolkien calls John Earle's "private gambol" at the end of *The Deeds of* Beowulf (from which Tolkien cribbed much of his account of the early critical history of the poem that he presented in the Oxford lectures and

The Loss of History and the Celebration of Uncertainty

But while Tolkien in his own work tried to understand the literary merits of *Beowulf* in what he saw as the poem's historical context – post-conversion, but in a culture in which the memory of ancestors and their culture (and their paganism) was preserved – the field itself moved rapidly away from history, both that of eighth-century Anglo-Saxon England and of the migration, and began to focus much more exclusively on the literary merits of the poem.[55] What followed was not pure New Criticism, particularly not immediately, but soon led to consideration of the poem in far more formalistic terms than had previously been the case. Clare Lees' assertion – which was the received opinion when I was in graduate school in the 1990s – that Tolkien was the first New Critic is incorrect,[56] but "The Monsters and the Critics" certainly opened the door to the purely literary and mostly un-historical approaches that would dominate criticism for the rest of the twentieth century.[57]

These approaches were what the field of English studies, in contradistinction to philology or even medieval studies, wanted: an ancient English poem at the very beginning of the syllabus that could nevertheless be analyzed without confusing and speculative history about either unappealing early medieval Christian converts or Dark Age warrior peoples (and soon, without all that difficult philology). "*Beowulf*: The Monsters and the Critics" was taken up by the New Critics after

---

from which – partially – he constructed the "Babel of Voices" in "Monsters"). Tolkien, Beowulf *and the Critics*, 81; *The Deeds of* Beowulf: *An English Epic of the Eighth Century Done into Modern Prose*, trans. John Earle (Oxford: Clarendon Press, 1892).

[55] Klaeber, *Klaeber's* Beowulf, cxxii–cxxv.

[56] Clare Lees, "Men and *Beowulf*," in *Medieval Masculinities: Regarding Men in the Middle Ages*, ed. Clare Lees (Minneapolis: University of Minnesota Press, 1994), 129–48. For a critique of Lees's assertion that Tolkien was a New Critic, see Michael D.C. Drout, "Introduction: Seeds, Soil and Northern Sky," in Tolkien, Beowulf *and the Critics*, 1–27 at 19–21. See also George Clark, *Beowulf* (Boston: Twayne Publishers, 1990), 8–11. One difficulty that may have confused Lees was the habit among postmodernist critics in the 1980s and 1990s of using the shorthand "New Critics" to refer to scholars of the previous generation whether or not these scholars had employed New Critical methodologies ("boogeymen," while more accurate, might not have been as rhetorically effective). John Niles's phrase "prison house of the text of the New Criticism, with its strategies of interpretive confinement" is perhaps emblematic; see also Lees, "Men and *Beowulf*," John Hermann's *Allegories of War*, and Gillian Overing's "Recent Writing on Old English: A Response." John D. Niles, "Introduction: *Beowulf*, Truth, and Meaning," in *A* Beowulf *Handbook*, ed. Robert E. Bjork and John D. Niles (Lincoln: University of Nebraska Press, 1997), 1–12, at 7; John P. Hermann, *Allegories of War: Language and Violence in Old English Poetry* (Ann Arbor: University of Michigan Press, 1989); Gillian R. Overing, "Recent Writing on Old English: A Response," *Æstel* 1 (1993): 135–49.

[57] Klaeber, *Klaeber's* Beowulf, cxxvii–cxxix.

the fact – in some cases decades after the fact – to justify, as much as one can for a poem like *Beowulf*, ignoring the historical materials and their relationship to things outside the "cultural world in *Beowulf*."[58] Criticism could then comfortably pursue the analysis of ambiguity, or patterns of light and dark, or arriving and departing, civilization and wilderness, raw and cooked.

Now, any critical history that produces Edward Irving's *A Reading of Beowulf* can hardly be considered a complete failure,[59] and in fact New Critical, Patristic and later Post-Modern approaches to *Beowulf* have led to insights about the poem. But escaping the surly bonds of history also had the insalubrious effect of sending *Beowulf* scholarship into some blind alleys and dead ends from which it has not been easy to escape: tenuous and tedious patristic work in which no passage of the *Patrologia Latin* is too obscure to have influenced the *Beowulf* poet in his engagement with the trivia of Christian philosophy; dull, bad New Criticism that wrings every last bit of possible meaning from a single word or compounding element that is as likely as not to have been used to get a line to alliterate; mechanical deconstruction of the most banal binary oppositions towards the end of demonstrating that, well, hegemons hegemonate. Bad criticism infests the scholarly bibliography of any work of art, and *Beowulf* is no exception. But what our research team found as we read the complete record of *Beowulf* criticism of the 1970s is that the *best* criticism, the papers that are still remembered and cited and pondered decades after they were published, is almost all in one way or another tied to history. In *Beowulf* studies, historical scholarship is *productive*. Fitting the poem into a cultural and historical context may limit some aspects of the critic's interpretive freedom, but these limitations end up producing better work than complete free-play. Indeed, beyond *Beowulf* studies, the so-called New Historicism arose because scholars rediscovered how essential history is for the understanding of culture and its artifacts.

But historical scholarship needs to be tethered to history, and if Tolkien dealt historical study an unintentional body-blow, the Toronto conference was close to being a knockout punch. After 1936 the analysis of the literary merits of the poem eclipsed historical approaches, but scholars still set the poem in particular times, places and cultural contexts. After 1981 Anglo-Saxonists quickly began to accept a *Beowulf* written anytime

---

[58] The formulation is John Hill's, and I use it here not to criticize his work (which has been extraordinarily fruitful) but because the phrase is the most succinct distillation of an approach to *Beowulf* that reads the historical (or quasi-historical) material solely in poem-internal terms and not in relation to the historical context of the poem's composition.

[59] Edward B. Irving, Jr., *A Reading of* Beowulf, revised ed. (Provo: The Chaucer Studio, 1999).

and anywhere. The great pernicious effect of the un-dateable *Beowulf* – the culmination of the rhetorical process that Tolkien began but which was taken to the extreme in the aftermath of the Toronto conference – is that history is still invoked and used in the explication of the poem, but in an oblique way that, for lack of a better word, I am going to call *wrong*. The *New* Historicism is somewhat better than the *No* Historicism that preceded it, but there are significant and obvious problems in logic with the development of historical readings on a text that might not belong to the time period that is being used for context.[60] In particular, arguments that are essentially political allegory, many of which are variants of the political allegories of John Earle[61] or Albert S. Cook,[62] can only work if the poem really belongs to the period in question. If *Beowulf* was written in the eighth century, then reading it as a Benedictine Reform production, as I did in my dissertation, is simply not correct,[63] and so is reading the poem as a reflection of the court of Offa or the Age of Bede if it really was composed in the tenth or eleventh centuries. But because the idea that the date of the poem is unresolvable is now so entrenched in contemporary *Beowulf* studies, we have no way of sorting among these readings except by the very poor metrics of our current political prejudices or our admiration for cleverness. By using only such criteria we almost always end up just giving the people (ourselves foremost among them) what they want.

That some excellent scholars even celebrate this uncertainty indicates the damage done by the unexpected consequences of the Toronto volume.[64] I applaud the optimism that makes a virtue of necessity, but I

---

[60] There has been excellent work done – and there is more to do – on the reception in Anglo-Saxon England of Old English texts, but it is difficult to make detailed, nuanced arguments that often hang on the connotations of a single word (the kinds of arguments most influential in English studies) if we have to think that the tenth-century context was that of the poem's being copied, with the scribe perhaps adding a line or two here and there. For all the work on reception theory, the differences between composing, compiling, adapting, and copying have not been well theorized.

[61] *The Deeds of* Beowulf.

[62] Albert S. Cook, "Aldhelm and the Source of *Beowulf*," *MLN* 40 (1925): 137–42.

[63] We can always hedge. As Patrick Wormald said to me at ISAS 1997 in Palermo: "you can always get away with saying that *Beowulf* was *received* in a later century, but that's rather less interesting, isn't it?"

[64] It is not surprising that an undateable *Beowulf* appeals to many non-technical critics who are not specialists on matters of philology, linguistics, and Germanic history, but there are also solid, technically adept Beowulfians like James Earl, Nicholas Howe, Roy Liuzza, and John Niles who to various degrees seem to be suggesting that the uncertainty is intrinsically a good thing. It is important to distinguish between refusing to accept as proven things that are only speculative and claiming uncertainty as a good in and of itself. I doubt scholars would express the same celebratory attitude towards uncertainty in physics, biology, chemistry … or medicine.

question whether we really need to refuse to weigh the evidence for the date of the poem. It is important to be humble about the extent of our ignorance, to question received wisdom, and to challenge dogma, but a celebration of a politically created uncertainty or an unwillingness to evaluate the evidence cannot be good in the long term for a field whose very existence is premised on the notion that the study of history and historical artifacts is of intrinsic value. Scholars play a risky game when they give the people what they want. Tolkien never meant to excuse the loss of history, and from their other published writings, it seems unlikely that most of the Toronto organizers wanted an un-dateable *Beowulf*, either. But "The Monsters and the Critics" and the Toronto Conference occurred at particular moments when arguments, or even just some of their elements, became amplified, thus triggering large-scale preference cascades. And so the field of *Beowulf* studies in the twentieth century was changed massively and not entirely for the better. However, the very fact of the massive changes wrought by 1936 and 1981 suggests that the new dogma about the un-dateability of the poem will not endure forever. You can live for a while on rhetoric and political power but, it is to be hoped, inconvenient facts will re-assert themselves and a new scholarly generation will arrive with different talents, prejudices, and pieties. Perhaps, then, reports of the death of a dateable *Beowulf* will turn out to have been greatly exaggerated.

9

A Note on the Other Heorot

Joseph Harris

In a series of papers, Leonard Neidorf has argued that Germanic heroic legend circulated in Anglo-Saxon England predominantly in the seventh and eighth centuries, manifesting itself in Latin testimonia, vernacular poetry, visual art, royal genealogies, and personal names.[1] These papers, together with conversations with their author, gave new impetus and purpose to a note I had been contemplating writing off and on for two or three of decades, a note on the *other* Heorot.

In two firmly historical passages Bede speaks of a place and a structure, the name of which is built on the word or name *Heorot*. And as unlikely as it seems, *Beowulf* scholarship has largely neglected to mention this potentially interesting fact. When I began research for this note, I thought that, against all probability, that neglect had been total; on the whole this initial belief has so far held true, with the unusual nineteenth-century exception of Daniel Henry Haigh, whose views I discuss below, together with brief modern allusions to Haigh. I cannot explain how this second Heorot has escaped the attention of *Beowulf* scholars – if it really has – and even the brashest scholar would be uneasy about too confidently asserting a negative, especially in such highly cultivated fields as Bede and *Beowulf*. I will at least affirm that this connection is not

---

[1] See Leonard Neidorf, "Germanic Legend, Scribal Errors, and Cultural Change," Chapter 2 in this volume. See also his "The Dating of *Widsið* and the Study of Germanic Antiquity," *Neophilologus* 97 (2013): 165–83; "Scribal Errors of Proper Names in the *Beowulf* Manuscript," *Anglo-Saxon England* 42 (2013): 249–69; and "Beowulf before *Beowulf*: Anglo-Saxon Anthroponymy and Heroic Legend," *Review of English Studies* 64 (2013): 553–73. His arguments concerning the circulation of Germanic legend build primarily upon H.M. Chadwick, *The Heroic Age* (Cambridge: Cambridge University Press, 1912) and Patrick Wormald, "Bede, *Beowulf*, and the Conversion of the Anglo-Saxon Aristocracy," in *Bede and Anglo-Saxon England: Papers in Honour of the 1300th Anniversary of the Birth of Bede*, ed. R.T. Farrell (London: British Archaeological Reports, 1978), 32–95; reprinted with "Appendix: *Beowulf*: the Redating Reassessed," in *The Times of Bede: Studies in Early English Christian Society and its Historian*, ed. Stephen Baxter (Oxford: Blackwell, 2006), 30–102.

noticed in the encyclopedic recent edition of Klaeber[2] or in the older commentaries known to me and so cannot, at the very least, be *well* known in our field.[3] The object of this note, then, is first simply to introduce (or reintroduce) the second Heorot into the discussion of the poem and then to comment in preliminary form on its potential relevance to the dating and provenance of *Beowulf,* as I understand that problem in the light of scholarship.

Bede's first passage runs as follows:

> Intravit autem praefata regis Osuiu filia Deo dedicanda monasterium quod nuncupatur Heruteu, id est, Insula Cervi, cui tunc Hild abbatissa praefuit ...
>
> (Now the aforesaid daughter of king Oswy entered the monastery called Heruteu, that is the Isle of the Hart, over which at that time Hild ruled as abbess, there to be consecrated to God ...)[4]

Bede's larger context in book 3, chap. 24, adds little of use to us: Penda and his heathen Mercians had raided Oswy's Northumbria with devastating results and even refused to accept tribute. Oswy ($ōs$-$wīu$; cf. ON *Wiwar,* OHG *Wiwa, Wiwila*) therefore turned to God, offering *Him* tribute: namely Oswy's virgin daughter Elfled/Ælfflæd ($ælf$-$fl\bar{æ}d$) and twelve estates for monasteries. The princess was one year old when she entered the monastery of Abbess Hild and spent two years there in the Insula Cervi. Meanwhile, Hild had purchased property, ten households' worth, at *Strēaneshalh,* i.e., Whitby; little Ælfflæd removed with her abbess to the new monastery and lived the rest of her life there as pupil, teacher, and successor to Hild as abbess. Bede tells us that the virgin passed to her heavenly Spouse at age 59. Modern historians tell us that a single fragmentary letter remains from Ælfflæd.

---

[2] *Klaeber's* Beowulf: *Fourth Edition,* ed. R.D. Fulk, Robert E. Bjork, and John D. Niles (Toronto: University of Toronto Press, 2008).

[3] Johannes Hoops, *Kommentar zum* Beowulf (Heidelberg: Winter, 1932), 21–5; R.W. Chambers, Beowulf: *An Introduction,* with a Supplement by C.L. Wrenn, 3rd ed. rev. (Cambridge: Cambridge University Press, 1959), see index; *A* Beowulf *Handbook,* ed. Robert E. Bjork and John D. Niles (Lincoln: University of Nebraska Press, 1997), see index (I reserve p. 225 for comment below); Andy Orchard, *A Critical Companion to* Beowulf (Cambridge: D.S. Brewer, 2003), see index; R.D. Fulk and Christopher M. Cain, *A History of Old English Literature* (Oxford: Blackwell, 2003), relevant pages 193–215 (*Beowulf,* esp. 195–201, main statements on origins).

[4] Baedae, *Opera Historica* with an English trans. by J.E. King, based on the version by Thomas Stapleton, 1565, 2 vols. (Cambridge, Mass. and London: Harvard University Press/Heineman, 1930/1962), 1: 452–3 (*Historia ecclesiastica gentis Anglorum,* book 3, chap. 24). Two other editions have been consulted: *Venerabilis Baedae Historiam ecclesiasticam gentis Anglorum,* etc., ed. Charles [Carolus] Plummer, 2 vols. (Oxford: Clarendon, 1896/1975); and *Bede's Ecclesiastical History of the English People,* ed. Bertram Colgrave and R.A.B. Mynors, rev. ed. Oxford: Clarendon, 1991.

Bede's second relevant passage, book 4, chap. 23, recounts the life and death of Hild, and here he mentions the earlier history of Heruteu:

> Post haec [Hild] facta est abbatissa in monasterio quod vocatur Heruteu; quod videlicet monasterium factum erat non multo ante a religiosa Christi famula Heiu, quae prima feminarum fertur in provincia Nordanhumbrorum propositum vestemque sanctimonialis habitus, consecrante Aidano episcopo, suscepisse.

> (After this she [Hild] was made abbess in the monastery called Hartlepool; which indeed had been made a monastery not long before of the devout handmaiden of Christ, Heiu, which is said to have been the first woman in the province of Northumberland that took the vow and dress of a nun's habit, being consecrated by bishop Aidan.)[5]

This passage confirms the name of the monastery and adds valuable information about its history before Hild's rule. We might notice here Bede's exact wording: Heruteu had, only a few years earlier, been made (into) a monastery. That at least seems a possible interpretation: just as Hild existed before she *facta est abbatissa*, so Heruteu existed before it *factum erat ... monasterium*.[6] The dates of these events are framed by Hild's life, 614–80, and Aidan's death in 651. The founding of the monastery Heruteu seems to have been about 640;[7] Hild may have taken over from Heiu about 649; Ælfflæd was dedicated at Heruteu in 655; Whitby was founded c. 657.

Despite the failure of *Beowulf* scholarship explicitly to notice Bede's Heruteu, there is nothing occult about the phonology; *herut-* is simply an older form of *heorot*. Setting out the *u*- and *a*-umlaut of *e* in Anglian, Campbell, for instance, uses *Herut-* from early Bede manuscripts as an example of the pre-umlaut phonology and juxtaposes it with a spelling *Heorut-*, where the umlaut is registered; and in historical grammars of English, *heorot/heorut* 'hart' is a regular example of both West Saxon and later Anglian back umlaut of *e*.[8] Luick, for example, juxtaposes just our forms to make the same point.[9] Hogg (like Luick) also uses the 'hart' word to illustrate the weakening and loss of medial unstressed vowels,

---

[5] Bede (King ed./trans.), 2:128–9.
[6] A second reference in the same passage sheds no more light on the founding of Heruteu: *Sed illa [Heiu] post non multum tempus facti monasterii, secessit ad civitatem Calcariam ...* "But not long after the making of the monastery ..."
[7] But see John Blair, "Hartlepool," in *The Blackwell Encyclopaedia of Anglo-Saxon England*, ed. Michael Lapidge, John Blair, Simon Keynes, and Don Scragg (Oxford: Blackwell, 1999), 230: "in the 640s."
[8] Alistair Campbell, *Old English Grammar* (Oxford: Clarendon, 1959), §210 (1–2) [88].
[9] Karl Luick, *Historische Grammatik der englischen Sprache*, vol. 1 in 2 parts (Stuttgart: Tauchnitz, 1964 [orig. 1914–21]), 1.1: §228, n. 5 [= I: 209].

yielding forms like *heoretas* and later *heort*.¹⁰ The word survives in all Germanic languages except Gothic (e.g., OS *hirot*, Du. *hert*, OHG *hir(u)z*, G. *Hirsch*, ON *hjǫrt*-), all deriving from a form like **herutaz*, IE **kerw-* (as in Lat. *cervus* 'stag,' Welsh *carw* 'hart').¹¹ Our place name duly appears in Sweet's list of oldest English words from Bede¹² and in the OE translation of Bede's *Historia*, where there is little of real interest to us about the variants.¹³ Latin manuscripts have a variant *heruteig, herutei*; the later alteration to *heortes ig* would seem to remodel the first element of the compound to match the morphology of *Cervi*.¹⁴

The second element, *eu* 'island,' is an early form equivalent to WS *īeġ, īġ*, Angl. *ēġ*. The derivation of *eu* is very complicated and need not detain us too long. I follow K.R. Brooks: PIE *ə́kwā-* 'water' (in Lat. *aqua*, OE *ēa*, OHG *ah(h)a*, etc.) was the basis for an adjectival formation, which in PGmc yielded a form like **a(y)wjō´-* fem. 'associated with water.'¹⁵ This word is missing in Gothic, but found in all the other Gmc languages, e.g., ON *øy, ey* 'island.' This element, in what Brooks calls the "curious nom. sg." form *eu*, is common in Bede's place names, and the manuscripts offer a few variant spellings (e.g., *-e, -ig*).¹⁶ Brooks surveys the eleven instances

---

¹⁰ Richard M. Hogg, *A Grammar of Old English*, vol. 1 Phonology (Oxford: Blackwell, 1992), §6.64 [247–8] and §6.68 [249]; Luick 1.1: §347 [= I: 317–18].

¹¹ I have consulted a number of etymological dictionaries, here especially C.T. Onions, *The Oxford Dictionary of English Etymology* (Oxford: Clarendon, 1966), s.v. *hart*.

¹² Henry Sweet, *The Oldest English Texts*, EETS, OS 83 (London: Oxford University Press, 1966 [orig. 1885]), 140, 144.

¹³ *The Old English Version of Bede's Ecclesiastical History of the English People*, ed. and trans. Thomas Miller, EETS, OS 95–6: 110–11 (London: Trübner, 1890–98). The variants in some form of *ea* (e.g., ms O *heortea*) seem to represent an interpretation of Bede's *-eu* as *ēa*; see below n. 17.

¹⁴ Sweet, *Oldest English*, 140, notes *ig* written over *eu* in the place name *lastenga eu* (book 3, chap. 23) in the same manuscript.

¹⁵ For the PIE form see K.R. Brooks, "Old English *ēa* and Related Words," *English and Germanic Studies* (Birmingham) 5 (1952–53): 15–66, at 41, ratified in Julius Pokorney, *Indogermanisches etymologisches Wörterbuch*, 2 vols. (Tübingen: Francke, 1959) I: 23.

¹⁶ Brooks's invaluable article undoubtedly offers the right explanation for *eu*, but Campbell, *Grammar*, 103 and n. 2, seems doubtful: "This form has been much discussed, but it can hardly be explained without assuming confusion of a form meaning 'island' with *ēa* water," citing Max Förster, *Der Flußname Themse und seine Sippe: Studien zur Anglisierung keltischer Eigennamen und zur Lautchronologie des Altbritischen*, Sitzungsberichte der Bayerischen Akademie der Wissenschaften, Philos.-hist. Abteilung, 1941, Bd. 1 (Munich: Verlag der Bayerischen Akademie der Wissenschaften in Komission bei der Beck'schen Verlagsbuchhandlung, 1941) [Vorgetragen in der Sitzung von 15. Januar 1927]. Förster's relevant pages appear to be 288–93. Förster (291) equates the *eu* forms with OE *ēa* 'water' (< PGmc *áXwō*) and accounts for i-umlauted forms like OE *īeġ* as folks-etymological substitutes, seemingly reversing Brooks's explanation. Marijane Osborn, "Traveling Home with Beowulf," in her (with Gillian R. Overing) *Landscape of Desire: Partial Stories of the Medieval Scandinavian World* (Minneapolis: University of Minnesota Press, 1994), 22 and 31,

of the *eu* spelling in Bede's place names and the variants and brilliantly accounts for all forms from the same root **aujō-*.

Though they appear not to communicate well with Beowulfians, students of English place names have not neglected Bede's Heorot. I take Ekwall as the great example: his *Concise Dictionary* lists variants down to *Hert* 1130–5 and *Herte, Hert* 1242, with the definition "the headland or peninsula on which [the modern town of 'old'] Hartlepool stands."[17] This later version of the name, appearing as early as 1180 (but first as *Hertepol, Herterpol*), "means 'the pool by Hart', the reference being perhaps to the bay south of the peninsula," and a detailed geographic-etymological treatment of *Hartlepool* follows in Ekwall. The later forms of the name and their (slightly tricky) etymology are not strictly relevant to our investigation, but it might turn out to be important that there seems to be a gap in citations of Heruteu, its variants, and derivatives between the OE period and the twelfth century. Other place-name scholars have the 'hart' etymology correct and several cite the standard OE form *heorot*, but only Victor Watts actually mentions the Beowulfian Heorot.[18] *Beowulf's* place name is after all fictional or legendary, but another reason it might be ignored by serious place-name scholars is that there is no dearth of real 'hart' place names in England, names like Hertford, Hartanger, Hartburn, Harter Fell, Hartest, Hartfield, Harthill, Hartington (OE *heorta-dūn* 'stags' hill'), but also, less obviously, forms like Hardstoft, Harford. All the forms just quoted from Ekwall are based on landscape features, but there are also some cultural additives to the natural features, as in Hartington Nb (*Hertweitun* 1171), which Ekwall explains as the "*tūn* by the stags' path." Ekwall's *Dictionary* lists at least one other pre-Conquest 'Hart Island' and an early post-Conquest one.[19]

---

uses the form *Heorot-ea* (attested in the OE translation) and a confusing interpretation of Ekwall on Hartlepool; yet an interpretation of *–eu* like that of Campbell, Förster, and Osborn might have facilitated the addition of *–pol* in the twelfth century. See also Eilert Ekwall, *The Concise Oxford Dictionary of English Place-Names*, 4th ed. (Oxford: Clarendon, 1960), s.v. OE *ēġ, īeġ* (161).

[17] Ekwall, *Dictionary*, 222.

[18] But Watts's allusion (*A Dictionary of County Durham Place-Names*, with contributions by John Insley [Nottingham: English Place-Name Society, 2002], 54–5) would seem to be an oblique negative reference to Haigh (see below): "Scholars have shied away from the possibility that a place might simply be called 'stag' although a hall in *Beowulf* is so named, the stag being a symbol of royalty. They have preferred to see *Hart* as an early example of back-formation, here from Hartlepool and *Hartness*." Ekwall, who does not bring the forms with the *–pol* suffix (which appear in the record later) into the "shortening" to eME *Hert* but does allow for influence from *Herthernyss* (c. 1050), is to be preferred.

[19] Hartland in Devon appears as *Heortigtun* in 880 (**heort+īeg+tūn*, later *tun* supplanted by *land* 'peninsula'), showing a development like that that led to Hartlepol (Ekwall, *Dictionary*, 222); and Harty, Isle of, in Kent (*Heortege*, etc.; 223).

The modern historians I have consulted have little to say of relevance to any Heorot/Heruteu comparison or relationship, but archaeology does shed important light on the monastery.[20] R. Daniels's 1984–85 excavations establish an *early period* in the evolution of the monastery from the mid-seventh century to mid-eighth century, and this is traced through four *phases*, the first contemporary with the founding c. 640 (or 640s), a second terminating about 700, a third beginning about 700, and a fourth about the second quarter of the eighth century; the *second period*, showing a different kind of construction and some contraction in size, reaches from the mid-eighth century toward the end of the century.[21] After this there is a gap in the archeological record of the monastery until the high middle ages. Daniels writes: "Heruteu disappears from the record and was reputedly destroyed by Viking excursions. There was no obvious trace of destruction found at Church Close and it seems more likely that the community just declined in the inauspicious climate of the late eighth century. There is some evidence that by the mid-ninth century the monastery had ceased to exist."[22] Some popular and local historians are much more certain about the Viking raid of c. 800,[23] but the only real evidence is Daniels' post-750 decline.

With this understanding of the birth, flourishing, and decline of the monastery of Heruteu, we need to revisit the place-name evidence. The modern village of Hart, a short distance inland from the headland that was the setting of the monastery, begins to appear in the records in the twelfth century and *Hartness* appears c. 1050. Ekwall derives *Hartness* in its older forms from *Heorotēġ* + *hērnyss*; so it refers not to the headland as

[20] Rosemary Cramp, "The Anglo-Saxon Period," in *Durham County and City with Teeside*, ed. John C. Dewdney (Durham: Local Executive Committee of the British Association, 1970), 199–206 [201 on 1968 excavations in Lumley St. in Hartlepool]; R.J. Cramp and R. Daniels, "New Finds from the Anglo-Saxon Monastery at Hartlepool, Cleveland," *Antiquity* 61 (1987): 424–32; R. Daniels, "The Anglo-Saxon Monastery at Church Close, Hartlepool, Cleveland," *The Archaeological Journal* 145 (1988): 158–210.
[21] Daniels, "Church Close" (1988), 163–73; a found coin, minted 735–58 (Cramp and Daniels, "New Finds," 428: of Eadberht, r. 737–58), is assigned to period 2 (173).
[22] Daniels, "Church Close" (1988), 202; Robin Daniels, "The Anglo-Saxon Monastery at Hartlepool, England," in *Northumbria's Golden Age*, ed. Jane Hawkes and Susan Mills (Stroud: Sutton, 1999), 105–12, at 105; Elisabeth Okasha, "The Inscribed Stones from Hartlepool," in *Northumbria's Golden Age*, ed. Hawkes and Mills, 113–25, at 113.
[23] Cramp and Daniels, "New Finds," 424, assign the decline of Heruteu to "the transference of royal patronage to *Streaneshalch*" despite the fact that Hild probably retained control. "The monastery at *Heruteu* then disappears from the record, but was supposed destroyed by the Vikings in the ninth century." Daniels' later articles disavow the Viking hypothesis; a good website voices ideas like Daniels', adding: "A tantalising glimpse of this abandonment was recently found at the Friarage Field excavation, where a layer of wind-blown sand covered the Saxon layers, showing that the site was abandoned to nature at the end of its life" (www.teesarchaeology.com/projects/saxon_monastery/index.html).

a 'ness' but to the 'obedience' (OE *hīernes* 'report; obedience, subjection, allegiance; jurisdiction, district') to Heruteu. As for the modern village of Hart, some local scholars wish (not implausibly) to posit priority for the simplex from *hert* 'stag'; but professionals are right in seeing that name as a back-formation. Ekwall does not use this technical term but instead speaks of ME *Hert* as "shortened" from OE *Heorotēġ* (Bede's *Heruteu*).[24]

The village of Hart, rather than Heruteu, is the connecting point for the only significant conjunction yet made between the Beowulfian and the Bedan forms, that of the eminent Victorian, the Rev. Daniel Henry Haigh (1819–79). The wild philology and inventive history of Haigh's book *The Anglo-Saxon Sagas: an Examination of their Value as Aids to History* is not unknown to students of the history of our discipline and is sometimes alluded to briefly and dismissively.[25] For example, Shippey and Haarder quote appropriate pages from Haigh, relating him cross-culturally to the forces of nationalism (or at least "local patriotism");[26] Niles makes a similar point.[27] Marijane Osborn treats Haigh more sympathetically, though not entirely accurately.[28] Haigh, ubiquitous in the nineteenth-century study of English antiquities, was also active in early runology, and R.I. Page has commented on his "fertile imagination."[29] Despite overactive

---

[24] Watts, *County Durham*, 54 ("back-formation"); also in A.D. Mills, *A Dictionary of British Place-Names* (Oxford: Oxford University Press, 1991), 229 (bis) and other place-name scholars. Watts, *County Durham*, 55, interprets the ME spelling *Herte* as *Herté*, the direct development from *heorot+ēġ* (other place-name scholars have similar interpretations). While this is not implausible as a stage (clearer in other locations) on the way to Hert/Hart, it may run afoul, first, of the unreliability of ME final *-e* in relation to phonology and, second, of the contradiction in Watts' own "back-formation."

[25] Haigh's book carries the further descriptive subtitle *A Sequel to the "History of the Conquest of Britain by the Saxons"* (London: John Russel Smith, 1861) with reference to his other book of the same year.

[26] T.A. Shippey and Andreas Haarder, Beowulf: *The Critical Heritage* (London/New York: Routledge, 1998), 317; T.A. Shippey, "'Local Patriotism and the Early Interpretation of *Beowulf*," in *Traditions and Innovations: Papers presented to Andreas Haarder*, ed. Flemming G. Andersen and Lars Ole Sauerberg (Odense: Odense University Press, 1994), 303–18, at 315–16 (but Haigh is misnamed "Walter"). I thank Tom Shippey for a wide-ranging email conversation around topics touched on in this article.

[27] John D. Niles, "Myth and History," *A Beowulf Handbook*, ed. Bjork and Niles, 225.

[28] Marijane Osborn, "Traveling Home," 22 (critique below). Osborn provides a more satisfactory brief treatment of Haigh in the context of local patriotism in "The Lejre Connection in *Beowulf* Scholarship," in *Beowulf and Lejre*, ed. John D. Niles and Marijane Osborn, with contributions by Tom Christensen and Marijane Osborn *et al.* (Tempe, AZ: ACMRS, 2007), 288.

[29] R.I. Page, "Runes and Non-runes," in his *Runes and Runic Inscriptions: Collected Essays on Anglo-Saxon and Viking Runes*, ed. David Parsons with a bibliography by Carl T. Berkhout (Woodbridge: Boydell Press, 1995), 166, also passim 161–79; Page, *An Introduction to English Runes* (London: Methuen, 1973), 8, 138–40.

imagination, however, Haigh was of real importance in the archeological history of Hartlepool.[30]

Osborn says that one aspect of Haigh's "thesis" is "worthy of further examination,"[31] and I agree. Haigh identified Heorot with the modern village of Hart and found in the poem extensive reflections of the surrounding countryside; but the name Hart is the only arguable part of Haigh's "thesis," and the larger context makes *Anglo-Saxon Sagas* impossible as scholarship. Haigh supposes that everything in *Beowulf* happens in England ("with two exceptions");[32] all the persons and places are located there, and everything in *Beowulf* is more or less historical. It is not the case, as Osborn (following Wadstein) asserts, that Haigh argued "that the English poet imagined the Danish hall Heorot ... and the lake of the monsters in terms of landscapes around the northern English town Hartlepool"[33] – which would at least be a plausible thesis though it would not explain the name and its relation to Heruteu. But this act of projected imagination is untrue to Haigh's book. For him it all actually *happened* and happened right *there*! He even finds traces of the attack of Ingeld and the Heathobards.[34] The name of the village of Hart, however, is not attested before the twelfth century, and as we have seen, the ME name is best explained as derived from that of the monastery and its

---

[30] For example, Daniel Henry Haigh, "The Monasteries of S. Heiu and S. Hild," *Yorkshire Archæological and Topographical Journal* 3 (1873–74): 349–91. Cf. Haigh's "Hart water" (350) and n. 16 above.

[31] Osborn, "Traveling Home," 22.

[32] Haigh, *Anglo-Saxon Sagas*, 3.

[33] Osborn, "Traveling Home," 22. Osborn's paraphrase is faithful enough to Elias Wadstein's passing remark at the beginning of an article with a deceptive title ("The Beowulf Poem as an English National Epos," *Acta Philologica Scandinavica* 8 [1933]: 273–91), an article actually on the name and identity of the Geats. But a footnote of Wadstein's (273, n. 2) makes it clear that his knowledge of Haigh is not direct but "according to P. Fahlbeck." Pontus Fahlbeck ("Forskningar rörande Sveriges äldsta historia: Beovulfqvädet såsom källa för nordisk fornhistoria," *Antiqvarisk tidskrift för Sverige*, Del 8 (1884), no. 2, pp. 1–87) has, for his part, *also* not read Haigh, whom he lists among the *Gautar* deniers; his honest footnote (27, n. 1) reads: "Haighs arbete ... känner jag endast genom andre" (I know Haigh's work only through others). Nevertheless, Fahlbeck cites Haigh a second time, again making clear his merely mediated acquaintance with the book (38), and here we find the origin of Wadstein's and Osborn's reasonable, but inaccurate, interpretation of what Haigh was doing: "Jag medgifver gerna, att de topografiska enskildheterna uti beskrifningen på Grendelträsket o. s. v. kunna af skalden hafva hemtats från hans egen omgifning — det tyckes vara öfverensstämmelsen härutinnan med en vis trakt i närheten af Hartlepool, som ledt Haigh till uppställandet af denna hypotes" (I admit readily that the topographic details in the description of Grendel's swamp and so forth can have been taken by the poet from his own environment: there seems to be agreement in them with a certain district in the neighborhood of Hartlepool, which led Haigh to the launching of this hypothesis).

[34] Haigh, *Anglo-Saxon Sagas*, 23.

precincts. But there was at least a pre-Conquest church at Hart, and it might be hasty totally to dismiss any connection with the name of the Beowulfian Heorot.[35]

The naming of a monastery from an antecedent place name is not mysterious. Place names come into being everywhere through different combinations of similar forces, and they can be applied to cultural institutions (as in Princeton, Cambridge, Oxford) and their buildings. It is interesting that Bede's nomenclature for monasteries, for example *Streaneshalh*, consists mostly of place names. The peninsula or headland at Hartlepool was of course occupied before Heiu's foundation, but neither archeology nor onomastics suffice to illuminate its uses before c. 640. Daniels' excavations turned up some traces of habitation before his first phase of construction, but these traces are too weak for any cultural characterization.[36] If any of the noble symbolic associations of the stag were relevant to the origin of the place name,[37] they may have been weakened by 640, except that we must remember the aristocratic nature of this early monasticism. Hild and Ælfflæd are examples. Some modern popular sources state that Heiu was an Irish princess, but that rests on too much imagination and an early conflation with Begu or Bega (whose name is also not Irish).[38] Elisabeth Okasha tentatively relates Heiu's

---

[35] *The Victoria County History of Durham*, vol. 3 (1928), http://www.victoriacountyhistory.ac.uk/counties/durham: "The Anglo-Saxon crosses and sundial in the church of Hart show that the vill existed before the Conquest ... The late D.H. Haigh in his work on *The Anglo-Saxon Sagas* (1861) elaborated the theory that Hart was the site of Heort or Heorot, the hall of Hrothgar in the Beowulf Saga ... The identification, however, has not been generally accepted." The old features of the church were not discovered until the 1880s (VCH's "Church" section further on). Daniels, "Hartlepool" (1999), 112, mentions that Hart, along with Billingham and Greatham, were monastic estates of (medieval) Hartlepool.

[36] Daniels, "Church Close" (1988), 160, 163.

[37] For a rich survey, Wilhelm Heizmann et al., "Hirsch," *Reallexikon der Germanischen Altertumskunde* 14 (1999): 588–612 (esp. 595–612); see also C. Susanek, "Heorot," *Reallexikon* ... 14 (1999): 392–4.

[38] Begu was a nun at Hackness (Bede, book 4, chap. 23; [King, ed./trans., 2: 137]), who had a vision on the night of Hild's death; Elisabeth Okasha (*Women's Names in Old English* [Farnham: Ashgate, 2011], 25, 67, 82) connects her name with OE *beag*. Bega was "the very mythical Irish saint Bega, whose name is preserved in St. Bees" (Plummer, *Baedae Historiam* II: 248; I: 431). Haigh ("S. Heiu and S. Hild," 349–50) rejected the identification of Heiu and Begu/Bega stemming from a twelfth-century manuscript but retained the romantic Irish origin of Bega, whose name he spells *Begu*, and identification with Bede's nun of Hackness; the name is from a bracelet relique and replaced an Irish name. Popular historians – but also Cramp and Daniels, "New finds," 424 – frequently miswrite "Hieu."

name to OE *hēah* 'high,'³⁹ and this chimes well with the name of Heiu's last foundation and home near Tadcaster, Healaugh.⁴⁰

Beowulf and *Widsith* of course agree that Hrothgar's hall was named Heorot, and *Beowulf* is explicit about the founding, building, and naming. In what relation does its name stand to that of the monastery? They have in common not only the content but the fact that they name a building or buildings and probably the immediate precincts; in fact both name institutions. But the name of Heorot – simply 'stag' – is unlikely to have developed organically out of a place name as the name of the monastery probably did. *Beowulf*'s Heorot could (like the later village name) be a back-formation from Heruteu, and a modern Father Haigh might imagine a *Beowulf* poet educated in the (double) monastery, along with Oftfor and other churchmen.⁴¹ Years later, writing the epic, our nostalgic poet would have named the foundation of the ancient hero Hrothgar after that of the Christian heroine Heiu. I do not believe that *Beowulf* was created in this way, however, and this theory is weak in several points, including the relationship to *Widsith*. The existence of *two* OE references to Heorot (neither derivable from the other), together with the legendary and real existence of Hrothulf's court at Lejre, seem to me to justify a place for the name in Anglo-Saxon heroic-legendary tradition.

The evidence that the name of the hall came directly from Denmark, along with the most important personal names and basic Scylding legend, is, however, not very strong. Capital and royal hall stand in complementary distribution: Lejre, unknown in England, is mentioned frequently in texts touching on the Norse Skjöldung legend, while Heorot is known only in England. Herben dug up, from an eighteenth-century map, two farm names which he gives as *Stor Hiort* and *Lille Hiorte*, not at Lejre but some distance away on Zealand;⁴² Sarrazin offered a strained argument for a Hartdale near Lejre.⁴³ In recent times – and much more significantly

---

³⁹ Okasha, *Women's Names*, 67, 84.
⁴⁰ King, ed./trans., 2: 128–29 (Bede, book 4, chap. 23); Haigh, "S. Heiu and S. Hild," 349–50 (on Heiu and Begu), 364 (Healaugh interpreted as "domain of Heiu"), 365 (on Heiu's gravestone); Haigh, "Note on the Healaugh Tombstone," *Yorkshire Archæological and Topographical Journal* 3 (1873–74): 408. Plummer adopts the speculation that the name Healaugh may preserve the name of Heiu (*Baedae Historiam*, II, 244).
⁴¹ Oftfor, whose name recalls the type *Wīdsīþ*, studied in both of Hild's monasteries, as well as in Kent, traveled to Rome, and ended as bishop of the Hwiccas (book 4, chap. 23 [King ed./trans., II: 130–3]).
⁴² Stephen J. Herben, Jr., "Heorot," *PMLA* 50.4 (1935): 933–45, at 943; Herben argues that the modern Lejre is not the ancient site. See Marijane Osborn, "The Lejre Connection in *Beowulf* Scholarship," in Niles, *Beowulf and Lejre*, esp. 290, n. 8, for a good refutation of Herben and other displacers of Lejre.
⁴³ Gregor Sarrazin, Beowulf-*Studien: Ein Beitrag zur Geschichte altgermanischer Sage und Dichtung* (Berlin: Mayer & Müller, 1888), pp. 22–3 (repeated in earlier and later

– John D. Niles has drawn attention to the brook, Hjorterende, near the sixth-seventh-century hall at Gammel Lejre.[44]

After all, naming a building for an animal, as in *Beowulf*, is not an especially common practice in real life or in legendary sources. In *Hrólfs saga kraka* the king lives in *Hleðrargarðr*, but this is just 'the *tūn* of Lejre.'[45] Norse mythology is rich in hall names, among them *Breiðablik, Glitnir, Gimlé, and Valaskjalfr*; it also has plenty of animals. But I am unaware of a close parallel to a building named something like "stag" pure and simple (but cf. Herben above). In the modern world we are used to the type "Eagle's Nest" but not "Eagle"; in late medieval cities we have the type "Zum Bären" (with reference to a sign), but not simply "Bär." An analogue close in time and type is Yeavering, *Adgefrin/Adgebrin* in Bede; Ekwall's convincing etymology is Lat. *ad* + Welsh *gafr* 'goat' + *bryn* (*fryn*) 'hill.' Compare the Bedan monastery *Ad Caprae Caput* = Gateshead, with the same name structure.[46] So I am driven back to Moritz Heyne's idea that the antlered gables made the whole hall look like a giant stag.[47] (If we were willing to indulge the fantasy of a horned hall imagined as a noble stag drinking at the runnel Hjorterende, we might achieve an explanation of the simplex.) The multivalency of the hart symbol – suggestive in one direction of aristocracy and royalty, in the other of the Christian reception of a classical image[48] – might have contributed to its double acceptability, to the founders of the monastery and to bearers of heroic legend. Many scholars have commented on the possible symbolic weight of the name in *Beowulf* itself, even if it ultimately belongs to tradition.

To conclude: does the introduction of Heruteu into the discussion contribute anything to the dating of *Beowulf*? If (despite the silence of Scandinavian sources) the name of the hall came to England with the Lejre legend, then little is gained in terms of chronology. The name Heruteu surely preceded the monastery and is probably merely a typical place name combining 'hart' with an aspect of actual topography (type: Hartford). If, however, the name Heorot first entered the oral legend behind *Beowulf* and *Widsith* in England, then we can claim some contribution to

---

writings); for an excellent digest of Sarrazin's writings on Lejre, see Niles, Beowulf *and Lejre*, 435–47.

[44] John D. Niles, "*Beowulf* and Lejre," Beowulf *and Lejre*, 169–233, at 190 (and 179–80).

[45] A consensus etymology and orginal meaning of *hleiðr* is traced by Tom Christensen, "The Name *Hleiþra* (Hleiðr, Lethra, Lejre)," in Niles, Beowulf *and Lejre*, 89, though Jan de Vries, *Altnordisches etymologisches Wörterbuch*, 2nd ed. rev. (Leiden: Brill, 1977) gave equal treatment to two competing etymologies, 236, both with ritual associations.

[46] Ekwall, *Dictionary*, s.v.: the OE translator "mistranslated" the Lat. 'goat' word (*capra*) as 'roe-deer' (*ræge*, fem. to *rāha* 'roebuck'); *caput* refers to a headland or hill.

[47] Moritz Heyne, *Ueber die Lage und Construction der Halle Heorot im angelsächsischen Beovulfliede; nebst einer Einleitung über angelsächsischen Burgenbau* (Paderborn, 1864), 45.

[48] Heizmann, "Hirsch."

dating, if only the kind of contribution that associates things in a social network. "Heorot" as the onomastic base for an institution and building is demonstrably in circulation at the time of the founding and flourishing of the monastery, 640–750, and these dates, perhaps expanded to include Daniel's "second period," the decline of the monastery, 750–800, take in the most likely years of *Beowulf*'s composition according to both older traditional scholarship and R.D. Fulk's more recent, magisterial work. From linguistic evidence, Fulk concludes that the greatest probability surrounds a date of composition around the year 700 in an Anglian kingdom south of the Humber.[49] Evidence that traditions in *Beowulf* were in circulation at this time includes a seventh-century man named Beowulf[50] and others named after figures from heroic legend, such as Hroðulf, Hygelac, Ingeld, and Ætla.[51] To these personal names we may now add the rather interesting name of an institution. The existence of a monastery named Heruteu in the seventh and eighth centuries (but not the ninth and tenth) does not in itself offer much evidence for the dating of *Beowulf*, but it is one additional piece of the puzzle supporting the likelihood of a date in the earlier rather than the later Anglo-Saxon period.

In any event, investigation of the other Heorot has left me with few answers and at least one teasing complex of questions. Gregory's famous letter to Mellitus (601) establishes for every Christian foundation during the conversion period the presumption that it *might* have been based on a pre-Christian holy place. Heiu's foundation of about 640 would seem to fall within the period when Gregory's recycling policy would have been respected, and archeology discovered at least some evidence of culture below the founding phase of the monastery. Evidence in the form of burial orientation and at least one report of grave goods from a pre-Christian phase of the Cross Close burial grounds led Daniels to these thoughts about pre-Christian Heruteu: "… there must have been a considerable imperative at work to result in the new Christian community respecting the same [north–south] alignment and using the same cemetery. Such an imperative may have been rooted in the status of Hartlepool as a royal estate and conjures up the possibility that it functioned as a relatively important royal centre in the first half of the 7th

---

[49] R.D. Fulk, *A History of Old English Meter* (Philadelphia: University of Pennsylvania Press, 1992), 381–92.
[50] See Neidorf, "Beowulf before *Beowulf*"; see also R.D. Fulk and Joseph Harris, "Beowulf's Name," in Beowulf: *A Verse Translation*, ed. Daniel Donoghue (New York: Norton, 2002), 98–100; and R.D. Fulk, "The Etymology and Significance of Beowulf's Name," *Anglo-Saxon* 1 (2007): 109–36. On the dating of the monk named Beowulf, see Chadwick, *Heroic Age*, 64–6.
[51] Wormald, "The Redating Reassessed"; Chadwick, *Heroic Age*, 42–4, 64–6; and see the appendix to Neidorf, "Beowulf before *Beowulf*."

century."⁵² Bede's language for the foundation – *quod videlicet monasterium factum erat non multo ante* – can be interpreted as "had been made *into* a monastery." Indeed, it is inevitable that *something* was "there" before the monastery, but was the something secular (say, a camp for deer hunters?) or sacral? Some symbolic valences of the hart harmonize with the latter, and it is hard to resist the *analogical* attraction of the good arguments for Lejre as a cult center⁵³ – though a direct connection might challenge even a Haighian imagination. On the other hand, Heruteu as a place name (lacking any of the usual words for shrines, *hearg*, etc.) hardly supports a cultic connection. And delicious venison may be motivation enough for the earlier settlement.

---

⁵² Daniels, "Hartlepool" (1999), 110.
⁵³ A famous passage in Thietmar von Merseburg (c. 1012) leaves no doubt that Lejre was a great political-cultic site (readily available in Niles, Beowulf *and Lejre*, 297–9 [ed. M. Osborn] and a theme throughout Niles' book), partly redeeming early writings by Gregor Sarrazin surveyed there (435–47, 288–9) and other relevant articles by Sarrazin, including "Die Hirsch-Halle," *Anglia* 19 (1897): 368–92. Still open is the question whether the *name* of Lejre (*Hleiðr*) had cultic reference or referred to "tents" or "booths" for some secular purpose (see Niles, Beowulf *and Lejre*, 89, esp. the n.); the most recent writer on the subject, Thorsten Andersson, "Lejre §1. Namenkundliches," *Reallexikon der Germanischen Altertumskunde* 18 (2001): 248–9), favors the secular, but my reading of his sources does not agree.

10

Beowulf and Conversion History

Thomas D. Hill

One of the more dramatic stories about the conversion of the Germanic peoples in the early middle ages concerns the pagan Frisian king (or duke) Radbod:

> Praefatus autem princeps Rathbodus, cum ad percipiendum baptisma inbueretur, percunctabatur a sancto episcopo Vulframno, iuramentis eum per nomen Domini astringens, ubi maior esset numerus regum et principum seu nobilium gentis Fresionum, in illa videlicet caelesti regione, quam, si crederet et baptizaretur, percepturum se promittebat, an in ea, quam dicebat tartaream dampnationem.
>
> Tunc beatus Vulframnus: "Noli errare, inclite princeps, apud Deum certus est suorum numerus electorum. Nam praedecessores tui principes gentis Fresionum, qui sine baptismi sacramento recesserunt, certum est dampnationis suscepisse sententiam; qui vero abhinc crediderit et baptizatus fuerit, cum Christo gaudebit in aeternum".
>
> Haec audiens dux incredulus – nam ad fontem processerat, – et, ut fertur, pedem a fonte retraxit, dicens, non se carere posse consortio praedecessorum suorum principum Fresionum et cum parvo pauperum numero residere in illo caelesti regno; quin potius non facile posse novis dictis adsensum praere, sed potius permansurum se in his, quae multo tempore cum omni Fresionum gente servaverat.[1]

(The aforesaid lord (princeps?) Rathbodus, when he began to learn about baptism, inquired of the holy bishop Wulfram, binding [him] by oaths in the name of God, [as to] where the number of kings, lords and nobles of the race of the Frisians was greater – in that region of heaven which if he should believe and should be baptized, [the bishop] promised [him] he would see – or in that [region] which one called hellish damnation.

Then the blessed Wulfram [responded]: Do not be mistaken, distinguished lord, the number of the elect is fixed by God. For your predecessors, lords of

---

[1] *Vita Vulframni episcopi Senonici* ["Life of St. Wilfram,"] ed. W. Levison, in *Passiones Vitaeque Sanctorum Aevi Merovingici*, ed. B. Krusch and W. Levison, Monumenta Germaniae Historica, Scriptorum Rerum Merovingicarum V (Hannover and Leipzig: Hahn, 1910), 668.

the Frisian people, who died without the sacrament of baptism, certain is the sentence of damnation. Who from now on will believe and has been baptized, will rejoice with Christ forever.

Hearing these things the duke [was] incredulous – for he had proceeded to the font – and as it is said, he drew his foot back from the font, saying that he was not able do without the fellowship of his predecessors, of the princes of the Frisians and dwell in the kingdom of heaven with a small number of poor [wretches]. Moreover it was not easy to give assent to new teachings, but rather [he would prefer] to remain [committed] to those which he had kept with all the Frisian people for a long time.)[2]

However one may respond to this narrative, one has to grant that it is a good story. The saint offers salvation and while Radbod apparently accepts the narrative of salvation, which the saint offers, he refuses it since accepting baptism would involve an irreparable break with his ancestors and the traditions of his people. The story powerfully dramatizes the absolute gulf between "paganism" and Christianity as it was defined by some Christians in the early medieval world. A good narrative involves conflict and one could hardly ask for more dramatic or absolute conflict than the story of the conversion, aborted at the last moment, of the pagan king Radbod.

A narrative also requires, or at least is much improved by, an interesting villain or opponent and while the story is part of a hagiographic narrative and thus is told from a Christian perspective, it is hard not to feel some sympathy for Radbod, who must chose between salvation in the company of Christians (and scholars assume Christian Franks whom he hated with particular intensity), and damnation with his own Frisian ancestors. He makes the wrong choice from the Christian perspective, but one can understand on a human level at the least why he acted as he did.

This is a good story and a dramatic story, but there is one problem with it from a historical point of view. As told it is unlikely to be true. To begin with, the narrative occurs in a saint's life written decades after Wulfram's mission to Frisia and indeed the saint's death. And to touch on a point which I will return to later – it is improbable that any missionary who brought the great lord to the point of baptism would be quite so unyielding when faced with Radbod's questions. He and his associates were in the power of Radbod, who could, after all, have them killed or tortured if he so chose. And the question which Radbod raised is one to which even the medieval church had no firm answer. Some authorities insisted (to paraphrase the Athanasian creed) that "extra ecclesiam nulla

---

[2] "Life of St. Wulfram"; for the convenience of the reader I am providing a translation.

salus" [outside of the church, there is no salvation], but there are real difficulties with this assertion.

Turning aside from the theological problems, which the narrative involves, the question that I would like to raise is what point the narrative of Wulfram's intransigence might serve. And just as Radbod fills the role of the interesting, almost tragic, villain who refuses salvation because of his loyalty to his family and nation, Wulfram is the hero of this story who will make no concession to the concerns of his potential convert. The currency of the story and the fact that it was celebrated in art argues that ecclesiastical writers and some at least among their audience were pleased by the zealous intransigence of the missionary bishop. After the conversion, Churchmen liked to imagine that their predecessors had made no concessions to their converts – that they spoke unhesitatingly for the most unyielding version of Christian absolutism. The tragic doomed loyalty of Radbod is set against the absolute rigor of the missionary bishop.

The story of the frustrated conversion of Radbod defines one mode of understanding the process of conversion among the Germanic peoples in the early middle ages. I would like to turn to another kind of conversion narrative that implicitly underlies *The Prose Edda*.[3] One of the most deservedly famous texts in Old Norse-Icelandic is Snorri Sturluson's *Prose Edda* – the prologue explicitly addresses the problem of pagan polytheism in the Northern world and argues that while it was tragic that the memory of the worship of the true God was lost, the stories of the gods and heroes of the Northern world are interesting and were the subject and indeed the basis of poetry among the kings and lords of the north. The remainder of *The Prose Edda* is a gathering of myth and discussion and illustration of various poetic forms and meters. *The Prose Edda* is a very rich text and has attracted a great deal of commentary – indeed scholars have offered very divergent interpretations of the mythic narratives that Snorri tells. But one larger problem concerns our understanding of Snorri Sturluson's attitude towards these myths and the religious tradition that underlies them. Some scholars have questioned whether he wrote the "Prologue"

---

[3] All quotations and citations of *The Prose Edda* are from the editions of Anthony Faulkes. Snorri Sturluson, *Edda: Prologue and Gylfaginning* ed. Anthony Faulkes (Oxford: Clarendon Press, 1982); *Edda: Skáldskaparmál*, ed. Anthony Faulkes (London:Viking Society for Northern Research, 1998); *Edda: Háttatál*, ed Anthony Faulkes (London: Viking Society for Northern Research, 1999). For the sake of clarity in this paper I will refer to this text as *The Prose Edda* in order to avoid confusion with *The Poetic Edda*, or *Elder Edda*, the collection of mythological and heroic poems in the Codex Regius. For an interesting discussion of the problem of Snorri's attitude towards the pagan past, see Christopher Abram, "Gylfaginning and Early Medieval Conversion Theory," *Saga Book* 33 (2009): 5–24.

– it is not found in all of the manuscripts of *The Prose Edda* – but even if we accept Snorri's authorship of the "Prologue," it is very hard to "read" Snorri's attitude towards this material. One can imagine Snorri as a reluctant Christian, a pagan sympathizer, who revered the old religion and lamented the advent of Christianity, but there is nothing in the *The Prose Edda* to support such a reading. Snorri seems amused and detached as a narrator and very rarely, if ever, makes any explicit value judgments about the myths that he narrates. Alternatively one could imagine Snorri as a devout Christian who was grieved and offended by the myths and poetry of the old Scandinavian world. But again – leaving aside the obvious question of why such a Christian would compose a text like *The Prose Edda* – there is very little Christian comment on this material outside of the Prologue.

One way of resolving the problem of Snorri's attitude towards pagan myth and pagan poetry, and one which can be supported from what we know about the conversion of Iceland, is to assume that the missionaries who converted the Scandinavian peoples were much less absolutist than Wulfram. One can imagine their preaching message as being something like "your ancestors were intelligent and wise people who knew much and achieved much, but I have come to teach you something better." They would, after all, have the precedent of Paul's preaching to the Athenians in Acts for such an approach (Acts 18:22–34). As for the problem of the salvation of the heathen, while there are Christian thinkers who would affirm this possibility, all the missionaries need to have done is to avoid Wulfram's insistence that all pagans, no matter how virtuous, were damned. There are obvious problems with this idea and, indeed, some famous Christian thinkers (the ones who come to mind are Dante, Langland, and Erasmus) either hedged their bets (Dante) or unequivocally argued for the possibility of the salvation of the heathen (Langland and Erasmus).

At any rate, while one could write a long and learned book about the historical problem of medieval Christianity and its relation to those outside the Church, an immediate question which might be raised is what these reflections have to do with the particular topic of this volume – the dating of *Beowulf*. At this point I propose to summarize arguments which I have published previously in papers in *Traditio*[4] and in *A Companion to Old English Poetry*.[5] The second paper was later reprinted in Daniel

---

[4] "The 'Variegated Obit' as an Historiographic Motif in Old English Poetry and Anglo-Latin Historical Literature," *Traditio* 44 (1988): 101–24.
[5] "The Christian Language and Theme of *Beowulf*," in *A Companion to Old English Poetry*, ed. Henk Aertsen and Rolf H. Bremmer Jr. (Amsterdam: VU University Press, 1994), 63–77.

Donoghue's edition of Seamus Heaney's translation of Beowulf that is published in the Norton series.[6]

The first paper makes the case that in lines 2879–80 in which the *Beowulf* poet speaks of Beowulf's soul seeking the "soðfæstra dom" (judgment of the righteous), these lines unequivocally mean that Beowulf was saved. The phrasing accords with formulaic convention in Christian-Latin and vernacular Christian religous and historical writing, in which the souls of good Christians are described as rising to the realms above, ascending to heaven, seeking the kingdom of God and so on, whereas secular lords and kings whose salvation is more problematical are simply defined as dying. When Beowulf dies his death is marked by an elaborate Christian obit and these obits conventionally (and as far as I know universally) mark the death of someone assumed to be among the saved.

The second paper is somewhat broader in scope and attempts to survey the problem. Rolf Bremmer invited the contributers to this volume to write essays directed at undergraduates summarizing and surveying various topics, and since the Christian language of *Beowulf* and its thematic implications were topics that I had given some thought to, I took advantage of this opportunity to restate and to some degree reargue views which had already been already been expressed by Charles Donahue[7] and Morton Bloomfield[8] and implied by J.R.R. Tolkien and Fr. Klaeber – and more recently by Geoffrey R. Russom.[9] In the 3,182 lines of *Beowulf*, with the exception of about fourteen lines (175–88), the poet consistently depicts Beowulf and the admirable characters of the poem as monotheists who pray, give thanks to God, and are aware both of the moral order which God has ordained and of divine judgment, but who say nothing specifically Christian. I did contribute a new word to the discussion – "Noachite" – to suggest that the religious context of *Beowulf* is not "pagan" or specifically "Jewish" or "Israelite" but patriarchal. Beowulf, Hrothgar, *et al.* know approximately what Noah and his good sons knew about God, but do not know anything of revealed religion – the religious tradition and teachings which were revealed to Abraham,

---

[6] Beowulf: *A Verse Translation*, trans. Seamus Heaney, ed. Daniel Donoghue, Norton Critical Edition (New York: W.W. Norton, 2002), 197–211.
[7] Charles Donahue, "Beowulf and Christian Tradition: A Reconsideration from a Celtic Stance," *Traditio* 21 (1965): 55–116.
[8] Morton W. Bloomfield, "Patristics and Old English Literature: Notes on Some Poems," *Comparative Literature* 14 (1962): 36–41. This paper was reprinted in part in *An Anthology of* Beowulf *Criticism* ed. Lewis E. Nicholson (Notre Dame: Indiana: University of Notre Dame Press, 1963), 367–72.
[9] Geoffrey R. Russom, "At the Center of *Beowulf*," in *Myth in Early Northwest Europe*, ed. Stephen O. Glosecki, Arizona Studies in the Middle Ages and the Renaissance 21 (Tempe, AZ: ACMRS in collaboration with Brepols, 2006), 225–40.

Moses, and the prophets, a tradition which culminated in the ministry, passion, resurrection, and ascension of Jesus Christ.

This hypothesis has the advantage of explaining what Klaeber described as "the peculiar spiritual atmosphere" of the poem[10] and conforms to the Anglo-Saxon and early medieval understanding of world history. The Germanic peoples of Europe were descended from Noah's son Japeth, and while "real" Germanic peoples were pagan polytheists who worshiped Thor, Odin *et al.*, an Anglo-Saxon Christian could have assumed that some at least of his ancestors maintained the patriarchal faith which Noah had taught Japeth and thus were still "Noachites." (The one explicit Christian comment in the poem, lines 175–88, is in my judgment an interpolation and I have distinguished scholars on my side in this matter. All editors agree that there are missing passages in *Beowulf*; interpolations are no more remarkable than omissions and these lines flatly contradict the tenor of *Beowulf* as a whole.)[11]

This argument, which I hasten to say was not an original one, has met with some agreement. The most common skeptical response is not so much that I and my predecessors are wrong in our specific claims, but rather that the *Beowulf* poet was not really interested in such theological issues and that the idea that the poem represents its characters as patriarchal or Noachite in their religious perspective is a kind of illusion occasioned by the poet's use of formulaic Christian language without his really thinking about its implications. This is an argument, which would involve detailed analysis of a number of passages in the poem, but my counter argument is a simple one. 3,182 lines are a lot of poetry and, if the poet was simply drawing unreflectively on Christian poetic formulas, there would be more than one counter example to cite against the argument. And, to repeat myself, lines 175–88 which speak of how the Danes did not know God flatly contradict the rest of the poem – if one accepts them as authentic one must concede that the poet was clumsy to the point of incoherence in presenting the religious ideas of the main characters in the poem.[12] And while there is much disagreement among *Beowulf* scholars there is a broad consensus that the poet was a consummate craftsman.

I began with two models of conversion history suggested by the contrast between the failed conversion of Radbod, and the detached, amused, but appreciative account of pagan mythic narratives told by

---

[10] *Beowulf and the Fight at Finnsburg*, ed. Fr. Klaeber, 3rd ed. (Boston: D.C. Heath and Co. 1953), cxxi, n. 2.

[11] For more detailed discussion see Hill, "The Christian Language," 68–71.

[12] For a different perspective on this problem, see Karl P. Wentersdorf, "*Beowulf*: The Paganism of Hrothgar's Danes," *Studies in Philology* 78 (1981): 91–119.

Snorri in *The Prose Edda*, and I have offered an explanation for the "peculiar spiritual atmosphere" of *Beowulf* – one might quite reasonably at this point wonder what this chapter has to do with the date of *Beowulf*. I must begin by saying that I am not able to provide conclusive new arguments concerning this well-worn question. However, if my analysis of the poem as a syncretic text, depicting heroes and wise men from the pre-Christian past as admirable characters who deserve and indeed achieve salvation, seems at least broadly plausible, I would like to situate this account of the spirituality of the poem in its larger literary historical context.

The notion of an absolute dichotomy between "paganism" and Christianity, what one might call "Wulframism" has and has had a certain currency and appeal. To begin with, it is very simple – students and scholars studying this period can relax and rejoice in a clear distinction that does not require qualification or modification. This is a worldview that is free from exceptions and is easy to understand, if not to sympathize with. Again, there is a certain strand of Christian thought, more current in the past than in the present, which essentially sympathizes with this view. This legend of Radbod and Wulfram became as popular as it did, because some Christian authorities accepted it and liked it. And, in terms of the reception of the story in modern scholarship, modern scholars who are either "liberal" in their Christian faith, or more firmly agnostic or atheistic, like the story because it reinforces certain preconceptions about the rigidity and intransigence of the early medieval church. For different reasons the story is endorsed from both the right and the left as it were.

But there are other aspects of Christian thought and what one might call Christian historiography that were also current and which are relevant to this argument in its larger context. Jean Daniélou devoted a considerable portion of his very productive scholarly career to studying some of the earliest generation of Christians, the Judeo-Christians as he called them – those Christians who like Peter, Paul, and the other apostles were ethnic and practising Jews who accepted Jesus as the Messiah. Daniélou argues cogently that the clause from the early creed, "descendit ad infernum / He descended into Hell" derives from their influence. As Jews they were concerned about the ultimate destiny of the heroes and heroines of Hebrew Scripture and found a plausible explanation of how these figures might be saved. When Jesus died he must have descended into the realm of the dead and once there he would surely have rescued his own. Thus a concern for those outside the community of the baptized "orthodox" Christians informed the shaping of some of the basic documents of the faith in the earliest generations of the Church.[13] And, of course, if the unbaptized Israelites were saved in Christ's descent into Hell, virtuous gentiles such as Job and Melchizedech must have been saved along with them – a theological "fact" which provides authority and precedent for the salvation of figures such as Beowulf.

While it is true that some great patristic authorities affirmed a quite absolutist version of Christianity, some figures seem to have accepted the possibility of good gentiles and philosophers being saved. Augustine, for example, in an epistle to his friend Deogratias, "roundly declares that God's truth may be and surely is granted to many souls throughout the world, not simply those within the orbit of Biblical religion."[14] And at least one figure, Gregory, seems to have been ready to make substantive concessions to pagan converts. In his letter to Mellitus, the first bishop of London, he urges Mellitus to make use of formerly pagan building sites and suggests that Mellitus recycle as it were pagan festivals by renaming them as festivals in honor of Christian martyrs, but allowing the lay folk to enjoy their traditional feasts and celebrations.[15] Gregory seems to have been relatively indifferent to what laymen thought or believed so long as they attended and participated in Christian worship. In time they, or at least their children, would become believing Christians so long as they participated in the life of the Church. One is tempted to accuse him of elitism and even cynicism, but one must admit that his approach worked and over time Northern Europe became Christian. It is impossible to know what Gregory would have said to Radbod, but one suspects that he would have found some more tactful answer than Wulfram did.

Two other famous late classical texts are at least broadly relevant to this argument. Boethius was a Christian philosopher and theologian, but, facing death on a false charge of treason, he wrote the *Consolation of Philosophy*, a text which deals with the problem of human suffering and free will from a philosophical point of view and which says nothing specifically about Christian issues and ideas. Indeed some scholars think that Boethius as he faced death reverted to philosophy and in effect abandoned Christianity, but the text was received as a Christian

---

[13] Jean Daniélou, *The Theology of Jewish Christianity*, trans. John A. Baker (London: Darton, Longman and Todd, 1964), 233–48.

[14] Henry Chadwick, *Augustine of Hippo: A Life* (Oxford: Oxford University Press, 2009), 152. Chadwick is paraphrasing the letter to Deogratias "Sincerissimo fratri et conpresbytero Deogratias Augustinus in Domino salutem," "(Epistola 102) *Corpus Scriptorum Ecclesiasticorun Latinorum* (*CSEL*) 33, 544–78; for further evidence of this aspect of Augustine's thought, see Chadwick, *Augustine of Hippo*, 160, citing Epistola 164 to Evodius, "Domino beatissimo fratri et coepiscopo Evodio Augustinus in Domino salutem," CSEL 43, 521–41.

[15] Bede, *Bede's Ecclesiastical History of the English People*, ed. Bertram Colgrave and R.A.B. Mynors (Oxford: The Clarendon Press, 1969), I, xxx, 107–8.

philosophical text throughout the medieval period and is so understood by some modern scholars. Received in these terms *The Consolation of Philosophy* provides authority and precedent for a Christian to create an imaginative text in which revelation as such is excluded. Again the *Saturnalia* of Macrobius was long thought to be a work of late pagan apologetics, but the most recent editor of the *Saturnalia* has made a strong case on historical grounds that Macrobius was a Christian composing a kind of nostalgic appreciation of classical Roman pagan literary culture and was hinting at a kind of synthesis of the late classical cult of the sun-god Apollo and the one god revealed in the person of Jesus Christ.[16]

Late classical Latin texts which reflect deliberate syncretism are only generally relevant to the *Beowulf* poet and if we consider *Beowulf* in the relatively narrow context of Anglo-Latin or Old English vernacular literature the poet's sympathetic depiction of "pagans," or to be more precise, pre-Christian Germanic monotheists who know little of revealed religion, is exceptional. But most Old English literature is explicitly Christian – we have only fragments of a far greater whole and the fragments we have were preserved in ecclesiastical foundations. *Beowulf* is the only relatively long secular Old English text we have and so the degree to which it was *sui generis* in its depiction of the pagan past or was relatively conventional can only be a matter of speculation. But, when we consider *Beowulf* in the larger context of the vernacular literatures of Northern and Western Europe in the early medieval period, *Beowulf* is much less exceptional. The two literatures which are particularly relevant to *Beowulf* are Old Irish and Old Norse-Icelandic – rich vernacular literatures which like *Beowulf* treat of the pre-Christian past of the Irish and the Scandinavian peoples respectively. Among the Icelandic texts which one might mention is *Vatnsdaela saga* in which the heroic pagan men of Vatnsdal worship "him who made the sun" until they are further instructed by the Christian bishop who converts them. Then there is "Þáttr Þiðranda ok Þórhalls," a brief text, but one that treats of the conversion with remarkable subtlety and sophistication and has been the subject of a very interesting paper by Merrill Kaplan.[17] The most important literary text in the context of this argument is *Njáls saga*, which retells the story of the conversion and which deals among other things with the heroic life and death of the hero Gunnar of Hlíðarendi, who is killed by his enemies

---

[16] Macrobius, *Saturnalia*, ed. and trans. Robert A. Kaster, Loeb Classical Library (Cambridge Mass.: Harvard University Press, 2011).

[17] For an edition of the "Þáttr Þiðranda ok Þórhalls," see *Olafs saga Trygguasonar en mesta*, ed. Ólafur Halldórsson, Editiones Arnamagnaeanae, Series A, Vol. 2 (Copenhagen: Ejnar Munksgaard, 1961),142–50; Merrill Kaplan, "Prefiguration and the Writing of History in 'Þáttr Þiðranda ok Þórhalls'," *Journal of English and Germanic Philology* 99 (2000): 379–94.

before the conversion. Skarp-Hedin and Hogni, Gunnar's son, have a vision in which they see Gunnar after his death and while he is certainly not in Christian heaven, he is equally certainly not in a place of suffering. And the second part of *Njáls saga* takes place in newly Christian Iceland and concerns the death of a beloved son who dies forgiving his slayers, the sacrificial death of Njál and his sons, and the ultimate reconciliation of the good men on both sides of the feud. *Njáls saga* is a deeply Christian work, but the first two hundred pages or so are concerned with Iceland before the conversion and with sympathetic characters who live and die as pagans.

In the field of Celtic studies, specifically Old and Middle Irish, there has been a great deal of good new published material on the problem of pagan and Christian syncretism. I have been particularly struck by the work of John Carey who has argued and documented a sustained and substantial effort of assimilating Irish antiquity and Irish paganism. Not only did Patrick and other saints of the tradition of Irish Christiantiy save (according to legend at least) the great heroes of the Ulster and Fenian cycle, but there are at least hints of genuine ecumenical dialogue between Christian saints and pagan religious teachers. At one point according to a story told about St. Columba, the saint and one of the Tuatha Dé Daanan spent the better part of a day in religious discourse with each other. After the mysterious visitor has left, Columba speaks to his disciples about the mysteries he has learned. Such stories reflect an attitude about as remote from Wolfram's absolutism and rejection of the religious or secular other, as one can imagine. To quote John Carey's comment: "The medieval Irish sought, with agile and audacious imagination, to find room for as much as possible of their old religion within the frame work of the new, sometimes with exotic or indeed unorthodox results."[18] Among the instances Carey cites is the Irish argument that the divine beings of the old religious order were sons and daughters of Adam and Eve, conceived and born before the fall, and hence sinless. The Beowulfian claim that a virtuous Germanic heroic monotheist was saved seems modest and moderate by comparison. The dating of the various medieval Irish and Irish Latin texts in which these claims are advanced is frustratingly obscure, but it seems clear that these ideas about the salvation of the just pagans and the validity of pagan Celtic tradition were current well before the eleventh century at a time when at least the memory of Irish paganism was part of the living cultural memory of Irish poets and story tellers.

---

[18] John Carey, *King of Mysteries: Early Irish Religious Writing* (Dublin and Portland, OR: Four Courts Press, 1998), 10.

And this is finally the point towards which my argument is directed. The various vernacular texts in Irish or Old Norse-Icelandic which treat the heroes of the pagan past sympathetically are not all dated to the era of the conversion itself, but they are all close enough to that era that the fact of the conversion and the problems which it raised were still an immediate part of the cultural memory of the various poets and saga writers who composed these texts. Snorri for example was writing about two hundred years after the formal conversion of Iceland and about a hundred and fifty years after the real conversion of Iceland, assuming for the sake of the argument, that it took a generation or so for those Icelanders committed to the old religion to accept the new faith. The Icelanders were an antiquarian people who knew very well that they had not always been Christian – the richness and the range of the pagan lore that Snorri knew is proof enough of that. The dating of the various Irish texts is more complicated since many of them are Old Irish texts which are preserved in Middle Irish form, but there is evidence that some of these texts are quite old – and in any case the conversion of the Irish took centuries to complete after the first efforts to convert Ireland by St. Patrick and his associates.

Arguments based on cultural and religious concerns do not normally allow firm conclusions, but I would argue that if *Beowulf* were composed in the tenth century, the poet was for whatever reason writing about theological concerns appropriate to an earlier age. By the tenth century, Anglo-Saxon England had been converted to Christianity for approximately three hundred years. An imaginative and sensitive poet could conceivably have been concerned about the fate of his pagan ancestors, but they would have been distant ancestors indeed by that time. And Beowulf, Hrothgar *et al.* are not even Anglo-Saxons and thus even more remote from a tenth-century poet. But an earlier poet would have felt the issue of paganism and conversion as a much more immediate concern and the effort the *Beowulf* poet put into depicting his patriarchal heroes, carefully situating them in a world which is neither pagan nor conventionally Christian, argues that he was deeply concerned about these issues. This is as far as I can go with this argument; it is possible for an individual poet to violate expectations and reopen debate about an ancient question. But even if we cannot finally resolve this question, there is the notion of the preponderance of the evidence. The term "preponderance" etymologically invokes the cliché of judgment as a balance and I would like to think that the elaborate concern of the *Beowulf* poet for the salvation of ancient heroes adds some weight to the early side of the scales in this matter.

11

Material Monsters and Semantic Shifts[1]

Rafael J. Pascual

In *Linguistic Means of Determining the Dates of Old English Literary Texts*, Ashley Crandell Amos expressed doubt about the vast majority of proposed linguistic dating criteria.[2] The book's pessimistic conclusions are generally not credible, since Amos evaluated criteria in terms of absolute certainty rather than relative probability; her positivistic disregard for probability resulted in negative conclusions that were both inevitable and meaningless.[3] Yet for all that she unreasonably doubted, Amos took a more sanguine view of semantic evidence, affirming that semantic change could be instrumental "in providing evidence for the date of composition of various Old English texts."[4] Many native Old English words gradually changed their meanings after the advent of Christianity, losing older connotations and assuming new ones in order to adapt to novel concepts and ideas. The semantic history of Old English words originally referring to monsters of Germanic folklore, in particular, may shed light upon the dating of *Beowulf*. Over time, some of these words lost their ability to refer to a wider range of (physical) monsters and began exclusively to mean (spiritual) "demon" or "devil." It is clear that some of these words cannot have had such a narrow range of meaning in *Beowulf*, however, where they are uttered by pagan characters ignorant of the Christian revelation and never by the poem's scripturizing narrator.[5] In this essay, I first argue that two words – *scucca* and *þyrs* – possess

---

[1] Thanks are due to Professor José Luis Martínez-Dueñas and Dr. Mercedes Salvador-Bello for their continuous encouragement, and to Frederic Estrada; and to Leonard Neidorf, without whom this chapter would not exist.
[2] Ashley Crandell Amos, *Linguistic Means of Determining the Dates of Old English Literary Texts* (Cambridge, Mass.: Medieval Academy of America, 1980).
[3] See R.D. Fulk, *A History of Old English Meter* (Philadelphia: University of Pennsylvania Press, 1992), 1–65.
[4] Amos, *Linguistic Means*, 155.
[5] On the scripturizing narrator of *Beowulf*, see Marijane Osborn, "The Great Feud: Scriptural History and Strife in *Beowulf*," *PMLA* 93 (1978): 973–81.

only their pre-conversion meanings in *Beowulf*, for if they had acquired a Christian meaning by the time of composition, the poet would have violated his own design. I then track the semantic development of *scucca* and *þyrs*, following them through their appearances in glossaries and other texts, in an effort to determine when they acquired their Christian meanings. The composition of *Beowulf*, we may conclude, probably antedates the semantic Christianization of *scucca* and *þyrs*.

The process whereby words originally used to denote folkloric monsters changed their meanings is the semantic correlate of a broader cultural process whereby the material monsters of the pagan era became the purely spiritual devils of orthodox Christianity. J.R.R. Tolkien acknowledged these processes in his classic study of the monsters in *Beowulf*, in which he remarked of the poem's date: "I accept without argument throughout the attribution of *Beowulf* to the 'age of Bede.'"[6] Tolkien's statement about the date, announced in such bold terms, has naturally been taken out of context; Roberta Frank, for example, uses it to make the ascription of *Beowulf* to the eighth century look like the product of a "faith-based initiative."[7] Although Tolkien says he accepts an early date "without argument," this does not mean that his reading of the poem as a product of the eighth century lacks a chronological argument. Tolkien observed that the monsters in *Beowulf* are not immaterial demonic entities, but "mortal denizens of the material world, in it and of it."[8] Grendel and his mother are given a Christian scriptural pedigree, but they are still the corporeal creatures of pagan times; they are not yet the spiritual demons one finds in Ælfric's *Lives of Saints*, for example. Tolkien claimed, in effect, that the representation of monsters as both Christianized and corporeal did not span the entire Anglo-Saxon period.[9] As we shall see, the evidence for such representation of monsters is reliably dated to the early Anglo-Saxon period, and it includes Aldhelm of Malmesbury's *De Virginitate*, Felix of Crowland's *Vita Sancti Guthlaci*, the Repton Stone, and various glossaries. Broad literary-historical considerations would suggest, then, that *Beowulf* was composed in a milieu closer to this early material – where we can find material monsters – than to late homiletic literature like Ælfric's *Lives of Saints*, which feature purely spiritual devils as the saints' main antagonists. The semantic history of *scucca* and *þyrs* lends strong philological support to this conclusion and enables us to formulate it rather more precisely.

---

[6] J.R.R. Tolkien, "*Beowulf*: The Monsters and the Critics," *Proceedings of the British Academy* 22 (1936): 245–95, at 262.
[7] Roberta Frank, "A Scandal in Toronto: *The Dating of Beowulf* a Quarter Century On," *Speculum* 82 (2007): 843–64, at 844.
[8] Tolkien, "*Beowulf*: The Monsters and the Critics," 262.
[9] See, for instance, Tolkien, "*Beowulf*: The Monsters and the Critics," 264–5, 278.

Semantic Shift

Arguments that attempt to date *Beowulf* solely on cultural grounds are unlikely to be persuasive today, especially if these arguments are propounded without, or in opposition to, philological evidence. The argument that *Beowulf* must be a post-Viking poem because it features Scandinavian characters would be more persuasive if any credible philological evidence could be brought forward in support of it. The absence of such evidence makes the theory that *Beowulf* was composed to unify the English and the Vikings difficult to credit.[10] An attempt to date *Beowulf* according to a literary criterion, such as its particular representation of monsters, would similarly fall flat if it did not accord with philological evidence and if some of the pertinent evidence could not be assessed probabilistically. For my purposes, such evidence is furnished by the semantic history of the masculine *n*-stem noun *scucca*. This word appears just once in *Beowulf*, in its dative plural form, and is uttered by Hrothgar, not by the narrator. After Beowulf cleanses Heorot of Grendel, Hrothgar says to him:

> Ðæt wæs unġeāra   þæt iċ ǣniġra mē
> wēana ne wēnde   tō wīdan feore
> bōte ġebīdan,   þonne blōde fāh
> hūsa sēlest   heorodrēoriġ stōd,
> wēa wīdscofen   witena ġehwylc*um*,
> ðāra þe ne wēndon   þæt hīe wīde ferhð
> lēoda landġeweorc   lāþum beweredon
> scuccum ond scinnum.[11]   (ll. 932a–9a)

Hrothgar here refers to Grendel and his mother as *scuccan*. Editions of *Beowulf* consistently define the word *scucca* as "demon, devil" in its unique occurrence in the poem.[12] "Demon" or "devil" is, without question, the word's invariable meaning when it is used by late Old English

---

[10] See, for example, John D. Niles, "Locating *Beowulf* in Literary History," *Exemplaria* 5 (1993): 79–109.

[11] "Until not long ago, I did not expect ever to experience consolation for my afflictions, when the best of halls stood sword-gory, blood-stained; a far-reaching woe for all the counselors, who did not expect to protect the people's hall against hostile *scuccum* and sprites." All translations from Old English are mine. The text of *Beowulf* cited throughout is *Klaeber's* Beowulf: Fourth Edition, ed. R.D. Fulk, Robert E. Bjork, and John D. Niles (Toronto: University of Toronto Press, 2008) [henceforth *Klaeber IV*].

[12] See, for instance, the glossary in *Klaeber IV*, s.v. *scucca*, p. 428. Given Fred C. Robinson's strong emphasis on the poem's two levels of knowledge (cf. *infra*), the definition "demon" for *scucca* in the glossary of Bruce Mitchell and Fred C. Robinson's edition of *Beowulf* (Malden, MA: Blackwell, 1998) will turn out to be highly ironic, as will be demonstrated below.

authors like Ælfric or Wulfstan.[13] But if the word has such a meaning in *Beowulf*, its appearance in the mouth of Hrothgar would imply that a pagan character is aware of Grendel's diabolical nature. The narrator refers to Grendel frequently as a devil, but the poet systematically avoids placing diabolical terminology into the mouths of his pagan characters. In fact, the characters are unaware of the motivation and genealogy of Grendel, as the following statement from Hrothgar makes explicit:

> nō hīe fæder cunnon,
> hwæþer him ǣniġ wæs　ǣr ācenned
> dyrnra gāsta[14]　(ll. 1355b–7a)

These lines remind us that although the narrator and the audience are aware of the genealogy of the monsters' descent from Cain, the Danes and the Geats are deprived of this knowledge. The pagan knowledge of the poem's characters and the Christian knowledge of the poet and his audience are contrasted in this passage. For Hrothgar, Grendel's nature and origin are a mystery, as is the reason for his attacks on Heorot. The Christian audience, on the contrary, understands Beowulf's fights as part of the Great Feud between God and His evil enemies – even though Beowulf himself and the other characters in the poem do not know it.[15]

There is an artistic purpose behind these two levels of knowledge. As Marijane Osborn and Fred C. Robinson, among others, have observed,[16] the *Beowulf* poet maintains a double perspective throughout the poem. He differentiates consistently between what he and his Christian audience know as opposed to the limited knowledge of the pagan characters of the story. Thus, while the audience is aware that the hostility of Grendel and Grendel's mother toward God reflects their descent from Cain, the pagan characters are ignorant of their descent and motivations. As the editors of *Klaeber IV* put the matter: "the pagan Danes and Ġēatas may think of him [Grendel] as no more than a kind of man-monster; but we in the audience are privileged to recognize him as a descendant of Cain and an

---

[13] See, for example, the usage of the word in *Wulfstan: Sammlung der ihm zugeschriebenen Homilien nebst Untersuchungen über ihre Echtheit*, ed. A.S. Napier (Berlin: Weidmann, 1883), 249, where the word is used in its nominative plural form as a synonym for *dēofol*. For Ælfric's usage, see further below.

[14] "They know of no father, whether any of such mysterious creatures had been born before him."

[15] See *Klaeber IV*, lxxvii.

[16] See Osborn, "The Great Feud"; Fred C. Robinson, "*Beowulf*," in *The Cambridge Companion to Old English Literature*, ed. Malcolm Godden and Michael Lapidge (Cambridge: Cambridge University Press, 1991), 142–59, at 149. See also Edward B. Irving Jr., "Christian and Pagan Elements," in *A Beowulf Handbook*, ed. Robert E. Bjork and John D. Niles (Lincoln: University of Nebraska Press, 1997), 175–92, at 188. Irving expresses strong skepticism about Robinson's approach to *Beowulf*, but he recognizes the existence of the two different levels of knowledge present in the poem.

embodiment of satanic evil."[17] The poet is surprisingly meticulous in his handling of monster lore. As Ruth Mellinkoff has pointed out,[18] he even differentiated between the terms used to refer to antediluvian monsters and those used to refer to monsters that survived the Flood.[19]

Consequently, Hrothgar's ignorance of Grendel's origin and true nature is hardly reconcilable with the translation generally assigned to the word *scucca* as pronounced by the Danish king: "demon, devil." Even Homer nods, but did the *Beowulf* poet err in this instance? The pagan characters consistently refer to monsters in spiritually neutral terms, such as *eoten*, *fēond*, or *sceaþa*, while the narrator uses spiritually charged terms such as *dēofol*, *hellegāst*, or *helrūne*. This distinction is maintained throughout the poem: is *scucca* a rare exception? As Tolkien has observed, "Any theory that will at least allow us to believe that what [he] did was of design, and that for that design there is a defence that may still have force, would seem more probable."[20] As has been stated above, many words of pagan origin underwent semantic change as Christian discourse saturated Anglo-Saxon culture; words lost their original meanings and took on new ones. One important reason why the word *scucca* in *Beowulf* is routinely glossed as "devil, demon" is surely that the two most important complete dictionaries of Old English, Bosworth-Toller and Clark Hall, give these words as the only meaning of *scucca*. This is not surprising, given that in the majority of its occurrences, the word *scucca* is used unambiguously as a synonym for "devil, demon." The list provided by Richard Jente in his study of Anglo-Saxon mythology confirms the regularity of this meaning.[21] The high incidence of *scucca* meaning "devil" in Old English religious texts has naturally led translators and editors to interpret its occurrence in *Beowulf* in similar terms. But as Herbert D. Meritt has pointed out, "Once a word enters a dictionary, the very fact of its niche there tends to induce its inclusion in later dictionaries and to give it a usually quite fitting garb of authenticity; not

---

[17] *Klaeber IV*, lxxvii.
[18] Ruth Mellinkoff, "Cain's Monstrous Progeny in *Beowulf*: Part II, Post-Diluvian Survival,"*Anglo-Saxon England* 9 (1981): 183–97, at 184.
[19] For more on this matter, see Niilo Peltola, "Grendel's Descent from Cain Reconsidered," *Neuphilologische Mitteilungen* 73 (1972): 284–91; Stephen C. Bandy, "Cain, Grendel, and the Giants of *Beowulf*," *Papers on Language and Literature* 9 (1973): 235–49, at 240; Peter Clemoes, "Style as the Criterion for Dating the Composition of *Beowulf*," in *The Dating of* Beowulf, ed. Colin Chase (Toronto: University of Toronto Press, 1981), 173–85, at 182; and Andy Orchard, *Pride and Prodigies: Studies in the Monsters of the* Beowulf *Manuscript* (Cambridge: D.S. Brewer, 1995; reprinted Toronto: University of Toronto Press, 2003), 58, 69.
[20] Tolkien, *"Beowulf*: The Monsters and the Critics," 255.
[21] Richard Jente, *Die mythologischen Ausdrücke im altenglischen Wortschatz* (Heidelberg: Carl Winter's Universitätsbuchhandlung, 1921), 150–3.

all of them deserve it."[22] In all probability, *scucca* does not mean "devil" in *Beowulf*, and this deviation from the norm has significant implications for the dating of the poem.

In order to assess the probable pre-conversion meaning(s) of *scucca*, a consideration of its relatively obscure etymology is necessary. In his unpublished 1961 Wisconsin dissertation, Stanley M. Wiersma analyzed the different etymological theories for *scucca*,[23] which I shall briefly summarize here.

Jacob Grimm related the Old English word to Gothic *skōhsl*,[24] "evil spirit," and this to Old Norse *skōgr*, "forest," thus interpreting the word to have served as a designation for a forest spirit in Anglo-Saxon paganism. Grimm also proposed that the original Indo-European root would have been **skaka*, "to shake." This derivation of *scucca*, however, is philologically unlikely, as Wiersma has pointed out.

The Dietrich-Kauffmann theory is interesting.[25] They relate *scucca* to the reconstructed Old English verb **scyccan*, "to lead astray," of which only a preterit form, *scyhte*, survives. According to them, all of these words would be related to Old High German *scuwo* and Old English *scuwa*, "shadows"; and these, in turn, to Old High German *schusel*, Old English *sceoh*, and Middle High German *schiech*, "fright."[26] On the basis of these meanings, Kauffmann believes that, out of fear of shadows, prehistoric Anglo-Saxons imagined shadowy, deceiving beings that they would have originally called *scuccan*.

The most plausible etymological explanation for *scucca* in philological terms, however, is the one suggested by the Holthausen-Wissmann theory.[27] The word would be the Old English variant of the Old Saxon word *scocga*, "see-saw, swing," and Old High German *scocc*, "a swaying movement," all of them related to Old Norse *skopa*, "to walk," ultimately related to the Indo-European stem **skeu-b*. The original pre-Christian meaning then seems to refer to a swaying or, as Grimm first suggested (cf. *supra*), shaking creature – even if Grimm's phonetic reconstruction was unlikely. The word as applied to Grendel and his mother by Hrothgar

---

[22] Herbert D. Meritt, *Fact and Lore about Old English Words* (Stanford: Stanford University Press, 1954), viii.
[23] Stanley M. Wiersma, "A Linguistic Analysis of Words Referring to Monsters in *Beowulf*," unpublished dissertation, University of Wisconsin, 1961, 323–30.
[24] Jacob Grimm, *Teutonic Mythology*, trans. James Steven Stallybrass, vol. III (London: George Bell and Sons, 1883), 1003.
[25] Wiersma, "Linguistic Analysis," 324–5.
[26] Wiersma, "Linguistic Analysis," 324–5.
[27] Ferdinand Holthausen, *Altenglisches etymologisches Wörterbuch* (Heidelberg: Carl Winter Universitätsverlag, 1963), 280: s.v. *scocca, scucca*. Wilhelm Wissmann, *Nomina postverbalia in den altgermanischen Sprachen* (Göttingen: Vandenhoeck & Ruprecht, 1932), 178.

would thus emphasize their elusive nature in the eyes of the Danes as wandering, stalking inhabitants of homeless fens and moors.

Some indication of the early semantics of *scucca* may be evident in the toponym *Scuccanhlau*, i.e., *Scuccan hlāw*, "the mound of the *scucca*," which is recorded in a charter of King Offa of Mercia to the Church of St. Alban's, dated A.D. 792.[28] That the word antedates Christianization and that consequently it did not always mean "demon, devil" is indicated by the fact that in this and in other toponyms, *scucca* tends to be associated with amiable places, such as paths, roads, knolls, and bridges.[29] On the contrary, when the word *dēofol* is used in topographical compounds, it is systematically associated with strange places or phenomena.[30] As Wiersma remarks, the nature beings of Anglo-Saxon paganism did not have exclusively negative connotations, and he interprets the word's pejorative use in *Beowulf* as a symptom indicating that *scucca* had already begun to be reinterpreted as a devil.[31]

In doing so, Wiersma missed the most important chronological implication of his superb etymological analysis. There was indeed, as he points out, a process of transfer whereby the morally ambiguous beings of Germanic folklore became identified with the purely evil spirits of Christianity in Anglo-Saxon England.[32] But the process did not consist of a single transition, as *Beowulf* crucially demonstrates. In *Beowulf*, a mid-point is presented where the creatures of Germanic popular belief, such as the *ylfe*, the *eotenas*, and the *orcnēas*, are "scripturized" and made the evil descendants of Cain – but not yet completely transformed into the fallen angels of orthodox Christian religion. As Tolkien puts it, by "scripturizing" them, the monsters began to "symbolize (and ultimately to become identified with) the powers of evil, even while they remain, as they do still remain in *Beowulf*, mortal denizens of the material world, in it and of it."[33] There is thus a curious mix of correct and incorrect analysis in John D. Niles's statement that the *Beowulf* monsters "recall [on the one hand] the night-striders of Germanic folk-belief: the poet identifies them with *scuccum ond scinnum*, 'demons and specters'. On the other, they are

---

[28] The charter is available only in a thirteenth-century manuscript by Matthew Paris, MS Cotton Nero D. i, f.148. See Walter de Gray Birch, *Cartularium Saxonicum: A Collection of Charters Relating to Anglo-Saxon History*, vol. I (London: Whiting and Company, 1885), 367–9; see also Wiersma, "Linguistic Analysis," 345, n. 178.
[29] Wiersma, "Linguistic Analysis," 328–9.
[30] Wiersma, "Linguistic Analysis," 329.
[31] Wiersma, "Linguistic Analysis," 330.
[32] Tolkien, "*Beowulf*: The Monsters and the Critics," 263–5.
[33] Tolkien, "*Beowulf*: The Monsters and the Critics," 262.

the devils of Christian belief."³⁴ Niles is correct in thinking that *scucca* recalls monsters of Germanic folklore, but incorrect in glossing the word as "demon." Only the poem's narrator and his Christian audience are aware of the demonic nature of the monsters. To the pagan characters, the diabolical and scriptural qualities of these monsters are unknown. Accordingly, to define *scucca* as "demon" or "devil" is to accuse the *Beowulf* poet of a stylistic inconsistency.³⁵ It is more probable that scholars have erred in defining this word than that the poet has erred in using it.

The *Beowulf* poet is surprisingly precise in his creation of two levels of knowledge about the monsters in his poem.³⁶ While the Christian narrator refers to the poem's monsters as *dēofla*,³⁷ *helrūnan*,³⁸ *hellegāst*,³⁹ *helle hæfton*,⁴⁰ *fēond on helle*,⁴¹ *Godes andsacan/andsaca*,⁴² and *hǣþen*,⁴³ the poem's characters never use such language; they are unaware of the diabolical nature of the monsters against whom they must struggle. Consequently, the word *scucca* in *Beowulf* cannot be the unambiguous synonym for *dēofol* that it is in (later) religious texts. As Robinson put it, to the characters "the monsters have meaning only in terms of the pagan's dark mythology of evil."⁴⁴ On these grounds, two conclusions appear justified. The first is that the word *scuccum* in *Beowulf* retains its original meaning and refers to a particular kind of deceptive, swaying creature of Germanic folklore. The second is that *Beowulf* probably was composed before *scucca* acquired the invariable meaning "devil."⁴⁵

---

34 Niles, "Pagan Survivals and Popular Belief," in *The Cambridge Companion to Old English Literature*, ed. Michael Lapidge and Malcolm Godden (Cambridge: Cambridge University Press, 1991), 126–41, at 138.
35 The words *scin/scinna*, "specter, sprite," also acquired the Christian meaning "devil." Nevertheless, editors and scholars accept the pre-conversion meaning for this instance in *Beowulf*, and consequently it has no bearing on the present argument. See Wiersma, "Linguistic Analysis," 319–23. See also Orchard, *Pride and Prodigies*, 36, where he translates it as "sprite."
36 See, for example, Orchard, *Pride and Prodigies*, 39.
37 "Devils, demons," genitive plural. See, for example, lines 756a and 1680a.
38 "One skilled in the mysteries of Hell," nominative plural, line 163a.
39 "Hellish creature," accusative singular, line 1274a.
40 "Captive of Hell," accusative singular, line 788a.
41 "Hellish enemy," nominative singular, 101b.
42 "God's adversaries," accusative singular and nominative singular, lines 786b and 1682b.
43 "Heathen", in line 986a, genitive singular, referring to Grendel.
44 Robinson, *Beowulf and the Appositive Style* (Knoxville: University of Tennessee Press, 1985), 32.
45 In view of what he said, Tolkien seemed to be conscious that this word did not refer to Christian demons: "Where it [*gāst, gǣst*] is genuine it applies to Grendel probably in virtue of his relationship or similarity to bogies (*scinnum ond scuccum*), physical enough in form and power, but vaguely felt as belonging to a different order of being, one allied to the malevolent 'ghosts' of the dead." ("*Beowulf*: The Monsters and the

Early Anglo-Saxon glossaries furnish compelling evidence for dating this word's semantic shift. As Meritt observes, the word *scocha* as it appears in the Épinal and Erfurt Glossaries is simply a spelling variant of *scocca/scucca*.[46] In the former, which is dated to the early eighth century,[47] *scocha* is given as a synonym for *thyctin* (i.e., *tyhtend*, "inciter, instigator"), which glosses Latin *lenocinium*, "enticement, allurement."[48] Quite remarkably, in the Corpus Glossary, which is dated to the late eighth century (see below), the same Latin word is glossed exclusively by *tyhten*.[49] That *scucca* or its variants are not provided as synonyms for *tyhtend* in the Corpus Glossary might well be due to the fact that *scucca*, originally used to refer to a deceiving and instigating creature of Germanic folklore, had already changed its meaning to "devil" by the end of the eighth century.[50] This possibility is in accord with the copious evidence

---

Critics," 279). Thus, according to Tolkien, the reason why Grendel is called a *gāst* or his kin is referred to as *scuccum* is because they were all associated with specters of Germanic folklore – which is not to say that they were demons from a Christian point of view. Niles ("Pagan survivals," 138) recognizes *scuccum* as a word referring to creatures of Germanic folk-belief, despite his translation.

[46] Herbert D. Meritt, *Some of the Hardest Glosses in Old English* (Stanford: Stanford University Press, 1968), 94–5.

[47] J.D. Pheifer, *Old English Glosses in the Épinal-Erfurt Glossary* (Oxford: Clarendon Press, 1974), xxiii, lxxxix–xc; see also Elias Avery Lowe, *Codices Latini Antiquiores: A Paleographical Guide to Latin Manuscripts Prior to the Ninth Century. Part II: Great Britain and Ireland* (Oxford: Clarendon Press, 1935), vi; Henry Sweet, *The Épinal Glossary, Latin and Old English, of the Eighth Century*, Early English Text Society, o.s. 79b (London: N. Trübner and Co., 1883), xi–xii; *The Oldest English Texts*, Early English Text Society, o.s. 83 (London: N. Trübner and Co., 1885), 3; Wallace Martin Lindsay, *Notae Latinae: An Account of Abbreviation in Latin MSS. of the Early Minuscule Period (c. 700–850)* (Cambridge: Cambridge University Press, 1915), 456; Karl Brunner, *Altenglische Grammatik nach der angelsächsischen Grammatik von Eduard Sievers neubearbeitet*, 2nd ed. (Halle: Max Niemeyer, 1951), §2. a. 3.

[48] See Pheifer, *Old English Glosses*, 31, L579. The gloss erroneously reads *lenocium*. This gloss, it should be noted, enhances the credibility of the Dietrich-Kauffmann etymology of *scucca* (cf. *supra*). Its assessment is, nevertheless, beyond the scope of the present essay.

[49] See Meritt, *Hardest Glosses*, 95. See also *The Corpus Glossary*, ed. Lindsay (Cambridge: Cambridge University Press, 1921), 105, L117.

[50] The word *scocha* also appears as a synonym for *tyctin*, glossing Latin *lenotium*, in the first of the three glossaries of the late eighth- and early ninth-century Erfurt manuscript. See the *Corpus Glossariorum Latinorum*, vol. V, ed. George Goetz (Leipzig: B.G. Teubner, 1893), 368, L47; see also Pheifer, *Old English Glosses*, 31, L579; for the date of the glossary, see Pheifer, *Old English Glosses*, xxvi. This glossary, however, is a direct copy of the Épinal made by a continental scribe (see Pheifer, *Old English Glosses*, xxv). As Wiersma points out ("Linguistic Analysis," 323), the *n*-stem noun *scucca* exists only in Old English, which means that the continental scribe probably did not understand it and therefore copied the word mechanically. The appearance of *scucca* there is accordingly not relevant.

of *scucca* meaning "devil" in texts composed for certain after the eighth century.

Of all the instances of *scucca* indubitably meaning "devil,"[51] the earliest in a reliably dated work occurs in Wærferth's translation of Gregory's *Dialogues*, which was produced at the behest of King Alfred sometime between his ascension in 871 and the early 890s.[52] In chapter XVIII of Book IV of this work, which deals with the doom of blasphemous young people, Gregory describes how a party of evil spirits came in search of a blasphemous young man's soul at the moment of his death. Although the Old English translation tends to render the Latin text rigorously,[53] Wærferth introduces the prepositional phrase *fram þām scuccum* when he describes how the young man tried to hide himself from these evil spirits.[54] It is clear that in this context the word *scucca* refers to the purely spiritual demons of Christianity, since their purpose is to punish the young man's soul and they cannot even be seen by the man's father, who is with him at the moment of his death. Thus, like the authors who post-date him, Wærferth uses the word *scucca* unambiguously to refer to the spiritual demons or devils of Christian belief. Because *Beowulf* was in all likelihood composed before the meaning of *scucca* became fixed as "devil" in the Christian sense of the word, Wærferth's work may provide us with a rather firm *terminus ad quem* for the poem's composition: the mid-to-late ninth century. The Corpus glossary, however, encourages us to move this *terminus* closer to the beginning of the ninth century, since it might express awareness that the semantic change of *scucca* had already taken place.

It appears that Amos was correct when she predicted that historical semantics might be instrumental in helping us to date the composition of vernacular poems. If the semantic trail left by Old English words originally referring to pagan monsters is further pursued, we may find additional reasons to move the *terminus ad quem* for *Beowulf* toward the

---

[51] See the list provided by Jente, *Die mythologischen Ausdrücke*, 150–1.

[52] See *Bischof Waerferths von Worcester Übersetzung der Dialoge Gregors des Grossen*, ed. Hans Hecht, Bibliothek der angelsächsischen Prosa 5 (Leipzig: Georg H. Wigland, 1900). For the date of composition, see David Yerkes, *Syntax and Style in Old English: A Comparison of the Two Versions of Wærferth's Translation of Gregory's Dialogues* (Binghamton, NY: Center for Medieval and Early Renaissance Studies, 1982), 9; and "The Translation of Gregory's *Dialogues* and its Revision: Textual History, Provenance, Authorship," in *Studies in Earlier Old English Prose*, ed. Paul E. Szarmach (Albany: SUNY Press, 1985), 335–43. See also Stanley B. Greenfield and Daniel G. Calder, *A New History of Old English Literature* (New York and London: New York University Press, 1986), 42; and R.D. Fulk and Christopher M. Cain, *A History of Old English Literature* (Malden: Blackwell, 2003), 66, 242 n. 17.

[53] See, for example, Fulk and Cain, *A History of Old English Literature*, 66.

[54] See *Übersetzung der Dialoge Gregors des Grossen*, ed. Hecht, 289, l. 17.

beginning of the ninth century. When Beowulf arrives at Hrothgar's court, he states that he will fight against Grendel by himself. The word he uses to refer to Grendel is þyrse (l. 426a),[55] the dative singular form of the masculine i-stem noun þyrs, which is usually translated as both "giant, ogre" and "demon."[56] Beowulf's utterance of this word is its only appearance in the poem. The etymology of þyrs, as Nora Chadwick and Wiersma have noted, is very complex, and its precise original meaning is not clear.[57] The evidence of *Maxims II*,[58] place names,[59] and etymology,[60] nevertheless indicate that the word was used to refer to some kind of pre-Christian fen-inhabiting monster of the Grendel type. Although þyrs came to be associated with Christian demons and devils, it is doubtful that this word possessed spiritual connotations by the time *Beowulf* was composed. The poem's hero, a pagan ignorant of revelation, is unaware of Grendel's diabolical nature. In fact, after landing in Denmark, Beowulf says to Hrothgar's coastguard:

> þū wāst, ġif hit is
> swā wē sōþlīċe   secgan hȳrdon,
> þæt mid Scyldingum   sceaðona iċ nāt hwylċ,
> dēogol dǣdhata   deorcum nihtum
> ēaweð þurh eġsan   uncūðne nīð,
> hȳnðu ond hrāfyl.[61]   (ll. 272b–7a)

Beowulf states explicitly that he does not know the nature of Grendel (*sceaðona iċ nāt hwylċ*) and calls him a "mysterious" (*dēogol*) persecutor. The poet here provides an artful reminder of the ignorance of the pagan characters concerning Grendel's origins. The phrase *uncūðne nīð* likewise

---

[55] For an informed discussion of the term þyrs as applied to Grendel, see Philip Cardew, "Grendel: Bordering the Human," in *The Shadow-Walkers: Jacob Grimm's Mythology of the Monstrous*, ed. Tom Shippey (Tempe, AZ: ACMRS, 2005), 200–5.
[56] See Joseph Bosworth and T. Northcote Toller, *An Anglo-Saxon Dictionary: Based on the Manuscript Collections of the Late Joseph Bosworth. Supplement by Thomas Northcote Toller* (Oxford: Clarendon Press, 1921). J.R. Clark Hall, *A Concise Anglo-Saxon Dictionary*, 4th ed. with a supplement by Herbert D. Meritt (Cambridge: Cambridge University Press, 1960), s.v. þyrs. The meaning "enchanter" is a late Old English development. See Wiersma, "Linguistic Analysis," 39.
[57] Nora Chadwick, "The Monsters and Beowulf," in *The Anglo-Saxons: Studies in Some Aspects of their History and Culture Presented to Bruce Dickins*, ed. Peter Clemoes (London: Bowes and Bowes, 1959), 171–203, at 173–4; Wiersma, "Linguistic Analysis," 34–8.
[58] See *The Anglo-Saxon Minor Poems*, ed. E.V.K. Dobbie. Anglo-Saxon Poetic Records, vol. 6 (New York: Columbia University Press, 1942), 56.
[59] Dorothy Whitelock, *The Audience of Beowulf* (Oxford: Clarendon Press, 1951), 72–3.
[60] Holthausen, *Altenglisches etymologisches Wörterbuch*, 375, s.v. dyrs.
[61] "You are aware, if it is as we have truly heard tell, that among the Scyldings a criminal, I do not know of what kind, a mysterious persecutor terrifyingly effects in the dark nights unprecedented enmity, humiliation, and slaughter."

implies that, unlike the poem's narrator and the audience, Beowulf and the pagans do not know the ultimate reason for Grendel's attacks.[62] Beowulf is unaware of Grendel's descent from Cain, his feud with God, and his diabolical nature. In fact, in 959b–60a, after he has killed Grendel, Beowulf says to Hrothgar *frēcne ġenēðdon / eafoð uncūþes*, "we daringly tested the power of an unknown creature." Because it is repeatedly stressed that Beowulf is unaware of the theological context of Grendel's attacks, it is improbable that *þyrs* should mean "demon" or "devil" when it comes out of his mouth.

In her paper on the nature of the *Beowulf* monsters, Nora Chadwick discusses a gloss for Latin *Orcus* found in the late eighth-century Corpus glossary.[63] As she points out, both H.M. Chadwick and Paul Grosjean agree to the range 770–800 as the *terminus a quo* for the compilation of this glossary. The terms this glossary gives as the nearest Old English equivalents for Latin *Orcus* are *þyrs* and *heldiobul* (i.e., *helldēofol*, "hellish devil").[64] This gloss indicates, then, that by the end of the eighth century, *þyrs* had developed the Christian meaning of "demon" or "devil." Because the pagan characters in *Beowulf* do not use diabolical terminology, it is unlikely that *þyrs* could possess such connotations when Beowulf utters it in reference to Grendel. For the *Beowulf* poet, an author attentive to theological nuance, the word *þyrs* must have been a straightforward term for an ogre or a giant. It is a term appropriate for speech that articulates the limited perspective of the pagan characters, but not for the theologically sophisticated narrator. The restricted semantic range of *þyrs* suggests that the composition of *Beowulf* probably antedated the compilation of the Corpus glossary, which took place at the end of the eighth century.

Material Monsters

As I mentioned in the introduction to this chapter, the changes of meaning evident in words like *scucca* and *þyrs* were the semantic aftermath of

---

[62] See Lapidge, "*Beowulf* and the Psychology of Terror," in *Heroic Poetry in the Anglo-Saxon Period: Studies in Honor of Jess B. Bessinger, Jr.*, ed. Helen Damico and John Leyerle (Kalamazoo, Michigan: Medieval Institute Publications, Western Michigan University, 1993), 373–402, at 382–3.

[63] For the date of the Corpus Glossary, see Chadwick, "The Monsters," 173, n. 3; see also *The Corpus Glossary*, ed. Lindsay, xiii; H.M. Chadwick, "Studies in Old English," *Transactions of the Cambridge Philological Society*, vol. IV, part II (Cambridge: Cambridge University Press, 1899), section xxi.5; and Paul Grosjean, "Remarques sur le *De Excidio* attribué à Gildas," *l'Archivium Latinitatis Medii Aevi* XXV (1955): 155–87, at 177.

[64] Jan H. Hessels, *An Eighth-Century Latin-Anglo-Saxon Glossary* (Cambridge: Cambridge University Press, 1890), 86, O231; see also *The Corpus Glossary*, ed. Lindsay, 127, O231.

a broader process of cultural change whereby material pagan monsters ended up giving way to purely spiritual Christian devils in the Anglo-Saxon imagination. A glance at other eighth-century Anglo-Saxon texts representing monsters sheds further light on these processes of semantic and cultural change. These texts provide weighty substantiation for the claim that words originally used to refer to pagan monsters still denoted material monsters rather than purely spiritual devils during the eighth century. They also enable us to get a better sense of the syncretic literary milieu in which *Beowulf* was composed.

As R.D. Fulk and Christopher M. Cain observed, "Anglo-Latin literature is the most narrowly datable of all, and in constructing a history of OE literature, it is Anglo-Latin texts that must provide the framework into which undated vernacular works may be tentatively inserted."[65] I begin, therefore, with Aldhelm of Malmesbury's *opus geminatum*, *De Virginitate*, which was composed around the year 700.[66] Because of the outstanding presence of dragons in *De Virginitate*, this Aldhelmian work has lent itself readily to comparison with *Beowulf*.[67] Although interest in dragons pervades medieval literature, certain features render the case of Aldhelm particularly pertinent to the study of monster lore in Anglo-Saxon England. For one, no Anglo-Saxon author is more enthusiastic about dragons than Aldhelm. In *De Virginitate*, Aldhelm enhances the prominence of his saints' struggles with dragons, sometimes altering his sources and reducing a saint's obstacles to focus our attention on the dragon fight.[68] The disparities between Aldhelm's treatment of dragons and those found in his sources may be due to Aldhelm's familiarity with representations of dragons in Old English verse.[69] Aldhelm's dragons are different from those in his sources, but similar to the dragon in *Beowulf*, in that they are characterized by their super-destructiveness, i.e., their hostility extends to an entire people or nation. It might well be that super-destructive dragons were a current motif in Old English verse tradition at the time Aldhelm was composing, and that both Aldhelm and the *Beowulf* poet modeled their dragons upon it. That there was

---

[65] Fulk and Cain, *A History of Old English Literature*, 35.
[66] On the dating of Aldhelm's *De Virginitate*, see *Aldhelm: The Prose Works*, ed. and trans. Michael Lapidge and Michael Herren (Cambridge: D.S. Brewer, 1979), 14–15.
[67] For such comparisons, see, for example, Margaret E. Goldsmith, *The Mode and Meaning of* Beowulf (London: The Athlone Press, 1970), 133–4; Michael Lapidge, "Beowulf, Aldhelm, the *Liber Monstrorum* and Wessex," *Studi Medievali* 23 (1982): 151–91, at 160–2; Paul Sorrell, "The Approach to the Dragon-Fight in *Beowulf*, Aldhelm, and the *traditions folkloriques* of Jacques Le Goff," *Parergon* 12 (1994): 57–87; Christine Rauer, Beowulf *and the Dragon* (Cambridge: D.S. Brewer, 2000), 57.
[68] Lapidge, "*Beowulf*, Aldhelm, the *Liber Monstrorum* and Wessex," 160.
[69] Lapidge, "*Beowulf*, Aldhelm, the *Liber Monstrorum* and Wessex," 157–8; "Aldhelm's Latin Poetry and Old English Verse," *Comparative Literature* 31 (1979): 209–31.

an exclusively insular dragon motif, and that it was in circulation in England only temporarily, is substantiated by the transitory custom of engraving dragon-like figures on the obverse of coins, as fourteen silver *sceattas* (600–750?) in Reary's list attest.[70] Such a custom is concomitant, as Clemoes has pointed out,[71] with a short period of predominance of insular motifs over continental sources in Anglo-Saxon art.

Closely related to the dragons' super-destructiveness is the issue of their materiality. In his introductory chapters to the prose *De Virginitate*, Aldhelm speaks in an almost allegorical manner of the "serpent of gluttony" and of the "ferocious adder of pride" (chapter XII).[72] Yet he does not forgo the materiality of his dragons for the sake of spiritual instruction. Their material presence means a real, physical menace for the entire populations they harass. Like the dragon in *Beowulf*, Aldhelmian dragons are "mortal denizens of the material world." Sylvester needs to use a collar in order to constrict the dragon he faces.[73] Hilarion burns up another dragon's scaly body.[74] Thus, even though the quasi-allegorical references in the introduction associate the dragons with pure evil, their physicality prevents them from becoming completely allegorical. This is exactly what Tolkien thought of the monsters in *Beowulf*,[75] and he argued that this mid-point between materiality and allegory was a sign of the poem's early composition.[76] That the same fusion is evident in *De Virginitate*, an Anglo-Latin work composed c. 700, supports the idea that a literary milieu conducive to the composition of *Beowulf* obtained in the earlier Anglo-Saxon period.

This early Anglo-Saxon fondness for material monsters appears to be corroborated in both the *Liber Monstrorum* (c. 650–750) and the Repton

---

[70] See Peter Clemoes, *Interactions of Thought and Language in Old English Poetry* (Cambridge: Cambridge University Press, 1995), 17–18.

[71] Clemoes, *Interactions of Thought and Language*, 18.

[72] *Aldhelm: The Prose Works*, ed. and trans. Lapidge and Herren, 69.

[73] *Aldhelm: The Prose Works*, ed. and trans. Lapidge and Herren, 82–4.

[74] *Aldhelm: The Prose Works*, ed. and trans. Lapidge and Herren, 88–9.

[75] See, for example, Tolkien, "*Beowulf*: The Monsters and the Critics," 259, where he states that "the balance is nice, but it is preserved. The large symbolism is near the surface, but it does not break through, nor become allegory." For more on this matter, see Alvin A. Lee, "Symbolism and Allegory," in *A Beowulf Handbook*, ed. Bjork and Niles, 233–54.

[76] See Tolkien, "*Beowulf*: The Monsters and the Critics," 265–6, where he observes: "Yet this theme plainly would not be so treated, but for the nearness of a pagan time. […] He [the *Beowulf* poet] was still dealing with the great temporal tragedy, and not yet writing an allegorical homily in verse. Grendel inhabits the visible world and eats the flesh and blood of men; he enters their houses by the doors. The dragon wields a physical fire, and covets gold, not souls; he is slain with iron in his belly."

Stone (c. 750).[77] The author of the former (probably a colleague of Aldhelm) reimagined Vergil's Report (*Fama*, in *Aeneid* IV.181) by transforming it from a metaphorical monster into a real, material one.[78] The sculptor of the Repton Stone, on the other hand, depicted a warrior fighting a large serpentine monster biting the heads off two other warriors. The materiality of this creature – who calls to mind Grendel's cannibalistic tendencies – is apparent. As Clemoes has remarked, the inspirational force behind such representation probably was the image of hell as a devouring mouth.[79] Like the author of the *Liber Monstrorum*, the stone carver went a step further by transforming a non-living entity (the mouth of hell) into a living, material one.

This image of hell as a devouring mouth is present in another eighth-century Anglo-Latin work which, like *De Virginitate*, has traditionally been compared to *Beowulf*: *Vita Sancti Guthlaci*, written by Felix of Crowland and commissioned by King Ælfwald of East Anglia (r. 713–49). The horde of fen-haunting demons which assails the saint is said to carry him *ad nefandas tartari fauces* (chapter XXXI).[80] Remarkably, these demons are addressed by St. Guthlac as *semen Cain*, i.e., "the seed of Cain."[81] As has been noted,[82] *Vita Sancti Guthlaci* is the only other Anglo-Saxon text where such identification between demons and the kin of Cain is established. The identification is based in part on an interpretation of Genesis, but more particularly on a tradition articulated in the Book of Enoch and other apocryphal texts.[83] Felix's antagonists are

---

[77] For the date of composition of the *Liber Monstrorum*, see Lapidge, "*Beowulf*, Aldhelm, the *Liber Monstrorum* and Wessex," 164–5; see also Orchard, *Pride and Prodigies*, 86. For the Repton Stone, see Martin Biddle and Birthe Kjølbye-Biddle, "The Repton Stone," *Anglo-Saxon England* 14 (1985): 233–92, at 289–90; Catherine E. Karkov, *The Art of Anglo-Saxon England* (Woodbridge: Boydell Press, 2011), 102–3; and Clemoes, *Interactions of Thought and Language*, 58–64.

[78] Lapidge, "*Beowulf*, Aldhelm, the *Liber Monstrorum* and Wessex," 168.

[79] Clemoes, *Interactions of Thought and Language*, 65

[80] See *Felix's Life of Saint Guthlac*, ed. and trans. Bertram Colgrave (Cambridge: Cambridge University Press, 1956), 104.

[81] *Felix's Life*, ed. Colgrave, 106.

[82] See Whitelock, *The Audience of* Beowulf, 80–1; Clemoes, "Style as Criterion," 183, and *Interactions of Thought and Language*, 19; Orchard, *Pride and Prodigies*, 85. See also Sam Newton, *The Origins of* Beowulf *and the Pre-Viking Kingdom of East Anglia* (Cambridge: D.S. Brewer, 1993), 143. Newton emphasizes the most important parallels between Guthlac's demonic opponents and the Grendel kin, observing "that some early eighth-century East Anglians, like the audience of *Beowulf*, believed that fens and marshes were haunted by the evil seed of Cain." He also calls attention to the East Anglian dialect word *Shuck*, a term derived from Old English *scucca* used to refer to a diabolic black dog of folklore (Newton, *The Origins of* Beowulf, 142–3).

[83] See *Felix's Life*, ed. Colgrave, 185; Clemoes, "Style as Criterion," 182–3; Robert E. Kaske, "*Beowulf* and the Book of Enoch," *Speculum* 46 (1971): 421–31; Ruth Mellinkoff, "Cain's Monstrous Progeny in *Beowulf*: Part I, Noachic Tradition," *Anglo-Saxon*

of a more immaterial nature than Aldhelm's, but they retain a material dimension. For one, the mere fact of having a human ancestor implies some element of corporeality. That Felix conceived of these monsters as having a physical existence is likewise suggested in an interesting detail: the monsters are said to inhabit haunted barrows excavated by greedy people in search of treasure.[84] Details such as these might have struck sober readers as superfluous, but they likely crept into the representation of the demons in Felix's work due to their circulation in contemporary vernacular poetry.

Quite a distinct situation is found when we get to Ælfric of Eynsham's late tenth-century hagiographical texts. His choice of antagonist tends to be either a completely evil Roman governor of the time of the persecutions or a purely immaterial devil whose goal is to bring about the spiritual failure of the saint. Remarkably, these purely spiritual devils are often referred to as *scuccan*. The word is particularly recurrent in Ælfric's homily on Job, where it is used to refer to the devil that tempts him.[85] How are we to explain the immense difference between the *scuccan* of Ælfric's work and the monsters found in several reliably dated products of the eighth century, which are remarkably similar to the *scuccum* found in *Beowulf*? The answer is simple: Anglo-Saxon England did not exist in stasis for three centuries. The literary culture of the eighth century differed substantially from the literary culture of the tenth century, and *Beowulf* clearly gravitates toward the eighth rather than the tenth. There are countless reasons for the cultural changes separating the earlier and later Anglo-Saxon period, but two have bearing here. One is that the Christianization of pagan language and phenomena – including monsters – did not occur overnight. The Anglo-Saxons of the eighth century were still relatively recent converts. A second factor is that the Benedictine Reform brought Anglo-Saxon England more in line with mainstream continental Christianity. The idiosyncrasies of the earlier period fall away in the orthodox world of Ælfric. *Beowulf* is better understood as a product of the same cultural context as *De Virginitate*, *Vita Sancti Guthlaci*, the *Liber Monstrorum*, and the Repton Stone – a context where the change from pagan material monsters to Christian spiritual devils was not yet complete.

England 8 (1979): 143–62; Mellinkoff, "Cain's Monstrous Progeny in *Beowulf*: Part II, Post-Diluvian Survival"; Orchard, *Pride and Prodigies*, 64–6, 76.

[84] *Felix's Life*, ed. Colgrave, 92–4.

[85] See *Ælfric's Catholic Homilies, the Second Series: Text*, ed. Malcolm Godden, Early English Text Society, s.s. 5 (Oxford: Oxford University Press, 1979), 260–7.

Conclusion

The transformation of material monsters into spiritual devils necessitated a semantic shift in the Old English words that were originally used to refer to material monsters. The semantic history of such words has important implications for the dating of *Beowulf*. If words such as *scucca* or *þyrs* are to be taken as referring exclusively to material monsters in *Beowulf* – which must be the case, given their context – then the dates when those words changed their meanings become plausible *termini ad quem* for the composition of the poem. It is worth noting that these are not the only words that have been said to retain their pre-conversion meanings in *Beowulf*. Tom Shippey has noted that the ō-stem noun *hrēow* must be understood as retaining its pre-conversion meaning, "sorrow," rather than the meaning it normally carries in later religious prose, "penitence."[86]

As Tom Shippey has also observed, the semantic history of certain words provides "absolute proof of nothing."[87] Such evidence merely contributes incrementally to the probability that *Beowulf* is an early composition, but its contribution is not negligible. Scholars desiring a post-eighth-century *Beowulf* may still cling to the claim that the language of heroic poetry is not the language of religious prose, and may "retreat to the safe haven of a *Mischsprache*,"[88] arguing for the possibility that in the so-called "poetic dialect" *scucca* and *þyrs* always retained their pre-conversion meanings irrespective of time. This is theoretically possible, but the evidence gives little reason to invest credence in such a counterintuitive and *ad hoc* explanation. Far less credence is required to accept the simple conclusion the semantic evidence suggests: namely, that the *Beowulf* poet used the words *scucca* and *þyrs* in the way he did because they still referred to material monsters exclusively – and that *Beowulf*, therefore, was composed at a time in the eighth century before those two words acquired their restricted, spiritual meanings.

---

[86] Tom Shippey, "Old English Poetry: The Prospects for Literary History," in *Proceedings of the Second International Conference of SELIM (Spanish Society for Medieval English Language and Literature)*, ed. Antonio León Sendra *et al.* (Córdoba: Servicio de publicaciones de la Universidad de Córdoba, 1993), 164–79, at 173–5. Other words which have been said to preserve their pre-Christian meaning in *Beowulf* are the jō-stem noun *synn*, "hostility," the ō-stem noun *fyren*, "pain, violence," and the neuter wa-stem noun *bealu*, "aggression"; see *Klaeber IV*, clii. See also Robinson, Beowulf *and the Appositive Style*, 56–7; Dennis Cronan, "Poetic Meanings in the Old English Poetic Vocabulary," *English Studies* 84 (2003): 397–425, at 400–405; and Fulk, "Old English *þā* "now that" and the Integrity of *Beowulf*," *English Studies* 88 (2007): 623–31, at 629.

[87] Shippey, "Prospects," 175.

[88] Shippey, "Prospects," 165.

12

Scandals in Toronto: Kaluza's Law and Transliteration Errors[1]

George Clark

Roberta Frank's presidential address ("A Scandal in Toronto") at the 2007 annual meeting of the Medieval Academy in Toronto, Canada, sparkled with wit, and imaginatively linked the search for the true date of *Beowulf* with an entertaining fable based on Conan Doyle's creation of a bumbling Dr Watson as straight man to the brilliant Sherlock Holmes. Turning Doyle upside down, Frank made Holmes – representing the "early daters" – the bumbler and Watson the true sleuth, carefully rebutting, almost in spite of himself, the Holmes-like conjectures of the "early daters."[2] Now published in *Speculum*, the address has lost none of its wit, but has gained an impressive set of notes documenting much of the history of the controversy over the date of the poem.[3] Frank's comments on that scholarship sometimes seem rather tilted toward a late dating, as when she quotes Bjork and Obermeier as recommending "a cautious and necessary incertitude," but that phrase concludes their discussion of the date, author, and audience of the poem.[4] Frank subsequently notes that Bjork and Obermeier take Fulk's metrical arguments as "seemingly the most reliable test" for dating the poem.[5] She does not quote the last sentence in Bjork and Obermeier's discussion of the date of *Beowulf* – "Advocates of a late *Beowulf*, however, must contend with the apparent absence of Scandinavian loan words in the poem, the

---

[1] Geoffrey Russom, Michael Lapidge, and the late Rand Hutcheson gave me much-appreciated advice. Leonard Neidorf's copy-editing saved me from a number of slips. All remaining errors are mine in fee simple.
[2] Thom Eberhardt's comic film, *Without a Clue* (1988), made Dr Watson (played by Ben Kingsley) the true detective and Holmes (Michael Caine) the blunderer.
[3] Roberta Frank, "A Scandal in Toronto: *The Dating of Beowulf* a Quarter Century On," *Speculum* 82 (2007): 843–64.
[4] Robert E. Bjork and Anita Obermeier, "Date, Provenance, Author, Audiences," in *A Beowulf Handbook*, ed. Robert E. Bjork and John D. Niles (Lincoln: University of Nebraska, 1997), 13–34, at 33; Frank, "Scandal," 846.
[5] Frank, "Scandal," 846; Bjork and Obermeier, "Date," 33.

presence of exclusively English forms of personal names, and Kaluza's law."[6] Frank's address and *Speculum* paper seem to accept the burden of proof Bjork and Obermeier imply rests with "late daters," including a new challenge, the evidence of paleography.

Although she somehow misses Geoffrey Russom's metrical case (not based on Kaluza's law)[7] for an early *Beowulf*, Frank cites almost every modern scholar who has written on the date of the poem. Her article, however, aims chiefly at refuting R.D. Fulk (the metrics of Kaluza's law) and Michael Lapidge (paleography and the confusion of letter forms).[8] Both scholars have made quite powerful cases for an early dating of *Beowulf* from very different bodies of evidence. For all its panache and wit, Frank's attempt to rebut Fulk fails and her case against Lapidge proves doubtful at best. Frank's conclusions rest on incomplete and inadequate examinations of the evidence presented by Fulk and Lapidge and inadequate documentation of her claims regarding the distribution of Kaluza I (hereafter K 1) verses in *Beowulf* and the appearance of Lapidge's literal confusions in the Exeter Book. Against Fulk's claim that the poem's high frequency of K 1 verses[9] in *Beowulf* indicates the poem's early date, Frank argues that a late poet salted heroic episodes and scenes in *Beowulf* with an appropriately archaic verse form. To support this claim that K 1 verses served as "a 'ye olde' sign," Frank cites some seventeen examples in part I of the poem, characterizes their contexts as "heroic," and finds that the praise of Beowulf's company on arriving at Heorot emphasizes their "old-style gladiatorial physical courage,"[10] although the passage confirms the affluence and social status of its heroes and thus implies their physical courage. Frank's Dr Watson notices some clusters of K 1 verses early in the poem and muses "[t]he hypothesis that the poem was of great age did not by itself explain such a distribution ... "[11] The argument fails logically: assuming the poem's age does not account for its

[6] Frank, "Scandal," 852, Bjork and Obermeier, "Date," 26. For a brief summation of arguments for and against the unity of the poem, see *Klaeber's* Beowulf: *Fourth Edition*, ed. R.D. Fulk, Robert E. Bjork, and John D. Niles (Toronto: University of Toronto, 2008), lxxxviii–xci and the notes thereon, especially n. 4, xci [hereafter, *Klaeber IV*].

[7] Geoffrey Russom, "Dating Criteria for Old English Poems," in *Studies in the History of the English Language*, ed. Donka Minkova and Robert Stockwell (Berlin: Mouton de Gruyter, 2002), 245–66.

[8] R.D. Fulk, *A History of Old English Meter* (Philadelphia: University of Pennsylvania Press, 1992), 381–92; Michael Lapidge, "The Archetype of *Beowulf*," *Anglo-Saxon England* 29 (2000): 5–41.

[9] Kaluza 1 verses – type 2A3 (ii) – have, like *morðbeala mára*, resolution in the first drop (- *bealo*) the second syllable of which must be etymologically light. I owe this succinct definition to Robert Fulk. See Alan J. Bliss, *The Metre of* Beowulf, rev. ed. (Oxford: Blackwell, 1967), 27–31.

[10] Frank, "Scandal," 859.

[11] Frank, "Scandal," 858–9.

disposition of K 1 verses, nor does assuming the poem's youth. A poet of the seventh or early eighth century, like a poet of the late tenth or early eleventh century, could have favored K 1 verses for heroic episodes; on empirical grounds, one might note that part I includes K 1 verses in "Hrothgar's sermon," an episode without heroic or archaic features. Although the second part of *Beowulf* seems richer in heroic actions than the first, part II proves poorer in those heroic verses. Frank or her alter ego, Dr Watson, introduce a new criterion for explaining the scarcity of K 1 verses in part II of *Beowulf*: the tone there is too bleak for an archaic and heroic verse form suitable for scenes of heroic celebration and ceremony.[12] However, the bleakest episode in part I, the Finnsburh episode, has an above par number of K 1 verses and the bleakest lines in the poem, the expression of grief and fear at Beowulf's funeral, has one in its opening (3149a). The evidence for these remarks appears below, along with an analysis of the actual distribution of K 1 verses in *Beowulf* as a whole and in its several main sections.

Against Lapidge, Frank (and Dr Watson) appeals first to E.G. Stanley's flawed argument that some of the literal confusions found in *Beowulf* appear in the gloss to the Arundel Psalter. Stanley apparently assumed that gloss was contemporaneous with the psalter (basically Gallican, a textual tradition that became widely known in England in the tenth and eleventh centuries), but as Guido Oess, the editor of the Arundel Psalter, pointed out in 1910, the gloss is largely copied from an earlier psalter in the Roman tradition (widely known in the early Anglo-Saxon period) and frequently mismatches the psalter text.[13] That the gloss to the Arundel Psalter predated the psalter itself was hardly surprising: as the Gallican tradition became general in England, some scribes deficient in Latin or industry glossed copies by imposing older, Roman glosses on the newer Gallican psalter MSS.[14] Frank buttresses this argument with her own claim that Cynewulf's signed poems have "all but one" of the literal confusions Lapidge finds in *Beowulf* and that one of them (**d** and **ð**) appears very frequently (nearly one instance per folio) in the Exeter Book. Frank leaves her readers to find the literal confusions in Cynewulf's work and the Exeter Book without a single reference to a specific folio or line in an edition of the texts. Here too, her claims deserve a more detailed examination. A fuller examination of "Lapidge errors" seems to confirm that *Beowulf* was copied into the archetype as a single poem, but the distribution and nature of K 1 verses in part II could be taken as

---

[12] Frank, "Scandal," 859.
[13] *Der Altengische Arundel-Psalter*, ed. Guido Oess (Heidelberg: Winter, 1910), 17, 18–23.
[14] George Clark, "The Date of *Beowulf* and the Arundel Psalter Gloss," *Modern Philology* 106 (2009): 677–85, at 683–4.

suggesting that different poets, perhaps at different times, composed the poem's two parts.

Kaluza's Law, Patterns, and Meaning

Frank's argument against Fulk's position claims, on the basis of a few observations, that the uneven distribution of K 1 verses in *Beowulf* implies that the audience would recognize those verses as archaic and that passages rich in K 1 verses express an outmoded worldview and set of values the poem's audience might appreciate but did not share.[15] These weighty claims rest on a rather light examination of the appearances of a verse form that is probably old but not necessarily archaic at the time when the poem first became a written text. Fulk finds 62 K 1 verses in *Beowulf*, but Frank generalizes on their distribution after noting the contexts of about one quarter of them. Tracking down the other K 1 verses reveals that the evidence contradicts Frank's conclusions on the distribution and significance of K 1 verses in *Beowulf*. Her conclusion goes well beyond the evidence that readers must find for themselves. Investigations often go seriously astray when the detectives involved identify a suspect and develop "tunnel vision," an inability to see clues leading elsewhere. Frank's Dr Watson seems just such a detective. For Dr Watson, finding 7 K 1 verses in 43 lines (195–222), 3 in 8 lines (1239–46), and another 6 in 97 lines (1063–1159) proves that the appearance of K 1 verses in *Beowulf* express the poet's conscious purpose and that purpose can be deduced from that same small data sample. Pure chance would distribute K 1 verses unevenly throughout the poem; a distribution without clusters and corresponding gaps in the occurrence of those verses would be wildly improbable.[16] The absence of clusters in a large sample indicates a non-random distribution. Further, non-random appearances of a given word or verse form may not represent conscious artistry: Chaucer's Pandarus, advising Troilus on his first love-letter, warns "And if thow

---

[15] Frank, "Scandal," 858–9, 863.

[16] The number of A type K 1 verses in *Beowulf* has been disputed: Bliss listed 62, Fulk excluded one of those (1534a) as "ambiguous," but added one (232a) for an unchanged total of 62; see Fulk, *A History of Old English Meter*, 160 and his "Old English Meter and Oral Tradition: Three Issues Bearing on Poetic Chronology," *JEGP* 106 (2007): 317–24, at 318 and 320. In his statistical table (at 320), he failed to include 232a in the total. Seichii Suzuki, *The Metrical Organization of 'Beowulf'* (Berlin: Mouton de Gruyter, 1996), 424, n. 29 disputed the inclusion of five *a* or on-verses from *Beowulf* (1122, 1243, 1534, 1778, 3149) but Fulk's contra-argument seems convincing and his figure of 62 is accepted here; see his "Review: *The Metrical Organization of Beowulf*," *International Journal of Germanic Linguistics and Semiotic Analysis* 3 (1998): 293–4. Frank accepts Suzuki's argument without noting Fulk's rebuttal; see 858, n. 84.

write a goodly word al softe, / Though it be good, reherce it nought to ofte" (2.1028–9).[17] Repetition may not be artful. English teachers, and the editors of learned journals, often have to point out to surprised students or scholars that they have repeated a favorite word rather too frequently. And as Beaty showed long ago, the *Beowulf* poet, having hit upon a "goodly worde" often repeats it, sometimes more than once, in the next few lines.[18] That tendency may apply to verse forms as well as diction. Barry Gewen's amusing and informed review of Michael Blastland and Andres Dilnot's *The Numbers Game* notes the authors' observation that clusters (whether of cancers or of K 1 verses) "occur naturally just as a coin tossed 30 times will probably produce at least one sequence of four heads or four tails" and advises the reader of the review "[t]attoo this on your arm: a pattern doesn't always mean a plan."[19]

To examine the distribution of K I verses in *Beowulf*, the poem might be arbitrarily divided into blocks of one hundred lines, and the overall distribution examined. Since line 2229 has been dropped from the poem's now standard edition, it has 3,181 lines (though the last is still numbered 3,182).[20] *Beowulf* may be divided into 31.8 hundred-line blocks (here rounded up to 32), and has 62 K I verses, hence the average distribution would be almost 2 (1.94) K 1 verses per block. The frequency of K I verses in apparently natural divisions in the narrative, e.g., parts I (1–2199) and part II (2200–3182, and the episode recounting Beowulf's return (which Magoun took to be a folk variant of the poem relating the hero's Danish adventures) can be compared.[21] Frank's generalizations about the distribution of K 1 verses in the poem can be tested against a wider view of the appearance of these verses in *Beowulf*.

In the following list of K 1 verses in the poem, off-verses are noted (b), but on-verses are unmarked; a K 1 verse identified by Fulk but not by Bliss is indicated with an F; a slash (/) separates the successive blocks of one hundred lines; three dots (. . .) within slashes indicate blocks with no K 1 verses. A boldface star (*) precedes the first K 1 verse in part II. The list: 76 / 136, 156, 193 / 208, 215, 222, 226, 232F, 236 / 328 / 430, 485 /. . . / 622, 640 / 715, 753, 767 /. . . / 994 / 1065, 1079 / 1116, 1121, 1122, 1147, 1171, 1177 / 1239, 1243, 1246, 1284 / 1317b, 1343, 1369b / 1463, 1476 / 1516

---

[17] See The *Riverside Chaucer*, ed. Larry D. Benson, 3rd ed. (Boston: Houghton Mifflin Co., 1987), 503.
[18] John O. Beaty, "The Echo-Word in *Beowulf* with a Note on the Finnsburg Fragment," *PMLA* 49 (1934): 365–73.
[19] Barry Gewen, "Books of the Times," *The New York Times*, February 6th, 2009, C 6.
[20] See *Klaeber IV*, xxix for the excision of line 2229.
[21] Francis P. Magoun, Jr., "*Béowulf* B: A Folk-Poem on Beowulf's Death," in *Early English and Norse Studies*, ed. Arthur Brown and Peter Foote (Methuen: London, 1963),127–40; and "*Béowulf* A': A Folk-Variant," *Arv* 14 (1958): 95–101.

/ 1602, 1619, 1676 / 1722, 1738, 1778 /. . . / 1906, 1940 / 2046, 2077 / 2108, 2120 / * 2250, 2265 / 2320, 2357 / 2419, 2429, 2456 / 2537, 2584 / 2607, 2618 / 2742/. . ./. . ./. . . / 3149. To sum up, in the whole poem 6 blocks have no K 1 verses, 6 blocks have 1, 11 blocks have 2, 6 blocks have 3, 1 block has 4, no block has 5, and 2 blocks have 6. In part I (1–2199), 3 blocks have no K 1 verses, 3 blocks have 1, 7 blocks have 2, 5 blocks have 3, 1 block has 4, no block has 5, 2 blocks have 6. In part II (2200–3182), 3 blocks have no K 1 verses, 2 blocks have 1, 4 blocks have 2, one block has 3, no block has more than 3. However, part II has a remarkably long gap between its last two K 1 verses. A diligent and imaginative scholar might readily suspect an artistic plan or deliberate design in the appearance of K 1 verses in *Beowulf* just as astrologists find the signs of the Zodiac in the night sky.

To take a broad view, the average frequency of K 1 verses per hundred-line block in the poem as a whole is almost 2 (1.94), but in part I, the average frequency is 2.23 per block, and in Part II, 1.32. K 1 verses appear quite densely from lines 193–236 (7 examples) and again from 1116–77 (6 examples); a lesser cluster 1239–46 (3 examples) may indicate the poet's enthusiasm for K 1 verses waned as the poem progressed, or his occasional realization that this verse form had appeared rather frequently. Parts I and II each have three blocks of one hundred lines with no K 1 verses, but part I is more than twice the length of part II. In part I no K 1 verses appear between lines 485 and 622 (a gap of 136 lines), lines 783 and 994 (gap: 211), and 1778 and 1906 (gap: 127), but in part II no K 1 verses appear between 2742 and 3149, a gap of 407 lines. Except for this extraordinary interval between K 1 verses, part II seems to distribute them more evenly than part I – the first six blocks have respectively 2, 2, 3, 2, 2, and 1 K 1 verses, about the whole poem average per block, but slightly (insignificantly) less than the average for the Part I (2.23:2). Constructing a unified theory for the distribution of K 1 verses in *Beowulf* seems difficult given this set of data, but Frank's theory (or theories) can be ruled out.

Frank's Watson finds that members of the "club" (K 1 verses) "mostly hung out in dark, martial, passages, haunts heavy with weapons and armor, with hall retainers, ships, battles, and smoke, the furnishings of a heroic society" and cites three clusters of such heroic verses, one including lines 193a, 208a, 215a, 222a, 226a, 232a, and 236a, another including lines 1239a, 1243a, and 1246a, and as well, the Finnsburh episode with its six examples between lines 1063 and 1159.[22] Considering these clusters, Dr Watson concluded that possibly "*Beowulf* was invoking semi-obsolete linguistic markers in order to paint a heroic past," and that K 1 verses

---

[22] Frank, "Scandal," 858.

were a "generic signal, a 'ye olde' sign ..."[23] The matter of *Beowulf* seems largely heroic in its surface narrative whatever meanings may lie below that literal matter, but part II seems more consistently heroic than part I though it has lower frequency of K 1 verses. Dr Watson had no trouble dismissing this *contretemps*: in the "Cimmerian gloom" of part II the poet could find "no one and no thing left to burnish" (859). Counting 3149a among the K 1 verses with Fulk (versus Suzuki who would exclude it) places a K 1 verse in the gloomiest passage in part II (or indeed the whole poem) as the Geats lament (*modceare mændon*) their dead king and dismal future at his cremation (3148b–55a). Moreover, the Finnsburh episode (1063–159), a bleak narrative that applies little burnishing to its events or actors, has six K 1 verses in only 97 lines (6.19 per hundred) exceeding the density of K 1 verses announcing Beowulf's propitious arrival in Denmark and at Heorot, lines 205–370 that have seven K 1 verses in 165 lines (4.24 per hundred). Had Dr Watson tested his theory by searching for a passage that seems neither heroic nor archaic, he might have turned to Hrothgar's "sermon" which lacks "ships, battles, and smoke" but includes something of the rhetoric of Christian exhortations to virtue, not a topic that should attract verse forms purportedly reserved for archaic and heroic passages. Hrothgar's sermon proper runs, one might say, from 1709 to 1784 and on this theory should have no K 1 verses. But the "sermon" has three (1722, 1738, 1778) in only 76 lines (a frequency of 3.94 per hundred lines against an average of 2.23 per hundred in part I). In sharp contrast, fitts 12 and 13, lines 791–990, report Grendel's defeat and flight, the expedition to the mere, the triumphant return to Heorot, the ancient and heroic story of Sigemund's exploits, Hrothgar's praise, and public wonder at Grendel's severed, weapon-proof arm, but these two hundred heroic and optimistic lines have no K 1 verses at all.

Frank's Dr Watson supports his tentative explanation that the *Beowulf* poet's K 1 verses, "semi-obsolete linguistic markers," called up "a heroic past" just as Anglo-Latin poets constructed "new hexameters of authoritative old ones," and Hellenistic poets mined Homer for archaic verse forms. "Watson wondered whether the verse type *morðbealu maga* acted similarly as a generic signal a 'ye olde' sign advertising the shard, the ruin, the blurred hieroglyph, as an embodiment of the classical high style."[24] Probably not. Though *morðbealu maga* and its metrical equivlaent *morðorbealu* (the *–or* is not syllablic, *o* should be underdotted) appears three times in *Beowulf* (136, 1079, 2742), the compound appears nowhere else in Anglo-Saxon poetry. Watson might have recalled at that point Holmes' dictum that "[s]ingularity ... is almost invariably a

---

[23] Frank, "Scandal," 859.
[24] Frank, "Scandal," 859.

clue."[25] Indeed, 35 of 62 (56%) of K 1 verses in *Beowulf* appear only in that poem and may have sounded newly forged rather than obsolete when the poem was first heard. One compound beginning a K 1 verse, *guðsearo* (215), also appears in *Andreas* (127) – a poem almost certainly influenced by *Beowulf*[26] – and nowhere else in the surviving corpus.

A.G. Brodeur argued, expanding on Klaeber's brief remarks, that the *Beowulf* poet's creation of new compounds illustrated his originality.[27] A late poet might form an unexceptional K 1 verse after the distinction between long and short endings had been lost by simply repeating a familiar verse but could hardly invent a number of new but correct K 1 verses. Yet the *Beowulf* poet seems to have done just that – and frequently.[28] Some of the compounds in these verses appear more than once in *Beowulf*. In part I, 30 of 49 (61%) K 1 verses begin with a compound found nowhere else in the poetic corpus, in part II, the figure falls to 5 of 13 (38%), a rather small sample that may suggest a lessened impulse toward metrical novelty. Part II begins with a distribution of K 1 verses close to that of part I, but has no K 1 verses between lines 2742 and 3149, a long and still unexplained gap which accounts for the lower frequency of K 1 verses in Part II as compared to Part I.

Though the distribution and nature of K 1 verses in the poem as a whole may offer some slender support for Magoun's claim that Parts I and II had separate origins, that distribution tells against his argument that the section of the poem often called "Beowulf's Return" is a folk variant of the first version of the hero's Danish adventures. Magoun did not define the limits of his folk tale variant (*Beowulf* A´ or A prime) which might be taken as extending from line 1888 to 2199 or be constrained to lines 1963–2151. In either case, the supposed variant narrative seems, in

---

[25] Frank, "Scandal," 862.
[26] See *Klaeber IV*, clxxv, n. 6 for a bibliography of important studies on this point. Of them, Anita Riedinger, "The Formulaic Relationship Between *Beowulf* and *Andreas*," in *Heroic Poetry in the Anglo-Saxon Period: Studies in Honor of Jess B. Bessinger, Jr.*, ed. Helen Damico and John Leyerle (Kalamazoo: Medieval Institute, 1993), 283–312, argues quite convincingly that *Andreas* was indeed directly influenced by *Beowulf*.
[27] Arthur G. Brodeur, *The Art of* Beowulf (Berkeley: University of California Press, 1960), 6–16; Brodeur cites Klaeber for the *Beowulf* poet's abundant compounds and the probability that many of them were "the poet's own coinage," at 6; see Beowulf *and the Fight at Finnsburg*, ed. Frederick Klaeber, 3rd edition with first and second supplements (Boston: D.C. Heath, 1950), lxii–lxiv, lxviii [henceforth *Klaeber III*].
[28] K 1 verses with opening compounds not found in other poems or in prose occur at lines 136, 222, 226, 232, 236, 430, 485, 715, 753, 767, 1065, 1079, 1121, 1122, 1147, 1239, 1243, 1246, 1284, 1317, 1343, 1516, 1619, 1722, 1940, 2046, 2108, 2120, 2320, 2357, 2429, 2618, 2742. Repeated appearances of an opening compound not found elsewhere: *morðbeala* 136 (as.), *morðorbealo* 1079 (as.), 2742 (as.); *fyrdsearu* 232 (ap.), 2618 (as.?); *drihtsele* 485 (ns.), 767 (ns.), 2320 (as.); *gomenwudu* 1065 (ns.), 2108 (as.); *freawine* 2357 (ns.), 2429 (ns.).

its distribution of K 1 verses, to be typical of the poem as a whole. Lines 1888–2199 have six K 1 verses in 212 lines (1906, 1940, 2046, 2077, 2108, 2120), a frequency of 2.8 per hundred; lines 1963–2151 have four K 1 verses (2046, 2077, 2108, 2120) in only 88 lines for a frequency of 4.4., but in either case, Magoun's hypothesized A´ – including Beowulf's account of his battles in Heorot at a minimum – seems rich in K 1 verses.

The editors of *Klaeber IV* conclude from the appearance of correct K 1 verses in all parts of *Beowulf* that the poem may be regarded, until contrary evidence appears, "as a unified composition in regard to its overall structure."[29] Since parts I and II have a significant number and relatively high frequency of K 1 verses and – significantly – no exceptional K 1 verses, both probably fall within the same limited period, but *Beowulf* I has a markedly higher frequency of K 1 verses than *Beowulf* II or any other Anglo-Saxon poem long enough to provide a comparable data sample. The higher frequencies (K 1 verses per hundred lines), in descending order, appear in *Beowulf* I, 2.23; *Beowulf* II, 1.32; *Exodus*, 0.847; *Judith*, 0.573; Cynewulf's poems, 0.499; *Andreas*, 0.465; *Maldon*, 0.308; Hutcheson's late corpus, 0.191; Alfred's poems, 0.111.[30] Taking *Beowulf* I and II together, the poem has 1.94 K 1 verses per hundred lines, more than double the frequency in *Exodus*. Except for *Beowulf* all Anglo-Saxon poems with more than a single K 1 verse have at least one that violates Kaluza's law. That part II might be the work of a marginally later poet, or a poet with different metrical preferences might seem a possibility, but now requires dividing part II at an uncertain boundary. As far as adherence to Kaluza's law goes, *Beowulf* I and II have more in common than either part has with any other Anglo-Saxon poem. Unity is therefore more probable than disunity.

In short, Dr Watson's theory of the distribution of K 1 verses in *Beowulf* fails to explain their presence in some contexts, their absence in others, and their relative frequencies throughout the poem. The distribution of K 1 verses in *Beowulf* does not depend on the subject matter of a passage or its tone.

Literal Confusions

Lapidge argues that a set of "literal confusions" (miswriting one letter for another) in the surviving MS of *Beowulf* arise from the difficulties later

---

[29] *Klaeber IV*, xci.
[30] The list of frequencies relies (excepting *Maldon*) on R.D. Fulk's "Old English Meter and Oral Tradition," 320; Fulk does not separate parts I and II as here; in calculating the frequency of K 1 verses in the whole poem, he does not include 232a (see 318 for this verse) hence a slight error in his frequency for K 1 verses in *Beowulf*.

scribes had in interpreting letterforms in an archetype written before 750. These "literal confusions" were **a** / **u** (3073, 357, 581, 2821, 2860, 2961, 158) [he suggested (in a private communication) some possible additions of which 1031 seems the most compelling]; **r** / **n** (250, 1520, 2251, 2755, 3154); **p** / **ƿ** [for *wynn*] (2814, 2854); **c** / **t** (2771, 1602, 3060); **d** / **ð** (1278, 1362, 1837, 2064, 2959, 1107, 1991) to which Lapidge adds (in note 75) 385, 472, 1198, 1528, 2869. To these, 414 should be added, as *Klaeber IV* confirms. Two literal confusions or literal ambiguities wrongly disambiguated probably appear in line 1278 where the archetype presumably read *deod* with **d** representing both the voiced plosive /d/ and the voiceless fricative that might have been represented as **ð** or **þ**. A later scribe wrongly took the final **d** as /θ/ and the initial **d** for a (voiceless) fricative, thus *deoð* (the archetype's *deod* for *deoð*, restored in *Klaeber III* and *IV*) became *þeod* in a double confusion. Two confusions of **d** and **ð** in line 1278 bring the total to fourteen. Some appearances of *sunu* (344, 1115, 1278, 1808), all or none of which could have been confusions of **a** and **u**, appear in the MS as *sunu* which *Klaeber IV* accepts. Omitting these and some other ambiguous cases leaves some thirty-two probable "literal confusions" though Lapidge suggests that other such confusions may appear in *Beowulf* **h** and **b** (780) and **f** and **ƿ** (2882). For most of these confusions, the sample seems too small to judge any possible significance in their distribution, but **a** / **u** (eight examples) appear both in the stints of scribes I and II with four examples each (with examples and in parts I and 2 evenly divided); **r** / **n** (five examples) appear twice in the work of scribe A, three times in B whereas **d** and **ð** appear more frequently in part I than in part II (14 against 2) which, adjusting for length, makes a ratio of about 7:2.

The literal confusions Lapidge points out appear equally (or nearly so) in the work of the poem's two scribes. An exclusion here or addition there of a probable Lapidge confusion would hardly alter this conclusion. Scribe A's stint makes about 61% of the poem and has seventeen or roughly 53% of the Lapidge confusions whereas Scribe B's 39% of the poem has fifteen or about 47% of those confusions. Conceivably, scribe A slightly excelled B in deciphering unfamiliar letter forms, but all parts of the poem presented both scribes with nearly equal opportunities for confusion. Part I (69% of the poem) has nineteen or 59% of its Lapidge confusions, part II (41% of the poem) has thirteen or 41%.

Assuming that the poem has thirty-two Lapidge confusions, their overall frequency would be almost exactly one per hundred lines. Taking Beowulf's return as running from 1888–2199 (just over three hundred lines), two Lapidge confusions (1991 and 2064) fall insignificantly short of the poem's average of one per hundred lines. Lapidge confusions appear in *Beowulf* at lines: 158, 250, 357, 385, 414, 472, 581, 1031, 1107, 1198, 1278, 1278, 1362, 1520, 1528, 1602, 1837, 1991, 2064, 2251, 2755, 2771, 2814, 2821,

2854, 2860, 2869, 2959, 2961, 3060, 3073, 3154. Dividing the poem into two hundred line blocks with slashes between blocks and with three dots between slashes for blocks with no Lapidge confusions, we have /158/ /250, 357, 385/ /414, 581 /. . ./. . ./ 1031, 1107, 1199/ 1278, 1278, 1362/ 1520, 1528 / 1602/ /1837, 1991, 2064/ 2251/. . ./ 2755, 2771/ 2814, 2821, 2854, 2860, 2869, 2959, 2961/ 3060, 3073, 3154/. Three blocks have no Lapidge confusions, three have one, two have two, six have three, none have four, none have five or six, one has seven. Except for the block running from lines 2800–999 with seven Lapidge confusions, this distribution seems random. Most remarkably, from 2755 to the end of the poem (427 lines or 13% of the poem) has twelve (37.5%) of Lapidge's literal confusions. This area of abundant literal confusions (copied by scribe B) coincides closely with the part of the poem (from line 2742 to the end) that has only one K 1 verse. Since Lapidge's literal confusions appear in all parts of the poem (like K 1 verses), the archetype of *Beowulf* probably included parts I and II (and "Beowulf's Return"), but the final 450 or so lines of the poem pose still unsolved problems for its students.

Frank notes Lapidge's argument for dating *Beowulf* from a set of five literal confusions, but counterclaims that those confusions appear in other MSS containing vernacular poems: "Cynewulf's signed works, the composition of which Lapidge and Fulk put between 750 and 850, provide multiple examples of all but one of these errors; the Exeter Book has almost as many **d** / **ð** confusions and alterations as it has folios" and remarks that only the confusion of **c** and **t** "appears to be missing."[31] Against the dozen or fourteen examples of **d** and **ð** confusions in *Beowulf*, Frank asserts that there are many more in Cynewulf's signed poems and indeed in the Exeter Book as a whole, but leaves the reader to verify her claim that she counted "approximately 100 examples in 123 folios" of the Exeter Book.[32]

Lapidge insisted that the co-occurrence of five literal confusions he noted indicated that the archetype of our *Beowulf* MS was written before 750. Frank's claim that finding four of those confusions in Cynewulf's signed poems invalidates Lapidge's argument if (and only if) those confusions can be shown to arise from the same cause as those appearing in *Beowulf*. All of Frank's four literal confusions in Cynewulf's work need examination, but the one richest in examples may come first. Lapidge, of course, assumed that the confusions of **d** and **ð** in *Beowulf* go back to an archetype in which **d** represented the voiced plosive and also frequently or regularly – and ambiguously – represented the voiced and voiceless allophonic continuants [θ] and [ð]. The confusions of **d** and **ð** in the Exeter

---

[31] Frank, "Scandal," 857.
[32] Frank, "Scandal," 857, n. 81.

Book, on the other hand, may have had a very different origin. Muir, the most recent editor, noting the literal confusions and corrections common in the work, suggests that a "possibility, which has not been entertained previously, is that one scribe, involved somewhere (and perhaps latterly) in the chain of transmission may have been a non-native (which is not to say non-Germanic)," and observes that many foreign monks worked in England at the time of the monastic reform.[33]

Muir lists the characteristic literal confusions of the Exeter Book as "especially *þ-wynn, p-wynn, s-wynn, n-h, s-f,* and *d-ð.*"[34] The number of confusions involving *wynn* seems remarkable especially given that the two graphic forms of **s** bears little visual resemblance to *wynn* (**p**) and only a topless version of **þ** (a rarity) would be confused with **p**.[35] Muir's list of literal confusions in the Exeter Book overlaps at only two positions with Lapidge's list for *Beowulf*: **p / p** and **d / ð**, a curiously frequent confusion in the Exeter Book. A foreign scribe whose native language did not include or had lost the continuants [θ] and [ð] could have frequently confused what should have been [d] with [ð]; that possibility seems all the stronger since another literal confusion, of **t** and **ð**, in the Exeter Book may well have the same origin in a foreign scribe's accent literally made literal. The Exeter Book MS has *wunat* for *wunað* (*Christ II* 590), the MS *bryttað* (682) was altered from *bryttat*, *wlitat* (1104) was altered to *wlitað*; in *Juliana* the MS *metet* was corrected to *meteð* (218). The confusions of **d**, **ð**, and **t** in the works of Cynewulf (including the unsigned *Christ III*) probably arise from an auditory confusion, a scribe's imperfect comprehension of English speech sounds and their graphic representation, not an archetype's use of **d** for both **d** and **ð**. The letter forms for **t** versus **d** and **ð** can hardly confuse the eye. Muir's hypothesis that a foreign scribe was involved in the transmission of these texts carries conviction. The scribe may have caught some of his mispronunciations or mishearings of English words turned into "literal confusions" when he looked back at his exemplar to pick up more text and noticed that he had not followed copy faithfully. He or another scribe may have proofread the work after its completion. At any rate, most of the literal confusions involving **d**, **ð**, and **t** in Cynewulf's poetry were corrected in the MSS. In *Beowulf*, one confusion of **d** and **ð** is corrected in the work of each of the two scribes; no confusions of **t** with **d** or **ð** and appear in *Beowulf*.

---

[33] *The Exeter Anthology of Old English Poetry*, ed. Bernard J. Muir, 2 vols. (Exeter: University of Exeter Press, 1994), I: 39.
[34] *Exeter*, ed. Muir, I: 38–40.
[35] If the emendation of *mwatide* (2226b) to *in þa tide* proposed in *Klaeber IV* be correct, *wynn* replaced an original *thorn*, almost certainly because of damage to the MS rather than a confusion of letter forms.

Cynewulf's works (including the unsigned *Christ* III), as witnessed in the Exeter and Vercelli books, have thirty-five confusions of **d** and **ð** of which only three appear in the Vercelli (1442 lines) and thirty-two in Exeter (2395 lines).[36] Exeter's error rate should have raised eyebrows in the scriptorium; indeed, twenty-one of those errors were corrected in the MS, while ten went uncorrected. The corrector (or the original scribe) may have been exasperated at line 364 (*Christ* 1) where the original reading *genyrwad* was altered in error to *genyrwað* by adding a cross stroke to the **d**, a confusion but not a correction (hence twenty-one and not twenty-two errors were corrected). Of the three confusions of **d** and **ð** in Cynewulf's work preserved in the Vercelli book, one was corrected in the MS (*Fates* 43). As Frank notices, Cynewulf's poems (including, as Frank did not, *Christ III*) have no examples of the confusion of **t** and **c**; the confusions of **d**, **ð** and **t** (the last not treated by Frank or commented on by Muir) in the Exeter Book (and perhaps the Vercelli Book) probably have a quite different origin from the confusion of **d** and **ð** in *Beowulf* and hence do not tell against Lapidge's argument on the archetype of *Beowulf*. At this point, Cynewulf's poems may not share the essential pattern of literal confusions Lapidge rightly insisted on as an indication of the archetype's archaic script (as compared to the script of the surviving MS of *Beowulf*). Of Lapidge's pattern of errors, confusions of **a** and **u**, of **p** and **ƿ**, and of **r** and **n** need exploring at this point.

In Cynewulf's Exeter Book poems, confusions of **a** and **u** appear in *Christ* at line 18 (MS *þa* for *þu*), 408 (*rodorus* was corrected to *rodoras* in the MS), 978 (the MS has *þu* for *þa*), 979 (MS *foldun* was altered in the MS to *foldan*), 1137 (Muir reports that "there is a cross stroke at the top of the **u** so that it resembles an **a**"). Though Lapidge counted seven instances of a possible confusion of **a** and **u** in *Beowulf*, four appeared in grammatical endings; Stanley objected that such variations can appear at any time and Gerritsen excluded such examples from his earlier analysis of of telltale errors in the text (but noted that in the Nowell Codex, the scribes confused the letter forms **a** and **u** only in copying *Beowulf*).[37] Gerritsen

---

[36] Confusions of **d** and **ð** corrected in Cynewulf's poems (including *Christ* III) preserved in the Exeter Book appear at: *Christ* 4, 47, 64, 118, 137, 257, 359, 364 (where the correct reading is altered in error), 482, 494, 518, 574, 846, 970, 1031, 1173, 1311, 1337, 1490, 1562; *Juliana* 325, 666. The uncorrected errors appear at: *Christ* 69, 539, 698, 710, 790, 795, 961, 1337, 1597 and *Juliana* 338; the Vercelli Book's record of Cynewulf's *Fates of the Apostles* and *Elene* has one corrected confusion of **d** and **ð**, *Fates* 43, and two uncorrected confusions at *Elene* 14 and 1294.

[37] See E.G. Stanley, "Paleographical and Textual Deep Waters: <a> for <u> and <u> for <a>, <d> for <ð> and <ð> for <d> in Old English," *ANQ: American Notes and Queries* 15 (2002): 64–72; and Johan Gerritsen, "Have with you to Lexington! The *Beowulf* Manuscript and *Beowulf*," in *In Other Words: Transcultural Studies in Philology*,

then rested his case on *wudu* for *wadu* (581) and *strade* for *strude* (3073).[38] Similar caution would bar 408 and 979 (in *Christ*) above leaving only the paired errors *þa* for *þu* in 18 and *þu* for *þa* in 978. Both *þa* and *þu* are grammatical words frequently appearing at or near the beginning of a verse clause where a scribe might need to understand the clause as a whole to know whether *þu* or *þa* was required. In line 978–79 … *þa wið holme ær / fæste wið flodum* … the MS reading *þu* would have made sense until the next half-line where the verb form is plural. At line 18–19, *Eala þu* [MS *þa*] *reccend / ond þu riht cyning / se þe locan healdeð* … a competent scribe should have realized that *reccend* is singular and the context demands *þu* and not *þa*. In both of these cases, *þa* and *þu* have metrically unstressed positions in the half-lines *þa wið holme ær* (xxPxP, Sievers B1) and *ond þu riht cyning* (xxPpx, Sievers C3): a foreign scribe (or a careless native) might have missed the difference between an unstressed *þa* or *þu*.

In *Beowulf*, Scribe B twice confuses **p** and **ǫ** (2814, 2854), but the Exeter Book scribe confuses, as Muir notes, "þ-wynn, p-wynn, [and] s-wynn;" the confusions of **p** and **ƿ** are in *Elene* (245, 996). In the Vercelli Book's Cynewulfian poems, the one confusion of **p** and **ƿ** is in *Juliana* (294), but Vercelli adds a confusion of **ƿ** and **ð** (*Andreas*, 65). Since an Exeter Book scribe had so much trouble with , the literal confusions of **p** and **ƿ** in *Elene* probably arise from his unfamilarity with this originally runic letter. The Vercelli Book shares Exeter's errors but with a reduced frequency. The large number of corrected literal confusions in Exeter may represent scribal proof-reading against the exemplar or the intervention of a copy-editor. Lapidge notices five confusions of **r** and **n** in *Beowulf*, two from part I and three from part II; though Krapp and Dobbie missed them, two appear in Cynewulf's Exeter Book poems (*Juliana* 601 and *Christ* 1146).

Frank claimed that since Cynewulf's signed poems share "all but one" of the literal confusions Lapidge maintains enable us to date *Beowulf* before 750, Cynewulf's work and *Beowulf* must be younger than Lapidge would have it.[39] That conclusion seems doubtful at best. First, Frank is correct that one of five "literal confusions" Lapidge notes in *Beowulf*, **c** / **t**, does not appear in the signed works of Cynewulf or in *Christ* III, usually taken to be his. Second, the confusion of **d** / **ð** / **t** suggests that these errors may well have their origin not from a exemplar which made **d** represent the voiced plosive /d/ and the voiced and unvoiced fricatives /ð/ and /θ/ but with a foreign scribe whose language had neither /ð/ nor /θ/. Third, the co-occurence of a confusion of **p** and **ƿ** in the Exeter Book (and

---

Translation and Lexicography Presented to Hans Heinrich Meier, ed. J. Lachlan MacKenzie and Richard Todd (Dordrecht: Foris, 1989), 15–34.
[38] Gerritsen, "Have with you to Lexington," 24.
[39] Frank, "Scandal in Toronto," 857.

Cynewulf's poem therein) and *Beowulf* may not suggest their exemplars date from the same period since the Exeter Book also and repeatedly confuses ƿ with þ and s; the Vercelli Book even confuses ƿ and ð. The scribe may have been unfamilar with the runic ƿ [wynn] – and the shared errors between Exeter and Vercelli hints that foreign scribes may have been involved in the transmission of both, though Vercelli has rather fewer of the same errors. Fourth, all the confusions of **a** and **u** in Exeter appear in grammatical endings or in two grammatical words (**þa** and **þu**) in unstressed positions, hence this "literal confusion" may not be based on letterforms. Nonetheless, those two examples might be counted as parallels to the Beowulfian confusions of **a** and **u** admitted as evidence by Gerritsen. Fifth, two confusions of **r** and **n** appear in the Exeter Book's Cynewulfian poems against five in *Beowulf*, the comparative frequency rate would be (counting *Christ* III and Cynewulf's poems in Vercelli) about 1.6 confusions in a thousand lines of *Beowulf* versus .5 per thousand in Cynewulf.

In conclusion, Frank's case against Fulk fails and her argument against Lapidge proves nugatory. The present study confirms the validity of the arguments mounted by Fulk and Lapidge against a variety of piecemeal objections. The regular and extensive adherence to Kaluza's law in *Beowulf* must reflect a subtle regularity in the poet's speech; it cannot be regarded as an artful attempt to evoke a bygone era. The *Beowulf* poet consistently observed distinctions of etymological length that were lost around 725 in Mercia for a simple reason: he composed before the pertinent desinences became phonologically indistinct.[40] The transliteration errors pervading the transmitted text of *Beowulf* provide independent confirmation that the poem had been committed to parchment early in the eighth century. The internal consistency of *Beowulf* – its spread of archaic metrical features and syntactic idiosyncrasies, not to mention its thematic unity – indicates that the poem was not substantially altered during its textual transmission.[41] The two scribes to whom we owe the poem understood

---

[40] See Fulk, *A History of Old English Meter*, 381–92; Fulk, "Old English Meter and Oral Tradition," 321. Leonard Neidorf and Rafael J. Pascual have recently demonstrated that the adherence to Kaluza's law in *Beowulf* must have been phonologically conditioned and that every alternative hypothesis fails to explain this phenomenon adequately. See Neidorf and Pascual, "The Language of *Beowulf* and the Conditioning of Kaluza's Law," forthcoming in *Neophilologus*.

[41] The bibliography in support of the unity of *Beowulf* is now considerable. On the immediate relevance of Kaluza's law and archaic metrical features to this question, see R.D. Fulk, "On Argumentation in Old English Philology, with Particular Reference to the Editing and Dating of *Beowulf*," *Anglo-Saxon England* 32 (2003): 1–26, at 16–24. On the syntactic and stylistic regularities that characterize the entirety of *Beowulf*, see Tom Shippey, *Old English Verse* (London: Hutchison Press, 1972), 37; Janet Bately, "Linguistic Evidence as a Guide to the Authorship of Old English Verse: A Reappraisal,

it slenderly and can hardly have introduced any artistic or substantial changes beyond their many inadvertent errors and misunderstandings.[42] We have the eighth-century poem, but with the imperfections of an eleventh-century transcription. The strongest evidence – metrical, linguistic, paleographical, and lexical – leads to the conclusion that the archetype of *Beowulf* was written before 750.[43] No comparable evidence so far adduced points elsewhere.

with Special Reference to *Beowulf*," in *Learning and Literature in Anglo-Saxon England: Studies Presented to Peter Clemoes on the Occasion of His Sixty-Fifth Birthday*, ed. Michael Lapidge and Helmut Gneuss (Cambridge: Cambridge University Press, 1985), 409–31; John D. Sundquist, "Relative Clause Variation and the Unity of Beowulf," *Journal of Germanic Linguistics* 14 (2002): 243–69; and R.D. Fulk, "Old English *þa* 'now that' and the Integrity of *Beowulf*," *English Studies* 88 (2007): 623–31. For literary-critical arguments for the unity of *Beowulf*, see Arthur G. Brodeur, "The Structure and the Unity of *Beowulf*," *PMLA* 68.5 (1953): 1183–95, as well as the literature reviewed in Thomas A. Shippey, "Structure and Unity," in *A Beowulf Handbook*, ed. Bjork and Niles, 149–74.

[42] See Leonard Neidorf, "Scribal Errors of Proper Names in the *Beowulf* Manuscript," *Anglo-Saxon England* 42 (2013): 249–69, at 264–7.

[43] In addition to the studies cited above, see R.D. Fulk, "Archaisms and Neologisms in the Language of *Beowulf*," in *Studies in the History of the English Language III: Managing Chaos: Strategies for Identifying Change in English*, ed. Christopher M. Cain and Geoffrey Russom (Berlin: Mouton de Gruyter, 2007), 267–87; Dennis Cronan, "Poetic Words, Conservatism, and the Dating of Old English Poetry," *Anglo-Saxon England* 33 (2004): 23–50; Leonard Neidorf, "Lexical Evidence for the Relative Chronology of Old English Poetry," *SELIM* 20 (2013): 7–48; and Rafael J. Pascual, "Material Monsters and Semantic Shifts," Chapter 11 in this volume.

13

Afterword: *Beowulf* and Everything Else

Allen J. Frantzen

Arguments about the date of *Beowulf* are more impassioned than the question seems to merit. Even so, the controversy has its uses. *Beowulf* is a great work, all agree, but it constitutes only a sliver of the poetic canon and is doubtless more important to Anglo-Saxon culture now than it was a thousand years ago. For all its glory, *Beowulf* provides no better an index to Anglo-Saxon poetry than *Hamlet* to Renaissance drama, which is to say that one can know both works well without knowing much about the corpus to which either belongs. It is to welcome and good effect, then, that several chapters in this volume link the date of *Beowulf* to the date of everything else, which, for purposes of this discussion, is the rest of Old English poetry.

At the Harvard conference, R.D. Fulk argued that the date of the poem's composition is less significant than the means used to hypothesize the date. The introduction to Fulk's Chapter 1 in this volume sums up an extended discussion regarding probability, proof, and linguistic evidence drawn from his *History of Old English Meter*. Fulk observes that the criteria for dating verse are not uniformly rigorous and that they have not been subjected to uniformly rigorous testing. Words can be counted and their forms analyzed, so that exceptions to linguistic and metrical criteria emerge quickly; in these cases, the relative probability of competing hypotheses can be readily gauged. In comparison, claims about the representation of Danes in Old English poetry, or assertions about the literary consequences of Scandinavian occupation, possess no probabilistic value. To make his point, Fulk compares diphthong lengthening to various forms of non-linguistic evidence. The rules of historical linguistics leave little room for doubting the difference between short and long diphthongs or the probability that the former predate the latter. Historical and cultural claims are more difficult to verify. "For instance," Fulk writes of *Beowulf*, "it has been argued that the poem was composed as part of an effort to forge a common culture for Englishmen and Scandinavians living side by side in Britain, and thus it is not likely to have been composed before the reign of Æthelstan." He regards the connection of the poem's date to a common English-Scandinavian culture as "just one among a very large number of possible contexts for the composition of the poem," adding that "it does not even seem the likeliest of those possibilities."[1] Fulk also points out that "credence in a hypothesis" is not invalidated "by the mere existence of an alternative hypothesis." All hypotheses have alternatives, but the alternatives are not equally probable.[2] There is a gap, then, between what is linguistically or historically possible (just about anything) and what is probable (a great deal less).

Fulk reminds readers that "the range of possible dates for the composition of *Beowulf* is not nearly as unconstrained as many literary scholars have acquired the habit of remarking as a matter of course."[3] The constraints to which Fulk refers were not established solely by metrical criteria, as he said pointedly in *A History of Old English Meter*.[4] These criteria were applied not only to *Beowulf* but also to *Genesis A*, *Daniel*, *Exodus*, and other verse. That Old English poems form a sequence established by their linguistic features is hardly a new idea, although in previous generations the sequence was part of a narrative that linked developing literary sophistication to the growth of Christianity. The chronology supplied by Hippolyte Adolphe Taine in 1865 is an example.[5] Even older is Benjamin Thorpe's treatment of the "Cædmonian Genesis" (1832).[6] In the nineteenth century the Germans were leading the way both in establishing phonological and metrical criteria and in challenging them, as Ashley Crandell Amos observes in *Linguistic Means of Determining the Dates of Old English Literary Texts*.[7] Amos cites Levin L. Schücking's 1917 essay as the first attack on "the reliability of all tests proposed for dating by linguistic criteria."[8] Although the linguists proposed chronologies similar to those hypothesized by Thorpe and others, their claims were

---

[1] R.D. Fulk, "*Beowulf* and Language History," Chapter 1 in this volume, p. 000. He cites John D. Niles, *Homo Narrans: The Poetics and Anthropology of Oral Literature* (Philadelphia: University of Pennsylvania Press, 1999), 134–40.
[2] R.D. Fulk, *A History of Old English Meter* (Philadelphia: University of Pennsylvania Press, 1992), 13–14.
[3] Fulk, "*Beowulf* and Language History," last paragraph.
[4] Fulk, *A History of Old English Meter*, 5.
[5] Hippolyte Adolphe Taine, *A History of English Literature* (New York: The Nottingham Society, n.d.).
[6] *Cædmon's Metrical Paraphrase of Parts of the Holy Scriptures, in Anglo-Saxon, with an English Translation*, ed. Benjamin Thorpe (London: Society of Antiquaries, 1832).
[7] Ashley Crandell Amos, *Linguistic Means of Determining the Dates of Old English Literary Texts* (Cambridge, Mass.: Medieval Academy of America, 1980), 13–17.
[8] Levin L. Schücking, "Wann entstand der Beowulf?" *Beiträge zur Geschichte der deutschen Sprache und Literatur* 42 (1917): 347–410. See Amos, *Linguistic Means*, 14 and n. 10.

based in part on a scientific, quantified approach to the dating of *Beowulf* that was antithetical to the prevailing spirit of "the affinity method," to use Leonard Neidorf's term for the cultural and historical approach that British and American scholars preferred.[9] There were long-standing tensions between new German methods and traditional British scholarly practices, and two world wars brought about by Germany did not make the methods of its leading philologists more welcome in England.[10] Writers in the post-war period emphasized affinities, just as nineteenth-century British scholars had done. Linguistic arguments were not as important as cultural arguments, whatever date they supported.

Both cultural and linguistic arguments were made at the 1980 Toronto conference, which has become a turning point in the dating controversy. One scholar who reported changing his views was E.G. Stanley, who noted that papers by Roberta Frank, R.I. Page, and Alexander Callendar Murray had persuaded him to shift his preferred date from the late ninth century to the early tenth.[11] He continued to support an "early" date, however, and "late" in his view meant 940 and after, i.e., from the death of Æthelstan or perhaps the battle of Brunanburh (939).[12] It is not clear what kind of a dividing line the king's reign might provide, but it could not be a line between a "pagan" or Germanic and a Christian phase, or between Viking and West Saxon political dominance. Stanley regarded late poems as "West Saxon" or sharing "West-Saxon colouring," but these criteria are unsuitably vague, reminiscent of the "Christian coloring" detected by those who saw the poem not as an expression of pan-Germanic paganism but as a hybrid.[13] Hybridity was eventually rejected in favor of a unified *Beowulf*; parts of the poem that had been seen as disconnected were now seen as forming what Murray calls "integral elements of a single conception." Murray claimed that "the implications [of unity] for dating the poem are obvious" and added that "the onus is on those who think to show that some element of the poem can be

---

[9] See Neidorf's introduction to this volume.
[10] Allen Frantzen, "By the Numbers: Anglo-Saxon Scholarship in the Twentieth Century," in *An Introduction to Anglo-Saxon Literary Culture*, ed. Philip Pulsiano and Elaine Treharne (Oxford: Blackwell, 2001), 472–95. See also Hans Sauer, "Anglo-Saxon Studies in the Nineteenth-Century: Germany, Austria, Switzerland," in *An Introduction*, ed. Pulsiano and Treharne, 455–71.
[11] E.G. Stanley, "The Date of *Beowulf*: Some Doubts and No Conclusions," in *The Dating of* Beowulf, ed. Colin Chase (Toronto: University of Toronto Press, 1981), 197–212, at 200–1 [henceforth *Dating*].
[12] Stanley, "Some Doubts and No Conclusions," 209.
[13] F.A. Blackburn, "The *Christian Colouring* in the *Beowulf*," PMLA 12 (1897): 205–25, reprinted in *An Anthology of* Beowulf *Criticism*, ed. Lewis E. Nicholson (South Bend: University of Notre Dame Press, 1963), 1–21.

dated only before the Viking age."[14] As this claim suggests, aesthetic judgments carried implications for the poem's date. A "composite" text could be early, but once the very same textual elements were seen as a forming a structural unity, it was "obvious" that the poem as a whole had to be a late work.

In the Toronto volume's most detailed inquiry into the language of *Beowulf*, Angus Cameron, Ashley Crandell Amos, and Gregory Waite concluded that "the evidence of language should not be neglected in any inquiry into the date and localization of *Beowulf*." They deferred judgment, anticipating "further analysis of the language of *Beowulf*, of Cotton Vitellius A.XV, and of other Old English texts and manuscripts," including new information "about the date and localization of both the poem and its manuscript."[15] Elsewhere in the volume, language, meter, and style were used to support claims for the poem's date. Thomas Cable saw nothing in his metrical evidence to rule out a ninth-century date.[16] He offered a time-line for twenty-two Old English poems that grouped the texts according to their use of Sievers types C, D, and E. Cable showed that the use of these types decreased from a high of 40% (*Exodus*; compare *Beowulf* at 38.3%) to a low of 14% (*Durham*).[17] Peter Clemoes used style to arrive at "the second half of the eighth century." "Style" sounds impressionistic, but there is nothing impressionistic about Clemoes' analysis of word order, metaphor, and point of view, and their distinctive operation in *Beowulf*.[18] Reviewing familiar points from previous scholarship, John C. Pope settled on the eighth century.[19] Colin Chase favored the ninth century.[20] Arguments for a late date came from Murray, who favored a tenth-century, post-Viking age *Beowulf*; from Kevin Kiernan, who advanced an argument about composite structure and the eleventh century; and from Roberta Frank and Walter Goffart. Chase summed up the state of the question, noting that a survey of over 80% of editions and

---

[14] Alexander Callendar Murray, "*Beowulf*, the Danish Invasions and Royal Genealogy," in *Dating*, 101–12, at 110–11.
[15] Angus Cameron, Ashley Crandell Amos, and Gregory Waite, with the assistance of Sharon Butler and Antonette DiPaolo Healey, "A Reconsideration of the Language of *Beowulf*," in *Dating*, 33–76, at 37.
[16] Thomas Cable, "Metrical Style as Evidence for the Date of *Beowulf*," in *Dating*, 77–82, at 82.
[17] Cable, "Metrical Style," 79–81. Cable finds *Exodus* closer to *Beowulf* in some regards than the latter is to *Genesis A*.
[18] Peter Clemoes, "Style as the Criterion for Dating the Composition of *Beowulf*," in *Dating*, 173–86, at 185.
[19] John C. Pope, "On the Date of Composition of *Beowulf*", in *Dating*, 187–96, at 195.
[20] Colin Chase, "Saints' Lives, Royal Lives, and the Date of *Beowulf*," in *Dating*, 161–72, at 170.

translations turned up only one author – Thorkelin – who "firmly commits himself to a date outside the range 650–800."[21]

There is, then, ample support for an early date in the Toronto volume. Yet the conference has been seen as marking a shift away from that view. The collection offers a case study in cognitive dissonance too great to be leveled within the limits of professional courtesy. When it is impolitic to choose, some people will abstain. Thus, rather than the build on the work of Cable, Clemoes, and Pope, among others, many Anglo-Saxonists opted for a new orthodoxy, which was that the date of *Beowulf*, and, by implication, of everything else, was undecideable, a view that could encompass many hypotheses.[22] Such pluralism was all the more likely because attitudes concerning the significance of meter and other linguistic criteria had already changed. In 1979 A.N. Doane commented on diminished confidence in the value of linguistic evidence. In a discussion of the language of *Genesis A* he contrasted "the confident standards which once placed the poem in a Northumbrian home in the late seventh or early eighth centuries," seen in B.J. Timmer's 1948 edition of *Genesis B*, to the "tentative guide to the reader" about language and date in Robert T. Farrell's 1974 edition of *Daniel*. Doane traced the "loss of confidence in linguistic evidence" to Kenneth Sisam's 1953 essay on dialect and "earlier" Old English verse, which showed that distinct layers of language could be unearthed in many texts and that forms were mixed in a "common stock" from which poets drew as often as they drew from the speech of their own regions.[23] Sisam argued that early poetry could be found in the south as well as in Northumbria or Mercia and that early verse was not necessarily Anglian.

As Sisam's concept of "common stock" was adapted and extended, the Old English poetic corpus eventually came to resemble a homogenous mass about which, with few exceptions, readers could draw no conclusions concerning either provenance or date – a view Sisam never held. With "common stock" as the new orthodoxy, incertitude became the new certitude, rather like the view of the agnostic who somehow knows there is no God. It was as if Sisam put paid not only to the idea that Anglian meant early as well as northern, but also, Doane seems to suggest, to the

---

[21] Colin Chase, "Opinions on the Date of *Beowulf*, 1815–1980," in *Dating*, 3–8, at 8.
[22] R.D. Fulk and Christopher Cain, *A History of Old English Literature* (Malden, Mass.: Blackwell, 2003), 198.
[23] *Genesis A: A New Edition*, ed. A.N. Doane (Madison: University of Wisconsin Press, 1978), 25–6, citing Kenneth Sisam, "Dialect Origins of the Earlier Old English Verse," in *Studies in the History of Old English Literature* (Oxford: Clarendon Press, 1953), 119–39.

idea that firm conclusions about dating poems were possible.[24] Ten years before Doane's edition, T.P. Dunning and A.J. Bliss concluded their discussion of structure and theme in "The Wanderer" this way: "The dating of Old English poetry is notoriously difficult; not only do all draw upon a single strong poetical tradition but all have survived in late West Saxon manuscripts. It would be unwise to place much confidence in any individual linguistic or metrical feature of 'The Wanderer.'"[25] If that held for "The Wanderer" in the words of A.J. Bliss, who juxtaposed "a single strong poetical tradition" (i.e., Sisam's "common stock") to "individual linguistic or metrical" evidence, others could be forgiven for assuming that the same held for *Beowulf*, not to mention everything else.[26]

Doane resisted this new orthodoxy, which owed something to Amos's work on the linguistic means of dating texts (1980).[27] Doane grouped *Genesis A* with *Exodus* and *Daniel* and distanced *Genesis A* from "the poems known to be late." He followed Robert J. Menner and Fr. Klaeber in associating *Genesis A* with *Beowulf* and offered that "any date in the eighth century seems reasonable," adding that the poem might be Northumbrian, Mercian, or southwestern.[28] It is hard to see how that conclusion failed to ramify, but it did. Many accounts of *Genesis A* in literary histories suggest an early date but say nothing about possible connections to *Beowulf*. The older volumes by G.K. Anderson (1949) and C.L. Wrenn (1967) comment on the significance of an early date for the poem, but, beyond comparisons of "Cædmon's Hymn" to the "creation hymn" of the *scop*, do not link the poem to *Beowulf*.[29] *A New Critical History of Old English Literature* by Stanley B. Greenfield and Daniel G. Calder (1986) suggests a date of "around 700" for *Genesis A* and mid-ninth century for *Genesis B*.[30] The account of *Genesis A* in *The Cambridge Companion*

---

[24] James W. Earl offered one of the bleakest assessments: "I now consider it axiomatic that *the problem of the poem's date is insoluble ...*" He also writes that "*we cannot safely use the poem to help us interpret Anglo-Saxon history; we cannot assume the poem is representative of any period, or even, finally, representative of anything at all.*" See Earl, Thinking About Beowulf (Stanford: Stanford University Press, 1994), 16–17. The italics are his.

[25] The editors found no evidence for an early date but did find some data that supported a late date. See *The Wanderer*, ed. T.P. Dunning and A.J. Bliss (London: Methuen, 1969; rpt. 1973).

[26] See Fulk, *A History of Old English Meter*, 273–4, on popular misunderstandings of Sisam's work that have allowed his conservative views to be enlisted in support of extreme arguments.

[27] See comments in Fulk, *A History of Old English Meter*, 5–6.

[28] *Genesis A*, ed. Doane, 37.

[29] George K. Anderson, *The Literature of the Anglo-Saxons* (Princeton: Princeton University Press, 1949; rev. 1966), 115–20. C.L. Wrenn, *A Study of Old English Literature* (New York: Norton, 1967), 98–103.

[30] Stanley B. Greenfield and Daniel G. Calder, *A New Critical History of Old English Literature* (NewYork: New York University Press, 1986), 207 and 210.

to Old English Literature (1991) offers dates for *Genesis A* ranging from seventh or eighth century to around 1000.[31] Little in these surveys indicates that *Beowulf* and *Genesis A* might have emerged in a shared literary culture that differed significantly from that of "The Wanderer" or "The Dream of the Rood," much less what that difference might mean. In this same spirit, surprisingly, Fulk and Cain observe that "the poem is often compared to *Beowulf* for the originality and inventiveness of its heroic diction" but do not elaborate.[32]

During the years bracketed by the studies mentioned above, the academic world changed. After World War II, historical criticism of the kind seen in the work of Thorpe and Taine began to seem naive. Unprecedented democratization of the classroom subjected the study of Old English to new pressures and influences. They included the advent of literary criticism that prized encounters with texts above familiarity with historical context; a widening literary canon; the loosening of degree requirements; and the waning of interest in foreign languages.[33] Philological study that presupposed knowledge of Latin and Greek and that deferred engagement with literary questions appeared obsolete. Whatever the "historical context" of "The Wanderer" or "The Dream of the Rood," or, for that matter, *Beowulf*, how much of that context could be fit into a two-semester survey of British literature? The answer: just as much as the introductions in *The Norton Anthology* could cover, and the more general the better. Literary histories of the type written by Taine were replaced by surveys based on genre and theme. It was safe to trace the development of prose along the path from Alfred to Wulfstan, but nobody wanted to support Thorpe's attempt to link "Cædmonian" verse to the age of Bede.

According to Fulk and Cain, the emergence of an undated and undatable *Beowulf* has had detrimental consequences. "*Beowulf* criticism tends still to be dominated by ahistoricizing, formalist approaches that contribute to the widespread impression of scholars in later periods that it is antiquated and out of touch with the wider concerns of the profession, and even of medieval scholarship." Moreover, "the insolubility of the problem" of the poem's date is regarded by many "as a congenial state of affairs," since a firm date would "constrain interpretation, discouraging certain views of the poem."[34] Several scholars have noted a comment by

---

[31] Malcolm Godden, "Biblical Literature: The Old Testament," in *The Cambridge Companion to Old English Literature*, ed. Malcolm Godden and Michael Lapidge (Cambridge: Cambridge University Press, 1991), 206–26, at 210.
[32] Fulk and Cain, *A History*, 114–15.
[33] Allen J. Frantzen, *Desire for Origins: Old English, New Language, and Teaching the Tradition* (New Brunswick: Rutgers University Press, 1983), 223–6.
[34] Fulk and Cain, *A History*, 198–9.

Nicholas Howe, in an afterword to the reissue of Toronto proceedings, which "celebrates the interpretive contexts opened up by the volume."[35] Howe wrote that "the reader can choose a date for the poem among the possibilities argued in these essays as well as in other sources."[36] Fulk and Cain suggest that the earlier the poem is dated, the less ironic its representation of the heroic world is likely to be. An early date frustrates critics who tend to read "against the grain" and "value particularly the ways in which texts resist interpretive closure and bare their own contradictions."[37] The gratifying resonance between modern skepticism and Anglo-Saxon skepticism vanishes if the poem is indeed early and if the poet presents an earnest (if critical) rather than an ironic view of heroic culture.[38] The chief benefit of an undatable *Beowulf*, as we see in Howe's remark, is access to the poem unfettered by historical constraints.[39] Many critics would remark on the advantages of a synchronic poetic canon for thematic criticism, and on its modernity. Later they would remark on its post-modernity.

A preference for "ahistoricizing, formalist approaches" also emerges in much feminist, gender, and post-colonial criticism, which bulks large relative to its modest contributions to knowledge of the text, its language, or its contexts. Some of this criticism is hostile to the heroic ethos itself, regards masculinity as toxic, and invites the view that *Beowulf* is an anti-heroic poem populated by weak men.[40] The poem's date matters to these claims, for it is more probable to find a self-doubting hero and failing heroic ethos at the end rather than the beginning of a tradition, or even in the middle. Contemporary medievalists are inured to projection and prolepsis even as they scorn it in older writers. Witness *Chaucer's Sexual Poetics*, in which Carolyn Dinshaw mocks the male-centered reading of two "sons," E.T. Donaldson and D.W. Robertson, Jr., while claiming that the Chaucer's Clerk reads "like a woman." He incorporates a double perspective, speaks from a marginal position, and demonstrates

---

[35] Leonard Neidorf, "The Dating of *Widsið* and the Study of Germanic Antiquity," *Neophilologus* 97 (2013): 165–83, at 167; see also Fulk and Cain, *A History*, 198.
[36] Nicholas Howe, "The Uses of Uncertainty: On the Dating of *Beowulf*," in *Dating* [reprinted in 1997 with this afterword], 213–20, at 220.
[37] Fulk and Cain, *A History*, 199.
[38] See, for example, the discussion of the poem's "social coherence," as seen by John Hill, and its "deliberately ambivalent" rendering of social institutions, as seen by Clare A. Lees, in Elaine A. Joy and Mary K. Ramsey, "Introduction: Liquid *Beowulf*," in *The Postmodern* Beowulf: *A Critical Casebook*, ed. Joy and Ramsey (Morgantown: University of West Virginia Press, 2006), xxix–lxvii, at xli–ii.
[39] Fulk and Cain, *A History*, 210–11.
[40] See Allen J. Frantzen, "Teaching *Beowulf* and Teaching Gender," in *Teaching* Beowulf *in the Twenty-first Century*, ed. Howell D. Chickering, Allen J. Frantzen, and R.F. Yeager (Tempe: ACMRS, 2014), 205–13.

"aggression" by resisting patriarchy. This seems to make him a feminist much like Dinshaw herself.[41]

Despite the vagueness of critical propositions and the convenient consensus that formed around an "insoluble" date, thorny matters of language and meter have not disappeared from the discussion of the poem's composition. In *A Beowulf Handbook*, Robert E. Bjork and Anita Obermeier note that arguments for an early date rest on "the apparent absence of Scandinavian loan words in the poem, the presence of exclusively English forms of personal names, and Kaluza's law." For Bjork and Obermeier these criteria do not "rule out a later date" than 685 to 825 A.D. But the authors cautiously add that anyone advocating a later date "must contend" with them, understatement worthy of an Old English poet.[42] The linguistic evidence supporting an early date takes more forms than those Bjork and Obermeier list, as one can see in Fulk's chapter in this volume. That evidence cannot be narrowed to any one criterion, for example, to Kaluza's law, and the idea of an early date then discarded if the results prove inconclusive. George Clark's Chapter 12 shows that the adherence of *Beowulf* to Kaluza's law cannot be dismissed as a mere product of stylistic preference.

Since there is a tendency to set metrical or linguistic evidence aside as inconclusive or contradictory, it is worth noting Thomas Bredehoft's exploration of the relationships between text and audience. This kind of investigation holds the promise of explaining what it might mean that *Genesis A* and *The Wanderer* came from, and address, different literary cultures and historical periods. Based in part on lexical parallels, ranging from phrases to whole lines, Bredehoft's arguments seek to establish relationships between Old English poems and poems and their audiences. This approach might profitably be connected to Janet Coleman's work on public reading and Middle English.[43] Bredehoft suggests that in early Old English poems the audience is perceived as "local" while the audience in Latin works is perceived as "distant." In the latter tradition, naming devices are necessary for contextualization. The poem is imagined from the outset as being read in or from a manuscript, while in the oldest Old English tradition that moment of inscription is not anticipated. "Anonymous presentation" – the poetic "I" declaiming before an assembled audience – means that no authorizing devices are needed.

---

[41] Carolyn Dinshaw, *Chaucer's Sexual Poetics* (Madison: University of Wisconsin Press, 1989), 134–6.

[42] Robert E. Bjork and Anita Obermeier, "Date, Provenance, Author, Audiences," in *A Beowulf Handbook*, ed. Robert E. Bjork and John D. Niles (Lincoln: University of Nebraska Press, 1997), 13–34, at 28.

[43] Janet Coleman, *Public Reading and the Reading Public in Late Medieval England and France* (Cambridge: Cambridge University Press, 1996).

Bredehoft traces the textualization of Old English poems to Alfred's time, the point at which he sees the formulas of the native tradition, which were preserved in the "classical" Old English poems, meeting continental, specifically Old Saxon traditions, and new "literate processes."[44]

Bredehoft notes that his views about dates of composition agree with those of Fulk. He sees a "classical" period responsive to oral composition and performance, the period of *Beowulf*, *Genesis A*, and *Daniel*, a finding that parallels Fulk's view that *Beowulf*, *Genesis A*, and *Daniel* are "the most [metrically] conservative of the longer poems." Bredehoft suggests that the signed epilogues of Cynewulf place the poet in the "second wave" of Old English poets rather than the first, since Cynewulf and others were thinking of poems as written rather than oral texts, as distant rather than "local," or what I would prefer to think of as immediate as opposed to mediated. Fulk also finds the works of Cynewulf and *Andreas* "measurably later."[45] Late poetry, in comparison, is highly literary and heavily indebted to textuality and imitation. Bredehoft offers *The Battle of Maldon* as an example.[46] In this assessment, *Maldon* loses its famous immediacy. Bredehoft does not see the poem as an "intersection between the Old English literary conventions of the heroic ethos and the events of 'real life' in an occasional poem," as it has been described.[47] Scholars often juxtapose *Maldon* to the literariness of *Beowulf*. Bredehoft suggests that the poet of *Maldon* imitated some "full-line formulas" found in *Beowulf* and manifested an old-fashioned literariness of his own.[48] These various forms of intertextuality, whether parallels, formulae, analogues, or borrowings, need to be defined and made systematic. As an example of the literary knowledge that might result, one can consult Peter Clemoes' *Interactions of Thought and Language in Old English Poetry*.[49] Clemoes' essay in the Toronto volume also draws multiple contrasts between the use of metaphor and point of view in *Beowulf* and those devices in other poems.

A consensus about the chronology of Old English poetry would in no sense be a return of the disciplinary wheel to a prior condition. Ideas of audience, textual transmission, and the hybridity of literary culture have

---

[44] Thomas A. Bredehoft, *Authors, Audiences, and Old English Verse* (Toronto: University of Toronto Press), xi. See also *The Saxon Genesis: An Edition of the West Saxon Genesis B and the Old Saxon Vatican Genesis*, ed. A.N. Doane (Madison: University of Wisconsin Press, 1991), 43–54.

[45] Bredehoft, *Authors, Audiences*, 200–1, referring to Fulk.

[46] Bredehoft, *Authors, Audiences*, 140–1.

[47] Katherine O'Brien O'Keeffe, "Heroic Values and Christian Ethics," in *The Cambridge Companion to Old English Literature*, ed. Malcolm Godden and Michael Lapidge (Cambridge: Cambridge University Press, 1991), 107–25, at 117.

[48] Bredehoft, *Authors, Audiences*, 136–7.

[49] Peter Clemoes, *Interactions of Thought and Language in Old English Poetry* (Cambridge: Cambridge University Press, 1995; rept. 2006).

developed in many directions since Sisam wrote, and those developments must engage linguistic evidence that has never disappeared from view. Systematic dating of the composition of Old English poems, however general the parameters, will require critical approaches to be more accountable. As the undefined stretches of Anglo-Saxon literary history become smaller, poems will be located within more limited periods. The result will be a more constrained kind of criticism. History will become something less like History and more like history, with all the restrictions the shift implies. Even as some critics have decried the assumption of universal truths by older forms of analysis, they themselves have been happy to read poems against a vague and idealized background. As Mechthild Gretsch noted, some writers borrow and transmit historical information so casually that it ceases to be meaningful as either history or criticism.[50] The promise of a narrower range of dates may emerge in new views of the knowledge that poetry both preserves and creates. In *Literary Knowledge*, Paisley Livingston contrasts knowledge within literary works (what they tell us about their own time) to knowledge they produce, or "knowledge of literature" (what they contribute to the time in which the reader exists – which is to say, what the reader makes of them). The corpus of Anglo-Saxon now seems to be tradition boiled down to what Livingston describes as "the relations between disembodied minds in an ideal library."[51] By narrowing possibilities for *Beowulf*, we can narrow them for other texts and construct reading worlds and performance worlds that include some Old English poems but not others. We can construct Old English verse in a diachronic rather than a synchronic pattern and shape it as an imaginative literary world we cannot have if, as now seems to be the case, all poems potentially interact with, influence, and are influenced by all others.

Some scholars will continue to multiply possibilities rather than assess probabilities, and new possibilities will lead to more of the same. Once the *Liedertheorie* was laid to rest, critics found other ways to fragment and even liquefy *Beowulf*. External evidence (historical or archaeological), like the date of composition and the poem's transmission, is inconsequential in these processes, since the interpretive result is predetermined by the assumptions on which the analysis is predicated. "Liquid *Beowulf*" is an example. "Liquid" refers to software-based modernity, with its speedy or "light" technologies, and to their consequences for a world

---

[50] Mechthild Gretsch, *Ælfric and the Cult of Saints in Late Anglo-Saxon England* (Cambridge: Cambridge University Press, 2005), 211–12.
[51] Paisley Livingston, *Literary Knowledge: Humanistic Inquiry and the Philosophy of Science* (Ithaca: Cornell University Press, 1988), 196. The parenthetical elaborations of Livingston's terms are my own.

order in which power is maintained, in the words of Zygmunt Bauman, by "traveling light, rather than holding tightly to things."[52] In such a world, *Beowulf* will either confirm "the tenuousness of everything" or be positioned in resistance to it.[53] It hardly matters which of these conclusions is reached, since the hypothesis is not assessed in probabilistic terms, and since the interpretive possibilities are endless. How would narrowing the date of composition to the eighth century affect the case for the poem's liquidity? Would a more specific historical context than the one we currently imagine make the poem less or more liquid, weigh it down with the "time and place" of "heavy modernism," or, equally plausibly, free it of weighty associations with the reign of Æthelstan and the synthesis of Scandinavian and Anglo-Saxon culture? No scholarly discovery will make *Beowulf* less liquid to someone determined to read the poem as a form of software. Nor will such a discovery alter interpretations determined to argue for, or for that matter, against the view that the poem associates power with women. The value of such assertions seems secondary to their value as demonstrations of the flexibility and ingenuity of contemporary criticism, a matter that has been clearly evident for some time.

The date of the composition of *Beowulf* matters little to readers who are concerned primarily with absorbing the poem into forms of knowledge the readers are already versed in, such as feminism or deconstruction or psychoanalysis. These readers sometimes imagine the poem as a ghost or a memory, or they personify it in some way so that it becomes a silent actor in their own interpretive drama or the analysand in their psychoanalytic transaction. If we are concerned instead with a more structured kind of knowledge within the poem, the date of *Beowulf* does matter. If we imagine the poem in dialogue with other works, then it does matter what the composer of *Beowulf* expected the audience to know. Such knowledge, a form of Livingston's "literary knowledge," would be valuable in decoding some of the poem's puzzling episodes. An example is James W. Earl's description of apocalyptic time, which contrasts the account of the Swedish–Geatish wars in *Beowulf* to the linear account of Beowulf's death. Earl observes that thirteen deaths occur in the war narrative, creating what he sees as "counterpoint" to the death of the hero. Earl describes this style as "conspicuously repetitive and unchronological," a form of "hammering at the deep patterns that repeat themselves, getting

---

[52] Zygmunt Bauman, *Liquid Modernity* (Cambridge: Cambridge University Press, 2000), 12–13, quoted in Joy and Ramsey, "Liquid *Beowulf*," xxxvii.
[53] Joy and Ramsey, "Liquid *Beowulf*," xxxviii.

to the heart of the issues" as do the prophetic books of the Bible.[54] If this is a serviceable description of a stylistic device, then we need to ask which of the poem's audiences would have recognized it and when.

This new group of essays on the dating of *Beowulf* will build confidence in assessing the dating of other poems as well. Many essays demonstrate the validity of philological dating criteria that can (and, in some cases, have been) applied to other texts. Studies that date *Beowulf* with reference to political and cultural developments, such as Anglo-Danish unity or West Saxon hegemony, cannot be held to the same standard of evidence. Sooner or later, those who want to argue from external evidence will have to deal with linguistic, metrical, semantic, onomastic, and paleographical evidence. Essays that do so in this collection provide models for studies that should shed light on the dating of everything else and in the process contribute to a relative chronology for Old English poetry. Once that chronology takes shape and is tested, it will, inevitably, constrain literary interpretation. Surely that is all to the good. Research should lead to knowledge that makes critical judgments more difficult, not easier, and should improve those judgments by requiring stricter and narrower comparisons. The literary knowledge emerging from this work will help us see the Anglo-Saxon world anew, a project all *Beowulf* scholars endorse.

---

[54] James W. Earl, "Prophecy and Parable in Medieval Apocalyptic History," *Religion and Literature* 31.1 (1999), 25–45 at 33–5.

Index

Alcuin 41, 43, 44, 55, 56, 61, 66
Aldhelm 41, 203, 214–17
alliteration 99–102, 104–5, 108–9
Asser 51, 120–2, 129, 134,
agnosticism 6–8, 16, 56, 158–60, 167–9, 174–7, 219, 243
Andreas 10, 11, 25, 27, 104, 226–7, 232, 244
Anglian genealogies 42, 49–53, 56, 115–16, 136
Anglo-Danish unity 3, 20–22, 204, 247
Anglo-Saxon Chronicle 26, 50, 106, 112, 120, 127–30, 134
Ælfred, King of Wessex 6, 10, 16, 51, 53, 56, 69, 98, 125, 133, 137, 211, 227, 244
Ælfric, Abbott of Eynsham 101–2, 109, 203, 205, 217
Ælfwald, King of East Anglia 42, 49, 50, 52, 216
Ætla 9, 43, 48, 55, 189
Æthelberht, laws of 26, 34
Æthelberht, King of Kent 49, 50, 115
Æthelstan, King of England 6, 20, 56, 236, 246
Æthelweard 51, 120, 125, 128–35
Æthelwulf, King of Wessex 38, 49–53, 112, 115, 118, 125–35

Bede, age of 2, 3, 4, 6, 16, 17, 169, 172, 176, 203, 241
Bede, *Historia Ecclesiastica* 26, 38, 50, 51, 115–17, 178–82, 189–90, 198
Beowulf, the hero 49, 71, 150, 152–3, 195, 201
Beowi 49, 52, 53, 56, 122
Biuuulf, the monk 48, 49, 61, 189
Boethius, Anicius Manlius Severinus 198–9
Boethius, Old English 53–4
Boethius, Meters of 10, 87, 103–4

Brunanburh, The Battle of 10, 80–2, 84–92, 94–6, 100–4, 133

Cain 205, 208, 213, 216
Cædmon's hymn 10, 240
Carolingian transmission 40, 45, 55
contraction 11, 25
Corpus glossary 8, 45, 210, 211, 213
Cynewulf 10, 11, 25, 27, 104, 105, 227, 229–32, 244

Daniel 10, 25, 92, 104, 105, 236, 239, 240, 244
Dæghrefn 65–8, 144, 153
Deniga 26, 39
dragon 62, 66, 71, 139, 147–8, 152, 173, 214–5

East Anglia 14, 42, 49–50, 52, 70, 78, 216
Ecg 26
Ecgþeo(w) 25, 26, 60, 65
Épinal-Erfurt glossary 8, 12, 38, 45, 210
Exodus 8, 10, 92, 104–6, 227, 236, 238, 240

Franks Casket 45–7, 55–6
Frisians 15, 49, 139–56, 191–2

gender 242–3, 246
Genesis A 8, 10, 11, 13, 25, 27, 45, 92, 104–6, 236, 239–41, 243–4
Gregory of Tours 140–1, 146
Gregory I, Pope 189–90, 198
Grendel 139, 146, 148, 153, 173, 185, 203–7, 209–10, 212–13, 215–16, 225
Grendel's mother 63, 139, 203–7
Guthlac A 33, 34, 92, 104, 106
Guthlac B 26, 104, 105
Guthrum 117–18, 134

Heliand, The 45, 105, 110
Heorogar 68–71
Heorot 46, 70, 74–5, 178–90
Hreow 218
Hrolfs saga kraka 68–70
Hroðmund 49, 52, 56, 69–72, 78
Hygelac 41–3, 49, 56, 61, 63, 65, 67–71, 73–4, 77, 139–56
hypermetric verses 87–8, 94, 100, 104, 108–9

Ingeld 43, 44, 46, 48, 54–6, 61, 63–4, 69–70, 73, 171, 185

Judith 10, 11, 81–4, 86–96, 101–3, 106, 227

Kaluza's law 11, 12, 17, 28–32, 56, 219–27, 233–4, 243
Kingship 15, 113–14, 125, 132, 156
Kuhn's laws 27

Lejre 68–70, 75, 184, 187–8, 190
lexical evidence 8, 9, 28, 89–94, 234
Liber Historiae Francorum 140–2, 146
Liber Monstrorum 41, 42, 49, 55, 56, 141–3, 146, 215–7
Liber Vitae Dunelmensis 48, 49, 60, 66, 68, 70, 75, 78

Macrobius 199
Maldon, The Battle of 10, 11, 80–2, 86, 88–90, 92, 94, 98, 100–4, 227, 244
Maxims I 9, 88, 92, 93, 104
Maxims II 212
Mercia 3, 6, 12, 16, 42–44, 49–52, 56, 134, 136, 163, 179, 208, 233, 239–40
Merewioing 14, 15, 23, 74–5, 77, 144
Missere 8, 92

namegiving, heroic-legendary 9, 47–9, 59–61, 75, 189
new criticism 174–7, 242
Njáls saga 199–200
Northumbria 3, 12, 46, 50, 60, 70, 119, 122, 179, 239–40

Offa, King of Mercia 3, 6, 16, 52, 134, 136, 163, 208
Old Saxon influence 98–100, 108, 244
Onela 68, 70, 150–2
Ongenþeo(w) 20, 25, 46, 70, 71, 152, 155

parasiting 10, 24
probabilism 16, 22–4, 35, 40, 56, 202, 204, 218, 235–7
proper names, corruption of 13, 39, 54, 55, 58, 59
  etymologically correct OE forms 14, 15, 20, 42, 46, 55, 65–8, 74, 220, 243

Radbod, King of Frisia 191–3, 196–8
Repton Stone 203, 215–17

Scealdwa 49, 52, 53, 56, 112, 121–4
Scucca 202–11, 213, 217–18
semantic change 45–6, 204–13, 218
Skaldic verse 21, 22, 33, 166
Soðfæstra dom 195
succession 15, 138–9, 145–50, 152, 155–6
Suhtor(ge)fædren 8, 45
Sturluson, Snorri 193–4, 197, 201

transliteration errors 13, 17, 23, 38, 39, 220–2, 227–34

Þeo(w) 20, 25
Þyrs 203, 212, 213, 218

Vatnsdaela saga 199
Vikings 3–4, 6, 16, 21, 22, 40, 46, 55, 183, 204, 238
Vita Sancti Guthlaci 41, 42, 43, 44, 50, 55, 203, 216–17
Vita Vulframni episcopi Senonici 191–2, 197

Wanderer, The 240–1, 243
weak adjective 27, 28
Wealhþeo(w) 25, 72, 145, 150
Wealh 45
Weland 40, 47, 53, 54, 68
Wessex 16, 44, 49, 51, 69, 98, 116–17, 124, 135
West Saxon royal genealogy 49–53, 112, 115–37
Wærferth 211
Widia 40, 48
Widsið 8, 44, 45, 46, 48, 49, 55, 56, 60, 61, 64, 66, 67, 70, 71, 72, 73, 141, 187
Wini(g)a 26
Wulfstan, Archbishop of York 205, 241

Yrmenlaf 62–5, 68

ANGLO-SAXON STUDIES

Volume 1: The Dramatic Liturgy of Anglo-Saxon England,
M. Bradford Bedingfield

Volume 2: The Art of the Anglo-Saxon Goldsmith: Fine Metalwork in Anglo-Saxon England: its Practice and Practitioners
Elizabeth Coatsworth and Michael Pinder

Volume 3: The Ruler Portraits of Anglo-Saxon England, *Catherine E. Karkov*

Volume 4: Dying and Death in Later Anglo-Saxon England,
Victoria Thompson

Volume 5: Landscapes of Monastic Foundation: The Establishment of Religious Houses in East Anglia, c. 650–1200, *Tim Pestell*

Volume 6: Pastoral Care in Late Anglo-Saxon England, *Edited by Francesca Tinti*

Volume 7: Episcopal Culture in Late Anglo-Saxon England,
Mary Frances Giandrea

Volume 8: Elves in Anglo-Saxon England: Matters of Belief, Health, Gender and Identity, *Alaric Hall*

Volume 9: Feasting the Dead: Food and Drink in Anglo-Saxon Burial Rituals, *Christina Lee*

Volume 10: Anglo-Saxon Button Brooches: Typology, Genealogy, Chronology, *Seiichi Suzuki*

Volume 11: Wasperton: A Roman, British and Anglo-Saxon Community in Central England, *Edited by Martin Carver with Catherine Hills and Jonathan Scheschkewitz*

Volume 12: A Companion to Bede, *George Hardin Brown*

Volume 13: Trees in Anglo-Saxon England: Literature, Law and Landscape,
Della Hooke

Volume 14: The Homiletic Writings of Archbishop Wulfstan,
Joyce Tally Lionarons

Volume 15: The Archaeology of the East Anglian Conversion,
Richard Hoggett

Volume 16: The Old English Version of Bede's *Historia Ecclesiastica*, *Sharon M. Rowley*

Volume 17: Writing Power in Anglo-Saxon England: Texts, Hierarchies, Economies, *Catherine A. M. Clarke*

Volume 18: Cognitive Approaches to Old English Poetry, *Antonina Harbus*

Volume 19: Environment, Society and Landscape in Early Medieval England: Time and Topography, *Tom Williamson*

Volume 20: Honour, Exchange and Violence in *Beowulf*, *Peter S. Baker*

Volume 21: *John the Baptist's Prayer* or *The Descent into Hell* from the Exeter Book: Text, Translation and Critical Study, *M. R. Rambaran-Olm*

Volume 22: Food, Eating and Identity in Early Medieval England, *Allen J. Frantzen*

Volume 23: Capital and Corporal Punishment in Anglo-Saxon England, *Edited by Jay Paul Gates and Nicole Marafioti*

Volume 24: The Dating of *Beowulf*: A Reassessment, *Edited by Leonard Neidorf*

Volume 25: The Cruciform Brooch and Anglo-Saxon England, *Toby F. Martin*

Volume 26: Trees in the Religions of Early Medieval England, *Michael D. J. Bintley*

Volume 27: The Peterborough Version of the Anglo-Saxon Chronicle: Rewriting Post-Conquest History, *Malasree Home*

Volume 28: The Anglo-Saxon Chancery: The History, Language and Production of Anglo-Saxon Charters from Alfred to Edgar, *Ben Snook*

Volume 29: Representing Beasts in Early Medieval England and Scandinavia, *edited by Michael D. J. Bintley and Thomas J. T. Williams*

Volume 30: Direct Speech in *Beowulf* and Other Old English Narrative Poems, *Elise Louviot*

Volume 31: Old English Philology: Studies in Honour of R. D. Fulk, *edited by Leonard Neidorf, Rafael J. Pascual and Tom Shippey*

www.ingramcontent.com/pod-product-compliance
Lightning Source LLC
Chambersburg PA
CBHW071203240426
43668CB00032B/2030